JUDAISM IN MUSIC
AND OTHER ESSAYS

Richard Wagner

TRANSLATED BY
William Ashton Ellis

University of Nebraska Press
Lincoln and London

Manufactured in the United States of America

♾ The paper in this book meets the minimum requirements of American National Standard for Information Sciences—Permanence of Paper for Printed Library Materials, ANSI Z39.48-1984.

First Bison Book printing: 1995

Library of Congress Cataloging-in-Publication Data
Wagner, Richard, 1813–1883.
[Literary works. English. Selections]
Judaism in music and other essays / Richard Wagner; translated by William Ashton Ellis.
p. cm.
Originally published: Richard Wagner's prose works; v. 3, The theatre. London: Kegan Paul, Trench, Trübner, 1907.
ISBN 0-8032-9766-1 (pbk.)
1. Wagner, Richard, 1813–1883—Aesthetics.   2. Musical analysis.   3. Music—History and criticism.   4. Opera.   I. Ellis, William Ashton, d. 1919.   II. Title.
ML410.W1A1267   1995
780—dc20
95-5274   CIP
MN

Reprinted from the 1894 translation of volume 3 (*The Theatre*) of *Richard Wagner's Prose Works,* published by Kegan Paul, Trench, Trübner & Co., Ltd., London. The volume title has been changed for this Bison Book edition.

CONTENTS

	PAGE
TRANSLATOR'S PREFACE	v
AUTHOR'S INTRODUCTION	1
ON THE "GOETHE-STIFTUNG"	5
A THEATRE AT ZURICH	23
ON MUSICAL CRITICISM	59
JUDAISM IN MUSIC	75
MEMENTOES OF SPONTINI	123
HOMAGE TO L. SPOHR AND W. FISCHER	145
GLUCK'S OVERTURE TO "IPHIGENIA IN AULIS"	153
ON THE PERFORMING OF "TANNHÄUSER"	167
REMARKS ON PERFORMING "THE FLYING DUTCHMAN"	207
EXPLANATORY PROGRAMMES	219
1. Beethoven's "Heroic Symphony"	221
2. Beethoven's Overture to "Coriolanus"	225
3. Overture to "Der fliegende Holländer"	228
4. Overture to "Tannhäuser"	229
5. Prelude to "Lohengrin"	231
ON FRANZ LISZT'S SYMPHONIC POEMS	235

CONTENTS.

	PAGE
EPILOGUE TO THE "NIBELUNG'S RING"	255
PREFACE TO THE "RING" POEM	274
A LETTER TO HECTOR BERLIOZ	285
"ZUKUNFTSMUSIK" ("MUSIC OF THE FUTURE")	293
ON THE PRODUCTION OF "TANNHÄUSER" IN PARIS	347
THE VIENNA OPERA-HOUSE	361
SUMMARY	387
INDEX	405

TRANSLATOR'S PREFACE.

S the present volume's subdivision into a number of shorter essays has given me the opportunity of prefixing a historical note to wellnigh each of them, only one or two points are left for treatment in a preface.

In the first place I have to justify the title chosen for the book as a whole : "THE THEATRE." Volumes I. and II. having each a distinctive title—in the one case taken from its longest essay, in the other from Wagner's own superscription—it seemed advisable that the remainder of the series should follow their example; for this Volume III., then, the question was simply "What?" For long I weighed the conflicting claims of "On Tannhäuser," "Judaism in Music," "Music of the Future" etc., etc.; but each of these would have been misleading as to the general character of the contents, while the third not only would have fathered upon the author a title invented by his enemies, but would have collided with Mr. E. Dannreuther's able translation of the "*Zukunftsmusik*" article and with the late Dr. Hueffer's somewhat ill-named brochure on Richard Wagner himself. Upon thinking over the chief characteristics of the present volume, however, it suddenly occurred to me that "The Theatre" would best meet the emergency, and for the following reasons. It forms a portion of the titles of two of the most important essays in this book, namely the second and the last; the matter of those two essays is largely supplemented by significant suggestions for theatrical management in the article that constitutes the centre of the volume, "On the Performing of Tannhäuser"; the "Preface to the 'Ring' Poem" contains an outline of the theatre proposed by the author whenever his tetralogy should come within measurable distance of a representation; and throughout the question of theatrical mismanagement and theatric reform is uppermost in Wagner's thoughts, perhaps more markedly here than anywhere else. Moreover, while OPERA AND DRAMA was chiefly occupied with the substance and form of the Artwork itself, the contents of this volume are very largely devoted to the general question of performance, in other words to THE THEATRE in its broadest sense.

Reserving a word about the period in Wagner's life covered by the accompanying essays, I may mention that they represent the whole of the prose-writings in volumes v., vi., and vii. of the *Gesammelte Schriften*—the remaining space of those volumes being filled by the poems of *Der Ring des Nibelungen, Tristan und Isolde* and *Die Meistersinger von Nürnberg*—also that the article on "Judaism in Music" belongs partly to an earlier, partly to a later period, for part of it was published before its author had commenced to write his *Oper und Drama*, and part five years later than the last essay included in this book (in fact, as will be seen on page 76, it belongs to vol. viii. of the *Ges. Schr.*, though this is my only departure from the original order).

Of all the present contents, it was this "Judaism" that created the greatest stir, both its earlier and its later publication gaining Wagner more and bitterer foes than anything else that came from his pen. Of course it was attributed to personal envy, though in 1850 one of the two musicians discussed was dead, and in 1869 not only were they both dead, but even Meyerbeer's artistic reputation was decidedly on the wane in Germany. Further, if one looks at the matter calmly and dispassionately, there was nothing so *very* dreadful in "Judaism in Music" about Meyerbeer, whilst Mendelssohn is handled in almost an affectionate manner, so far as concerns his personality.

In the later section of "Judaism in Music" Wagner himself has given us the history of what the earlier brought down upon his head; his fate with the publication of 1869 may be gathered from a glance at the catalogue of the British Museum. There we find ten Replies in German, of varied character, two alone being at all moderate: namely a pamphlet by a Herr J. Lang, called "An Attempt at reconciling Richard Wagner with the Jews," and another "published by the Alliance Israélite Universelle," written by "E. Liéser," an obvious pseudonym (Eleazar), and entitled "The Modern Jew-haters and J. Lang" etc. In the rest the argument mostly takes the following lines: "To us the prophet of the music of the future seems great in only one respect—the naïvety and consistency with which he pursues his literary, poetical and musical humbug, as no poet and composer before him." This sentence comes from a pamphlet called "*R. Wagner und das Judenthum: von einem Unparteiischen*"—the "impartial" (*unparteiisch*) is very funny!

I have said that there are ten of these Replies in the archives of the British Museum, not including a pamphlet of about seventy pages written by Dr. Puschmann in 1872 to prove that Richard Wagner was *mad*, and suggesting that he was positively criminal, one of Puschmann's chief points being that the Bayreuth master was possessed with the "persecution-illusion." This number gives one a very inadequate idea of the hubbub raised, however, for C. F. Glasenapp tells us that a collector amassed no less than *one hundred and seventy* different pamphlets, many of which must have been written in pure ignorance of the text itself, since the edition of Wagner's brochure had not been exhausted by 1876 (the date of Glasenapp's first Life of Wagner) and we can scarcely suppose that one half of those who bought it, promptly sat down to polemise against it. A constantly-recurring cry was, in so many words, the following: "Your attack of 1850 had been noticed by no one; nobody knew you were the author, as you had used a pseudonym; *therefore* you had no need to reprint it in 1869, and you are not telling the truth when you say it has brought upon you the persecution which you allege." In fact, some went so far as to deny that Brendel was ever assailed for having opened the columns of the *Neue Zeitschrift für Musik* to the question in 1850, whereas Glasenapp has since given us the names of the teachers in the Leipzig Conservatoire who signed a petition to the Directors to "immediately discharge" Franz Brendel from his post at that institute: these names are Rietz, Becker, Böhme, David, Hauptmann, Joachim, Klengel, Moscheles, Plaidy and Wenzel. Moreover Brendel himself—and mind you, Brendel is well known to have been the soul of honour, and to have owned the clearest, coolest judgment—Brendel supplies us with unimpeachable evidence of the "notice" aroused at the time. On the 4th of July, 1851, he writes in his *Neue Zeitschrift* as follows: "*Das Judenthum in der Musik.*—Readers will remember the article bearing the above title in No. 19 of the 33rd volume of this paper; they will probably remember also a Reply which followed soon thereafter, in No. 31, after Dr. Krüger had already spoken some words of conciliation in No. 27. The matter was by no means thereby set at rest. But as that first article had called up a veritable tempest, had given rise to now friendly, now hostile notices in a crowd of other papers, and finally had occasioned the sending to me of many expectorations (*sic*) of diverse tendencies, destined for these columns, I held it wisest to let the matter rest a while, to give the heated passions time to cool. Only to *one* voice, representing the opposite view, did I think it my duty to give space, and therefore accepted the article in No. 31. Further discussions I did not desire for the moment, and I therefore laid aside all the other manuscripts received by me, including a tolerably lengthy article from London and a short rejoinder by Herr Freigedank himself. It was not my object to stifle the question; I only wished, as said, for calm discussion, and not the voice of passion. One reason alone would have sufficed for my not closing the matter for good, namely that in the said Reply of No. 31 Herr Freigedank was wholly *misunderstood*. Though I could not agree with him on every point, still less could I agree with his opponent." Brendel goes on to explain his reading of Wagner's words, agreeing with what he says about "the common Jew," i.e. the Polish Jews who swarmed in Leipzig and Dresden. Presently he comes to this very important point: "To the educated Jew, as to every other man, the way stands open to the highest thing; but the question is, whether they have taken the right road. They have often assimilated our Culture in a high degree, and have appeared in a productive capacity. They have mixed with us to such a point that they are hardly to be recognised, inwardly or outwardly. These are facts. But Freigedank replies that most of them have thereby fallen into a hopeless contradiction, i.e. of possessing our culture and yet remaining Jews, of wishing to be Jew and Christian in one person. They do not see that to make our culture their own to the very bottom, they must give up their earlier standpoint, their individuality. They wish for this as a ready-made result, without having gone through the inner labour, the gigantic struggles of, for instance, the German spirit. They look upon this Culture as a thing one can take possession of in ease and comfort, without knowing that it all is only to be bought by 'sweat, anguish and the full cup of suffering and sorrow.' This is the chief offence of the cultured Jew, and upon this view is based the main idea of Freigedank's whole essay."

I cannot make a longer quotation from this very able article of Brendel's, but the upshot of it is that with Wagner's main lines he agrees, though he considers that "a few harsh expressions" might well have been omitted. It is as unnecessary as it would here be impertinent for me to give my own opinion of the larger question, further than to remind the reader that Richard Wagner was essentially and typically an Aryan; but I wish to lay stress upon the fact that the 1850 article *was* noticed, and very keenly, at the time of its publication. The next point is: Did people guess it was written by Wagner? About this, also, there can be no question, for (1)—the "Hebraic art-taste," mentioned on page 79, is to be found in an article of Uhlig's (signed "T. U.") in the *Neue Zeitschrift* for April 23, 1850; this article discusses Meyerbeer's *Prophète*, which had just been produced at Dresden under the personal direction of the composer, and the quoted term occurs in the following connection: "If this [namely, certain wobbling arpeggios for the voice] is dramatic song, then Gluck, Mozart, Cherubini and Spontini ought to have made their studies in the New Market at Dresden or the Brühl at Leipzig . . . To a good Christian such vocal phrases must needs appear, in the best case, far-fetched, overdone, unnatural, tricky; nor is it likely that a propaganda of Hebraic art-taste, carried on with such means as these, will have success." Now it would be absurd to imagine that none of Meyerbeer's myrmidons promptly brought this article, in the most important musical journal of the day, to the notice of their chief; and everyone at Dresden could tell him that Uhlig was one of Wagner's disciples — the initials "T. U." forming no disguise at all, as Uhlig's full name appears often enough in the journal. This alone would rouse suspicions that either Wagner or one of his adherents, and probably Uhlig, had written the "Judaism" article which appeared a few months later. But (2)—Wagner had only just published his *Art-work of the Future*, and the article's style must very soon have been compared with that of the book, for we find Liszt writing him on April 9, 1851: "Can you tell me, under the seal of the most absolute secrecy, whether the famous article on Judaism in Music in Brendel's paper is by you?" And (3)—upon pages 47 and 87 of *Opera and Drama*, referring to Meyerbeer, expressions will be found such as to have left no doubt in anyone's mind about the authorship of the article in question. It is impossible to suppose that these clues should have escaped the vigilance of Meyerbeer and his understrappers.

The point as to the article's effect upon Wagner's prospects at German theatres may be settled in a word or two. It is historically ascertainable that the tone adopted by German papers toward Richard Wagner (the *Grenzboten*, for instance) underwent an almost instant change; it is also known that in Germany a majority of the newspapers have long been in the hands of the Jews; it is further known that, even with papers owned by thoroughbred Germans, the influence of Meyerbeer was supreme. Under these circumstances it is idle to deny that "Judaism in Music" was the cause of a very large part of Wagner's difficulties in gaining acceptance for his dramatic works; though it is far more likely that the war was waged by the adherents of Meyerbeer and Mendelssohn as such, than that the "persecution" proceeded from the Jewish nation itself, for we find that he won many a private friend among the Jews,—to say nothing of theatrical audiences.

I fear that the above may have given this particular article an undue prominence among the contents of the present volume; but it was almost the only one that needed a longer notice than could conveniently be embodied in the text.

To the article "On the Performing of Tannhäuser" I desire to add a note. On pages 179-81 Wagner speaks of the passage for Tannhäuser, "*Zum Heil den Sündiger zu führen*" etc., saying that "it is accompanied by whispered phrases for all the singers on the stage." Though there does not exist in the British Museum a copy of the original score (1845), the 1860 edition shews that this whole passage was meant to be accompanied by the other singers; but a note is added, to the effect that, if necessary, Tannhäuser may take it as a solo. In the present authorised version (pianoforte and vocal score, arranged by Joseph Rubinstein, pages 194-6) it will be seen that later experiences proved to Wagner the advisability of *definitely* establishing this passage as a solo.— Further, upon page 187 there will be found an allusion to "Walther's solos in the Minstrels' Tourney"; these have now been excised, probably at the time of the Paris revision.

TRANSLATOR'S PREFACE. xi

With regard to the "Preface to the 'Ring' Poem," it would have been better to place this in its chronological order, i.e. last but one in the volume. The reason for its appearing where it does, is that Wagner deemed advisable to print both poem and preface in the same volume of the *Ges. Schr.*, viz. :—volume vi., and I have not thought it wise to depart from the order chosen by him, except for very cogent reasons.

As to the translation, I may state that the articles: "Homage to L. Spohr and W. Fischer," "On the Performing of Tannhäuser," and "A Letter to Hector Berlioz" had already appeared in *The Meister*, Nos. XII, XIII to XV, and I, respectively. In each case, however, I have carefully revised my earlier work, in fact, almost re-written it.

And now, for a final word about the whole volume, I have to say that it represents a very important epoch in Richard Wagner's life. Whilst Volumes I and II cover a period of barely two years' literary activity, this Volume III—without including *Judaism in Music*, which has been misdated by a curious error either of the author or of his German publisher—extends over a period of more than twelve years. During this time Wagner was occupied with the dramatic poems already mentioned, and with their musical composition, completing that of *Das Rheingold*, *Die Walküre*, half of *Siegfried*, *Tristan und Isolde*, and the overture to *Die Meistersinger*. It was a period that began full of promise, and ended in despair; characteristics which are reflected by the writings themselves, for one finds it hard to attribute to the same mood the article "A Theatre in Zurich" and that "On the Vienna Opera-house," though they have many features in common. In 1851 it still seemed possible to Wagner that many and many an artist would answer his inspiriting call, and help forward his "artwork of the future" in the widest sense, i.e. by creating and performing works of a style such as he upheld: in 1863 he has given up all hope, not only of finding fellow-workers in the creative field, but even of getting his own *Ring* performed. He had been permitted, at last, to return to his native land, only to find that there was no room in it for a man like him. From the spring of 1863, when *Tristan und Isolde* was definitely struck off the engagement-list of the Viennese Opera-house, to the spring of 1864, when an enlightened monarch called him to his side, and the prophetic question of page 282 fulfilled itself—this was the darkest year in Richard Wagner's life. With Volume IV, commencing with "State and Religion" and "German Art and German Politics," we shall find that the clouds have rolled away, never again to gather with quite such ominous force.

WM. ASHTON ELLIS.

LONDON, *Christmas* 1894.

AUTHOR'S INTRODUCTION.*

OR the arrangement of the contents of these two volumes I have been obliged, in some measure, to neglect the strictly chronological sequence. These writings fall in that period of my life which was chiefly occupied by the conception and execution of the poem for my grand *Bühnenfestspiel:* "DER RING DES NIBELUNGEN"; in fact some of them belong even to the time of its musical working-out, whilst an epilogue, penned quite recently, sums up its fate.

At that epoch of my life I had already relinquished any further systematic pursuit of the problems started in my anterior, more circumstantial writings; it was therefore due to mere occasional incidents, that I tried from time to time to continue formulating my thoughts upon the question at issue.

The nature of these occasional incidents will be easily recognised by the reader; to tell the truth, they mostly came as a disturbance even to myself, and it was almost with repugnance that I answered to each stimulus as it arose. Yet there was already one advantage to be reaped: namely, I no longer needed to construct on abstract lines, but could let my main ideas entrench themselves behind just those concrete cases which offered the incitement. I fancy that in this consists the great good fortune of our modern Journalism, giving it an importance quite unknown

---

* "Einleitung zum fünften und sechsten Bande," i.e. "Introduction to the fifth and sixth volumes" of the *Gesammelte Schriften* (1872), which contain, besides the prose-writings that will appear in this Volume iii of the present series, the whole text of the *Ring des Nibelungen*.—TR.

in earlier times, and a virtual ascendence over Book-writing proper. There is something very fascinating in taking the most trivial occurrence of the day to demonstrate the correctness of a pet idea of one's own, especially since one may assume that in this form it will find the speediest route to an attention commonly denied it when set forth in its abstract nakedness. The worst of it is, however, that the thought is generally misunderstood on these occasions, because the preponderance of interest in the very Stuff which supplied the peg on which to hang it, so seldom and so scantily leaves room for calm consideration. To myself this has been brought home the plainest by the sort of understanding which has befallen my article on "Judaism in Music." To very few has it occurred, that it was not the generally-avowed experience which I haply sought to shew in a new and lurid light, but that I had felt prompted to link to this quite common experience the development of a thought which, in truth, lay far indeed from the supposed intention of dealing out a monstrous insult. On the other hand I have had to reap the experience, that at any rate the newspaperism of the day tries hard to make itself, and keep itself, interesting by following a course the opposite of my own ; here, in setting up an æsthetic, a philosophic, or a moral maxim, one merely endeavours to so far commend one's principles that the aim of a purely personal animosity, whence the thing derives its only life, may be hid beneath them.* Thus it comes, that anyone who is honestly concerned for the thought itself, cannot escape being thrown on one common heap with those who merely take the thought as pretext ; for just his eagerness to demonstrate his thought, makes him forget all heed of personal considerations.

The more incorrectly, then, this class of individual utterances on theoretic problems is judged at its appearance on the surface of the daily press, so much the more proper

* The allusion is of course to Dr Hanslick, about whose methods and whose book "*Vom Musikalisch-Schönen*" it will be seen that Wagner has something to say in his Appendix to *Judaism in Music.*—TR.

must it seem for precisely such works to be presented in a grouping of the kind which I have here allowed myself; they thus are for the first time placed in the needful light, where the later judge is appealed-to merely on the essential thoughts indwelling in them.

In a similar sense the instructions for the performance of two operas of mine may still seem worth regarding, notwithstanding that these jottings were originally meant to serve nothing beyond a thoroughly practical purpose of the moment. That that practical aim has stayed so entirely unattained, however, has more particularly determined my present publication of these works. In fact I almost might rest content with one reason, for wishing that these directions should be examined a little closer: namely to give the reader some faint idea of how I felt, when I discovered that they had not been honoured with the smallest consideration, nay, not even thought worth reading, by the very people for whom they were written and to whom they were addressed. Especially had an ample supply of the instructions for the performance of *Tannhäuser*—which I had had set up in nice neat type—been sent by me to all the theatres which gave that opera, for distribution to their respective managers and executant artists. Most perplexed was I, then, at hearing later that even so profoundly earnest an artist, as the too early departed *Ludwig Schnorr*, had not the smallest knowledge of this "Address"; until at last a hazard solved for me the riddle. I myself had run out of my last copy of the pamphlet, and this caused me to inquire of the management of a Court-theatre, with which I then was in closer relations, for one of the six I earlier had forwarded to it.* All six copies were discovered happily locked up and well-preserved among the archives: not one of them had even been cut, yet they had been stored as property securely under bolt and bar.

Well, I am afraid that many of the following essays— all of which I published in their day—may have met the

---

* This theatre would appear to be that of Munich, and the date the early part of 1865.—TR.

same fate as those directions for the performance of *Tannhäuser*. But I must leave it to the kindly reader, for whom I now resuscitate them as from the grave, to judge whether I have a serious interest in presenting him with just these variations of the one great theme that turned on me its attention, and in presenting them in a manner which may not be altogether logical, yet to me appears to suit the circumstances.

ON THE "GOETHE-INSTITUTE."

Über die „Goethestiftung."

A LETTER TO FRANZ LISZT.

In Letter 59 of the Correspondence of Wagner and Liszt, *dated April 18, 1851, Wagner says:* "*I wanted to write you about your* Goethe-Stiftung, *but must wait for a calmer moment in order to do justice to your grand idea.—I doubt whether the proof-sheets will still be needed? However, they are already on their way to Leipzig."—The work was a pamphlet of about 150 pages (by Liszt)* " De la Fondation Goethe à Weimar," *evidently submitted to Wagner in a 'proof' state, for its publisher was F. A. Brockhaus, Leipzig. In Letter 60, May 17, Liszt writes:* " *I have received your* Goethe-Stiftung *letter, and sincerely thank you for it. I may mention, in passing, that it will probably take two years of time and trouble to make the idea a reality. But I will spend them on it, since I am fully convinced that without my activity, even on this soil, the thing will melt into air just as has already happened at Berlin. What do you say to publishing your letter (with a few trifling modifications and additions), just in its present form of a letter addressed to me, in some paper whose columns stand open to you?" To which Wagner replies in Letter 61, of May 22 (his birthday), in terms which are well worth reading through; here I can only quote one sentence:* " *As regards my last letter to you, I beg you to be assured that I wrote it absolutely without any ulterior aim."*

Liszt's project seems to have fallen through; for it must not be confounded with the Goethe-Gesellschaft, started June 1885, or the Goethe-Museum, opened July 1886, i.e. a few days before Liszt's death.—Wagner's letter (the accompanying) eventually appeared in the Neue Zeitschrift für Musik, *March 5, 1852.*—TR.

DEAR FRIEND,
　　　　　I still owe you an account of my views about your sketch for a "Goethe-stiftung." *

Is there any need for me to assure you in advance, that I thoroughly endorse the unconditional praise bestowed by the public journals on the fire and beauty of your conception of that idea? Looking quite aside from your exceptional situation toward the question, and the fact that in that situation you approach the subject from a far nobler and worthier standpoint than those who properly should stand far closer to it than yourself,—this witness must be borne you: that you alone have rightly grasped at all the aim and efficacy of a "Goethe-stiftung."

Since yours I have read many proposals on this subject, among others recently the article by Schöll in the *Deutsche Museum*, where the funds of the "*Goethestiftung*" are point-blank claimed for the support of the plastic arts. This, and many another consideration, now lets me see the undertaking in a somewhat different light from that which it necessarily must have taken for you. I may tell you

---

* "Goethe-foundation," or "Goethe-institute." Neither translation being exactly satisfactory, I prefer to use the German title, particularly as Wagner nearly always places it between inverted commas.—To this letter, on its appearance in the *N.Z.f.M.*, the following editorial footnote was appended: "We believe we shall afford our readers a subject of great interest by publishing this letter, originally in nowise meant for publication. In it the author already places himself on the standpoint which he indicated in his contribution to No. 6 of our issue for this year. In view of the new and broader lines which we have traced for the *Zeitschrift*, and shall keep resolutely before us, to us the letter seems quite in place. For Liszt's plan of a *Goethestiftung* see Volume 34, No. 25, of this paper." The last reference is to a résumé of Liszt's pamphlet, by T. Uhlig in June 1851; the "contribution" of Wagner's is the article on "*Musical Criticism*," a translation of which will be found on page 59 et seq. of the present volume.—TR.

quite openly, that I entirely disbelieve in the coming about of a "*Goethestiftung*," at least in its ever coming about in your sense. You desire a union, where the most absolute disunion is conditioned by the very nature of things. Our *Art* being completely splintered into separate *arts*, each of these bespeaks the supremacy for itself alone; and with just the same right as any of the others, each several art will know to make itself a title, at least to being the one most needing help.

We have no Poetry (*Dichtkunst*), but merely a poetical Literature: had we a genuine art of poetry, then all the other arts would be contained therein, and from it would draw the first prescriptions for their practice. Poetical Literature at present helps itself entirely alone: through the medium of the book-trade it stretches far and wide, and makes of itself a paper currency; much the same is the case with our literature-music. Painter and sculptor, on the other hand, find it much more difficult. To be sure, they too have learnt to convert their art into literature; engravings and lithographs circulate their works among the public, through the art-trade. But, seeing that with their productions the plastic original is by far the more important object, than e.g. the author's manuscript of a literary poem, which can only have intrinsic value as a curiosity, and not as an artwork,—seeing further, that this original can only consist of *one* example, and that the sale of this costly specimen is just the difficulty for the sculptor or painter, since the art-feeling and art-rewarding princes of the Renaissance are disappearing day by day, whilst the money-princes of our time are turning a more and more indifferent back,—these artists must necessarily be the first to look round them for the founding of societies and unions, and towards the active efficacy of contributions. These art-unions are becoming more and more the actual breadgivers of plastic art, and in the eyes of our plastic artists a "*Goethestiftung*" can naturally mean naught else but a joint-stock Goethe Art-union: members for this union will be found in largest numbers, and with openest purses, if one holds on every Goethe-anniversary an art-lottery—as some one will be sure to propose in the end. To such demands our plastic artists see themselves compelled by Want; and it would be hard indeed to dispute the justice of their plea, since in truth they base it on a salient feature (*Moment*) of their art, namely that its products consist in original exemplars which cannot be multiplied without losing their real artistic qualities. They can tell the poets and musicians that to *them*, once they wish to quit Literature for actual Life, our countless theatres and concert-rooms stand open, where " if only they know how to catch the public taste " they may get their works multiplied and paid-for at any time and any place, through the medium of performances; whereas their own works are simply damned to monumental singleness, and should therefore commend themselves to a special protection such as must appear entirely unneedful for the poet or musician.

If, then, no higher aim were to be taken in eye, when discussing the employment of a "*Goethestiftung's*" funds one could justly pay regard to nothing but the plastic arts; and the experiences reaped in this quarter have at any rate decided you, as well, to make proposals for the satisfaction of *every* class of artists. Yet a higher aim exists withal, and plainly do you speak it when you insist in general on the furtherance of such works as, by their very character, can *not* be left for recompense to the public's ruling taste, and therefore need peculiar exertions, on the side of a higher art-intelligence, to further them. Unmistakably you aim at the assistance of artistic tendencies whose idiosyncrasy makes it difficult for themselves to break a path. But here you cannot possibly have in eye the plastic arts; no, only poetry and music, in so far as they depart from Literature and make towards the physically enacted Artwork.

The plastic artist, for the recognition, success and reward of his performance, has solely to do with that finely cultured art-intelligence which is deemed intrinsically capable of recognising new and individual tendencies, and which you therefore call upon to contribute to their furtherance: but he never comes in contact with, and least of all into dependence on, the actual public. This public, which that artist leaves quite unregarded, is the very one, and almost the only one, the poet turns-to with his work for physical portrayal; and in view of *it* alone, can a special furtherance from the side of art-intelligence be deemed either necessary or efficacious.

Now, if poetry and music remain mere literature, they have absolutely no need for special furtherance, such as through a Goethe-union; and the plastic artist is perfectly right, to wish it denied them so long as the whole operations of the "*Goethestiftung*" are to be confined within the circle of this art-intelligence, and are not to pass over into a helpful relation with the genuine public. But if poets and musicians are concerned to turn the paper artwork into a really represented one, to reach beyond the literary formulas of thought to the only operative actuality of the art-*phenomenon*, then the question before us becomes immensely altered; for it suddenly grows into a question of *how the poet is to be furnished with those organs of realisement* which it costs the plastic artist—in his mechanical apparatus—so little trouble to procure. The painter and sculptor has within his hands the means of setting up an artwork completely knowable and finished—just as he conceived it, and according to his sole capacity for carrying it out: with him, to look at the purely practical aspect of the thing, there can only be a question of compensation for expenditure of time and technical material,—a material which he can be sure of getting for his ready money. Is this business portion of the matter settled; has he procured his material and made his time, or been recouped for its expenditure: then the purely social problem of the existence of his artwork is solved, and he has only further to commend it, in all its unmistakable reality, to the judgment of those persons versed in art. The subsequent question, how high shall be the reward for the enjoyment of his artwork as an intellectual product? is quite another matter, and has nothing to do with the furtherance of his artwork up to the point of bringing it into a state where unbiased judgment is possible thereon.—How does it stand, on the contrary, with the work of the poet and musician, when it is about to leave the literary formulas of thought for the certainty of plain and physical show?

Let us first take the poet, alone, within our ken.—He thrusts toward actuality of his artwork—in the sense of the actuality of works of plastic art—in Drama only; and indeed, not in the literary drama, but in drama *actually presented on the stage.* Now, how do the organs of this scenic representment compare with the mechanical instruments and materials of the sculptor or painter? Exactly as organism with mechanism in general. The realising organs of the poet are nothing less than human artists; and the art of dramatic portrayal, again, is a unique, a through and throughout living art. Where is the poet to find these artists, the sole enablers of his work, and where this art to realise his thoughts; those media which, in the form of tools and works of mechanism, stand ready to the plastic artist's hand wherever modern civilisation has spread itself? Painter and sculptor make answer: At our theatres, of which almost every town possesses one at least.—The affair would thus be made short work of, were it not that experience suggests a second question: Whether these theatres really hold an art-material which offers to the poet, whom we are viewing in the sense of the "*Goethe-stiftung*," just as sure and reliable organs for the realisement of his aim as the sculptor has at his disposal in clay and stone and chisel, or the painter in canvas, oils and paintbrush? Who would ever think of answering this question with a Yes?

Since it is precisely of a " Goethe "-institute that we are speaking, the experience cannot lie so very far from us, methinks, that our greatest poet just *did not* find those same artistic organs for the realisement of his highest aims. We see this poet's inner shaping-impulse driving him at every epoch towards its fullest utterance in actual Drama;

we see him giving his whole heart, with endless care and trouble, to the attempt to win that realising organ from and in the materials of the existing Theatre; we see him turn away at last in desperation from that torture,—in purely literary work, in scientific ferretings (*im wissenschaftlichen Tichten und Trachten*), to gain imaginary artistic rest and reparation,—and yet we can entertain a moment's doubt as to whether, for a poet in the Goethian sense, the organs for realising the poetic artwork are painlessly and lightly to be won, or in fact may anywhere be found at all?—Certainly there are stages to hand, and in every town and almost every night they are played on: but there is likewise to hand a Literature that draws its noblest breath almost solely from the impossibility in which our genuinely poetic writers find themselves, of getting these theatres to realise their aims. Our theatres stand in absolutely no relation with the noblest spirit of our nation: they offer a distraction for tedium, or a recreation from the toils of business, and thus maintain themselves by a function wherewith the true poet has positively naught in common; the stuff for their productions they borrow from abroad, or from imitations dressed-up for no other purpose than the function just denoted; their artistic media of portrayal, again, are trained for nothing but this end—and, faced with this phenomenon, the poetic spirit stands in utmost chill of resignation, cast back upon itself and condemned to find its only, its imaginary embodiment, in pen and paper, or printer's ink.

Now, what would the painter or sculptor answer us, if we told him: Content yourself with pencil and paper, and forego all colour and brush, all stone and chisel; for these belong not to the artist, but to public industry?—He would reply that he was thereby robbed of all possibility of realising his artistic thought, and bound down to merely hinting, but never carrying out that thought.—We then might make rejoinder: Very well, you shall be allowed the tools of industry, just as you refer the poet to our industrial theatres; adapt your aim to the means and ends of the painter of shop-signs or the hewer of gravestones, and you'll have precisely the same task before you, as you assign to the poet when you direct him to our stage. Should you find your aim completely marred hereby and made ununderstandable, we give you this further admonition: content yourself, just like us, with merely sketching out your thought; sell your sketch to the art-dealer, and you will have the advantage of seeing it circulated far and wide, in thousands of cheap lithographs or engravings! Mind you, this is what the poet of our day has also to be pleased with; you surely can't ask more than he, and under the protection of a "*Goethestiftung*" too?—In truth the plastic artist asks for more; he wants the furtherance of an already realised artwork: the sculptor wants his statue in bronze or marble made feasible, the painter his picture in colours on canvas, and to see this feasibility assured him by the warrant of a market for his artwork. The reason why he wishes the poet excluded from the competition, is because he merely looks upon him as a literarian to whom materials are easily procurable, and who already through the book-trade can reach his goal—be it reward or recognition: the thing the plastic artist despises from the bottom of his heart,—a purely literary ministration,—with *that* the poet is to be once for all content, and, for sake of this required contentment, to be shut out from competing.

How were it, if the poet—particularly should he take a rational view of the meaning of a "*Goethestiftung*"—stepped up to us and said he would *not* content himself with a purely literary rôle, he would no longer merely draft his thoughts in the literature-poem, but wished to see them embodied in a scenic artwork and realised as vividly as the painter now sets forth his thought in the oil-colours of his picture, or the sculptor in the marble of his statue? How were it, further, if he called *Goethe* as witness to the bootlessness of our existing Theatre, and implored that before all other things he should be provided with the artistic organ for that needful realisement, in a *Theatre* answering to the essence of his aim; since it is impossible for the poet to provide *himself* with a theatre in the same easy fashion as the plastic artist obtains the technical materials for presentment? Perchance the plastic artist, too pleasantly wrapt-up in self, might regard this claim as overstated and not in consonance with his own. The poet, however,—provisionally relying on the fact that this institute happens not to be proposed in honour of Dürer or Thorwaldsen, but of *Goethe*,—would then have to press him somewhat closer, and explain that the poet's work, without its realisation on the boards, would be placed in the most inequitable position towards the public verdict, as compared with the realised artwork of the painter, and that such a false position—at least in the sense of a "*Goethestiftung*" —would be a crying indignity; moreover, that the only reasonable object of a "*Goethestiftung*" would be to take thought for providing the means whereby the several art-branches might be placed on an equal footing as to their *power of manifestment*, and that in the present case it would have to act with all the greater energy, as it was a matter of correcting the mis-placement of the *art of poetry* —in homage to the memory of our greatest poet.

I know not whether the plastic artists will comprehend and assent to this; at present, however, that need not trouble us, for we may hope that they are not the leaders of *ton* at a "*Goethestiftung*."

Let us give our next thought to the musician, and come to speedy terms about his position towards the "*Goethestiftung*."—For the realisement of his ampler conceptions, to the musician there stand open two ways to publicity: the concert-room and—again—the theatre. What he writes for smaller circles is on all fours with poetic literature, which also is declaimed and read aloud, and with which we here will have nothing to do. In Germany the concert-room, with its orchestra and choir of singers, is for the most part so constituted that it may pass as offering the absolute musician a completely fitting organ for his aims: in this genre the Germans have remained original; neither Frenchmen nor Italians dispute with them the field. All the national genius applied in this direction is already furthered fittingly enough; means and end are here in thorough harmony, and even though our concert-institutes afford a more æsthetic criticism much food for thought, yet this lies in the nature of the genre which here is cultivated, but not in any technical disqualification which a "*Goethestiftung*" ought to help remove. We therefore can take the musician within our purview only from the point where he comes in contact with the poet, and shares his fate in respect of our stage: in this department, then, he comes entirely within the category of the poet; and all we have said about the latter, as touching the Theatre, may be equally applied to the musician.—

After all these premises, let me come to a conclusion.

If the "*Goethestiftung*" sets for itself no other goal than a yearly distribution of prizes for sculpture, painting, literature and music, turn and turn about: then in my opinion it does not in the slightest further Art, but merely makes it easier than they are accustomed to, for individual artists to find a market for their wares. In such an office the "*Goethestiftung*" would inevitably sink by degrees to the level of our existing art-unions; for bare sake of material maintenance, the institute could not help becoming in time an art-lottery under the firm of "Goethe."

But according to your explicit aim, the office of the "*Goethestiftung*" is to consist in a *furtherance* of Art. So that one can only go on to argue about the meaning of this "furtherance": and it is here that I'm at variance with you; this time indeed—so I believe—as the realist with the idealist.—A merely material assistance to the artist in disposing of his work, and even the assignment of an artistic prize, can never have that ideal effect, in furthering Art, which nevertheless you keep alone in view: the assumption of such an effect is already itself the too advanced ideal, whose realisement, again, can only be a thing of thought and not of actuality. He who does not feel within himself the necessity of art-creation, he whom this necessity does not force to doing, and who is first to be spurred to production through the possibility of a pecuniary reward or an honourable mention, he will never bring to pass a genuine artwork. But an other possibility must be offered the artist, if he is to win the courage, nay the capability, for creating: and that is *the possibility of bringing his planned and thought-out work to a Show in keeping with his Aim,—to a show in which this aim of his can first be truly understood, i.e. be felt.* If this material is not at the disposal of an artist, then he certainly must give up his aim: thus the artwork is nipped in the very bud, or to put it more correctly, the artistic aim cannot even be so much as taken.—To offer *this* possibility you decidedly intend: but as to the way in which it is to be offered we are not of one mind, for *you presuppose existing means of realising the artwork, while I dispute their existence or their adequacy.*—Let me therefore proceed to the statement of what, in my opinion, a Goethe-union would have to regard, and finally to further, in this matter.

A society which, in honour of the memory of Goethe and from the standpoint of pure artistic intelligence, should set itself the task of furthering Art, would in the first place have to espy where any art-line was suffering from a difficulty, or indeed a complete obstacle, in the way of that possibility of adequate physical manifestment to which I have referred above; and next to turn its whole united force of will and knowledge to lightening that possibility, or in sooth to first creating it. After a closer scrutiny the society would find, to its astonishment, that precisely the art in whose honour it first had met together, was the most, in fact the only one, in need of furnishing with that possibility. To the sculptor, the painter and the musician (so long as the latter abjures the stage) either mechanism or artistic fellowship affords the needful means for realising his artistic aim. If a genius of these arts feels in himself the thrust and aptitude for a new and individual departure (*Richtung*), there is nothing whatever in the way of his pursuing it; for he stands possessed of the means for fully shewing forth his aim, and it could only be ascribed to his own inaptitude, or the unsoundness of his departure, if he failed to make himself understood, or could not win a fellow-feeling for his aim ; nor in the latter case would any encouragement, would any union in the world avail to help him, since nothing here can further but the advice of brother artists and the harvest of his own experience. Precisely the same is the case with the poet who contents himself with literature, for the manifestment of his thought: in pens, ink and paper there stand at his disposal the simple means of making himself entirely intelligible—for just so far as he chooses, and no farther than himself intends ; they offer not the smallest obstacle to his striking out new paths.

But quite otherwise—as we have seen—does it stand with the genuine poet, who wishes to bring his poem to unfailing show in Scenic Drama : for him the means of realisement, in the present condition of our Theatre, are rightdown not forthcoming. The fallacy here, however, the thing which leads our eye from the true state of affairs, is that these means *appear* to be forthcoming. Undoubtedly there are theatres, and on their boards are even played * from time to time the best works of dramatic art of bygone ages ; so that, in view of this circumstance, one commonly hears put the thoughtless question : Why are our poets no Goethes and Schillers ; who can be blamed that no geniuses like these are born again ?—It would lead me too far, were I to attempt a radical reply to the confusion of mind whence such remarks proceed : for the moment let us be content with recording that, true enough, there has nothing of importance been done on our stage since Goethe and Schiller, also that it occurs to no one to search for the reason anywhere but in an absolute decay of the nation's genius. How were it, though, if from this very phenomenon I drew a proof that simply the faulty or unsuitable means of dramatic representation have brought about that more than apparent decay ? I have already

* How ?—this, at any rate, is asked by few, and surely least by our plastic artists !—R. WAGNER.

mentioned that Goethe, vanquished by the impossibility of grappling with the Theatre in *his* sense, withdrew from it altogether. Naturally, this failure of courage, on the part of a Goethe, passed down to his poetic heirs; and their compulsory abandonment of the Theatre was the very reason why, even in poetic Literature, they lost more and more the true creative faculty. Goethe's power of artistic shaping waxed strong in direct ratio to its application to the reality (*Realität*) of the stage, and in the same degree did it slacken and grow feeble as, with loss of nerve, he turned it back from that reality. This nervelessness became an æsthetic maxim of our younger poet-world; which lost itself in an abstract literary impotence for shaping, in exact measure as it contemptuously turned its back upon the stage and left it to the exploitations of our modern industrial playwrights.

But after the knowledge we have gained of it, it is precisely this stage that should be handed over to the poet, and in the endeavour would lie the only reasonable object of a Goethe-union; especially as it is through this means alone that it can attain the aim of influencing the artistic culture of the *Folk* as well, whom the plastic artist cannot reach at all, and the poet only when he lifts his *thought* to a visible and tangible (*sinnfälligen*) artistic *deed* in represented Drama.—With our Theatre, in the hopeless corruption into which it has fallen since just those fruitless efforts of Goethe's, the nobler spirit of our poetic powers can have nothing at all to do, without it means to taint itself: here it meets, for ruler and lawgiver, an evil system which it is unable to get-at without disfiguring itself beyond all recognition. Any new and individual departure, however, such as you wish the "*Goethestiftung*" to further or incite in general—any such line as this, the poet cannot even dream of striking through the medium of our Theatre. As the co-ordinate organs are entirely lacking on our stage, inasmuch as the Existing gives to *him* the law, not he to *it*, so his new line would only be misunderstood; for he would fain express an aim for which the sole enabling means of expression were wholly absent. Wherefore, confronted with the impossibility of its expression, he never arrives at even taking such an aim; *and this explains most simply the decay of our poetic spirit.*

Laying everything together, then, the "*Goethestiftung*," as a beginning, can only propose to bring about one thing: the founding of a Theatre * in the noblest spirit of our nation's poetry, i.e. *a Theatre that shall serve as a fitting organ for realising in dramatic art-work the most idiomatic outcomes of the German mind.*—Only when such a Theatre was forthcoming, only when the poet had found in this Theatre the realiser of his aim, and through that possibility of realisement had been given the zest and power for taking up poetic aims which at present, in the impossibility of their realisement, he cannot so much as entertain:—only *then* could one justly entertain the thought of challenging the plastic arts to compete with poetry. I for my part, however, am convinced that, in presence of the livingly enacted artwork of the poet united in Drama with the musician and thereby raised to the utmost fulness of his powers of utterance, the painter and sculptor would abjure all competition, and bow in reverence before an artwork compared wherewith their own works—which now, with so much apparent justice, they wish regarded as the only genuine artworks—could only seem the lifeless *particles* of Art. It would then perchance occur to them, that they must likewise weld these particles into a whole; and for this whole they would have to let the *architect* prescribe the laws, from whose binding guardianship they now with so much idle pride continue to withdraw themselves. As to the position of this at present so utterly neglected Architect, the virtual poet of the plastic arts, to whom sculptor and painter are to bear themselves in like manner as

---

* "Theater"—perhaps one should point out that Wagner uses this word not as referring to the mere building, but to the means of performance in general, actors, management, &c. &c.—TR.

musician and performer to the actual Poet,—as to the
position of this Architect thus inducted to his worthiest
office, towards the realised artwork of the Poet, we then
should have to come to terms; and here at last we should
light on a common field of action whereof we certainly
have no conception now. To fill that field with life, a
"*Goethestiftung*" would haply not alone suffice; but to
have instigated a search for it, would be more in keeping
with the views of Goethe, than any fresh encouragement
and outward furtherance given to our splintered art-depart-
ments in their obvious inward impotence for life.— —

Thus there would only remain, to give you my ideas
about the establishing of that Theatre itself. Allow me,
for to-day, to express myself with the utmost brevity on
this point, and to say that amid all circumstances, at every
place and with any quality of means, I deem possible the
gradual formation of a Theatre in consonance with our
aim, provided *one thing* be determined in advance: namely,
that this is to be an **original-theatre**. With this hint I
must leave the matter for the present, since the unfolding
of my plan for the establishment of such a theatre would
lead me much too far; but I am ready and willing to set
this forth at length, so soon as ever it is expressly asked
for.— — —

Here, dear Liszt, you have the upshot of what my acquaintance with your brochure on the "*Goethestiftung*" has
aroused in me. I believe I have hit your meaning, though
you express it somewhat differently. Two aspects seem to
have intercrossed in your proposal, an ideal and a real one,
which cannot fully blend together. In the ideal you almost
share my point of view: the quadrennial festival [*] appears
to me to offer in broad outline what might some day issue
from the realisation of my plan; only, that I should keep

---

[*] Liszt had proposed a *musical* festival, to be held in the Wartburg every fourth year, in addition to the annual competition for prizes in the four respective arts.—TR.

the *drama* more in eye. On the real side you feel constrained, through the claims of our present artist-castes, to make concessions which probably have been extorted from you by the desire to stir a wide-spread interest. But let us look squarely at this matter, and recognise that we shall effect no lasting good if we begin by wishing to please everyone at once. Let us draw a smaller circle and first take a definite aim in view, thus holding to the root of the noble future tree we long for. This root is here the Theatre: that stands, in Weimar's, at your hand; it needs wellnigh nothing but the will, to soon reach a goal which in itself would be already the fittest "*Goethestiftung*." For this, however, you well can do without a wider Goethe-union: if they wish to help you, let them look at home and set to work on their own plot of ground; let them follow your example in the theatre. If they achieve the same elsewhere, so much the better, and the goal will then be reached in ever wider circles. But you may easily rest content with Weimar for the present, and if the Goethe-committee leaves you in the lurch, why! let them go; they would only be shewing that they can be of no further use to you. Let these people found an art-lottery under the title of a "*Goethestiftung*": found you meantime a *genuine Goethestiftung*, and call it how you choose!

I can't help thinking that I have struck your secret wish. If so, then may this letter serve you as a buttress to your will, a special reinforcement of your universal aim. Only in this sense, at least, have I told you my mind.

Prolix as this communication may appear, yet I am alive to the many gaps it still leaves in the exposition of its subject. To make it quite complete, to convince on every hand, at least according to my powers, I should have had to swell it out into a book; which after all would not be read by those I wish to get at, or if read, would be made over to a prudent disregardal on their part. In the maintenance of a real or affected disregard for whatever, taken honestly, might challenge them to a little unselfish deliberation, our artists and art-scholars of to-day are great indeed; for this they draw the aptitude from the lucky circumstance that they know everything already: everything, that is, which they comfortably can stow within their separate-artistic pigeon-holes. But you, best friend, I refer—for supplement of to-day's communication—to my soon forthcoming book on "Opera and Drama," at whose close I reason out my views anent the ineptitude of the modern Theatre, more especially in Germany. For the moment, however, I must think of the close of the present letter, before it likewise swells into a book. So I will make it short and to the point, by merely crying you the heartiest Farewell of

     Yours,

          RICHARD WAGNER.

Zurich, May 8, 1851.

A THEATRE AT ZURICH.

(1851).

Ein Theater in Zurich.

In Letter 61 to Liszt—already cited—Wagner writes: "You will by now have received my little pamphlet, 'ein Theater in Zurich': much of it, nay the most part, will not do for you, since the conditions here are far too unlike those at Weimar. My ideas of the field of operations for an 'original-theatre,' however, will be made tolerably clear to you by the little work. In case the question should arise in your mind—Do I wish to altogether exclude everything foreign?—I reply to it in advance: Certainly for the present, and until the main object is attained; but not for all future time. The main object consists in the theatre, such as I suggest, training itself to an entire, an individual self-dependence, through its own originality" &c. Minor references to the pamphlet occur in a letter to Uhlig and another to F. Heine, both dated the middle of April '51, shewing that it was written about three weeks before the article on the "Goethe-stiftung."

This "little work" was published in Zurich, and considerable portions of it were reprinted in the Neue Zeitschrift of June 27, July 4, and July 11, 1851.

TRANSLATOR'S NOTE.

THEATRE-SEASON is over. Six months ago a number of stage-artists, from the most diverse regions of the world, arrived in Zurich at the summons of a manager: this troop is now dispersing in all directions. Just as in the spring of last year, various impresarios are again competing for the lease of the theatre-building for the coming winter: after duly depositing the caution-money the solidest-seeming applicant will obtain the lease, and with it, not the mandate, but the permission to collect a company from far and near, in order to let its members scatter again next spring—should no bankruptcy have meanwhile intervened—to all the points of the compass. In the course of the coming winter-months this director will make it his business to meet the wishes of the public by as rapid and varied a production as possible, of pieces that have been well received elsewhere. In the most fortunate event, he will have assembled a personnel among which some individuals will earn particular favour—a circumstance enabling him to give frequent repetitions of certain pieces; in a sorrier case, it will be impossible to take such interest in any member of his troop, and he then will give us all the more motley a mixture of theatric novelties, as their breathless change must serve to win from curiosity that support which a particular liking of the public for this or that performer is unable to lend the undertaking. What will be the success of this director?

Let us take our answer from the success of the last undertaking.

The director who has just left us, made it his object last autumn to get together a particularly good stage-company: which means, in other words, that he determined to spend a larger sum in salaries. That in consequence of this determination he was able to engage some excellent talent, he must certainly attribute to a stroke of luck; since experience teaches that, for however great a wage, superior artists are very seldom to be found. Equipped with a good personnel, he scrupulously offered the public what it wished for, and what the character of his company permitted. After getting over its initial distrust, the public shewed an interest no smaller than, judging by earlier-made experiences, one might reasonably expect. The result of this undertaking, however, was nothing but its undertaker's forfeiting the larger portion of a not inconsiderable sum, which had been set aside at the outset; and he now departs with the satisfaction of knowing that a whole winter through, for the loss of his money, he has provided the Zurich public with theatrical performances as good as possible. Any inducement to continue this experiment, unselfish at least in its issue, has not been offered him from any quarter.

After the above experience, what can be the views and intentions of the impresario who will bear away the prize from the competition, at present taking place, for the only thing which confers a right and might to manage the theatre—the lease of the playhouse?—If he goes systematically to work, he must first weigh all the circumstances, and decide whether he will pursue the path so lately opened by the departing manager: namely, engage as good a company as possible, and shirk no sacrifice of money to this end. The experience just made here must necessarily turn him off from that; only personal vanity could tempt him to suppose that in his hands, and with his special cleverness, *that* might perhaps succeed, which was wrecked through some failing of another. The next spring would open his eyes to the fact, that any failings of his forerunner were by no means personal to the director, but arise necessarily from the unalterable position of every theatric manager toward his personnel and the public— thus from the general relations of this sort of stage—and are not to be avoided by the greatest cunning on his part. Thus in the most favourable event he would only make over again the experiences of the last management, and would ascertain, to boot, that the Zurich public last winter shewed itself precisely as interested in the theatre as is possible for it under existing circumstances; but that this interest is not sufficient to entirely cover the costs of his undertaking. So that if the coming director strikes the path just indicated, we shall be the richer by no fresh experience, while this director too—with or without a bankruptcy—will certainly have grown poorer by a sum of money.

It is rather to be supposed, then, that the next director, so soon as he views the matter in cold blood, will only think of his outgoings and profits. If he goes systematically to work, he will before all things lower his salary-list, intentionally select a middling personnel, and so arrange his productions with these forces as to speculate on nothing but the public's curiosity. After every fresh enticement the public will leave the theatre in disappointment; the director, however, will constantly bestir himself to lure the disappointed into a new curiosity-trap; until all his dainties are exhausted, the director straps his bundle, and—another theatre-season is over, leaving behind it the utmost indifference in respect of all theatric art.

But there remains a third possibility, namely that the future stage-director will lay aside all system, and leave himself and his undertaking to sheer "good luck": he engages just whatever comes his way, and presents just what presents itself. At the same time he reckons on favouring chances, such as good or bad weather, a scandal in the town, a pretty actress and her lover, and incidents and things like these; all which he exploits according to a system of his own, till at last the police give him his marching orders—unless he should first have been called to a special post at one of the great Court-theatres. In any case, even after the end of *this* theatrical director, there would again be opened here a fresh contention for the lease.

How comes it, now, that the theatre never rouses a higher form of attention than that which leaves to mere hazard in what sense it shall be conducted, and whether an impresario shall to-day bestir himself to give us something good, or to-morrow another shall make it his lamentable duty to woo fortune with something bad? Without doubt there lies at the bottom of this phenomenon a great lack of interest in the Theatre itself, and this lack of interest must rest on a profound inner dissatisfaction with the Theatre's doings; a dissatisfaction which dwells unconsciously within the public breast, and to bring which to its consciousness may prove indeed a not unweighty task.

I will attempt to discharge this task, and at like time to bring to consciousness a need which necessarily must shew itself in utmost clearness, if the means for its satisfaction are ever to be fathomed and devised.

The interest in the Theatre, as we have just seen, is not of such a kind that the public has felt disposed to voluntarily support an undertaking which fulfilled all that was possible under existing circumstances, in any other way than by a payment for admission to certain performances —such payment not sufficing in and by itself to fully cover the undertaking's costs. Without a moment's regret, one witnesses the dispersal of a company to which one cannot refuse its meed of praise; to no one does it occur to instigate proceedings for its retention, but indifferently one leaves to chance the fate of the next theatrical season. Yet this general indifference to the fate of the Theatre, taken with the circumstance that during the winter the public often attends the performances in large numbers, does not point to a dislike for the Theatre on the whole; but rather a half conscious, half unconscious doubt whether, even if more substantially supported, a theatre at Zurich could ever be brought to yield anything really good.

This doubt must certainly be harboured with full consciousness by those who are in a position to visit the larger cities of Europe from time to time, and involuntarily allow the imposing effect of the theatrical productions * there to influence their judgment on the doings of the theatre at home. It is not in the least to be wondered at, if the same dramatic works which so completely dazed them there by wealth of trappings, by opulence of scene and brilliant virtuosity of players, should produce so sobering an impression on them when reproduced on the local stage that they find first this and that, and at last everything quite insupportable, and finally turn away in utter apathy, resolving to make themselves amends on their next trip to Paris or Naples. To be sure, the less well-to-do section of the public,—more fettered to its native soil, and thus kept aloof from the constant revival of comparisons between the doings of those great theatres and of the little one at home —does not feel the contrast so directly; nevertheless it unconsciously feels a dissatisfaction, such as needs must follow on the unclear impression left by every imperfect thing, even when the exact nature of its imperfections is not divined. In our theatrical productions this public is presented with an object which cannot address it clearly and plainly, for the simple reason that the needful means of expression are not forthcoming. It is confronted with features reckoned for quite other circumstances, and quite other people, than our own and ourselves. Let us sum in a word the whole ailment wherewith almost every theatre of Europe is stricken, even unto death: it consists in this, that with very few exceptions, among which only the first opera-houses of Italy can be included, *there is no Original-theatre but that of Paris, and all the rest are merely its copies.—*

With the exceptions above-referred-to, Paris is the only city in the world where such pieces alone are performed, as have been expressly written and accurately calculated for the boards on which they reach portrayal. The character

* "Vorstellungen"—as this word and "Aufführungen" are used in a sense not quite the same as that of "Darstellung" (performance, or representation), I have thought it better to render them by "productions" whenever their particular employment does not absolutely *exclude* the idea of what we call in England a "first night."—TR.

of each of the many Parisian theatres, its resources, the compass and arrangements of its stage, the peculiarity of the 'talent' belonging to it at the moment, afford their dramatic authors the definite means of expression through which they are to bring their subject to a hearing; and this subject, again, decides itself according to the idiosyncrasy of this particular theatre's public, on the one hand, and just those expressional means on the other. These conditioning, and at like time enabling circumstances hold equally good for every Paris theatre, from the paltriest Vaudeville of the suburbs right up to the sumptuous Grand Opéra itself. Never would it occur to one of these theatres, to produce a piece not written expressly for it; and, through this perfect harmony between means and end, so sure a feeling for the true essence of a good and intelligible dramatic representation has been engendered among performers and public alike, that any occasional attempts with foreign pieces have been foredoomed to certain failure.*

Thus has theatric Paris become the only genuine producer of our modern dramatic literature. In the first place, its productions are reproduced in the provincial towns of France, and already there, with all the defects of a decreasing originality; but beyond this, all the German theatres live almost exclusively on an imitation of the Paris stage. The larger German theatres as a whole have taken their modern grafting of dramatic art from nowhere but abroad, and, supported by parade-struck Courts, they spend the most enormous sums on bringing the products of Parisian theatres to reproduction on their stage; at the present day one goes so far as to copy the Paris productions with the most scrupulous pains, even to the minutiæ of scenery, machinery and costumes. Yet how null and void these copies are, however great the cost, everyone feels at once, who has visited the theatres in Paris where those pieces are to the manner born. He finds that at the

---

* By reference to Wagner's article "*Le Freischutz*" (translated in *The Meister*, No. xxv) it will be seen that the author had formed this opinion as early as 1841.— TR.

largest German theatres, and in the most favourable event, one has merely been able to copy the veriest externals of those productions; and that the special idiosyncrasy of talent for which the dramatic composition was originally reckoned, has been watered past all knowledge. He notices further that, even could the character of the original productions be copied on German stages, yet those productions win their full vivacity of colour and impressiveness only where they step into life amid a social surrounding and before a public—in short, under conditions of time and place which have absolutely nothing in common with our own, and are thoroughly alien to our views and habits.

In order to put my meaning in the clearest light, let me instance the enormous difference between a German and an Italian audience. The Italian opera-theatres have preserved their originality, and that in dealing with a public which nowadays seeks nothing in the theatre but the most sensuous distraction. Throughout the make-believe of drama this public pays its sole attention to the most brilliant passages of the evening's star, be it the prima donna or her male rival in the art of song; the remainder of the opera it as good as doesn't heed, but spends the larger portion of the evening upon paying and returning visits in the boxes, and upon private conversations carried on aloud. Faced with this behaviour of the public, the opera-composers have grown accustomed to devote their artistic productivity merely to the aforesaid rôles; while they treat all the opera's groundwork, namely the choruses and rôles of so-called minor personages, with the most deliberate negligence, filling it out with banal, everlastingly repeated, absolutely nothing-saying stopgaps, intended just to make a bustle during the public conversation. A German audience, on the contrary, is wont to give the performance its continuous attention; it therefore receives with the same interest as the principal rôles, or at least with the same struggle for interest, that nothing-saying tonal noise, and thus takes as sterling golden coin what the composer had issued with full consciousness as pewter tokens. Now, how must we appear to that Italian stranger? Very ridiculous, to be sure! and that's extremely vexing: for at the bottom of our attentive listening to his spurious artwork there lay, in truth, an honourable artistic sense of good manners. However, let us learn from this to what a pitch of poverty and helplessness we now have sunk!

If I here have given a glimpse of the general situation of the German Theatre, in its dearth of all originality, a still more mournful sight will greet our eye when we survey the only field of activity lying open to a theatre such as that of Zurich.

At the more eminent theatres of Germany not only are original Paris products reproduced, but on their form and nature German playwrights and composers have modelled dramatic works in which they have tried to localise, in a measure, the foreign content of those pieces. In this fashion there has come to light an unedifying, hybrid genre, which has drawn notice to itself only through its content mirroring the moods and interests of the place and season for and in which these pieces are calculated and composed. Berlin, Vienna, Hamburg and other of the greater theatre-cities have in this way turned out pieces which, in view of the immediate local and temporal relations whose specific interest served them as subject-matter, have been able for a time, and for as far as those relations reached, to interest as novelties pure and simple, albeit no artistic merit could ever be adjudged them. If one looked at these pieces a little closer, one was bound at last to recognise the original of their copy; an original which primarily lay far outside the circle of relations for which the copy had been trimmed up. From that original, one had borrowed principally the form; but this whole form had earlier emanated from a content which, in its most important features, was as different from the new and substituted content as, for instance, are Paris and the Parisians from Berlin and the Berliners. The necessary variance between stuff and form mostly operated on the German piece-maker in *this* direction :—

that he must try to arrange his own new-chosen stuff to fit
the form he copied; whereby it happened that the stuff
itself was twisted into the most complete un-nature, an
utter caricature. So that this pseudo-original product had
to seek its real effect in sheer externals; and these were
either more or less witty allusions to local events of the
day, or the very definite personality of special favourites
among the 'talent.'

Now, what has been prepared in this wise as theatric
fodder for the flabby and indifferent appetite of the public
of the larger German cities, serves next—together with the
more direct copies of Parisian productions—for almost
the solitary food of the public of smaller theatre-towns, in
whose ranks one must number Zurich. Here one misses
all those references, which gave a certain sort of interest to
the "points" of that theatric aftermath in the cities where
it still could shew a glimmer of originality. Of these
productions nothing effective can be left for *here* but the
most inartistic, coarsest features, in addition to that interest
in the personality of performers who entirely for themselves, again, and without a shred of connection with the
fictitious artwork, bestir themselves to absorb the public's
attention in any way they think proper.

However, the more debased the sphere of execution in
which these efforts move, so much the easier is it for means
and end of the performance to maintain a certain harmony,
and for this simple reason: that here it must seem permissible for the performer to display his personality, and
that alone, with all the force he knows of; an end that
can have been the only one which hovered, more or less
consciously, before the author of the piece himself. In this
sphere and to this end have the real bread-bringers of our
theatres plied their trade, from Herren Friedrich and
Kaiser down to the royal Prussian upper-court-poetess
Frau Charlotte Birchpfeiffer. Whoever may want to gain
a calm and clear idea of the despicable nature of these
piece-makers' stage-products, let him compare their sham
original pieces, such as "A hundred-thousand Thalers"

&c. with the genuine Parisian originals on which they are modelled, or let him set Ch. Birchpfeiffer's adaptation of Hugo's romance "Nôtre-Dame" by side of the adaptation which was given at the Parisian *Théâtre de l'Ambigu comique*; he then will feel the unexampled desolation of our theatric art, in which one has come to be content with the vilest copies of copies vile themselves!

From this debased foundation, on which there yet is shewn a certain harmony in what is done, the representations of a theatre such as that at Zurich move up to undertaking feats which they are the less competent to achieve, the higher do those feats mount up before them; and for the simple reason that they were calculated for quite other forces than stand here at disposal. The discrepance of the expressional means increases in direct ratio as the expression's fictive end is lifted higher; and that for reasons which I have already hinted at in general, but here must scrutinise a little closer.

In the first place I have to adduce a fact observed in the winter just gone by. On the part of the public the director of the theatre was point-blank dissuaded from giving certain greater, nobler dramas; on the other hand, as regards Opera he was principally asked for pieces of the so-called "grand" variety. This observation characterises the whole present attitude of the public toward the Theatre, and alike the notion which actual performances have given it, of the Theatre's essence. The higher-pitched task, which one did not trust the performers to accomplish in the Play, one coolly imposes on them for the Opera. But, with this remarkable predilection for Opera, one involuntarily confesses to holding it a lower art-genre than the Play; and as regards the ministrations of Opera nowadays, at any rate, one is absolutely right. It is impossible for the higher class of play to win a genuine interest, unless that interest be roused by the Action, by the Characters which vindicate that action, and finally by the truthful, the soul-engrossing Representment of those characters. In the play there therefore lurks the genuine backbone, the true intent, of all dramatic art: only when this has fully evolved and been given due scope, can the higher expression—that of musical delivery—be naturally joined therewith, as a thing both craved and justified. To seek this inner kernel of the Drama, in face of our theatric doings, the public has been absolutely unaccustomed; and for the aforesaid reason, that it has never been presented with original products, racy of its soil and sprung from those ever-present moods and bearings which it feels with all its soul. The public of our theatre has been solely offered foreign goods, which have never made its heart to beat, but merely laid claim to its outmost sensuous interest through their own most outward side. Now, this outward side is the absolutely least exciting or engrossing in the higher class of Play; much rather in the very lowest class, since there the personal caprice of the performer must be allowed to go even the length of caricature so as to make an effect. In Opera, on the contrary, the outward appeal to the senses has so thoroughly established itself in power, that a purely material amusement of the nerves of hearing was bound to become the musical composer's virtual aim. A play cannot enthral in any other way than through an intimate adoption of the poet's aim; in the realisement of this aim the spectator's whole soul-phantasy must take its share, because—in just the spectacle (*Schauspiel*)—that Phantasy has not for helpmeet so exquisite a stimulus of Feeling, as in the musical drama. In Opera, however, the poetic aim is merely used as pretext; whereas the virtual aim resides in that ear-entrancing method of delivery, which may well exert a purely outward fascination without kindling in the inner soul one single spark of interest. —

Wherefore in its desire to see performed, not higher-class plays, but by all means the Grand Opera, the public gives voice to its profound contempt for theatric art in general; a contempt in which it is perfectly justified, since it has never made the acquaintance of a Theatre in living artistic relation with its own views and tempers. For Art, however, there remains the shocking humiliation, that, plied as a mere means of livelihood, she has to adapt herself to the public's craving from the outset,—to this craving which, all ignorant of the higher dignity of Art, can only go out to her on her most frivolous side. In theatrical productions, whose dramatic kernel one spurns from ignorance or lack of sympathy, the demands of the paying and thus dictating public have to be answered with a putting forward of the outermost of husks, cut loose from all the core and pulp of Art; and the real focus of the performances, the only thing which can draw the public's outward interest, remains "Grand Opera" so-called.

Now, this gold-bedecked Grand Opera is in and by itself a mere husk without a kernel: to wit a florid, glittering display of the most sensuous expressional means, without an aim worth the expressing. In Paris, where this genre acquired its modern finish, and whence it is being transplanted to our stage, there has been distilled from all the native arts of luxury and delectation a dazzling extract, which has gained at the Grand Opéra a consistence unapproached elsewhere. All the rich and notables, who settle in the monstrous world-metropolis for its out-of-the-way amusements and distractions, are driven by ennui and unsated cravings to the sumptuous chambers of this theatre, there to get set before them the fullest draught of entertainment. The most astounding pomp of decorations and stage-costumes unfolds itself in startling multiplicity before the swooning eye, which turns its greedy glance, again, to the most coquettish dancing of the amplest ballet-corps in all the world; an orchestra of unrivalled strength and eminence accompanies in sonorous fill the dazzling march of never-ending masses of chorus-singers and *figurants*; between whose ranks at last appear the most expensive singers, schooled expressly for this theatre, and claim the overwrought senses' residue of interest for their special virtuosity. As pretext for these seductive evolutions a dramatic aim is also dragged-in by the ears—its tantalising motive borrowed from some murderous, or Devil's scandal;

and this whole clinking, tinkling, glittering, glistening show * is paraded as "Grand Opera."

Now, at a theatre like that of Zurich, what remains of this intoxicating wonder-drink, when it is reached down to the thirsting public for an after taste? Nothing but the flat and stately sober dregs.—All that made this opera precisely a "grand" opera, all that raised the rank effect of these productions to something quite apart from the lesser genre,—the giant wealth and variety of sensuous accessories,—all this falls away on our theatre, because of poverty and inadequacy of means of exhibition; and of all the stately edifice there is nothing left but the exiguous scaffold, which had absolutely no intrinsic object in itself, but was simply there to serve for propping out the gorgeous drapings. Merely *that* can be brought before us, which there was only used as pretext; the real aim, that made this pretext serve it, must remain quite unimparted to us.

If in the effect of such maimed theatric rites we must recognise an ignominious self-deception on the part of the public, on the other side we have yet to consider what an artistically demoralising influence the concernment with tasks so inachievable must exert on the performers. In the first place, the lack of requisite and fitting means of represenment forbids any giving the chosen work in its entirety. Though the build of this work—with its aim directed merely to material and sensuous excitation—was not the organic structure of a genuine artwork, yet it was so pinned together through mechanical expedients, that the pretext of a uniting dramatic 'intention' was mostly built into it with quite observable purpose. Where, however, this Grand Opera's intrinsic aim—to serve as a showstall for resplendent means of expression—was so completely reached as at the Paris theatre, there this very pretext might easily be dropped, upon occasion; and we see that, without the slightest damage to the real value of the seeming artwork, on certain nights merely single Acts of such operas are given, then followed by the per-

* "Klingen, Schwirren, Flittern und Flimmern."—

formance of any other work you please. But where this opera's intrinsic aim cannot be reached at all, as at our local theatre, there we are, strictly speaking, confined to that bare pretext; and to lift it somehow into an intrinsic aim, must consequently become the foremost care of the performance. Only, just this pretext is certain here to be withdrawn into utter hopelessness of recognition, since the inadequate means impose the most appalling cuts and shortenings; so that what is left, obtains a position quite other than it had in its connexion with the parts excised, and the scenes retained can only appear as the unintelligible fragments of a whole become unknowable.* Add to this the further evil, never yet sufficiently explored, that those works are only given us in translations, which, unlovely in themselves, are mostly made entirely unintelligible through their clumsy and bad array beneath the notes: and we may infer at last the spirit in which the performers approach their task. Completely indifferent to an aim whereof they are ignorant, they rehearse their parts as mere vocal instruments; since hardly one of them knows the content of his own song-talk, still less does he heed the verbal meaning of his fellows; so that the character of a situation, and its bearing on themselves, remain entirely strangers to them. In such circumstances, moreover, each day makes them more indifferent whether this or that scene, this or that connecting link—which may be inconvenient to them for such and such reasons (principally that of over-hurried study)—is also dropped at last, or whether these or those conscious faults occur; for after all one can advance the so insulting, and yet completely warranted excuse: "The public will never notice it!"

Now just as, in compliance with the public's liking for Grand Opera, the performers have here accustomed themselves to leave entirely out of count the higher dramatic aim where it had merely been employed as pretext, so

---

* Who among my readers can truthfully vouch that he has ever understood the plot of "Robert the Devil," for instance, from its representations in this town?—R. WAGNER.

they end quite naturally by carrying this indifference into the performance of works in which that aim exists as a genuine thing; of works which therefore dispense with the material fillip to the senses, alone intended in the expressional means elsewhere. After what has been said above, one may imagine in how irreconcilable a contradiction the habits of the performers must stand to the task herewith proposed them! Here their incapacity can only be so utter, that the public turns unmoved and wearied from the representation of such works, and puts up rather with the flattest products; in which the unconsciously felt contrast between means and end does not at any rate come out so nakedly.—If we reckon further, that, with the public's necessary lack of inner interest in these really most unsatisfying performances, its outward interest, i.e. its money at the doors, can only be attracted through a whetting of its curiosity or its love for motley change; and if we perceive that, to this end, there must be always something new brought out, or at the smallest, something other: then we shall also conceive that the whole restless activity of an everlastingly harried troop of players must needs consume itself in an exertion absolutely profitless to Art. Never is it possible for performers or managers to devote their care to the *how* of the productions, but always to the protean *what*. Any conception and execution of an artistic plan, must be abandoned from the outset; the eternal Want (*Noth*) is to give something new and other, at last no matter in what guise: for—on this alone depend the takings, the payment of wages, the provision of the necessaries of existence.

What, then, is the mutual sentiment between Theatre and Public; and, in the given circumstances, what can it not but be? Let us say it frankly out: a reciprocal contempt!—The public can pay no honour to an art which is never in the position to enthral and satisfy it; unenlightened as to the grounds of this its dissatisfaction, it is only able to dupe itself into a superficial interest when, on occasion and from a purely personal liking for this or that performer, it signals an applause as to whose intrinsic value it never takes the slightest thought. The theatrical performers cannot respect the will and judgment of a public which, through the very character of its interest in the theatre, makes impossible to them the development of aptitudes whereof the practice of their art affords them an instinctive consciousness; they are aware that the public gives its interest merely to the most superficial unfoldings of art, that it is to be bribed by the cheapest claptrap, and —as for any knowledge of the upshot of their doings— may be held the veriest gaby. How often in their representations things happen of such monstrous folly, that the performers needs must laugh in their sleeves when they remark that the public is not one whit upset! Thus even the bestowed applause can by no means be taken as the encouraging reward and acknowledgment of an effort to do the right, but merely as the reckoned and besought result of employing certain stock-devices; one receives it as a matter of course, and when it hangs fire—mostly through some accident—one feels justified in indignation. If the public could only witness these indignant outbursts a little oftener, it would soon be taught how dishonouring and disrespectful are the relations between itself and the priests of our theatric art of nowadays: it would perceive that, just as for *it* the Theatre is an inwardly despised purveyor to its entirely superficial craze for entertainment, for that purveyor, in turn, *itself* is but a lightly to be cozened victim of the most self-seeking speculation.

However, we may almost assume that the relation here disclosed does not need to be unmasked to the public so absolutely for the first time, and that it is wellnigh as much aware of its actual standing toward the Theatre, as the stage-personnel is acquainted with *its* toward the public. At least, this assumption is unequivocally vouched-for by the public's aforesaid utter indifference to the fate of the local theatre here, which takes for it the semblance of a beggar to whom one mechanically reaches out an alms without so much as looking him in the eye, and thoroughly untroubled as to his physiognomic personality. This will also explain the entire lack of interest even in the riddance of so mutually dishonouring a situation : were the smallest spark of respect or love forthcoming, one would take thought for means to elevate so unseemly a relation. Since nothing of the kind occurs, and any attempt to establish a nobler relation between the Theatre and Public on the present basis must appear fruitless out and out, we certainly need not wonder either that the public abides in its state of inward indifference, or that the theatre does not of itself soar up to a position whence it might conquer that indifference ; for one thing here conditions the other, and no real blame attaches to either, as both phenomena have their grounds in a wider relation—whose present discussion would lead to naught.

There is only one thing to be wondered at, namely : how so thoroughly unseemly a relation, so strongly and so injuriously affecting the public taste as that I here have touched on, should have hitherto escaped the watchful eyes of thinking men and carers for the public weal ; and thus that no one has as yet come forward with suggestions for the appointment of a Board (*Behörde*) to whom should be committed the task of finding a more satisfactory solution of the Theatre-question, in the interest of public morals.

It is far from any wish of mine, to think of the Theatre as an educational institute for the public. This idea, which certainly has been conceived by some, tells of an absolute disdain for the public, together with a degrading estimate of Art herself—who in Drama attains her highest, her most peculiar glory. Were it expedient to educate the public by aid of theatrical performances, then it would first be necessary to settle who is to be the educator, and what is to be laid down as the divine evangel according whereto dramatic art is to be employed as means, and public taste to be formed as end. Neither this gospel, nor that educator, should we find on any reasonable path.—If we rightly gauge the station of each several Board in so organised a State as that of Zurich, however, this authority should be the conscious organ for reaching an end demanded by a need in common, as its satisfaction. Surely the fact that the public has never hitherto felt with requisite strength the real need of a Theatre, can be the only assignable ground for this other fact: that there exists as yet no Board entrusted with the task of satisfactorily arranging the affairs of the Theatre. Up to to-day the Theatre has passed for a class of entertainment that one sought from purely accidental personal liking, without connecting it with any object to which one might suppose oneself pledged by considerations of an inner need in common. Merely insofar as the social entertainment offered by the Theatre was one whose very nature set it in the circle of a wider-spread publicity, did it draw the attention of an authority which is entrusted, in the interest of public safety, with the prevention of nuisances such as might spring from heedless conflict with that public interest. Wherefore the only authority through which Theatre and Public have been brought into contact, from the burgher standpoint, is the Police.

Now if we look a little closer, we have first to attest a feature which may well be regarded as the symptom of a common higher need, in the sense we mean; and this is the undeniable fact that in the course of the six winter months a majority of the inhabitants of Zurich, from tenderest youth to hoariest age, assembles in the theatre several times a week, and often in large numbers at a time, with the object of procuring itself a common entertainment, though mostly in very diverse moods. That this entertainment as a rule could only be of the kind I have described above, is the thing which heretofore has withdrawn from this sight the gaze of thinking and public-minded men; because they could nowhere find in it the point they might deem fitted for the accommodation of a higher associate end. But the question now arises, whether the simple fact of that often numerous attendance does not already reveal a need, which merely from ignorance of nobler pleasures at present exhibits itself as feeble and incapable of shaping, yet in which there well may lie a higher furthering attribute if only the pivot of its inner bent were found and brought to consciousness. Before all else, then, it cannot be denied that in the Theatre, under the circumstances just cited, we have a 'moment' of public life informed with a 'motive' which needs culture to become a higher ethical force.* After noting this, the next duty would be to carefully examine whether that culture-needing motive were withal a motive capable of cultivation ; so that, in case one could not convince oneself of this, one might use all one's disposable powers to prevent so crippled a thing from offending and injuring the healthy spirit of publicity, insofar as the public interest is made over to the guardianship of every public-minded burgher,—or if that motive already shewed promise of an aptitude for cultivation, one might put forth all one's powers to aid in its maturing.

Thus our first business would be to prove the existence of that aptitude, and prove it from a need already manifested by the public. This proof is quite undoubtedly afforded by the simple experience that in those isolated cases where, through any special pains or lucky circumstance, one succeeded in giving the theatrical productions an approximate stamp of perfection, by setting a real artistic end in passable harmony with the means forthcoming †—there the public was surprised into betokening a satisfaction which evidently avouched the existence of an inner need within it ; a need which could not come as yet to common consciousness, only because those cases shewed themselves so very rarely, and must be choked into complete oblivion by the mass of unsoundness in general affairs theatric. If therefore, in face of these customary

---

* " Ein Moment des öffentlichen Lebens . . . dem ein bildungsbedürftiges Motiv für höhere Gesittung innewohnt."

† Reference should be made to *Letters to Uhlig*, No. 18 (dated Zurich, October 22, 1850), where Wagner gives a fairly long account of his own intervention in these performances, and adds : " But I must withdraw, because with the best will in the world I do not see how a répertoire can be kept up, which should prevent that being pulled down on the one side which I am building up on the other."—TR.

affairs, the best-trained minds have adopted the despairing view that in the Theatre there may lie indeed a motive of culture, but its development is impossible amid existing circumstances: then our further concern would only be to prove that this impossibility is nothing absolute, but overcomable in circumstances depending merely on our definite and operative will; and thus, that the ripest evolution of the cultur-able motive indwelling in the Theatre is an altogether certain possibility. Should this proof succeed, it then would rest with every public-minded citizen who took pleased knowledge of it, to ponder well what profit for the public weal might be gathered from that knowledge. And this profit would have to be safeguarded thus: that the public, the only right decisor in this matter, be moved to combine for the appointment of a managing committee, which should consult together on the means for realising the demonstrated possibility, and bring those means to bearing.

This organ, which in itself could be no absolute education-board in the sense of that already functioning, would nevertheless come in contact at one supremely weighty point with the immediate interest of the Educational Council. So as to accurately denote this point—which lies not alone in the flourishing of general public culture, but also in making practicable the means whereof this culture is the end—I will allow myself to offer a brief review of what, in keeping with local conditions, I feel justified in holding necessary and possible for development of the cultural motive indwelling in the Theatre.

To arrive at a thorough exposure of the standing faults in our local theatre, I started by remarking that its doings entirely lacked originality, and were mere copies of productions which—in relations quite different from those prevailing here, amid quite other manifestations of the public mind, than those intelligible to us, and especially through executive means quite other than we have at hand —had stepped into life on a soil far distant from our own, as original efforts. Let us therefore begin the recital of our possibilities in this Theatre matter with the unwavering assertion, that *no theatre can bring its operations to a salutary issue, unless its doings are before all else original.* Altogether in consonance with the means of theatric execution standing at disposal, must be tempered the artistic ends to be realised thereby. To closely prove his means, to judge their capacity when put to the utmost strain, and to rule his end entirely by the possibility of reaching it through those means : this is the task before the creative artist who above all desires to bring his aim to understanding. It will then be the performers' answering task, to take up this aim into themselves and realise it to the top of their bent; they themselves will become artists, only in degree as they comprehend that aim and share in its realisation. Where an artistic aim thus realised is set before the public, there remains no loophole for criticising means; the public no longer has to wish or care in this regard, no more comparisons to draw with others: but means and end have become *one*, i.e. they have gone up into the Artwork—which now, as an aim intelligible by Feeling, turns solely to the feeling of this Public, by it to be *enjoyed.*—Even the scantiest means are equal to realising an artistic aim, provided it rules itself for expression through those means. The artistic quality of an aim does not consist in its being realisable only through exceptionally ample means, but in its taking the means which stand alone at its service under given circumstances, and bringing them to the highest development whereof they are capable. If we ponder well what kind of artistic aim it must be, that has to employ in this sense the means of portrayal at all procurable for Zurich, we shall perceive that it must decidedly be such an one as answers in general to our thinkings and beholdings, and therefore realises precisely what we may wish and claim with any rhyme or reason: namely artworks easily understandable by us, because peculiar to our nature and holding up to it a faithful mirror.

As for the practical realisation of the idea here given in general terms, this can be effected only through a transition from our wonted methods. I shall be better understood, if I at once proceed to unfold my plan in its most salient features.

The care of the moment can simply be the provision of means, i.e., in the first place, the provision of a dramatic personnel in proportion to Zurich's theatre-going forces. This personnel would have to be strenuously sought and chosen with an eye to its consisting, not so much of artists already soaked with the modern stage-routine, but rather of young, still trainable recruits to the arts of Play and Song. In keeping with our present monetary resources, the quality of this personnel would have to be brought within the bounds of possible excellence through the number of its members being limited. Only such members should be engaged, to wit, who shewed both aptitude for acting and a natural disposition for song. This personnel would therefore have so to be combined, that its members coupled either an already fairly developed talent as actors with a still to be cultivated gift for song, or an already better practised singing-organ with an as yet to be developed capability for acting; so that we should not obtain a double company, parcelled between Play and Opera, but one simple and harmonious group of dramatic artists.— Upon the evolution of our dramatic style of representment the evil influence of a total severance of the art of acting proper, from that of operatic song, is so great and so obvious to a little thought, that it needs but be mentioned here, and not explained in detail. The employment I am about to propose for the aforesaid personnel, however, will shew how the apparent unsuitableness of such a union may be avoided; and on the other hand, how an all-round perfect bringing-out of forces may be attained. For the moment let us keep our eye on this alone: through procuring a single personnel we concentrate our pecuniary resources on a smaller number of good members, instead of squandering them on the engagement of a double number of mediocrities.

In the present condition of the Theatre, a sound foundation of dramatic art subsists in the Play alone: not till every performer can effectively interpret a good play, do they gain the faculty of rendering the musical drama also in a manner befitting dramatic art in general. The aforesaid personnel would thus have first to busy itself with representing plays of such a kind that it might thereby grow aware of the natural stipulations of every drama, and at last attain the faculty of thoroughly fulfilling them. To this end, and with a view to the development of our further plan, such pieces must be chosen as not only are completely suited to the forces available, but move within a sphere of expressional means so tempered that the speaking tone need never rise above a pitch allowable, without injury to their voice, for performers who are also destined to sing.—I must here content myself with remarking, that plays which contain moments of such passionate declamation that they tax the speaking-organ with an excessive strain, already overstep the line which must stay drawn round pure play-acting; for beyond this line only the singing-organ, with the mighty aid of tone-art, can bring forth an expression setting passion in the needful light of beauty. Arrived at this line in the development of its powers of dramatic expression, our artist-personnel must therefore leave its pure concernment with the Play, and step into the realm of Musical Drama; in which, commencing with the next of kin, it has to unfold its forces to their utmost attainable pitch of dramatic portraiture. Wherefore one should choose for production those existing operas which form the proper link between this genre and spoken comedy. Precisely of this class we possess admirable works, which may certainly rank as the most natural and wholesome things that have ever been done in Opera. But in this regard the greatest care must be bestowed on bringing the texts, translated from a foreign tongue, into exact accordance with the musical expression; to this end they should be scrupulously revised, since the existing translations mostly do away with that accordance, maintained in the original.—

Up to this point, the originality of the doings of our theatre would have been displayed merely in this one respect: that no artworks were brought to a production there but such as the fellowship of artists, according to the measure of its powers, was really able to *make its own* through an adequate representment. Though this gain would already be an immense advance upon our present theatric usage, and though this feature alone would almost fully suffice to afford the public far nobler and more satisfying joys than now can be the case: yet the very nature of the thing would bring with it the impossibility of stopping at this stage. Not merely for sake of a display of originality on principle, but for the simple reason that the number of existing works adapted for our purpose is extremely limited, we should have to stride onward to the manufacture of dramatic works themselves. Here, if we had no intention of letting the theatre fall back into its ancient plight, there would arise a veritable Want. Yet we need never fear this Want, but bid it welcome as the only thing that can lead us to true creative Deeds. Let us see how this arisen Need would have to be contented.—

We have first of all to note an astounding phenomenon: the increased spread of intellectual artistic aptitude, as result of our progressive culture, together with the seemingly constant decrease of productivity in respect of really significant artworks. There has come about an incredible disproportion between the strength of actually extant productive forces and the feeble worth of open products. So widely is poetic and musical ability—furthered through every natural channel of art-experience—to be met with nowadays, that a closer consideration of the extraordinary dearth of public artistic productivity can only fill one with amazement. If we go to the bottom of this phenomenon, we recognise with startling plainness the ruinous influence exerted by the centralisation of our public art-supplies at a few solitary points of European intercourse. With rare exceptions, our whole public craving for theatric art is fed with the crumbs that Paris throws us from its groaning board. The ill effect which we have just seen exerted by this evil circumstance upon the nature of the productions of more or less every theatre, be it even of highest rank, has told with growing rigour on the productive forces of native art; and in such a way, that they have more and more diverted their creative impulse from the Theatre. For the portrayal of art-creations peculiar to their mind and soul, they have seen that the Theatre offers neither means nor disposition: the alien in these public theatricals, the unakin to their own being, has estranged them from the Theatre, and forced their creative trend away from it. Whereas we see that none but counterfeiters of the foreign have laboured for the present stage, the native idiosyncrasies of art-productiveness have more and more withdrawn from the Theatre, to leave it as the chosen arena for speculation on the most superficial crazes of a more or less unthinking public. The German spirit, whose peculiar inwardness prevents it from parleying with any but a public quite familiar, has completely lost itself in an almost exclusively literary sphere of art; it is in Literature that we have to seek it out—on the one hand to fathom its fill of riches, on the other to wrest from it the avowal of a need, which it can only still, in truth, before a full publicity and in the genuine Artwork. So comes it, that our most individual poetic forces are deployed almost nowhere but in the literary-Lyric: while our broadcast musical faculty consumes itself almost solely in setting the countless poems which have sprung from out that Lyric, and thus has wellnigh made itself a Literature of its own. In this Literature, however, we recognise the richest and most varied forces, immeasurably surpassing, for individuality and true artistic capability, the hectic glamour of the whole art-herodom of Paris. What is brought to light in Paris nowadays, owes its origin hardly at all to an individual artistic force, but merely to a brilliant technical routine; and to none is this plainer than to the German art-genius, thrown back on its own inside for nurture, as it turns its back in loathing on the shallow inwards of those high-famed art-producers and their world-spread works. But just what fits *these* out so bravely for the public eye, is altogether lacking for the freer development of native art: namely a public art-institute in keeping with our spirit, our forces, and our idiosyncrasies; an institute that not only should help our art-creations to the light of day, but, through offering the possibility of such a furtherance, should supply the first incitement to take dramatic art in hand at all.

Let us keep Zurich in eye, and particularly in its weighty bearing on the whole of German Switzerland. Are there no creative artistic forces here? Unknown they may be, but surely not un-existing. We so often pay for the longed acquaintance with great celebrities, nowadays, with an undeception: were it not a nobler toil, to draw the unknown native forces, if not exactly into the cold glare of idle fame, yet within the warming glow of public love? Shew we them but the way, and how quickly shall we make the intimacy of a home-bred host whereof we hitherto had never dreamt! But this way consists in the longing which we manifest them; and this we can only manifest to them by shewing them the furthering means, in that same art-institute we have in view as a source of pleasure to ourselves.

In the orderly series of productions of already extant works, for whose completely fitting representment it has trained itself by rational use and progressive strengthening of its forces, the dramatic artist-personnel, above described, will exhibit to our native artists a pattern for the first guidance of their own creative forces and aims. The theatre—which indispensably needs original products, if it is to render justice to its higher station—must do all it can to shew our poetic heads and musical talents the artistic path on which they are to satisfy that need at like time with their own, their need of quitting a merely literary career. In this way not only will hidden forces be drawn to light, and new ones woken, but they will also be intensified to a power they never could have gained before they spent themselves on the most consummate art-genre, the actually enacted Drama.

From the very outset, then, a cry must go forth to poets and musicians, from the nearest of blood to the farthest of kin, to furnish works expressly for this theatre, now given over to their creative energy; works reckoned, both in general idea and feasibility of perfect representment, for the actual forces of this stage. The highest result, to answer this more and more intense and more extended operation of our forces, would at last consist in this: that the dramatic works of the past need less and less be called upon for aid, and the doings of the ever-living forces of the present would make a reaching back to older things seem day by day less needful. And who shall dispute the possibility of this result? Do we not see by every Paris theatre, and each theatre of Italy, that this result must be an altogether natural one; that it merely depends on the individuality of our spirit, to give our works that hallowedness which the products of those theatres can never own before our Feeling?

But on the exponent artists, too, this converse with the productive Present must have a quite specific influence. Just as the works enacted by them would more and more consist, in time, of original products and nothing else: so also would their personnel, on principle, have gradually to shape itself into one entirely belonging and peculiar to ourselves. I mean by this, the gradual extinction of the player-class as a specific caste dissevered from our civic life, and its ascension into an artistic fellowship in which the whole civic society, according to aptitude and liking, would more or less take part. With a progressive finer culture of our citizen society, the absolute aloofness of the player-class must become more and more untenable. A man who his whole life through concerns himself with the representant player's art alone, can only be most one-sided in his culture; the unbroken exercise of his art, without any change of inducement or stimulus thereto, must become at last a sheer business routine, and end by taking all the character of a handicraft, if he has to put it to mere money-making. On the other hand the burgher society which never concerns itself with the practice of art, leaves a large portion of its noblest faculties undeveloped, to its utmost loss, and accustoms itself to a radically false notion of Art's essence—a notion based on a certain pedantic crudity. In this its attitude, the public can but confound the doings of Art with the productions of Industry; it pays for both with its money, and in face of Art herself, degraded in its notion to a branch of Industry, it stays bare of all artistic culture. Art is only then the highest 'moment' of human life, when it is no 'moment' sundered from that life, but a thing with all its varied manifestments completely knit in Life itself. We are nearer to this social humanising of Art, or this artistic ripening of Society, than perhaps we fancy—if only we bestow on it our whole full will; and Zurich, of all places, shall furnish me the proof for my assertion.

The educational authorities here have already made it their duty to assign to the training of the body a weighty share in the maturing of youth: technically conducted gymnastic exercises take their place beside the scientific curriculum; athletic competitions are arranged, and public prizes awarded for bodily adroitness. On another side we see a rapid spread of singing unions, the uncommonly meritorious work of Nägeli: almost every parish has brought its vocal forces to a pitch of ductility which only needs to be given a dramatic bent, to heighten their significance for the common culture. Already this bent exists in one department of the public life; on any occasion for a public festival, be it earnestness or mirth, one snatches quite of itself, and wellnigh in first line, at the arranging of processions in characteristic dress; pictures from the Folk-life or from history, carried out with great fidelity and speaking naturalness, make out the chief attraction of these pageants. Still more decidedly does this dramatic bent of the nation's open culture shew forth in certain country districts, where youth and riper years alike engage in the performance of plays right out. Though we have here to recognise an inherited primeval custom of the Folk, yet, as regards both subject and expression, we are already definitely confronted with the influence of certain modern developments in the player's art, upon this Folk's-play; and this influence may easily give rise to mischief and perversion, if that art be not itself held down to a healthier evolution than now is taking place.

With so many symptoms of a natural taste for art, and notably for dramatic art, as we encounter here in public life—it should escape no one charged with conscious furtherance of the common weal, how necessary for evolution of the existing germs it is, that their indwelling bent be guided to one common goal. This goal is none other than the full exercise of dramatic art, in a plenitude made possible by the art-experience of to-day. Through a far-seeing application of the organs of public culture, one would have to work towards the reaching of this goal; and here is the point where the educational authorities would come into immediate contact with that Commission for managing the Theatre. So soon as one intended to develop to their fullest all those cultural factors in our public teaching-institutes which make for an artistic training beside the purely scientific, the educational authorities would have to be pointed to that Theatre-commission as the natural ally for yielding them the most vital aid in the solution of their task. In the more mature dramatic artists of this theatre—raised in our proposal to a state of highest honour—there would of itself be found the teachers for developing those artistic faculties which needs must bud in our young people from the very liking woken in them by the inspiring sights and sounds of the theatre. One has heretofore deemed better to keep our young folks away from the theatre, in its present state: if the theatre, however, were made capable of functions such as I have just denoted, we should rather enjoin upon our youth to visit it. Hitherto it has been held a misfortune in any burgher family of standing,* for one of its members to let himself be swept into the player-class: in future the dread of such a misfortune would be absolutely impossible, since any player-class would have more and more to cease existing, and each qualified person would satisfy his tastes and exercise his talents without quitting his ordinary social station, or entering a class that made impossible his fulfilment of a civic calling. For at the goal of this new theatrical departure, the Theatre, in its present shape, would have vanished into air ; it would have ceased to be an industrial institute offering its goods for sale as often and as pushingly as possible. Perchance the Theatre would then make out the highest social rallying-point of a public art-communion from which all taint of Industry had been completely wiped away, and wherein the unique end would be the making tell our ripest faculty for artistic execution alike with that for art-enjoyment.

It would take me too far just now, were I to set forth in detail my plan for establishing the important point last touched on—that of education. Maturely as I have reflected on this point in general, and easy as it might be for me to propose the simplest media for its carrying out, yet the chief part of the matter could only be definitely settled after making close acquaintance with local circumstances; therefore I must content myself with having merely afforded an incitation. Only as to the nighest way for taking in hand my general plan, have I still to impart my views in brief.

I have spoken of constituting a suitable Commission for Theatrical Affairs. This Commission, in my opinion, might be formed most naturally in the following manner.— An appeal should be addressed to the friends of dramatic art in Zurich and the surrounding districts: these would have to agree, in any way they pleased, as to whether they would lend assistance to founding a Theatre in the sense

---

* A matter of our author's own experience, seeing that his uncle Adolph Wagner was always strongly opposed to Richard Wagner's sisters adopting the stage as a profession.—TR.

above-denoted. Should their decision prove favourable, voluntary contributions towards the support of the undertaking for a year, in the first place, would have to be signed for, and a committee must be chosen to see that the sum subscribed was expended *on attaining the object for which they had combined.* A committee chosen *in this sense and to this end* would form quite of itself the Commission which I had in view for the Theatre.—Now the first care of this Commission would be to bring the sum-total of the subscriptions into combination with the theatre's ascertainable average takings for a winter half-year. These takings, however, must forthwith be rated by a different standard from that prevailing hitherto: in behalf of a choicer repertory, and for special sake of more carefully prepared productions, the number of performances must be materially reduced, in comparison with what has been the wont; two, or at most (and only in certain favouring cases) three, performances in course of the week (perhaps with doubling the former number of concerts given throughout the winter) are almost more than sufficient for the theatre-goers of Zurich. The estimated receipts from these performances —which, for obvious reasons, would surely not be smaller than the theatre has taken heretofore—would form with the sum subscribed the fund for procuring such a *simple* company as I have described above, and for its maintenance during *one whole year.*—The undertaking should commence with the beginning of the summer half-year. In this summer season the united company would have to mature itself in every department of dramatic art, under properly-appointed guidance, and to practise with thorough artistic carefulness the dramatic works intended for presentation to the public in the winter; nor must the diligence of its efforts for perfection of practice be even then relaxed.—The result of this winter half-year would afford the theatre-friends of Zurich a very simple indication as to whether it was worth while prolonging the support they had furnished in the first year. Should the result be satisfactory, and the whole undertaking thus consolidate itself:

then in wider and wider circles, and finally by the State itself, there would be found an ever greater inducement to employ the institute, in the aforesaid sense, for the artistic training of youth. In course of time there would evolve an ever larger number of native 'talents,' who would be in a position to fill the eventual gaps in the theatric personnel, without thereby abandoning their civic station and entering a separate player-class; till at last, as the institute continued flourishing, the whole active personnel would consist of nothing but the flower of a native burgher-artisthood; and quite of itself the theatre would thus attain a self-supporting station, wherein it would have sloughed the last traces of a branch of industry.—

This goal is so new and significant, the conceivable result so uncommon and far-reaching, that many for this very reason will not believe it possible of attainment, particularly as the means I propose are so simple and so few.

Whosoever knows my elsewhere published views concerning the relation of our modern Civilisation to genuine Art, might wellnigh wonder to see me engaged in an attempt whose success ought to seem to just myself the most impossible. Nevertheless I have held it necessary to uncover every possibility of a nobler prospering of public art amid our present conditions, because in truth there still lies open a large field of possibility within them, and a field which has by no means yet been measured out. Not till it has been ascertained *that our public is unable to embrace the Will to realise this possible thing*, can it plainly appear whether—together with the impossibility of this Will—the function which I have imagined for Art on the basis of our modern Civilisation is likewise a proved impossibility. Should such be the result, then our Civilisation would itself have passed the verdict on its incapacity for any higher work of humanising.—

What I have set forth, is in itself an actual possibility: on whether those who possess the powers for its realisation shall gain faith in it for themselves, depends its attainment. I by no means flatter myself that through my mere exposition I can found that needful faith: on a purely theoretic path to get at an essential notion, rooted in widespread habit, and move it to complete reversal—is the hardest, and generally the most resultless undertaking. Were it possible for me to bring before the public the full artistic Deed, in all its convincing directness, I certainly should be beyond a doubt as to the victory of my view; for the character of every Public, is to be mistrustful only of a fancy-picture: confronted with the actual phenomenon, it decides with unfaltering sureness. But the artistic phenomenon meant by me, is only to be brought to pass by the force of a common Will; to have roused this Will in a handful of men of willing hearts and thinking heads, may for the present, as far as my conscience goes, be my solitary success. May I thus at least have won a few fellow-knowers and sharers of my aim; and may the zeal arise in these, to win fresh partners in their knowledge! A favouring issue of their zeal would in truth be no small warrant for a happy future, and a Future quite in the sense of those who devote their civic energies to a reasonable preservation and advancement of the Existing.

ON MUSICAL CRITICISM.

Über Musikalische Kritik.

A LETTER TO THE EDITOR
OF THE
NEUE ZEITSCHRIFT FÜR MUSIK.

This letter originally appeared in the Neue Zeitschrift für Musik (*editor, Franz Brendel*) *of February 6, 1852. Together with the letter on the* "Goethe-Stiftung," *it was reprinted as a pamphlet, entitled* "*Two Letters* (Zwei Briefe) *by R. Wagner," and published by Bruno Hinze, Leipzig, 1852.*

TRANSLATOR'S NOTE.

HONOURED FRIEND,
You wish me to give you my opinion as to what share a "Journal for Music" should take in the process which our music of nowadays has necessarily to undergo, and in what manner that share may be made contribute to a common good?

It is impossible for me just now, and I heartily wish it may prove unneedful at any time, to occupy myself with further literary work. Still, I will try to come to terms with you on the question posed above, and indeed in the only way open to me: namely that I should tell you my opinion as resulting from my own particular views, and prompted by a matter which I have been doomed to see remain a wish, but not as any absolute maxim to be bound on you by hook or crook. I shall therefore tell you what *I* would do, if circumstances and moods imposed on me the publication of a Journal for Music; only by my keeping to this altogether individual standpoint, can my wish to gain your friendship for my opinion remain an unembarrassed one.

In the first place I candidly admit to you, that there was a period when I never set eyes on a musical journal of any kind, and that I have since had reason to regard that period—at least in this respect—as one of the happiest in all my life. This was the time when, as Kapellmeister in Dresden, I devoted all my zeal to the rendering of musical works of art; when I therefore believed I might set all my hopes, for the prospering of Art, on the immediate representations conducted by me, on the practical realisement of my artistic aims. At that time all gossiping and scribbling about Art went so strongly against my grain, that it was at utmost this distaste itself that could induce me, on and off, to speak out my mind. I have just called that period of my life a happier one: this it was because I was able to deceive myself. What I wanted then, however, I could never carry-out to my full satisfaction; of all the circumstances which hindered me,* I may select two for my present purpose: the complete confusion of the *public's* taste, and the brainlessness and dishonesty of the *critics*.—The true artist turns the liefest to the full emotional candour of the purely-human heart: should he not find it among our theatre-public, as experience needs must teach him, then he is compelled to look round for aid from the side of cultured art-intelligence, for the critic's mediation. Thus a speedy surfeit of the public drove me at last, and irresistibly, into this needy attitude toward Criticism; and here it was—where I sought it myself, and therefore could no more dismiss it of set purpose—that I was forced to learn the whole nature of our Modern Criticism, and to deliver my first attack against *it* almost alone. What art-writings I have published since, are in nowise an appeal to the public—such as many have thought necessary to impute to me—but I turn away in them from the modern Public, which I have had to give up as a senseless and heartless mass, and take arms against our Criticism: that is to say, against uncritical, bad criticism; the criticism which is led by neither Feeling *nor* true Understanding, and bases its continuance on nothing but the ruin of the mass; lives on this ruin, and for dear life's sake increases it. I say: I turned *against* this criticism, but not *towards* it; for any wish to better it, can never come to a man who has already been forced to give the public up as lost,—the public which at least is will-less in its degradation, whereas Criticism persists in its depravity on wilful principle. Notwithstanding, and as is inevitable with merely literary works, I have after all addressed myself *to* criticism alone: this means, however, to the newly to be gathered criticism of healthy Reason (*Vernunft*), namely of the Understanding which never for one instant consciously gives up healthy *Feeling*,

---

* In the *N.Z.f.M.* there appeared: "and whose broader connexion I have recently designated in a '*Communication to my Friends.*'"—Tr.

as its perennial feeder; thus not to the critical routine of the old method—that method which at most upholds itself on the selfsame confusion and dulness of feeling as we observe in the public—but to the throughly un-routined beholdings of those *men of culture* who feel as dissatisfied as myself with both the modern Public and the Criticism of nowadays.

Since that time I have again lain hand on journals both musical and devoted to art-interests in general, as I felt that I must search elsewhere than among the public— where I had sought them hitherto—for the human beings to whom I might turn for the contentment of my new need of discourse. For I had learnt that it was quite premature, and therefore fruitless, to endeavour to bring the Artwork itself before the unbiased Feeling, while such a feeling was absolutely non-existent as regards the proposed new features of a living art; but that one must before all set to work at destroying this Feeling's *bias,* so deadly a hindrance as we find it, for the artist, in our present public system. Now if I was bound to perceive that the cause of this sentimental bias lay deep-rooted in our political and social Life itself, and that nothing but an entire transformation of this Life could bring about the natural birth of *that* Art which I had taken in eye; if, for a clearer understanding of my intrinsic aim, I had to place this requisition in the forefront, and lay on it the principal emphasis, as in the first writings of my newer period ("*Art and Revolution,*" and "*The Art-work of the Future*"): on the other hand, I could not but be aware withal that in that new-birth of Art from Life a second might must take its share, a might which had to manifest as *the conscious Willing of that art.* To wake this conscious Will precisely in those who feel dissatisfied with our art and criticism of nowadays, could but appear to me the principal task for the Artist of the Present; for only from the fellow-longing of others, and at last of many, can spring the force to feed his higher effort, his effort directed toward the Art-work itself.

But this Will cannot be grasped till we have become completely clear, as regards the phenomena of modern art-life, that the reason why they do not satisfy us is no mere accidental one—e.g. an unconditioned running-dry of artistic faculty—but rather an entirely ' necessary,' a cause conditioned by a whole vast aggregate : and this clear insight we at present can only gain upon the path of Criticism; mind you, a Criticism able to both distinguish and combine, a healthy, nerved by Feeling, a revolutionary Criticism— and not that modern impotence for sifting and uniting, that pure conserver of traditions, that Criticism gone sick for Restoration. The first thing we must compass, then, is a close agreement as to the attributes of modern art and the causes of these same unsatisfying attributes ; until this agreement is established with the most regardless candour, we shall only fall into ever greater confusion as to What we wish in place of present art ; whereas so soon as we have fully cleared our minds on this nighest thing, quite of itself shall we gain that force of Will which I have just called a necessary sharer in giving birth to the Art of the Future, albeit its last empowering conditions are only to be found *in Life itself.*

So you see, my honoured friend, I surely do not minimise the worth of Criticism's help towards the highest ends of Art. And indeed! how could I, providing in my stress for Life I take count of the time and circumstances in which we live, and recognise, as recognise I must, that just in face of *our* life each effort must stay fruitless if the essential characteristics of precisely our epoch—this epoch that gives room to criticism alone, and not to Art—be not taken into full consideration ? Do we not live, then, merely in that we live exactly to-day and under the conditions of the Present ; and does not our noblest strife, itself, the strife for annulment of all the grounds of Criticism, proceed from just this Present ? Is not our wish, to annul the character of the Present, just a wish that wins its only nurture from *our* Present ; and can we bring it otherwise to ripe result, than in the very forms the Present affords us as the only ones intelligible?

Precisely the most decisive, because the most immediately necessary stroke for birth of the new art, according to my most strong conviction, may very well—nay, with almost the only prospect of success—be at present dealt in a journal dedicated to this end; and the question now could solely take the form: How far, and under what conditions, a "Journal for—*Music*" might be fitted for the meeting-point of critical forces operating in this sense?

Let me answer just this question, in accordance with my own particular views.

To start with, I may tell you that when recently the wish has risen within me, as risen it has from time to time, to speak aloud my mind on this or that phenomenon of our art-life, I have sought in vain for a journal such as I could deem really suitable for the reception of what I had drawn up: I either had to take the best that came, or I suppressed my communication altogether.—Our Æsthetic journals are not devoted to *artistic*, but to *literary* interests, and are therefore just as different in what they want (if they want anything at all) from what *I* want, as Literature itself is different from Art. They never come into contact with true Art, but over and over again with Criticism; they live entirely in a paradise (*von der erdenklichsten Möglichkeit*) of Criticism, and, since they heap critique on top of critique, their activity resembles that of the various classes of police in Russia—where one is set to watch the other, because one takes it for granted that each is playing blackguard tricks. As the Folk, or rather the human being proper, compares with these polices, so does true Art compare with that complexus of art-literary-critical journals: just as in the bureaux of those various polices one would hold the genuine Man for raving mad, if he wanted to express his natural feelings, so the man who genuinely wished for Art in these literature journals could only seem an equally eccentric monomaniac.

For, let those various polices extend their field of vision to the utmost, yet they end by merely soaring to the concept, *Police in general*: exactly as our literature-journals reach their utmost tether in the concept, *Literature in general.**

Now our modern music has at least this advantage over literature proper, that it must be throughly perceptible by the senses, must sound out, to be existent; a Journal for Music could therefore boast the proud pre-eminence, that it at any rate concerned itself with the sensible appearance of an art which without this sensibility can not be seized at all: whereas poetic literature, for instance, exists by very reason that it exists apart from sentience. Certainly, that Music should have needed a literature to busy itself with her, and pave the way to an understanding of her—thus,

---

* "That between our critical literates and the Russian police there subsists a very definite kinship, you may learn for yourself, by the way, from a recent review of my '*Opera and Drama*' in the *Grenzboten*; where the critic (to be sure, the most unmannerly of his métier) refers to an actress of whom I say that, so as not to be betrayed into unnaturalness by the look of the Iambic verses in her rôles, she had them written out in prose. For this behaviour the critic threatens her, after the event, with the birch-rod—or, as he puts it, with the "dust-broom" [*Staupbesen*, and "*Staubbesen*"]. You see, with what ruthless opponents we have to do: so let us be on our guard! From the frontier (*Grenze*) on which they have posted themselves, they send their runners (*Boten*) left and right; and should the Russian police march-in some fine day from the right, we may be pretty sure of being denounced by them. The terrors of the chastisement they then would demand for us *men*, you may easily judge by what they have suggested for a tender *woman*!"—This footnote occurred in the *N.Z.f.M.*, but was not reprinted in the Ges. Schr. In Letter 55 to Uhlig (Feb. 15, '52) Wagner writes: "For the edition in pamphlet form of my letter to Brendel, I should like added to the footnote (relating to the *Grenzboten*) something which I had forgotten, but which for clearness' sake ought not to remain forgotten." He then directs that after "left and right" there should be inserted: "and so know how to manage in any event; just as lately they denounced me on the left hand to the democrats as an aristocrat in disguise, and to the centre of our civilisation, the Jews, as their bitterest persecutor, so we may be sure that, should the Russian police march in from the right, they would likewise hand us over to it, after recommending their own literary rubbish to its best protection."—The passage in *Opera and Drama*, which so roused the critic's indignation, will be found on page 242, Vol. ii, of the present series.—TR.

that "Journals for Music" should find a place among us
—ought in itself to have opened our eyes to the weak side
of *this* art too; just as the weak side of all our "plastic"
arts, Architecture, Sculpture and Painting, has displayed
itself in their requiring a literary-journalistic intervention,
for their understanding. The present business, however, is
simply to get so far ahead in one's literary intervenings on
behalf of Music, that this weak side shall be completely
bared, the attributes of our music proved faulty by sheer
reason of their need of literary intervention, the cause and
character of this faultiness set forth exactly, and thus the
honest Will be placed on record:—to ransom Music from
her unrightful station and bring her to the only right one,
where some-day she shall need *no more* a literary intervention for her understanding. Thus the activity of a journal
"for Music" would forthwith gain a character immediately
directed to the life of Art; a character that would mark it
for one of the happiest, and under present circumstances
the most useful, in Art's sincerest interest.

In your recent deliverances you give us, honoured friend!
the assurance that you have pushed on as far as I have
here denoted, and alike a promise to henceforth spend
your literary energy in none but the sense I have just set
down. I confess to you, that before this declaration of
yours I had not been in a position to build any hopes on
the efficacy of a Journal for Music. Every new appearing
of a musical paper could only inspire me with feelings
of either wrath or laughter: the fresh-won possibility of
gabbling and scribbling about music an extra once, and
of taking the old gabble and scribble and over-gabbling and
over-scribbling it; then the disgustingly industrial character of the whole thing, which eventually turned quite
away from Music, to nothing but music-goods and music-
thrummers (two species which are one and the same for
me, as also for you at bottom), till it arrived at last at
music-making wheels and cylinders,—all this revealed to
me the utter Byzantinism which our musical affairs had
reached, whereby, in my eyes, there was nothing left for

them but the impotence of eunuchs. Through your declaration, however, you proposed to break entirely with these affairs, i.e. to withdraw from their influence and fight their selves, to the best of possibility, until you had destroyed them. Let us come to terms, then, as to how alone that result should be striven for, and what must be the practical path to strike thereto.

If our Music is to be set free from the false position which compels her to seek a literary interpreter, in my opinion it can only be done by giving her the widest meaning originally connoted by her *name*. We have accustomed ourselves to limiting our idea of "music" to the mere art, and now at last to the mere artifice, of *Tone*. That this is an arbitrary restriction, we know very well; for *that* people which invented the name of "*Music*," connoted by it not only *the arts of poetry and tone*, but each several artistic manifestment of the inner man, insofar as to the senses he conveyed his feelings and beholdings, in ultimate persuasiveness, through the organ of ringing speech.* The whole bringing-up of Athenian youth fell therefore into two divisions: into *Music* and—*Gymnastic*, i.e. the epitome of all those arts which bear on the most consummate expression through bodily show itself. Thus in "Music" the Athenian imparted himself to the *ear*, in Gymnastic to the *eye*; and only the adept *both* in Music and Gymnastic, was held by them for a *really* cultured man. Just as, dwarfing into the Politician, Man at last gave up the pains to shew himself fair of body, and consequently left Gymnastic to those who made its practice a profession,—till we now have got so far, that we recognise this art as the exclusive property of our ballet-dancers and funambulists: this selfsame Man gave up the really sounding Music when he could no longer practise aught but philosophic Criticism, so that at the time of the Alexand-

---

* "Insoweit er seine Gefühle und Anschauungen in letzter überzeugendster Versinnlichung durch das Organ der tönenden Sprache ausdrucksvoll mittheilte."—

rines, when Poetry had definitely turned to Literature, the music of Sound was practised by none but flutists and players on the lyre. What these latter give out, down to the present day, we un-thinkers by routine at all events still call it "music"; let us recognise, however, that we do so with no better warrant than for our employment in modern life, for instance, of the terms "Right," "Duty" and "Morals"* in a sense diametrically opposed to their primary significance!— Now our Music, in her noblest line, has already taken a development which must necessarily lead her to her sterlingest of meanings, through marriage with the *art of poetry*; and it is just that line, and just this necessity, which I have consciously observed and noted down [elsewhere]. If in a Journal for Music we with equal consciousness adopt that line, if we demonstrate this necessity as inherent in every morsel of her essence, and thus in all we say insist on the regaining of "Music's" truest and only vindicable meaning—whereby she is the closest union of the arts of Poetry and Tone, the fittest and most satisfying utterance of the inner man, his feelings and beholdings, through the organ of ringing speech—then in a "Journal for Music," of all others, we are in the right place; and no happier name could we possibly find to denote the art for which we fight, than just the name of "*Music*."

If on this point we agree, and resolve henceforth to battle for this "Music" and none else, then we primarily avow thereby that we at once have nothing in the least to do with our music *of to-day*, excepting in that we wage war to the death against it as an absolute separate-art, i.e. we mercilessly demonstrate its faultiness, and the void and nullity at last resulting from this faultiness, as shewn us in the total of its recent features. If we ponder well what is to be understood by this, we shall be forced to the conclusion that the Journal we mean must be cleansed from all the contents of a "musical paper" of heretofore: in it the phenomena of that modern separate-art should find no

* "*Sitte*"—its original meaning being "custom, habit, manners."—TR.

more consideration—ay, no more mention—except when either their trend toward *genuine* Music, as we understand it, is to be shewn, laid stress on, reinforced and strengthened in them, or when the diametrically opposite trend is to be exposed and plainly brought to book, as the erroneous, the faulty, the bare of sense and *Vernunft*. For no other reason whatever, ought any kind of musical affair to be given a line of notice in this Journal; and the mercantile, industrial character which has hitherto spread itself so vilely, over even our musical papers, must downright vanish from it and leave no trace behind.

Filled with this spirit, the Journal will then be forced, quite of itself, to confess a longing to also take the *poet* up into it; for he it is who has necessarily to join himself with the sterling tone-artist, so as to help into light that full agreement whence there once shall bloom the blossom of veritable *mus-ic art* (musischen Kunst). Wherefore we have to turn to that class of poet who yearns to quit the rut of literature-poetics, for his own true satisfaction, as much as the tone-artist longs from out his solitude towards the poet. To this Poet have we to open wide our arms, for we dare not feel a rightful hope till *him* we can embrace with fullest love. His watchful leaning toward us, his gradual approach, alone can yield the earliest sign that from *our* standpoint we are on the right, the saving path to our own contentment: so long as we are unable to detect this leaning, to spy out this approach, we may also rest assured that ourselves are still held captive in that lonely separation whereout, on *his* side, we want to lure the literary poet. The poet can make no overtures to us, till he has been rid of the selfsame repugnance against the sheer music-maker as that we feel against the unmixt literarian; and he will nurse this repugnance for just so long as he sees us lend a shadow of support to modern tone-jugglery. But the first poet who stretches forth his hand to us, may be our witness that we have really and completely stepped out of the old rut, and altogether freed ourselves from our unproductive egoism.

When the union of poet and tone-artist shall have once been reached and made fast, their joint labours will open an incommensurable field for the most fruitful artistic discussion. In a book just published, "Opera and Drama," I have already sketched this field in broader outline: what I hinted there in general traits, or merely in a few swift touches, I am inwardly convinced can only become the rich possession of my poetic and tone-artist comrades when they themselves devote their experiences, their knowledge and convictions, to the tillage of that field. In what they have already made a matter of their personal observation, each on his several path, will they win the implement for ploughing up the fill of truths that lies buried from our gaze till now—of truths we all must behold and know, if we mean to turn our forces in full consciousness to the single Artwork of the Future, such as Life shall one day bid appear in answer to its sovereign call, in achievement of its highest satisfaction.

What we harvest thus, will be full *knowledge* of true "mus-ic art," of "*Music*" in its broadest meaning; a meaning wherein Poetry and Tone-art are knit as one and indivisible. Not yet, however, should we have reached our final goal; for hereunto we should have reaped ourselves mere *knowledge*: this knowledge could never verify its truth, till necessarily and instinctively it thrust onward to an *activation* of the known, a begettal of the *real artwork itself*. To become entire artists, we now should have to face from "Music" toward "*Gymnastic*," i.e. the actual, physical art of bodily portrayal; the art which turns alone our Willed into an actual Canned. Till irresistibly we feel this thrust within us, we shall also have to admit that we are not yet completely at one, not ripe as yet for real knowledge of Art's nature; poets and tone-artists each, we should for just so long be not yet genuine "μουσικοὶ," but, for all our efforts to the contrary, still naught but "Literati." And only when the full force of our united Will bids us will none other than the *most vivid exhibition* (die *sinnlichste Darstellung*) of our art, may we deem the goal of our redemption-fight victoriously reached.

Up to this instant, it has never even in a dream occurred to one among the posse of our Literarians, to touch the question ear-marked here. For them our whole public art of representment *must* be exactly as it is to-day; and, side by side with the repulsive features of our theatres and concerts, they flit and fluster in their garb of printer's black as though all that appeals to the senses, there outside, could by no manner of means be their concern. Certainly, as now they are, it indeed is no concern of theirs: but the very fact that they don't think needful to trouble their heads about it, is what stamps their literary doings with the seal of utter contemptibility. On and off, perchance, we hear a moan sent up from this fungoid growth of Literature—a moan which almost takes the semblance of a sigh: but it is not the sigh of yearning to become a Man, not the low growl of indignation, the roar of anger at an infamous sensuality in the features of our public art—merely the groan of cowardice and impotence. Yet here it is a question of buckling to, not waiting to see how the will of God and the Directors may some day dispose our theatres and kindred institutes; but boldly and resolutely laying hand on the weapon wherewith the worthlessness of our public representant-art shall be put an end to. This courage will spring up in us when we have become entire "μουσικοί"; and into our hand will this weapon leap, so soon as we win over to our side that executant artist who yearns to quit the comediandom and music-thrumming of nowadays, just as *we* had longed to leave our own dishonouring station. And by this artist's casting in at last his lot with us—through Want (*Noth*) and Free-will sped to will with us the realisement of the Artwork—have *we* to judge if poet and tone-artist have truly reached the unerrable path of healing.

The goal of the joint efforts of these three artists, poet, tone-setter, and performer, can therefore be alone an artwork realised by its bodiliest presentment to the senses—

thus, in contrast to the only sort we know as yet, the Artwork of the Future; albeit, on the other hand, the Life of the Future itself alone can place that Artwork in our grasp. To prepare that artwork for the life of the future—in *this* resides the most reasonable occupation for the Artist of the Present; just as in this occupation lies the only surety for that artwork's finally appearing in that life. But ere itself has stepped into full life, we none of us have reached our goal. When this is reached in the real Artwork, however, when the thing we willed stands before our Feeling with a cogence past mistaking, then also is our Criticism at end; then from critics are we ransomed into artists and art-enjoying men. And then, my honoured friend, you may close your Journal for Music: it dies, because the Artwork lives!*—

A task so uncommon, so never-yet-been, and yet imposed on us by the Necessity of our times—can a Journal for Music fulfil, in my opinion. In your Will it rests, to hold this task unshakenly before your eyes; in the ability of your present and future colleagues, to fulfil it. Gladly ready am I to range myself among them; only, it is my fondest wish to learn that I should be a superfluity. To my unit self I can bear witness that, according to my powers, I have in every fashion done my best to break a pathway for the new departure; to yourself and comrades my purely artistic, alike with my quill-driving works will probably† serve, for some time to come, as stuff and subject for discussion and development of that departure: so that I may tell myself that in advance I have done my share for your journal. Great then would be my delight, if you shouldn't require me at all as an active contributor; not only because just now I feel the utmost need to turn my undisturbed attention toward a purely artistic project

---

* "Stark war die Noth, sie starb—doch Siegfried, der genas." *Siegfried*, act i.—TR.

† Seeing that Uhlig, among others, was on the staff of the *Neue Zeitschrift*. —TR.

of large dimensions, but especially because I thereby should gain the certainty that my convictions anent the essence of Art were no longer those of a lonely unit, but had become the reaped possession of an utmost-waxing number of likeminded friends. Nevertheless I won't deny that it may also from time to time become a need of mine, to impart my theories about some artistic matter: alas! it has too keenly been brought home to me, that often *thus* alone are misunderstandings to be corrected! May you keep me, then, a friendly welcome!

So, with the heartiest good wishes for the prosperity of your undertaking on its new lines, I commend myself to your constant friendly feeling, as

Yours
sincerely,

Zurich, January 25, 1852.

RICHARD WAGNER.

JUDAISM IN MUSIC.

Das
Judenthum in der Musik.

Judaism in Music *originally appeared in the* Neue Zeitschrift für Musik *of September 3 and 6, 1850, above the signature "K. Freigedank" ("K. Free-thought"). Its subsequent history is sufficiently set forth in the accompanying* "Explanations." *I ought to say, however, that I have taken the form in which these Explanations are arranged, not from the* Gesammelte Schriften, *but from the pamphlet published by J. J. Weber, Leipzig, in 1869. In the* Ges. Schr. *the article itself appears in Vol. v.—where its title-page bears the obvious printer's error "(1852)"—whereas the "Explanations," i.e. the dedication and appendix, are given in their due chronologic order, therefore in Vol. viii. For the English reader I believe the connected form will prove the more convenient.*

I may add that, before publishing it above his own name in 1869, Wagner carefully revised the wording of the original article—not without stating the fact in that edition. As the present version is from the text of 1869 (unaltered in the Ges. Schr., *except for such clerical changes as the substitution of "k" and "z" for the "c" in words of Romanic derivation, and "unsere" for "unsre") I have indicated in footnotes all the really important variants.*

TRANSLATOR'S NOTE.

SOME EXPLANATIONS CONCERNING "JUDAISM IN MUSIC."

(To Madame Marie Muchanoff, née Countess Nesselrode).

MOST HONOURED LADY!

In the course of a recent conversation you put me an astonished question, as to the cause of the hostility—incomprehensible to yourself, and so manifestly aiming at depreciation—which encounters all my artistic doings, more particularly in the daily Press not only of Germany, but of France as well, and even England. Here and there I have stumbled on a like astonishment in the Press itself, in the report of some non-initiated novice : one believed one must ascribe to my art-theories a singularly irritant property, since otherwise one could not understand how I, and always I, was degraded so persistently, on every occasion and without the least remorse, to the category of the frivolous, the simply bungling, and treated in accordance with that my appointed station.

The following communication, which I allow myself in answer to your question, not only will throw a light hereon, but more especially may you gather from it why I myself must engage in such elucidation. Since you do not stand alone in your astonishment, I feel called to give the needful answer to many others besides yourself, and therefore publicly : to no one of my friends, however, could I delegate the office, as I know none in so sheltered and independent a position that I durst draw on him a hostility like that which has fallen to my daily lot, and against which I can so little defend myself, that there is nothing left for me but just to shew my friends its reason.

Even I myself cannot engage in the task without misgivings: they spring, however, not from terror of my enemies (since, as I have here no residue of hope, so also have I naught to fear!) but rather from anxiety for certain self-sacrificing, veritably sympathetic friends, whom Destiny has brought to me from out the kindred of that national-religious element of the newer European society whose implacable hatred I have drawn upon me through discussion of peculiarities so hard to eradicate from *it*, and so detrimental to our culture. Yet on the other hand, I could take courage from the knowledge that these cherished friends stand on precisely the same footing as myself, nay, that they have to suffer still more grievously, and even more disgracefully, under the yoke that has fallen on all the likes of me: for I cannot hope to make my exposition quite intelligible, if I do not also throw the needful light on this yoke of the ruling Jew-society in its crushing-out of all free movement, of all true human evolution, among its kith and kin.

In the first place, then, I bring under your notice an essay which I wrote and published somewhat over eighteen years ago.*

---

* This last sentence, naturally enough, was omitted in the Ges. Schr., where the two constituents of the pamphlet were relegated to their respective periods, and where the Dedication was separated from the Appendix merely by a line (*G.S.* Vol. viii).—TR.

JUDAISM IN MUSIC.*

(1850)

N THE 'NEUE ZEITSCHRIFT FÜR MUSIK' not long ago, mention was made of an " Hebraic art-taste ": an attack and a defence of that expression neither did, nor could, stay lacking. Now it seems to myself not unimportant, to clear up the matter lying at bottom of all this —a matter either glossed over by our critics hitherto, or touched with a certain outburst of excitement.† It will not be a question, however, of saying something new, but of explaining that unconscious feeling which proclaims itself among the people as a rooted dislike of the Jewish nature; thus, of speaking out a something really existent, and by no means of attempting to artfully breathe life into an unreality through the force of any sort of fancy. Criticism goes against its very essence, if, in attack or defence, it tries for anything else.

Since it here is merely in respect of Art, and specially of Music, that we want to explain to ourselves the popular dislike of the Jewish nature, even at the present day, we may completely pass over any dealing with this same phenomenon in the field of Religion and Politics. In

---

* To the opening of this article the editor of the *Neue Zeitschrift* appended the following footnote : " However faulty her outward conformation, we have always considered it a pre-eminence of Germany's, a result of her great learning, that at least in the scientific sphere she possesses intellectual freedom. This freedom we now lay claim to and rely on, in printing the above essay, desirous that our readers may accept it in this sense. Whether one shares the views expressed therein, or not, the author's breadth of grasp (*Genialität der Anschauung*) will be disputed by no one."—TR.

† " Erregtheit "—in the *N.Z.* this stood as " Leidenschaftlichkeit," i.e. " passion."—TR.

Religion the Jews have long ceased to be our hated foes,—thanks to all those who within the Christian religion itself have drawn upon themselves the people's hatred.* In pure Politics we have never come to actual conflict with the Jews; we have even granted them the erection of a Jerusalemitic realm, and in this respect we have rather had to regret that Herr v. Rothschild was too keen-witted to make himself King of the Jews, preferring, as is well known, to remain "the Jew of the Kings." It is another matter, where politics become a question of Society: here the isolation of the Jews has been held by us a challenge to the exercise of human justice, for just so long as in ourselves the thrust toward social liberation has woken into plainer consciousness. When we strove for emancipation of the Jews, however, we virtually were more the champions of an abstract principle, than of a concrete case: just as all our Liberalism was a not very lucid mental sport †—since we went for freedom of the Folk without knowledge of that Folk itself, nay, with a dislike of any genuine contact with it—so our eagerness to level up the rights of Jews was far rather stimulated by a general idea, than by any real sympathy; for, with all our speaking and writing in favour of the Jews' emancipation, we always felt instinctively repelled by any actual, operative contact with them.

Here, then, we touch the point that brings us closer to our main inquiry: we have to explain to ourselves the *involuntary repellence* possessed for us by the nature and personality of the Jews, so as to vindicate that instinctive dislike which we plainly recognise as stronger and more overpowering than our conscious zeal to rid ourselves thereof. Even to-day we only purposely belie ourselves, in this regard, when we think necessary to hold immoral

---

* In the *N.Z.* this clause ran: "thanks to our pietists and Jesuits, who have led the Folk's entire religious hatred toward themselves, so that with *their* eventual downfall Religion, in its present meaning (which has been rather that of Hate, than Love), will presumably have also come to naught!"—Tr.

† "Nicht sehr hellsehendes (in the *N.Z.* "luxuriöses") Geistesspiel."—Tr.

and taboo all open proclamation of our natural repugnance against the Jewish nature. Only in quite the latest times do we seem to have reached an insight, that it is more rational (*vernünftiger*) to rid ourselves of that strenuous self-deception,* so as quite soberly instead to view the object of our violent sympathy and bring ourselves to understand a repugnance still abiding with us in spite of all our Liberal bedazzlements.† To our astonishment, we perceive that in our Liberal battles‡ we have been floating in the air and fighting clouds, whereas the whole fair soil of material reality has found an appropriator whom our aërial flights have very much amused, no doubt, yet who holds us far too foolish to reward us by relaxing one iota of his usurpation of that material soil. Quite imperceptibly the " Creditor of Kings " has become the King of Creeds, and we really cannot take this monarch's pleading for emancipation as otherwise than uncommonly naïve, seeing that it is much rather *we* who are shifted into the necessity of fighting for emancipation from the Jews. According to the present constitution of this world, the Jew in truth is already more than emancipate: he rules, and will rule, so long as Money remains the power before which all our doings and our dealings lose their force. That the historical adversity§ of the Jews and the rapacious rawness of Christian-German potentates have brought this power within the hands of Israel's sons—this needs no argument of ours to prove. That the impossibility of carrying farther any natural, any 'necessary' and truly beauteous thing, upon the basis of that stage whereat the evolution of our arts has now arrived, and without a total alteration of that basis—that this has also brought the public Art-taste of our time between the busy fingers of the Jew, however, is the matter whose grounds we here

---

* " Selbsttäuschung"; in the *N.Z.* "Lüge," i.e. "lie."—Tr.
† "Vorspiegelungen"; in the *N.Z.* "Utopien."—Tr.
‡ In the *N.Z.* "auf gut christlich," i.e. "like good Christians."—Tr.
§ "Elend" may also mean "exile." In this sentence the *N.Z.* had " Romo-Christian Germans," in place of " Christian-Germanic potentates."— Tr.

have to consider somewhat closer. What their thralls had toiled and moiled to pay the liege-lords of the Roman and the Medieval world, to-day is turned to money by the Jew: who thinks of noticing that the guileless-looking scrap of paper is slimy with the blood of countless generations? What the heroes of the arts, with untold strain consuming lief and life, have wrested from the art-fiend of two millennia of misery, to-day the Jew converts into an art-bazaar (*Kunstwaarenwechsel*): who sees it in the mannered bricabrac, that it is glued together by the hallowed brow-sweat of the Genius of two thousand years?—

We have no need to first substantiate the be-Jewing of modern art; it springs to the eye, and thrusts upon the senses, of itself. Much too far afield, again, should we have to fare, did we undertake to explain this phenomenon by a demonstration of the character of our art-history itself. But if emancipation from the yoke of Judaism appears to us the greatest of necessities, we must hold it weighty above all to prove our forces for this war of liberation. Now we shall never win these forces from an abstract definition of that phenomenon *per se*, but only from an accurate acquaintance with the nature of that involuntary feeling of ours which utters itself as an instinctive repugnance against the Jew's prime essence. Through it, through this unconquerable feeling—if we avow it quite without ado—must there become plain to us *what* we hate in that essence; what we then know definitely, we can make head against; nay, through his very laying bare, may we even hope to rout the demon from the field, whereon he has only been able to maintain his stand beneath the shelter of a twilight darkness—a darkness we good-natured Humanists ourselves have cast upon him, to make his look less loathly.

The Jew—who, as everyone knows, has a God all to himself—in ordinary life strikes us primarily by his outward appearance, which, no matter to what European nationality we belong, has something disagreeably* foreign to that nationality: instinctively we wish to have nothing in common with a man who looks like that. This must heretofore have passed as a misfortune for the Jew: in more recent times, however, we perceive that in the midst of this misfortune he feels entirely well; after all his successes, he needs must deem his difference from us a pure distinction. Passing over the moral side, in the effect of this in itself unpleasant freak of Nature, and coming to its bearings upon Art, we here will merely observe that to us this exterior can never be thinkable as a subject for the art of re-presentment: if plastic art wants to present us with a Jew, it mostly takes its model from sheer phantasy, with a prudent ennobling, or entire omission, of just everything that characterises for us in common life the Jew's appearance. But the Jew never wanders on to the theatric boards: the exceptions are so rare and special, that they only confirm the general rule. We can conceive no representation of an antique or modern stage-character by a Jew, be it as hero or lover, without feeling instinctively the incongruity of such a notion.† This is of great weight: a man whose appearance we must hold unfitted for artistic treatment—not merely in this or that personality, but according to his kind in general—neither can we hold him

---

* This adverb (*unangenehm*) was preceded in the *N.Z.* by another, "unüberwindlich," i.e. "unconquerably"; whereas "instinctively" (*unwillkürlich*) was absent from the next clause.—TR.

† Note to the 1869, and later editions :—"To be sure, our later experiences of the work done by Jewish actors would afford food for many a dissertation, as to which I here can only give a passing hint. Since the above was written not only have the Jews succeeded in capturing the Stage itself, but even in kidnapping the poet's dramatic progeny; a famous Jewish "character-player" not merely has done away with any representment of the poetic figures bred by Shakespeare, Schiller, and so forth, but substitutes the offspring of his own effect-full and not quite un-tendentiose fancy—a thing which gives one the impression as though the Saviour had been cut out from a painting of the crucifixion, and a demagogic Jew stuck-in instead. On the stage the falsification of our Art has thriven to complete deception; for which reason, also, Shakespeare & Co. are now spoken of merely in the light of their qualified adaptability for the stage.—The Editor" (i.e. Richard Wagner).

capable of any sort of artistic utterance of his * [inner] essence.

By far more weighty, nay, of quite decisive weight for our inquiry, is the effect the Jew produces on us through his *speech*; and this is the essential point at which to sound the Jewish influence upon Music.†—The Jew speaks the language of the nation in whose midst he dwells from generation to generation, but he speaks it always as an alien. As it lies beyond our present scope to occupy ourselves with the cause of this phenomenon, too, we may equally abstain from an arraignment of Christian Civilisation for having kept the Jew in violent severance from it, as on the other hand, in touching the sequelæ of that severance we can scarcely propose to make the Jews the answerable party.‡ Our only object, here, is to throw light on the æsthetic character of the said results.—In the first place, then, the general circumstance that the Jew talks the modern European languages merely as learnt, and not as mother tongues, must necessarily debar him from all capability of therein expressing himself idiomatically, independently, and conformably to his nature. § A language, with its expression and its evolution, is not the work of scattered units, but of an historical community : only he who has unconsciously grown up within the bond of this community, takes also any share in its creations. But the Jew has stood outside the pale of any such community, stood solitarily with his Jehova in a splintered, soilless stock, to which all self-sprung evolution must stay denied, just as even the peculiar (Hebraïc) language of that stock has been preserved for him merely as a thing defunct. Now, to make poetry in a foreign tongue has hitherto been impossible, even to geniuses of highest rank. Our whole European art and civilisation, however, have remained to the Jew a foreign tongue ; for, just as he has taken no part in the evolution

---

* In the *N.Z.* "purely human" stood in the place of "his."—TR.

† The clause after the semicolon did not exist in the *N.Z.*

‡ This sentence occurred as a footnote in the *N.Z.*, and the next sentence was absent.—TR.

§ In the *N.Z.*, "in any higher sense."—TR.

of the one, so has he taken none in that of the other; but at most the homeless wight has been a cold, nay more, a hostile looker-on. In this Speech, this Art, the Jew can only after-speak and after-patch—not truly make a poem of his words, an artwork of his doings. In particular does the purely physical aspect of the Jewish mode of speech repel us. Throughout an intercourse of two millennia with European nations, Culture has not succeeded in breaking the remarkable stubbornness of the Jewish *naturel* as regards the peculiarities of Semitic pronunciation. The first thing that strikes our ear as quite outlandish and unpleasant, in the Jew's production of the voice-sounds, is a creaking, squeaking, buzzing snuffle*: add thereto an employment of words in a sense quite foreign to our nation's tongue, and an arbitrary twisting of the structure of our phrases—and this mode of speaking acquires at once the character of an intolerably jumbled blabber (*eines unerträglich verwirrten Geplappers*); so that when we hear this Jewish talk, our attention dwells involuntarily on its repulsive *how*, rather than on any meaning of its intrinsic *what*. How exceptionally weighty is this circumstance, particularly for explaining the impression made on us by the music-works of modern Jews, must be recognised and borne in mind before all else. If we hear a Jew speak, we are unconsciously offended by the entire want of purely-human expression in his discourse: the cold indifference of its peculiar "blubber" ("*Gelabber*") never by any chance rises to the ardour of a higher, heartfelt passion. If, on the other hand, we find *ourselves* driven to this more heated expression, in converse with a Jew, he will always shuffle off, since he is incapable of replying in kind. Never does the Jew excite himself in mutual interchange of feelings with us, but—so far as we are concerned —only in the altogether special egoistic interest of his vanity or profit; a thing which, coupled with the wry expression of his daily mode of speech, always gives to such excitement a tinge of the ridiculous, and may rouse

* "Ein zischender, schrillender, summsender und murksender Lautausdruck."

anything you please in us, only not sympathy with the interests of the speaker. Though we well may deem it thinkable that in intercourse with one another, and particularly where domestic life brings purely-human feelings to an outburst, even the Jews may be able to give expression to their emotions in a manner effective enough among themselves: yet this cannot come within our present purview, since we here are listening to the Jew who, in the intercourse of life and art, expressly speaks *to us*.

Now, if the aforesaid qualities of his dialect make the Jew almost * incapable of giving artistic enunciation to his feelings and beholdings through *talk*, for such an enunciation through *song* his aptitude must needs be infinitely smaller. Song is just Talk aroused to highest passion: Music is the speech of Passion. All that worked repellently upon us in his outward appearance and his speech, makes us take to our heels at last in his Song, providing we are not held prisoners by the very ridicule of this phenomenon. Very naturally, in Song—the vividest and most indisputable expression of the personal emotional-being—the peculiarity of the Jewish nature attains for us its climax of distastefulness; and on any natural hypothesis, we might hold the Jew adapted for every sphere of art, excepting that whose basis lies in Song.

The Jews' sense of Beholding has never been of such a kind as to let *plastic* artists arise among them: from ever have their eyes been busied with far more practical affairs, than beauty and the spiritual substance of the world of forms. We know nothing of a Jewish architect or sculptor in our times,† so far as I am aware: whether recent painters of Jewish descent have really created (*wirklich geschaffen haben*) in their art, I must leave to connoisseurs to judge; presumably, however, these artists occupy no other standing toward their art, than that of modern

* In the *N.Z.* "durchaus," i.e. "altogether."—Tr.
† "In our times" did not appear in the *N.Z.* article.—Tr.

Jewish composers toward Music—to whose plainer investigation we now will turn.

The Jew, who is innately incapable of enouncing himself to us artistically through either his outward appearance or his speech, and least of all through his singing, has nevertheless been able in the widest-spread of modern art-varieties, to wit in Music, to reach the rulership of public taste.—To explain to ourselves this phenomenon, let us first consider *how* it grew possible to the Jew to become a musician.—

From that turning-point in our social evolution where Money, with less and less disguise, was raised to the virtual patent of nobility, the Jews—to whom money-making without actual labour, i.e. Usury, had been left as their only trade—the Jews not merely could no longer be denied the diploma of a new society that needed naught but gold, but they brought it with them in their pockets. Wherefore our modern Culture, accessible to no one but the well-to-do, remained the less a closed book to them, as it had sunk into a venal article of Luxury. Henceforward, then, the *cultured Jew* appears in our Society; his distinction from the uncultured, the common Jew, we now have closely to observe. The cultured Jew has taken the most indicible pains to strip off all the obvious tokens of his lower coreligionists: in many a case he has even held it wise to make a Christian baptism wash away the traces of his origin. This zeal, however, has never got so far as to let him reap the hoped-for fruits: it has conducted only to his utter isolation, and to making him the most heartless of all human beings; to such a pitch, that we have been bound to lose even our earlier sympathy for the tragic history of his stock. His connexion with the former comrades in his suffering, which he arrogantly tore asunder, it has stayed impossible for him to replace by a new connexion with that society whereto he has soared up. He stands in correlation with none but those who need his money: and never yet has money thriven to the point of knitting a goodly bond 'twixt man and man. Alien and apathetic stands the educated Jew in midst of a society he does not understand, with whose tastes and aspirations he does not sympathise, whose history and evolution have always been indifferent to him. In such a situation have we seen the Jews give birth to Thinkers: the Thinker is the backward-looking poet; but the true Poet is the foretelling Prophet. For such a prophet-charge can naught equip, save the deepest, the most heartfelt sympathy with a great, a like-endeavouring Community — to whose unconscious thoughts the Poet gives exponent voice. Completely shut from this community, by the very nature of his situation; entirely torn from all connexion with his native stock—to the genteeler Jew his learnt and payed-for culture could only seem a luxury, since at bottom he knew not what to be about with it.

Now, our modern arts had likewise become a portion of this culture, and among them more particularly that art which is just the very easiest to learn—the art of *music*, and indeed *that* Music which, severed from her sister arts, had been lifted by the force and stress of grandest geniuses to a stage in her universal faculty of Expression where either, in new conjuncton with the other arts, she might speak aloud the most sublime, or, in persistent separation from them, she could also speak at will the deepest bathos of the trivial. Naturally, *what* the cultured Jew had to speak, in his aforesaid situation, could be nothing but the trivial and indifferent, because his whole artistic bent was in sooth a mere luxurious, needless thing. Exactly as his whim inspired, or some interest lying outside Art, could he utter himself now thus, and now otherwise; for never was he driven to speak out a definite, a real and necessary thing, but he just merely wanted to speak, no matter what *; so that, naturally, the *how* was the only 'moment'

* In the *N.Z.* "but he just merely wanted to speak" appears to have been skipped by the printer, leaving a hiatus in the sense; moreover, after "no matter what," there occurred: "sheerly to make his existence noticeable."
—Tr.

left for him to care for. At present no art affords such plenteous possibility of talking in it without saying any real thing, as that of Music, since the greatest geniuses have already said whatever there was to say in it as an absolute separate-art.* When this had once been spoken out, there was nothing left but to babble after; and indeed with quite distressing accuracy and deceptive likeness, just as parrots reel off human words and phrases, but also with just as little real feeling and expression as these foolish birds. Only, in the case of our Jewish music-makers this mimicked speech presents one marked peculiarity—that of the Jewish style of talk in general, which we have more minutely characterised above.

Although the peculiarities of the Jewish mode of speaking and singing come out the most glaringly in the commoner class of Jew, who has remained faithful to his fathers' stock, and though the cultured son of Jewry takes untold pains to strip them off, nevertheless they shew an impertinent obstinacy in cleaving to him. Explain this mishap by physiology as we may, yet it also has its reason in the aforesaid social situation of the educated Jew. However much our Luxury-art may float in wellnigh nothing but the æther of our self-willed Phantasy, still it keeps below one fibre of connexion with its natural soil, with the genuine spirit of the Folk. The true poet, no matter in what branch of art, still gains his stimulus from nothing but a faithful, loving contemplation of instinctive Life, of that life which only greets his sight amid the Folk. Now, where is the cultured Jew to find this Folk? Not, surely, on the soil of that Society in which he plays his artist-rôle? If he has any connexion at all with this Society, it

---

* In the *N.Z.* this sentence was continued by :—"and this was just the proclamation of its perfect *faculty* for the most manifold Expression, but not an *object* of expression in itself (*nicht aber ein* Ausdruckswerthes *selbst*). When this had happened, and *if one did not propose to express thereby a definite thing,* there was nothing left but to senselessly repeat the talk ; and indeed " &c.— Perhaps I may be forgiven for again recalling Wagner's own parrot, from the *Letters to Uhlig* (see Preface to Vol. ii. of the present series).—TR.

is merely with that offshoot of it, entirely loosened from the real, the healthy stem; but this connexion is an entirely loveless, and this lovelessness must ever become more obvious to him, if for sake of food-stuff for his art he clambers down to that Society's foundations: not only does he here find everything more strange and unintelligible, but the instinctive ill-will of the Folk confronts him here in all its wounding nakedness, since—unlike its fellow in the richer classes—it here is neither weakened down nor broken by reckonings of advantage and regard for certain mutual interests. Thrust back with contumely from any contact with this Folk, and in any case completely powerless to seize its spirit, the cultured Jew sees himself driven to the taproot of his native stem, where at least an understanding would come by all means easier to him. Willy-nilly he must draw his water from this well; yet only a *How*, and not a *What*, rewards his pains. The Jew has never had an Art of his own, hence never a Life of art-enabling import (*ein Leben von kunstfähigem Gehalte*): an import, a universally applicable, a human import, not even to-day does it offer to the searcher, but merely a peculiar method of expression—and that, the method we have characterised above. Now the only musical expression offered to the Jew tone-setter by his native Folk, is the ceremonial music of their Jehova-rites: the Synagogue is the solitary fountain whence the Jew can draw art-motives at once popular and *intelligible to himself*. However sublime and noble we may be minded to picture to ourselves this musical Service of God in its pristine purity, all the more plainly must we perceive that that purity has been most terribly sullied before it came down to us: here for thousands of years has nothing unfolded itself through an inner life-fill, but, just as with Judaism at large, everything has kept its fixity of form and substance. But a form which is never quickened through renewal of its substance, must fall to pieces in the end; an expression whose content has long-since ceased to be the breath of Feeling, grows senseless and distorted. Who has not had occasion to convince himself of the travesty of a divine service of song, presented in a real Folk-synagogue? Who has not been seized with a feeling of the greatest revulsion, of horror mingled with the absurd, at hearing that sense-and-sound-confounding gurgle, jodel and cackle, which no intentional caricature can make more repugnant than as offered here in full, in naïve seriousness? In latter days, indeed, the spirit of reform has shewn its stir within this singing, too, by an attempted restoration of the older purity: but, of its very nature, what here has happened on the part of the higher, the reflective Jewish intellect, is just a fruitless effort from Above, which can never strike Below to such a point that the cultured Jew—who precisely for his art-needs seeks the genuine fount of Life amid the Folk—may be greeted by the mirror of his intellectual efforts in that fount itself. He seeks for the Instinctive, and not the Reflected, since the latter is *his* product; and all the Instinctive he can light on, is just that out-of-joint expression.

If this going back to the Folk-source is as unpurposed with the cultured Jew, as unconsciously enjoined upon him by Necessity and the nature of the thing, as with every artist: with just as little conscious aim, and therefore with an insuperable domination of his whole field of view, does the hence-derived impression carry itself across into his art-productions. Those * rhythms and melismi of the Synagogue-song usurp his musical fancy in exactly the same way as the instinctive possession of the strains and rhythms of our Folksong and Folkdance made out the virtual† shaping-force of the creators of our art-music, both vocal and instrumental. To the musical perceptive-faculty‡ of the cultured Jew there is therefore nothing seizable in all the ample circle of our music, either popular or artistic, but that which flatters his general sense of the intelligible: intelligible, however, and so intelligible that he may use it for his art, is merely That which in any degree approaches

* In the *N.Z.* "wondrous"; † "unconsciously"; ‡ "capacity," as also in the preceding sentence where now stands "fancy."—TR.

a resemblance to the said peculiarity of Jewish music. In listening to either our naïve or our consciously artistic musical doings, however, were the Jew to try to probe their heart and living sinews, he would find here really not one whit of likeness to *his* musical nature; and the utter strangeness of this phenomenon must scare him back so far, that he could never pluck up nerve again to mingle in our art-creating. Yet his whole position in our midst never tempts the Jew to so intimate a glimpse into our essence: wherefore, either intentionally (provided he recognises this position of his towards us) or instinctively (if he is incapable of understanding us at all), he merely listens to the barest surface of our art, but not to its life-bestowing inner organism; and through this apathetic listening alone, can he trace external similarities with the only thing intelligible to his power of view, peculiar to his special nature. To him, therefore, the most external accidents on our domain of musical life and art must pass for its very essence; and therefore, when as artist he reflects them back upon us, his adaptations needs must seem to us outlandish, odd, indifferent, cold, unnatural and awry; so that Judaic works of music often produce on us the impression as though a poem of Goethe's, for instance, were being rendered in the Jewish jargon.

Just as words and constructions are hurled together in this jargon with wondrous inexpressiveness, so does the Jew musician hurl together the diverse forms and styles of every age and every master. Packed side by side, we find the formal idiosyncrasies of all the schools, in motleyest chaos. As in these productions the sole concern is Talking at all hazards, and not the Object which might make that talk worth doing, so this clatter can only be made at all inciting to the ear by its offering at each instant a new summons to attention, through a change of outer expressional means. Inner agitation, genuine passion, each finds its own peculiar language at the instant when, struggling for an understanding, it girds itself for utterance: the Jew,

already characterised by us in this regard, has no true
passion (*Leidenschaft*), and least of all a passion that might
thrust him on to art-creation. But where this passion is
not forthcoming, *there* neither is any calm (*Ruhe*): true,
noble Calm is nothing else than Passion mollified through
Resignation.* Where the calm has not been ushered in by
passion, we perceive naught but sluggishness (*Trägheit*):
the opposite of sluggishness, however, is nothing but that
prickling unrest which we observe in Jewish music-works
from one end to the other, saving where it makes place for
that soulless, feelingless inertia. What issues from the
Jews' attempts at making Art, must necessarily therefore
bear the attributes of coldness and indifference, even to
triviality and absurdity; and in the history of Modern
Music we can but class the Judaic period as that of final
unproductivity, of stability gone to ruin.

By what example will this all grow clearer to us—ay,
wellnigh what other single case could make us so alive to it,
as the works of a musician of Jewish birth whom Nature had
endowed with specific musical gifts as very few before him?
All that offered itself to our gaze, in the inquiry into our
antipathy against the Jewish nature; all the contradictoriness of this nature, both in itself and as touching us; all
its inability, while outside our footing, to have intercourse
with us upon that footing, nay, even to form a wish to
further develop the things which had sprung from out our
soil: all these are intensified to a positively tragic conflict
in the nature, life, and art-career of the early-taken FELIX
MENDELSSOHN BARTHOLDY. He has shewn us that a
Jew may have the amplest store of specific talents, may
own the finest and most varied culture, the highest and
the tenderest sense of honour—yet without all these pre-
eminences helping him, were it but one single time, to call

---

* "Die durch Resignation beschwichtigte Leidenschaft." In the *N.Z.* this
ran : "der Genuss der Sättigung wahrer und edler Leidenschaft," i.e. "the
after-taste of true and noble passion satisfied." The change, or rather advance,
of view-point is highly significant.—TR.

forth in us that deep, that heart-searching effect which we await from Art* because we know her capable thereof, because we have felt it many a time and oft, so soon as once a hero of our art has, so to say, but opened his mouth to speak to us. To professional critics, who haply have reached a like consciousness with ourselves hereon, it may be left to prove by specimens of Mendelssohn's art-products our statement of this indubitably certain thing; by way of illustrating our general impression, let us here be content with the fact that, in hearing a tone-piece of this composer's, we have only been able to feel engrossed where nothing beyond our more or less amusement-craving Phantasy was roused through the presentment, stringing-together and entanglement of the most elegant, the smoothest and most polished figures—as in the kaleidoscope's changeful play of form and colour †—but never where those figures were meant to take the shape of deep and stalwart feelings of the human heart.‡ In this latter event Mendelssohn lost even all *formal* productive-faculty ; wherefore in particular where he made for Drama, as in the Oratorio, he was obliged quite openly to snatch at every formal detail that had served as characteristic token of the individuality of this or that forerunner whom he chose out for his model. It is further significant of this procedure, that he gave the preference to our old master BACH, as special pattern for his inexpressive modern tongue to copy. Bach's musical speech was formed at a period of our history when Music's universal tongue was still striving for the faculty of more individual, more unequivocal Expression: pure formalism and pedantry still clung so strongly to her, that it was first through the

---

* In the *N.Z.* "from Music."—TR.

† A slight change has been made by our author in the construction of this sentence, since the time of the *Neue Zeitschrift* article ; but, while improving the general 'run,' it has given rise to almost the sole instance of a "false relation" in all his prose.—TR.

‡ Note to the 1869, and subsequent editions: "Of the Neo-Judaic system, which has been erected on this attribute of Mendelssohnian music as though in vindication of such artistic falling-off, we shall speak later."

gigantic force of Bach's own genius that her purely human accents (*Ausdruck*) broke themselves a vent. The speech of Bach stands toward that of Mozart, and finally of Beethoven, in the relation of the Egyptian Sphinx to the Greek statue of a Man: as the human visage of the Sphinx is in the act of striving outward from the animal body, so strives Bach's noble human head from out the periwig. It is only another evidence of the inconceivably witless confusion of our luxurious music-taste of nowadays, that we can let Bach's language be spoken to us at the selfsame time as that of Beethoven, and flatter ourselves that there is merely an individual difference of form between them, but nowise a real historic distinction, marking off a period in our culture. The reason, however, is not so far to seek: the speech of Beethoven can be spoken only by a whole, entire, warm-breathed human being; since it was just the speech of a music-man so perfect, that with the force of Necessity he thrust beyond Absolute Music—whose dominion he had measured and fulfilled unto its utmost frontiers—and shewed to us the pathway to the fecundation of every art through Music, as her only salutary broadening.* On the other hand, Bach's language can be mimicked, at a pinch, by any musician who thoroughly understands his business, though scarcely in the sense of Bach; because the Formal has still therein the upper hand, and the purely human Expression is not as yet a factor so definitely preponderant that its *What* either can, or must be uttered without conditions, for it still is fully occupied with shaping out the *How*. The washiness and whimsicality of our present musical style has been, if not exactly brought about, yet pushed to its utmost pitch by Mendelssohn's endeavour to speak out a vague, an almost nugatory Content as interestingly and spiritedly as possible. Whereas Beethoven, the last in the chain of our true music-heroes,

---

* In the *N.Z.* this stood: "he yearned to pass beyond Absolute Music and mount up to a union with her human sister arts, just as the full and finished Man desires to mount to wide Humanity."—TR.

strove with highest longing, and wonder-working faculty,* for the clearest, certainest Expression of an unsayable Content through a sharp-cut, plastic shaping of his tone-pictures: Mendelssohn, on the contrary, reduces these achievements to vague, fantastic shadow-forms, midst whose indefinite shimmer our freakish fancy is indeed aroused, but our inner, purely-human yearning for distinct artistic sight is hardly touched with even the merest hope of a fulfilment. Only where an oppressive feeling of this incapacity seems to master the composer's mood, and drive him to express a soft and mournful resignation, has Mendelssohn the power to shew himself characteristic—characteristic in the subjective sense of a gentle † individuality that confesses an impossibility in view of its own powerlessness. This, as we have said, is the tragic trait in Mendelssohn's life-history; and if in the domain of Art we are to give our sympathy to the sheer personality, we can scarcely deny a large measure thereof to Mendelssohn, even though the force of that sympathy be weakened by the reflection that the Tragic, in Mendelssohn's situation, hung rather over him than came to actual, sore and cleansing consciousness.

A like sympathy, however, can no other Jew composer rouse in us. A far-famed Jewish tone-setter of our day has addressed himself and products to a section of our public whose total confusion of musical taste was less to be first caused by him, than worked out to his profit. The public of our Opera-theatre of nowadays has for long been gradually led aside from those claims which rightly should be addressed, not only to the Dramatic Artwork, but in general to every work of healthy taste.‡ The places in our halls of entertainment are mostly filled by nothing but that section of our citizen society whose only ground for change of occupation is utter 'boredom' (*Langeweile*): the

* "Wunderwirkenden Vermögen" and "eines unsäglichen Inhaltes" did not occur in the *N.Z.*—Tr.

† "Zartsinnigen"—in the *N.Z.* "edlen," i.e. "noble."—Tr.

‡ The last clause, "but in general" &c., was absent from the *N.Z.* article.—Tr.

disease of boredom, however, is not remediable by sips of Art; for it can never be distracted of set purpose, but merely duped into another form of boredom. Now, the catering for this deception that famous opera-composer has made the task of his artistic life.* There is no object in more closely designating the artistic means he has expended on the reaching of this life's-aim: enough that, as we may see by the result, he knew completely how to dupe; and more particularly by taking that jargon which we have already characterised, and palming it upon his ennuyed audience as the modern-piquant utterance of all the trivialities which so often had been set before them in all their natural foolishness. That this composer took also thought for thrilling situations (*Erschütterungen*) and the effective weaving of emotional catastrophes (*Gefühlskatastrophen*), need astonish none who know how necessarily this sort of thing is wished by those whose time hangs heavily upon their hands; nor need any wonder that in *this* his aim succeeded too, if they but will ponder well the reasons why, in such conditions, † the whole was bound to prosper with him. In fact, this composer pushes his deception so far, that he ends by deceiving himself, and perchance as purposely as he deceives his bored admirers. We believe, indeed, that he honestly would like to turn out artworks, and yet is well aware he cannot: to extricate himself from this painful conflict between Will and Can, he writes operas for Paris, and sends them touring round the world—the surest means, to-day, of earning oneself an art-renown albeit not an artist. Under the burden of this self-deception, which may not be so toilless

---

* Whoever has observed the shameful indifference and absent-mindedness of a Jewish congregation, throughout the musical performance of Divine Service in the Synagogue, may understand why a Jewish opera-composer feels not at all offended by encountering the same thing in a theatre-audience, and how he cheerfully can go on labouring for it; for this behaviour, here, must really seem to him less unbecoming than in the house of God.—R. WAGNER.

† To the *N.Z.* article there here was added a foot-note: "'Man so thun!' sagt der Berliner," i.e. "'It's to be done!' as they say in Berlin."—TR.

as one might think,* he, too, appears to us wellnigh in a tragic light: yet the purely personal element of wounded vanity turns the thing into a tragi-comedy, just as in general the un-inspiring, the truly laughable, is the characteristic mark whereby this famed composer shews his Jewhood in his music.—

From a closer survey of the instances adduced above—which we have learnt to grasp by getting to the bottom of our indomitable objection to the Jewish nature—there more especially results for us a proof of the *ineptitude of the present musical epoch.* Had the two aforesaid Jew composers † in truth helped Music into riper bloom, then we should merely have had to admit that our tarrying behind them rested on some organic debility that had taken sudden hold of us: but not so is the case; on the contrary, as compared with bygone epochs, the specific musical powers of nowadays have rather increased than diminished. The incapacity lies in the spirit of our Art itself, which is longing for another life than the artificial one now toilsomely upheld for it. The incapacity of the musical art-*variety*, itself, is exposed for us in the art-doings of Mendelssohn, the uncommonly-gifted specific musician; but the nullity of our whole public system, its utterly un-artistic claims

---

* This subsidiary clause did not exist in the *N.Z.*—TR.

† Characteristic enough is the attitude adopted by the remaining Jew musicians, nay, by the whole of cultured Jewry, toward their two most renowned composers. To the adherents of Mendelssohn, that famous opera-composer is an atrocity: with a keen sense of honour, they feel how much he compromises Jewdom in the eyes of better-trained musicians, and therefore shew no mercy in their judgment. By far more cautiously do that composer's retainers express themselves concerning Mendelssohn, regarding more with envy, than with manifest ill-will, the success he has made in the "more solid" music-world. To a third faction, that of the composition-at-any-price Jews, it is their visible object to avoid all internecine scandal, all self-exposure in general, so that their music-producing may take its even course without occasioning any painful fuss: the by all means undeniable successes of the great opera-composer they let pass as worth some slight attention, allowing there is something in them albeit one can't approve of much or dub it "solid." In sooth, the Jews are far too clever, not to know how their own goods are lined !—R WAGNER.—In the *Neue Zeitschrift* this note formed part of the body of the text.—TR.

and nature, in the successes of that famous Jewish opera-composer grow clear for any one to see. These are the weighty points that have now to draw towards themselves the whole attention of everyone who means honestly by Art: here is what we have to ask ourselves, to scrutinise, to bring to plainest understanding. Whoever shirks this toil, whoever turns his back upon this scrutiny—either since no Need impels him to it, or because he waives a lesson that possibly might drive him from the lazy groove of mindless, feelingless routine—even him we now include in that same category, of "Judaism in Music." * The Jews could never take possession of this art, until *that* was to be exposed in it which they now demonstrably have brought to light—its inner incapacity for life. So long as the separate art of Music had a real organic life-need in it, down to the epochs of Mozart and Beethoven, there was nowhere to be found a Jew composer: it was impossible for an element entirely foreign to that living organism to take part in the formative stages of that life. Only when a body's inner death is manifest, do outside elements win the power of lodgment in it—yet merely to destroy it. Then indeed that body's flesh dissolves into a swarming colony of insect-life: but who, in looking on that body's self, would hold it still for living? The spirit, that is: the *life*, has fled from out that body, has sped to kindred other bodies; and this is all that makes out Life. In genuine Life alone can we, too, find again the ghost of Art, and not within its worm-befretted carcase.—

I said above, the Jews had brought forth no true poet. We here must give a moment's mention, then, to HEINRICH HEINE. At the time when Goethe and Schiller sang among us, we certainly know nothing of a poetising Jew: at the time, however, when our poetry became a lie, when every possible thing might flourish from the wholly un-

---

* In the *N.Z.* this ran: " of Judaism in *Art*, whereto the actual Jews have merely given its most obvious physiognomy, but in nowise its intrinsic meaning. The Jews could never take possession of our art" &c.—TR.

poetic element of our life, but no true poet—then was it the office of a highly-gifted poet-Jew to bare with fascinating taunts that lie, that bottomless aridity and jesuitical hypocrisy of our Versifying which still would give itself the airs of true poesis. His famous musical congeners, too, he mercilessly lashed for their pretence to pass as artists; no make-believe could hold its ground before him: by the remorseless demon of denial of all that seemed worth denying was he driven on without a rest,* through all the mirage of our modern self-deception, till he reached the point where in turn he duped himself into a poet, and was rewarded by his versified lies being set to music by our own composers.—He was the conscience of Judaism, just as Judaism is the evil conscience of our modern Civilisation.

Yet another Jew have we to name, who appeared among us as a writer. From out his isolation as a Jew, he came among us seeking for redemption: he found it not, and had to learn that only *with our redemption, too, into genuine Manhood*, would he ever find it. To become Man at once with us, however, means firstly for the Jew as much as ceasing to be Jew. And this had BÖRNE done. Yet Börne, of all others, teaches us that this redemption can not be reached in ease and cold, indifferent complacence, but costs —as cost it must for us—sweat, anguish, want, and all the dregs of suffering and sorrow. Without once looking back, take ye your part in this regenerative work of deliverance through self-annulment †; then are we one and un-dissevered! But bethink ye, that one only thing can redeem you' from the burden of your curse: the redemption of Ahasuerus—*Going under!*

---

* In the *N.Z.* there appeared : "in cold, contemptuous complacency," and the sentence ended at the "self-deception"—a footnote being added, as follows: "What he lied himself, our Jews laid bare again by setting it to music." Moreover in place of "seemed" there stood "is," and in the next sentence the predicate "evil" did not occur.—TR.

† In the *N.Z.* : "an diesem selbstvernichtenden, blutigen Kampfe."—TR.

APPENDIX TO "JUDAISM IN MUSIC."*

IN the year 1850 I published in the *Neue Zeitschrift für Musik* an essay upon "Judaism in Music," † wherein I sought to fathom the significance of this phenomenon in our art-life.

Even to-day it is almost incomprehensible to me, how my recently departed friend FRANZ BRENDEL, the editor of that journal, made up his mind to dare the publication of this article: in any case the so earnest-minded, so throughly staunch and honest man, taking nothing but the cause in eye, had no idea that he thus was doing aught beyond just giving needful space to the discussion of a very notable question connected with the history of Music. However, its result soon taught him the kind of people he had to do with.—In consequence of the many years of rightly and deservedly honoured work which Mendelssohn had spent in *Leipzig*—at whose Musical Conservatorium Brendel filled the post of a Professor —that city had received a virtual Jewish baptism of music: as a reviewer once complained, the blond variety of musician had there become an ever greater rarity, and the place, erewhile an actively distinguished factor in our German life through its university and important book-trade, was learning even to forget the most natural sympathies of local patriotism so willingly evinced by every other German city; it was exclusively becoming the

---

* The above title I have introduced in order to mark the division between the article of 1850 and that of 1869.—TR.

† Note to the 1873 edition (*Ges. Schr.*, vol. viii)—"See volume v of my Collected Essays and Poems."—In the 1869 edition this paragraph ran as follows: "The essay which appears above—unchanged in its essentials—I published somewhat over eighteen years ago in the '*Neue Zeitschrift für Musik*,' as mentioned in my opening statement."—TR.

metropolis of Jewish music. The storm, which now rose over Brendel, reached the pitch of menacing his civic life itself: with difficulty did his firmness, and the quiet strength of his convictions, succeed in forcing folk to leave him in his post at the Conservatoire.

What helped him soon to outward peace, was a very characteristic turn the matter took, after the first imprudent foam of wrath on the part of the offended.

Should occasion arise, I had by no means intended to deny my authorship of the article: I merely wished to prevent the question, broached most earnestly and objectively by myself, from being promptly shifted to the purely personal realm—a thing, in my opinion, to be immediately expected if my name, as that of a "composer indubitably envious of the fame of others," were dragged into play from the outset. For this reason I had signed the article with a pseudonym, deliberately cognisable as such: K. Freigedank [i.e. "K. Freethought"]. To Brendel I had imparted my intention in this regard: he was courageous enough to steadfastly allow the storm to rage around himself, in place of conducting it across to me—a course of action which would have freed him at once from all the pother. Soon I detected symptoms, nay plain indications, that people had recognised me as the author: no charges of the kind did I ever oppose with a denial. Hereby folk learnt enough, to make them entirely change their prior tactics. Hitherto, at any rate, only the clumsier artillery of Judaism had been brought into the field against my article: no attempt had been made to bring about a rejoinder in any intelligent, nay even any decent fashion. Coarse sallies, and abusive girdings at a medieval Judæophobia—ascribed to the author, and so shameful for our own enlightened times—were the only thing that had come to show, beyond absurd distortions and falsifications of the article itself. But now a change of front was made. Undoubtedly the higher Jewry was taking up the matter. To these gentry the chief annoyance was the notice roused: so soon as ever my name was known, one had to fear that its introduction would merely increase that notice. A simple means of avoiding this result had been put into their hands, through my having substituted for my own name a pseudonym. Now it seemed advisable henceforward to ignore me as the essay's author, and at like time to smother all discussion of the thing itself. On the contrary, I was very well attackable on altogether other sides: I had published essays on Art and had written operas, which latter I presumably should like to get performed. On this domain a systematic defamation and persecution of me, with total suppression of the disagreeable Judaism-question, at any rate held out a promise of my wished-for chastisement.

It would surely be presumptuous of me—seeing that, at that time, I was living at Zurich in complete retirement—to attempt a more exact account of the inner machinery set in motion for the inverse Jewish persecution, then commenced against myself, and later carried into ever wider circles. I will merely recite experiences that are already public property. After the production of *Lohengrin* at Weimar, in the summer of 1850, certain men of considerable literary and artistic standing, such as ADOLF STAHR and ROBERT FRANZ, auspiciously came forward in the Press, to direct the attention of the German public to myself and work; even in musical papers of dubious tendency there peeped momentous declarations in my favour. But, on the part of each several author this happened exactly and only *once*. They promptly relapsed into silence, and in further course behaved, comparatively speaking, even hostilely towards me. On the other hand, a friend and admirer of Herr Ferdinand Hiller, a certain Professor BISCHOFF, shot up in the *Kölnische Zeitung* as founder of the system of defamation henceforward carried-out against me: this gentleman laid hold on my art-writings, and twisted my idea of an "Artwork of the Future" into the absurd pretension of a "Music of the Future" ("*Zukunftsmusik*"), a music, forsooth, which would haply sound quite well in course of time, however ill it might sound just now.

Not a word said he of Judaism; on the contrary, he plumed himself on being a Christian and offspring of a Superintendent. I, on the other hand, had dubbed Mozart, and even Beethoven, a bungler; wanted to do away with Melody; and would let naught but psalms be sung in future.

Even to-day, respected lady, you will hear nothing but these saws, whenever people talk of "Music of the Future." Think, then, with what gigantic pertinacity this ridiculous calumny must have been kept erect and circulated, seeing that in almost the entire European Press, despite the actual spread and popularity of my operas, it crops up at once with renovated strength—as undisputed as irrefutable—so soon as ever my name is mentioned.

Since such nonsensical theories could be attributed to me, naturally the musical works which thence had sprung must be also of the most offensive character: let their success be what it might, the Press still held its ground that my music must be as abominable as my Theory. This was the point, then, to lay the stress on. The world of cultured Intellect must be won over to this view. It was effected through a Viennese jurist, a great friend of Music's and a connoisseur of Hegel's Dialectics, who moreover was found peculiarly accessible through his—albeit charmingly concealed—Judaic origin.* He, too, was one of those who at first had declared themselves for me with a wellnigh enthusiastic penchant (*Neigung*): his conversion took place so suddenly and violently, that I was utterly aghast at it. This gentleman now wrote a booklet on the "Musically-Beautiful," in the which he played into the hands of Music-Judaism with extraordinary skill. In the first place by a highly-finished dialectic form, that had all the

* In the *Deutsche Rundschau* for January of this year (1894) Dr Hanslick says (p. 56): "It would simply be flattering to me, to be burnt by Pater Arbuez Wagner on the same pile with MENDELSSOHN and MEYERBEER; unfortunately I must decline this distinction, since my father and all his ancestors, so far as one can trace them, were arch-Catholic peasant-sons, moreover from a countryside where Judaism has only been known in the shape of a wandering peddler."—TR.

look of the finest philosophic spirit, he deceived the whole Intellect of Vienna into supposing that for once in a way a prophet had arisen in its midst: and this was the desired chief-effect. For what he coated with this elegant dialectic paint were the trivialest of commonplaces, such as can gain a seeming weight on no other field than one, like that of Music, where men have always merely drivelled so soon as they began to æsthetise about it. It surely was no mighty feat, to set up the "Beautiful" as Music's chief postulate: but, if the author did it in such a manner as to astonish all men at his brilliant wisdom, then he might succeed in doing a thing by all means harder, namely in establishing modern Jewish music as the sterling "beautiful" music; and at a tacit avowal of that dogma he arrived quite imperceptibly, inasmuch as to the chain of Haydn, Mozart and Beethoven he linked on Mendelssohn in the most natural way in the world—nay, if one rightly understands his theory of "the Beautiful," he implicitly allotted to the last-named the comforting significance of having happily restored the due arrangement of the Beauty-web, to some extent entangled by his immediate predecessor, Beethoven. So soon as Mendelssohn had been lifted to the throne—which was to be achieved with special grace through placing by his side a few Christian notabilities, such as Robert Schumann—it became possible to get a good deal more believed, in the realm of Modern Music. Above all, however, the already-pointed-out main object of the whole æsthetic undertaking was now attained: through his ingenious booklet the author had rooted himself in general respect, and had thereby gained a position which gave importance to him when, as a bewondered æsthete, he now appeared as a reviewer, too, in the best-read political paper, and straightway pronounced myself and my artistic doings completely null and nugatory. That he was not at all misled by the great applause my works obtained among the public, must give him but a larger nimbus; item, he thus succeeded (or others succeeded through him, if you will) in getting just this tone about me adopted as the fashion, at least so far as newspapers are read throughout the world—this tone which it has so astonished you, most honoured lady, to meet where'er you go. Nothing but my contempt for all the great masters of Tone, my warfare against Melody, my horrible mode of composition, in short "The Music of the Future," was thenceforth the topic of everybody's talk: about that article on "Judaism in Music," however, there never again appeared a word. On the other hand, as one may observe with all such rare and sudden works of conversion, this [*Dieser*—? "he"] produced its effect all the more successfully in secret: it [?"he"] became the Medusa's head which was promptly held before everyone who evinced a heedless leaning toward me.

Truly not quite uninstructive for the Culture-history of our day would it be, to trace this curious propaganda a little closer; since there hence arose in the realm of Music —so gloriously occupied by the Germans heretofore—a strangely branched and most dissimilarly constructed party, which positively seems to have insured itself a joint unproductivity and impotence.

You next will surely ask, respected lady, how it came that the indisputable successes which have fallen to my lot, and the friends my works have manifestly won me, could in no way be used for combating those hostile machinations?

This is not quite easy to reply-to in a word or two. In the first place, however, you shall learn how matters went with my greatest friend and warmest advocate, FRANZ LISZT. Precisely through the splendid self-reliance which he shewed in all his doings, he furnished the ambushed enemy, ever alert for the puniest coign of vantage, with just the weapons they required. What the enemy so urgently wanted, the secreting of the to them so irksome Judaism-question, was quite agreeable to Liszt as well; but naturally for the converse reason, namely to keep an embittering personal reference aloof from an honest art-dispute— whereas it was the other side's affair to keep concealed the motive of a dishonest fight, the key to all the calumnies launched-out on us. Thus the ferment of the whole commotion remained unmentioned by our side, too. On the contrary, it was a jovial inspiration of Liszt's, to accept the nickname fastened on us, of "*Zukunftsmusiker*" ("Musicians of the Future"), and adopt it in the sense once taken by the "*Gueux*" of the Netherlands. Clever strokes, like this of my friend's, were highly welcome to the enemy: on this point, then, they hardly needed any more to slander, and the title "Zukunftsmusiker" cut out a most convenient path for getting at the ardent, never-resting artist. With the falling-away of an erewhile cordially-devoted friend, a great violin-virtuoso on whom the Medusa-head would seem to have also worked at last, there began that seething agitation against Franz Liszt, who magnanimously heeded no attack, whence'er it came —that agitation which prepared for him the undeception and embitterment wherein at last he put an end for ever to his splendid efforts to found in Weimar a furthering home for Music.

Are you, honoured lady, less astonished at the persecutions to which our great friend was subjected, in his time, than at those which have taken myself for mark?—Perhaps what might mislead you, then, is that Liszt had certainly drawn down on himself the envy, above all, of his German colleagues left behind him, through the brilliance of his outward artistic career; moreover, through giving up the racecourse of the Virtuoso, and through his hitherto having made mere preparations for an appearance as creative musician, that he had given fairly intelligible rise to a doubt, so easy to be nursed by envy, as to his real vocation for that status. I believe, however, that what I shall refer-to later will prove that at the real bottom of the matter this doubt, no less than was the case with my own imputed theories, gave but the merest pretext to the war of persecution: in the one case as in the other, it would have sufficed that they should be looked into more closely, and compared with a correct impression of our doings, for the question to have been at once removed to quite another standpoint; then, one could have criticised, discussed, and spoken for and against—in the long run *something* would have been the upshot. But that's just what all the talk was *not* about; and just this closer viewing of the new appearances one did not want to let occur. No, with a vulgarity of expression and insinuation the like whereof has never shewn itself in a kindred case, the whole army of the Press indulged in such a howling and a shrieking, that any human decency of argument was quite past thinking of. And thus it is that I assure you :—what Liszt has encountered, also, is a proceed of the workings of that article on " Judaism in Music."

However, even we ourselves did not discover this at once. At all times there are so many interests opposed to new departures, nay making for an out-and-out crusade against each thing implied therein, that we, too, believed we here had but to do with *vis inertiæ* and an art-traffic jogged from out its wonted ease. Since the attacks proceeded for the most part from the Press, and indeed from the great and influential political Daily-press, those of our friends who had been made anxious by the public's being given a bias against Liszt's ensuing first appearance as instrumental composer, thought it their bounden duty to take corrective steps: but, leaving out of count a few blunders which were thus committed, it soon grew evident that not even the most sober notice of a Lisztian composition could find an entry to the greater journals, all places here being taken in advance and in a hostile sense. Now, who will tell me seriously that this attitude of the great papers evinced an apprehension of possible harm to be wrought the good German art-taste through a new departure? I have lived to find that in one of these respected sheets it was impossible for me to even mention Offenbach in the way befitting him: in this instance, who can dream of a care for the artistic taste of Germany? So far had the matter got: we were completely barred-out from the greater German Press. But to whom belongs this Press? Our Liberals and Men of Progress have terribly to smart for being cast by the Old-Conservative party into one pot with Judaism and its specific interests: when the Ultramontanes ask what right has a Press conducted by the Jews to interfere in matters of the Christian Church, there lies a fatal meaning in the question, which at any rate is founded on an accurate knowledge of the wires that pull those leading journals.

The remarkable thing about it is, that this knowledge is patent to everyone else; for who has not made the experience for himself? I am not in a position to say how far this state of things applies to larger matters of Politics, though the Bourse affords a tolerably open index to the situation: but on this realm of Music given over to the most disgraceful cackle no man of insight has the smallest doubt that everyone is subject to a very curious discipline, whose following in the remotest circles, and with uniform punctiliousness, lets one argue to a most energetic management and organisation. In Paris, in particular, I was amazed to find this watchful management a positively open secret: there everyone has some astounding tale to tell you of it, especially as touching the extremely minute precautions against the secret being openly denounced at least, now that it is exposed to indiscretion through too many sharing in its knowledge; so that every tiniest cranny, through which it might leak into some journal, has now been stopped, were it only by a visiting-card in the keyhole of a garret. Here too, then, everyone obeyed his orders precisely as in the best-drilled army while a fight is on: you have already made acquaintance with this platoon-fire of the Paris press, aimed against me under command of Care for Good Taste in Art.—In London, some years ago, I met more frankness on this point. As immediately on my arrival the musical critic of the *Times* (I beg you to remember what a colossal world-sheet I here have named!) rained down on me a hail of insults, so in the further course of his effusions Herr Davison did not hesitate to hold me up to public odium as blasphemer of the greatest composers for reason of their Judaism.* By this disclosure he at any rate had more to win than lose, for his own standing with the English public: on the one side, because of the great esteem which Mendelssohn enjoys in England, above all places; on the other, perhaps, because of the peculiar character of the English nation, which to experts seems more grounded on the old testament, than on the new.—Only in St. Petersburg and Moscow did I find the terrain of the musical press still overlooked by Jewry: there I lived to see a miracle—for the first time in my life, was I taken up by the newspapers quite as much as by the public, whose good reception, I may add in general, the Jews had nowhere been able to spoil for me save in my father-city, Leipzig, where the public simply stayed away.

Through its ridiculous aspects this portion of my story has almost betrayed me into a jesting tone, which I must give up, however, if I am to permit myself, respected lady, to finally draw your attention to its very earnest side; and this, in your eyes, will probably commence exactly where we look away from my persecuted person, and take in eye the effects of that singular persecution upon the spirit of our Art itself.

To strike that path, I first must touch once more expressly on my personal interest. Just now I mentioned incidentally, that the persecution put upon me by the Jews had not as yet been able to estrange the public from me, and that everywhere the public welcomed me with warmth. This is correct. I here must add, however, that that persecution at all events is calculated, if not to bar my *way* to

---

* Without in any way attempting to defend the late Mr J. W. Davison for his sometimes savage, sometimes jocular attacks on Richard Wagner in 1855, it should not be forgotten that our author confessedly knew very little English, and therefore must have largely depended on his London friends (of that time) to read Davison's articles into German for him—a proceeding open to all the usual dangers attendant on translation—while, on the other hand, a most clumsy and injudicious personal attack had been opened on Davison in an American paper, even before Wagner's arrival in this country and certainly without his knowledge, by one of those London friends (the late Fred Praeger).—TR.

the public, yet to make it so difficult that on this side too, at last, the success of the enemy's efforts may very well promise to become complete. You already see that although my earlier operas have broken an entrance to almost every German theatre, and are given there with steady success, each of my newer works encounters an impassive, nay, a defiant attitude on the part of those self-same theatres: my earlier works, forsooth, had forced themselves upon the stage *before* that Jewish agitation, and their success was no longer to be got the better of. But, so the story ran, my new works were composed on the lines of my later-published "senseless" theories; I thus had fallen from my earlier state of innocence; and no one more could listen to my music. Just as Judaism in general could only root itself among us through profiting of the defects and weaknesses in our social system, so also here the agitation lightly found a soil—ingloriously enough for us!—already laid-out for its ultimate success. In whose hands is the conduct of our theatres, and what tendence do these theatres pursue? On this point I have spoken my mind both often and enough, and only the other day again, in a larger treatise on "German Art and German Politics," I set forth at some length the multifarious reasons for the downfall of our theatric art. Do you imagine that I therewith made myself a favourite in the spheres concerned? Only with the greatest reluctance, as they themselves have verified, do theatrical administrations nowadays embark on the production of a new work of mine.* They *might*,

---

* It would be not uninstructive, and at any rate would afford a glimpse into our art-affairs, if I gave you particulars of the behaviour which, to my genuine astonishment, I had lately to experience on the part of the two largest theatres, those of *Berlin* and *Vienna*, with regard to my "*Meistersinger.*" In my negotiations with the manager of these Court-theatres it needed some little time before I saw through the dodgery employed there, and found that not only were they trying to *get out of* giving my work, but also to prevent its being given elsewhere. You thence would plainly see that it is a question of a fixed determination, and that a veritable terror was manifestly felt at the bare idea of a new work of mine appearing. Some-day, perhaps, it may entertain you to hear a few more details from my region of experiences.—R. WAGNER.

however, have their hands forced through the universally favourable attitude of the public toward my operas; how welcome then must be the excuse so lightly to be drawn from the fact that my later works, you see, are so universally contested by the Press, and especially by its most influential section! Don't you already hear the cry sent-up from Paris, why on earth one should think necessary to attempt the in itself so difficult task of importing my operas into France, seeing my artistic rank is not so much as recognised in my native land?—This state of matters, however, is still further aggravated by my actually not offering my later works to any theatre; on the contrary, to my haply sought consent to the production of a new work I am compelled to attach conditions never held needful before— namely the fulfilment of certain demands, intended to insure me a really correct performance.* And here I touch on the most serious aspect of the commingling of the Jewish essence in our art-affairs.

In that essay upon Judaism I concluded by shewing that it was the feebleness and incapacity of the post-Beethovenian period of our German music-producing, that admitted of the commingling of the Jews therein: all those musicians of ours who found in the washings of the great plastic style of Beethoven the ingredients for preparing that newer, shapeless, sickly mannerism, ground down and plastered with the semblance of solidity, wherein they plodded on in mawkish comfort, without a life, without a strife—all these I set down as thoroughly included in my sketch of Music-Jewdom, let them belong to any nationality they pleased. This singular community it is, that nowadays embraces nearly everyone who composes music, and— alas! too—who conducts it. I fancy many of them were honestly confused and frightened by my writings: it was on their sincere bewilderment and perplexity that the Jews, enraged by my aforesaid article, laid hold for sake of

---

* Only through my momentarily letting fall these demands out of imperative regard for my publisher, could I lately move the *Dresden Court-theatre* to undertake the production of my *Meistersinger*.—R. WAGNER.

promptly cutting short all decorous discussion of my remaining theoretic essays, seeing there had already been shewn some notable beginnings of such a thing on the part of honest German musicians. With that pair of catchwords was stifled every fruitful, every explanatory and formative debate and mutual clearing of the ground.—In consequence, however, of the devastations wrought by the Hegelian Philosophy in German heads, so prone to abstract meditation, the same feeble spirit had taken lodgment on this domain [i.e. of Philosophy] as well as on its annexe, of Æsthetics, after Kant's great thought—so intelligently used by Schiller as basis for æsthetic views upon the Beautiful—had been pushed aside by a dreary jumble of dialectic nothings. Even on this side, however, I met at first an inclination to enter honestly upon the views laid down in my art-writings. But that above-named pamphlet of Dr Hanslick in Vienna, upon the "Musically-Beautiful," just as it had been composed for a definite purpose, had also been brought with hottest haste into such celebrity that one can scarcely blame a blond and pure-bred German Æsthetician, Herr Vischer—who had plagued his brain to find a writer for the rubric "Music" in a grand 'system' he was working out—if he associated himself, for convenience and safety's sake, with the so very much belauded Vienna Music-æsthete: for his grand work he handed over to him the execution of that article on a subject which he confessed to knowing nothing about.* So the musical Jew-Beauty took its seat in the heart of a full-blooded German system of Æsthetics, a fact which helped the more to increase the renown of its creator, as it now was lauded by the journals at the top of their voice, but, owing to its great un-entertainingness, was read by no one. Under enhanced protection through this new and altogether Christian-German fame, the musical Jew-Beauty was now uplifted to a thorough dogma; the most intricate and hardest

---

* This was told me long ago, at Zurich, by Professor VISCHER himself; in what degree of personal directness the co-operation of Herr Hanslick was drawn upon, I was not informed.—R. WAGNER.

questions of Musical Æsthetics, whereon the greatest philosophers had always expressed themselves with doubt and hesitancy whene'er occasion called for serious judgment—these questions were henceforward taken up by Jews, and by bamboozled Christians, with such confidence that to anyone who really wanted to think about the thing, and particularly to account for the overpowering effect of Beethoven's music on his feelings, it must almost seem as though he were listening to the wrangle for the Saviour's garments at the foot of the Cross—a subject the famous bible-student, David Strauss, might presumably expound with just as great discernment as Beethoven's Ninth Symphony.

Now this all must have at last the broader issue, that any attempt of ours to fortify the ever-slackening nerves of Art—as against this fussy, unproductive twaddle—was met not only with the natural obstacles which uprear themselves in every age, but also with a fully-organised Opposition, wellnigh the only function wherein the elements involved had power to shew activity. If *we* seemed silenced and resigned, in the other camp there went on nothing that could properly be regarded as a Willing, an Endeavouring or Producing: rather did the very party which pinned its faith to pure Jew-music-beauty let anything take place that pleased, and every new calamity *à la Offenbach* rain down upon our German art-life, without so much as turning on its side—a thing which they, at any rate, will find quite "selbstverständlich" ["self-intelligible"]. On the contrary if anyone, like myself for instance, was prompted by some emboldening chance to lay hand on given artistic forces and lead them into energetic action, you must have heard, respected lady, the hubbub raised on every side. Then came real fire and flame within the tents of modern Israel! Above all, once more, was it astonishing to hear the contemptuous, the quite dishonouring tone —inspired, as I believe, not simply by blind passion, but by a shrewdest reckoning of its inevitable effect upon the patrons of my undertakings; for who does not feel hurt at last by the disdainful tone employed in general toward a man one honours with the highest trust 'fore all the world?* Everywhere and in every combination necessary to employ for complex undertakings, the quite natural elements of ill-will on the part of persons unconcerned (or perhaps, of those too vitally concerned) are present: how easy is it made then, by that contemptuous attitude of the Press, for these people to set my undertaking in a dubious light even in the eyes of its protectors ! Can anything like this occur in France, to a Frenchman honoured by the public; in Italy, to an acclaimed Italian composer? This thing, which could happen only to a German in Germany, was so new that certainly the reasons for it are for the first time now to be sought out. You, respected lady, were filled with wonder at it; but those who, for the matter of that, are unconcerned with this seeming strife of bare art-interests, and yet have other grounds for hindering undertakings such as those I set on foot—these people wonder not, but find the whole thing natural enough.†

So the result is this: an ever more persistent hindrance of each enterprise that might lend my works and labours an influence on our present state of musical and theatric art.

Is that anything of consequence?—In my opinion, *much*; and I believe I am saying this without pretension. That I

---

* The reference is evidently to King Ludwig II of Bavaria.—Tr.

† Of this you may form a very adequate notion, and of the way in which these last-named gentry employ the fashionable tone in my regard to obstruct all furtherance of each my enterprise, if you will only take the trouble to peruse the feuilleton of the recent New-Year's number of the "*Süddeutsche Presse*," just sent to me from Munich. Herr Julius Fröbel there calmly denounces me to the Bavarian Government as founder of a sect that proposes to do away with State and Religion, and replace it all by an Opera-theatre whence to reign; a sect, moreover, that makes for satisfaction of "'Tartuffian lust" (*Befriedigung* "*muckerhafter Gelüste*").—The deceased Hebbel once described to me the peculiar lowness of the Viennese comedian Nestroy, by saying that a rose must necessarily stink if this person had but smelt at it. How the idea of Love, as keystone of Society, may figure in the brain of a Julius Fröbel, we here may see with like effect.—But don't you understand, again, how cleverly a thing like this is reckoned to rouse that disgust which makes the slandered man himself disdain to smite the slanderer?—R. Wagner.

may venture to set a certain store by my own efforts, I perceive from this one fact:—how earnestly all comment is avoided, on those publications to which I have been impelled from time to time in this regard.

I told you how, at first—before the commencement of this so expertly mantled agitation of the Jews against myself—there had been shewn beginnings of an honourably German treatment and discussion of the views I had laid down in my writings upon Art. Let us suppose that this agitation had not supervened, or—to give everyone fair play—that it openly and honourably had kept to its immediate cause: then we reasonably might ask ourselves what shape the thing would have taken, on the analogy of kindred episodes in the life of unmixed German Culture? I am not so optimistic as to imagine that very much would have been the issue; but surely something was to have been awaited, and at any rate something other than the actual result. If we rightly understand the signs, the period of concentration had set in, both for poetic Literature and for Music, when the legacies of matchless masters, who in serried ranks make out the great re-birth of German Art itself, were to be realised for the common good of all the nation, of all the world. In what preciser sense this conversion would be operated—that was the only question. And it was for Music that it shaped itself the most imperatively: for here, above all through the later periods of Beethoven's creation, a whole new phase of evolution had entered for the art, a phase that overtopped all views and suppositions nursed by her before. Under the lead of Italian vocalism, Music had become *an art of sheer agreeableness*: one thus entirely denied to her the power of giving herself a like significance with the arts of Dante and Michael Angelo, and had hence dismissed her, without more ado, to a manifestly lower rank of arts. *Wherefore from out great Beethoven there was now to be won a quite new knowledge of her essence; the roots, whence Music had thriven to just this height and this significance, were to be followed thoughtfully through Bach to Palestrina; and thus* there was to be founded a quite other system for judging her *æsthetically*, than that which took its reckonings from a musical evolution lying far outside these masters' path.

A correct feeling on this matter was instinctively alive in the German musicians of this period; and here I name you ROBERT SCHUMANN as the most thoughtful and most gifted of them all. By the course of his development as composer one may visibly demonstrate the influence which the alloy of Jewish essence, above referred-to, has exerted on our art. Compare the Robert Schumann of the first, with the Robert Schumann of the second half of his career: there plastic bent to shaping, here turgid blurring of the surface, with end in sickliness dressed-out as mystery. And quite in keeping is it, that Schumann in this second period looked peevishly, morosely and askance on those to whom in his first period, as Editor of the " *Neue Zeitschrift für Musik*," he so warmly and so amiably held out his German hand. By the bearing of this journal, in which Schumann also (with a like sagacious instinct) set his pen in motion for the great object that behoves us, you may see at once with what a mind I should have had to commune, if with him alone had I had to come to terms about the problems that aroused me: here do we meet, in truth, another tongue than that dialectic Jewish jargon which has been at last transplanted to our new Æsthetics; and— this I maintain!—in that tongue one might have come to a helpful understanding. What was it, then, that gave the Jewish influence this might? Alas! a cardinal virtue of the German is alike the fount of his defects. The quiet, stolid self-reliance that is ingrained in him to the point of warding off all sentimental qualms, and prompts so many a loyal deed from out the even tenour of his unspoilt heart —this very quality, if linked with but a small deficiency of needful fire, may easily degenerate into that astounding passiveness (*Trägheit*) in which, amid the continued neglect of every loftier region of the German spirit on the part of high political powers, we nowadays see plunged the most, nay almost all the minds that still stay faithful to the

German nature. Into this passivity sank Robert Schumann's genius too, when it became a burden to him to make stand against the restless, busy spirit of the Jews; it fatigued him to have to keep watch on all the thousand single features which were the first to come under his notice, and thus to find out what was really going on. So he lost unconsciously his noble freedom, and his old friends —even disowned by him in the long run—have lived to see him borne in triumph by the music-Jews, as one of their own people!—Now, honoured friend of mine, was *this* not a result worth speaking of? At any rate its mentioning will spare our throwing light on pettier subjugations, which, in consequence of this most weighty one, were everyday the easier to achieve.

But these personal successes find their supplement in the realm of Associations and Societies. Here, too, the German spirit shewed itself aroused to act according to its natural bent. The idea, which I have designated as the task of our post-Beethovenian period, for the first time actually united an ever-growing number of German musicians and music-lovers for objects which gained their natural significance through taking up that task. To the excellent Franz Brendel—who with faithful perseverance gave the impetus, and was rewarded by the fashionable scoffs of Jewish papers—to him is to be ascribed the positive fame of having recognised the needful thing on this side too. But the defect inherent in our German system of Association was bound to shew itself the sooner here, as a Union of German Musicians not only set itself in competition with the powerful sphere of organisations conducted by the Government and State—in common with other free associations, condemned to like effectlessness—but further, with the mightiest organisation of our times, with Judaism itself. Manifestly any larger *Union* of musicians could only expect to help forward the formation of a German style, in music, by the practical expedient of altogether 'model' performances of weighty works. For this, one needed *means*; but the German musician is poor: who's going to help him? Certainly not a disputation and debate about art-interests, which can have no sense amid a crowd, and easily may lead to ridicule. The leverage we lacked, however, belonged to Judaism. The theatre to the dandies and young Israel of the coulisses, to the music-Jews the concert-institutions: what was there left for us? Just one small music-sheet, which printed a report of our biennial meetings.

As you see, respected lady, I herewith certify the total victory of Judaism on every side; and if now once more I raise my voice against it, it certainly is from no idea that I can reduce by one iota the fulness of that victory. As on the other hand, however, my exposition of the course of this peculiar episode in German Culture seems to affirm that the whole thing is the result of that agitation provoked among the Jews by my earlier article, you may not be very distant from a new astonished question: namely, Why on earth did I stir up this agitation through that my challenge?

I might excuse myself by saying that I was prompted to that attack, not by any pondering of the "*causa finalis*," but solely through the incentive of the "*causa efficiens*" (as the philosophers express it). Certainly, even at the time of inditing and publishing that essay, nothing was farther from my mind than the notion that I could combat the Jews' influence upon our music with any prospect of success: the grounds of their latter-day successes were already then so clear to me, that now, after a lapse of over eighteen years, it affords me some measure of satisfaction to prove my words by its re-publication. What I may have proposed to effect thereby, I should be unable to clearly state; wherefore I fall back on the plea that an insight into the inevitable downfall of our musical affairs imposed on me the inner compulsion (*Nöthigung*) to trace the causes of that fall. Perhaps, however, it lay near my heart to join therewith a hopeful divination: this you may gather from the essay's closing apostrophe, with which I turn towards the Jews themselves.

Just as humane friends of the Church have deemed possible its salutary reform through an appeal to the downtrod nether clergy, so also did I take in eye the great gifts of heart, as well as mind, which, to my genuine refreshment, had greeted me from out the sphere of Jew society itself. Most certainly am I of opinion that all which burdens native German life from that direction, weighs far more terribly on intelligent and high-souled Jews themselves. Methinks I saw tokens, at that time, of my summons having called forth understanding and profounder stir. If dependence, however, is a great ill and hindrance to free evolution in every walk of life, the dependence of the Jews among themselves appears to be a thraldom of the very utmost rigour. Much may be permitted and overlooked in the broad-viewed Jew by his more enlightened congeners, since they have made up their minds to live not only *with* us, but *in* us: the best Jew-anecdotes, so very entertaining, are told us by themselves; on other sides, too, we are acquainted with the frankest, and therefore at all events *permissible*, remarks of theirs about themselves as well as us. But to take under one's wing a man proscribed by one's own stock—*that*, in any case, must be accounted by the Jews a rightdown mortal crime. On this side I have had some harrowing experiences. To give you an idea of the tyranny itself, however, let one instance serve for many. An undoubtedly very gifted, truly talented and intellectual writer of Jewish origin, who seems to have almost grown into the most distinctive traits of German folk-life, and with whom I had long and often debated Judaism in all its bearings—this writer made the later acquaintance of my poems "*Der Ring des Nibelungen*" and "*Tristan und Isolde*"; he expressed himself about them with such warm appreciation and clear understanding, that he certainly laid to heart the invitation of my friends, to whom he had spoken, to publish openly his views about these poems that had been so astonishingly ignored by our own literary circles. *This was impossible to him!*—

Please gather from these hints, respected lady, that, albeit I this time have merely answered your question as to the enigmatic reasons for the persecutions I have undergone, particularly on the part of the Press, I nevertheless should not perhaps have given my answer this almost wearisome extension, were it not that even to-day a hope which lies within my deepest heart, though wellnigh inexpressible, had added its incentive. If I wished to give this hope expression, before all I ought not to let it bear the semblance of reposing on a perpetual concealment of my relations with Judaism: this concealment has contributed to the bewilderment wherein not only you, but almost every sympathising friend of mine is placed to-day. Have I myself given rise to this, by that earlier pseudonym; nay, have I made over to the enemy's hands the strategic means for my own defeat: then I now must open to my friends what had long been too well known to my opponents. If I suppose that this openness alone is able, not so much to bring me friends from out the hostile camp, as to strengthen them to battle for their own true emancipation: then perchance I may be pardoned, if a comprehensive view of our Culture's history (*ein umfassender kulturhistorischer Gedanke*) screens from my mind the nature of an illusion that instinctively has found a corner in my heart. For on one thing am I clear: just as the influence which the Jews have gained upon our mental life—as displayed in the deflection and falsification of our highest culture-tendencies—just as this influence is no mere physiologic accident, so also must it be owned-to as definitive and past dispute. Whether the downfall of our Culture can be arrested by a violent ejection of the destructive foreign element, I am unable to decide, since that would require forces with whose existence I am unacquainted. If, on the contrary, this element is to be assimilated with us in such a way that, in common with us, it shall ripen toward a higher evolution of our nobler human qualities: then is it obvious that no screening-off the difficulties of such assimilation, but only their openest exposure, can be here of any help. If from the so harmlessly-agreeable realm of Music—as our newest Æsthetics have it—an earnest impetus has been haply given this by me, that fact itself, perhaps, might be reckoned not unfavourable to *my* view of Music's weighty office; and you, in any case, best-honoured lady, might find herein an apology for my having detained you so long with a theme so seemingly abstruse.

Tribschen, near Lucerne, New-Year 1869.

RICHARD WAGNER.

MEMENTOES
OF
SPONTINI.

Erinnerungen
an
Spontini.

SPONTINI'S DEATH (1851)—to anyone who surveys the evolutionary course of modern operatic music — removes a notable phenomenon, which consisted in this: that those three opera - composers who represent the three chief tendencies of this art-genre, were still living at one time; we mean SPONTINI, ROSSINI and MEYERBEER. Spontini was the last link in a chain of composers whose first link is to be found in GLUCK; what Gluck wanted and was the first to undertake on principle, namely the utmost possible dramatising of the opera-cantata, that, so far as it was reachable in the musical opera-form, Spontini carried out. Just as Spontini had declared by word and deed that he could never go beyond the point already reached by him, there appeared Rossini who bade entire farewell to the dramatic aim of Opera and took up instead, and developed farther, the frivolous and absolutely-sensuous element that lay within the genre. Beyond this tendency there was another characteristic difference between the operations of the two composers, namely that Spontini and his forerunners determined the public's line of taste through their making for Art on principle (*grundsätzliches künstlerisches Wollen*), whilst this public took pains to understand and adopt these masters' aim; whereas Rossini led the public away from this æsthetic trend, took it by its weakest side, of sheer distraction-hunting curiosity, and assigned it, from the artist's standpoint, the right to determine what should entertain it. Had the dramatic composer down to Spontini stood sentinel before the public in the interest of a higher artistic aim, through and since Rossini the public has been brought into a bespeaking and prescribing attitude towards the artwork; an attitude wherein, at bottom, it can no longer gain a new thing from the artist, but merely a variation of just its own demanded theme.—Meyerbeer, starting from the Rossinian line, made the public's ready-found taste his artistic lawgiver; nevertheless, confronted with a certain measure of art-intelligence, he tried to give his art-procedure the appearance of something characteristic and on principle: he added the Spontinian to the Rossinian line, and thereby necessarily twisted and distorted each. Indescribable is the repugnance felt by both Spontini and Rossini against the despoiler and commingler of art-tendencies belonging severally to themselves; just as to the genially sans-gêne Rossini he appeared a hypocrite, so Spontini considered him a trafficker in the most inalienable mysteries of creative art.

During Meyerbeer's triumphs our eye has often been led instinctively to the retreat of these marvellously isolated masters—now barely figuring any more in actual life—who from out the distance looked upon the Incomprehensible, to them, in this phenomenon. Above all, however, was our vision riveted by the art-figure of Spontini, who might regard himself with pride, but not with sorrow—for a huge disgust at present doings warded him from that—as the last of the dramatic composers who with earnest enthusiasm and lofty Will had addressed their efforts to an artistic Idea, and sprang from a time when universal respect and reverence had taken an, often hearty and helpful, interest in endeavours to realise that Idea.

Rossini's strong and opulent nature has outlived the consumptive variations of Bellini and Donizetti on his own voluptuous theme, the theme he had made over to the operatic world as centrepiece of public taste. Meyerbeer's successes live among us, spread broad across the opera-world, and give the thinking artist a riddle to rede, as to what may really be the class of public arts in which to rank the operatic genre.—But Spontini—is dead, and with him a great, an inestimable and noble art-period has now quite visibly descended to the grave: it and he belong henceforth no more to Life, but—only to Art-History.—

Let us bow in deep and reverent homage before the grave of the creator of the *Vestale*, the *Cortez* and the *Olympia!*

The above notice I had written for a Zurich journal, in a strain inspired by the earnestness of the moment, immediately upon receipt of tidings of Spontini's death. In later years, among the reminiscences of my life as Dresden Kapellmeister, I arrived at jotting down the peculiar circumstances in which I had come into very close contact with Spontini in the year 1844. These had stamped themselves so sharply on my memory, that this very fact allowed me to ascribe them a marked and singular physiognomy, sufficient to make them worth preserving not merely for myself. And however striking may seem the contrast between these reminiscences and the serious meditation which precedes them, yet I believe the attentive reader will detect no intrinsic contradiction, but rather will gather from the close of my recital that I did not need the mere news of his death, to prompt me to a very high esteem and earnest judgment of Spontini.—

For the late autumn of 1844 we had decided on a careful study of the "Vestale," for its resumption into the repertory of the Dresden Court-theatre. Since we might count on a large measure of excellence in the rendering of this opera, through the co-operation of Frau SCHRÖDER-DEVRIENT, and since Spontini had just suffered great indignities in Berlin, causing him to turn his back on it forever, I had suggested to Herr von LÜTTICHAU, Intendant of the Court-theatre, to pay him a demonstrative compliment, well-intentioned in the circumstances, by inviting him to take personal direction of his so justly celebrated work. This was done, and I, as being entrusted with the conduct of the opera, was specially commissioned to open negotiations with the master. It would seem that my letter, though written in my own French, had inspired him with a particularly good opinion of my eagerness for the undertaking, for, in a most majestic answer, he expressed to me his special wishes as to the arrangements to be made in honour of his assistance. As regards the singers, since he knew a Schröder - Devrient was numbered with them, he outspokenly declared his mind at rest; for the choruses and ballets, he anticipated nothing would be omitted in their due equipment; he also supposed that the orchestra would entirely satisfy him, as he assumed he would find in it the needful tale of first-class instruments, "garnished," as he expressed it, "with 12 good double-basses" ("*le tout garni de douze bonnes contre-basses*"). This clause quite broke my heart, for that one calculation, set down in figures, gave me a sufficient idea of the sturdiness of his remaining suppositions; and I hurried to the Intendant, to prepare him for the negotiations not going off so easily as could be wished. His horror was sincere and great; means must promptly be devised, for breaking off the invitation. Frau Schröder-Devrient heard of our distress: knowing Spontini fairly well, she laughed like a goblin at the naïve imprudence with which we had rushed on this petition, and found in a slight ailment she just was suffering under, the means of rescue which she placed at our disposal as pretext for an apparently considerable delay. Spontini, I must tell you, had pressed for an energetic hastening of our project, since he was most impatiently awaited in Paris and had little time to spare for the contentment of our wishes. Taking advantage of this, I now had to spin the web of innocent deceit wherewith to decoy the master from definitely accepting the invitation already addressed to him. We breathed again, held our rehearsals, and had just reached the day before the snugly plotted dress-rehearsal, when about midday a carriage drew up before my house; dressed in a long blue coat of frieze, the master, wonted else to move with all the dignity of a Spanish grandee, came rushing into my room without announcement, produced my letters, and pointed out from our correspondence that he had by no means declined our invitation, but, rightly understood, had distinctly fallen in with all our wishes. I forgot all possible embarrassments of the future in the truly hearty joy at seeing the wondrous gentleman within my doors, at hearing his work conducted by himself; and I promptly resolved to do all that in me lay, to bring about his satisfaction. I told him this with the frankest ardour: he smiled, with almost the sweetness of a child, when he observed it; but when, to bear him over any doubt of my sincerity, I simply begged him to conduct in person the rehearsal appointed for the morrow, he suddenly began to hesitate, and appeared to be pondering many a difficulty ahead. In great excitement, however, he gave no clear expression to his thoughts; so that it was no easy matter for me to elicit from him what plan I must adopt, to move him to accept the direction of this rehearsal. After a little reflection, he asked me what sort of baton we used for conducting with: with my hand I indicated, as near as possible, the length and thickness of a moderate-sized stick of ordinary wood, which the band-attendant served out to us each day wrapped round with fresh white paper. He sighed, and asked me if I thought it feasible to get made for him by next day a baton of black ebony, of most portentous length and thickness, which he outlined for me by his arm and hollow hand, and bearing at each end a fairly large white knob of ivory. I promised to see to his having at any rate an instrument that should look just like it, for the very next rehearsal, and another made of the precise material he desired, for the performance itself. Surprisingly calmed, he wiped his forehead, gave me permission to announce his acceptance of the direction for the morrow, and departed to his hotel after once more stamping on my memory his requirements in that matter of the baton.—

I half believed I was dreaming, and went off in a flurry to spread the news of what had happened and was to happen; we were trapped. The Schröder-Devrient offered herself as scapegoat, and I entered into the minutest details with the stage-cabinet-maker about the baton. This turned out so far well, that it had the becoming length and thickness, was black to look on, and bore great knobs of white. So, after all, we reached the real rehearsal. Spontini shewed obvious discontent with his place in the orchestra, and before all things wished the oboes placed behind his back; as this single change would momentarily have called up great confusion in the seating of the band, I promised to arrange it for him after the rehearsal. He said no more, and grasped his baton. In an instant I understood why he had laid so much weight on its form: for he did not take it by one end, like the rest of us conductors, but grasped it fairly in the middle with his whole fist, and manipulated it in a way to shew one plainly that he looked on the baton as a marshal's staff and used it, not for beating time with, but commanding. Now in course of the first scene there ensued a perplexity which became the more incurable, as the master's confounding of the German tongue was of the greatest hindrance to his properly conveying his instructions to either orchestra or singers. But we soon remarked thus much, that he was chiefly bent on ridding us of any notion that this was the final rehearsal, inasmuch as he had made up his mind to the opera's being studied radically afresh. The general despair was by no means trifling, especially on the part of my good old Choir-director and Manager, FISCHER—who had previously been most enthusiastic for the invitation of Spontini—when he became alive to this unavoidable upsetting of the repertoire; at last it passed over into open rage, blinded by which he saw nothing but some new chicane in each proposal of Spontini's, and

replied thereto with unmasked German gruffness. Once
Spontini beckoned me to his side, to whisper me about
a chorus just that moment ended: "*mais savez-vous, vos
chœurs ne chantent pas mal.*" Fischer had watched us
with mistrust, and asked me in a fury: "what has the old
—— —— again?" I had the greatest trouble in even
somewhat calming down the so speedily reversed enthu-
siast.—The greatest delay was caused by the evolutions of
the Triumphal March, in the first Act. Above all the
master gave loudest outcry to his utter dissatisfaction with
the indifferent demeanour of the People during the proces-
sion of the Vestal virgins; to tell the truth, he had not observed that everyone, in accordance with our stage-instructions too, had fallen on his knees at the approach of the
priestesses, since nothing merely cognisable to the eye was
existent for the excessively short-sighted master; what he
required was, that the religious homage of the Roman
army should be altogether drastically evinced by a sudden
prostration of everybody at once, and more particularly by
a crash of spears upon the ground. This had to be practised times without number; but always a few lances
would come clattering down too early or too late; he
himself went through the manœuvre a few times with the
baton on his desk; it was of no use, the crash was not decided and energetic enough. Now I distinctly remembered
the wonderful precision and wellnigh terrifying effect
wherewith similar evolutions had been carried out in the
performance of "Ferdinand Cortez" at Berlin, making a
great impression upon me in earlier years, and I saw at
once that our habitual gentleness in such manœuvres
would need a most solicitous and time-destructive sharpen-
ing-up, if it were ever to content a master so fastidious in
his least requirements. At the end of the first Act, indeed,
Spontini actually mounted the stage, to give the Dresden
Court-theatre's artists—whom he believed to be around
him—a circumstantial explanation of the reasons why he
must insist on a serious postponement of the opera, so as
to gain time for bringing the performance into keeping

with his own ideas, through rehearsals of all kinds. But everyone was already on the point of leaving; the singers and stage-manager had scattered to the winds, to vent their feelings on the misery of the situation in their own way: merely the carpenters, the lamp-cleaners and a few chorus-singers had drawn a semicircle round Spontini, to watch the remarkable man deliver a wonderfully impassioned peroration on the necessaries of true theatric art. I intervened in this terrible scene; pointed out to Spontini, in a friendly and submissive manner, the needlessness of his emotion; assured him that everything should go according to his wish, and especially would we get Herr EDUARD DEVRIENT—who, from his Berlin days, was well posted in the authentic staging of the *Vestale*—to drill the chorus and supers into the rites becoming a reception of the Vestal virgins; and so I bore him out of the undignified situation in which I had been horrified to find him caught. This calmed him; we sketched out the plan for a series of rehearsals after his own heart; and in truth I was the only one to whom, in spite of all, this turn of affairs was not unwelcome, since the almost burlesque features in much of Spontini's behaviour yet gave me an insight into the uncommon energy with which—although in strange, but gradually more explicable distortion—a goal of theatric art wellnigh lost-sight-of in our times was still pursued by him with might and main.

We began all over again with a pianoforte rehearsal, in which the master was to communicate his special wishes to the singers. To tell the truth, we heard little that was new from him; he gave us fewer hints as to details of rendering than remarks as to the general conception, and I noticed incidentally that he had accustomed himself to paying marked deference to singers of renown, such as Schröder-Devrient and TICHATSCHEK To the latter he merely forbade the word "Braut" ("Bride") wherewith *Licinius*, in the German translation, had to address "Julia"; this sounded dreadful to his ear, and he could not comprehend how anything so common, as the twang of this word, could be employed for music. To the less talented and somewhat inexperienced singer of the High Priest, however, he gave an exhaustive lecture on the conception of that character, saying he must take it from the recitative dialogue with the Augur; here he would see, to wit, the whole thing was based on priestly trickery and reckonings of the profit to be drawn from superstition. The Pontifex gives one to understand that he is not afraid of his adversary, even at the head of all the Roman army, since, should the worst come to the worst, he has his machinery ready to re-light the extinguished fire of Vesta by a miracle if must be; whereby, even though Julia thus escape a sacrificial death, yet the power of the priesthood would be kept intact.—In speaking of the orchestra I had asked Spontini to tell me why, though making lavish use of the trombones everywhere else, he had left them silent, of all places, in the magnificent Triumphal March of the first Act; quite astounded, he asked in turn : "*est-ce que je n'y ai pas de trombonnes?*" I shewed him the engraved score, whereon he begged me to introduce trombones into this march, and have it written out, if possible, in time for the next rehearsal. He also said: "*j'ai entendu dans votre 'Rienzi' un instrument, que vous appelez 'Bass-tuba'; je ne veux pas bannir cet instrument de l'orchestre: faites m'en une partie pour la Vestale.*" I was delighted to carry out his wish, with moderation and discretion. When he heard the effect for the first time, at rehearsal, he threw me a truly tender glance of thanks, and the impression made on him by this not very difficult enrichment of his score was so lasting that he sent me afterwards a most friendly letter from Paris, begging me to forward him a copy of this instrumental addition; only, his pride did not allow him to admit, in the expression used to signify his wish, that he was asking for anything from my own pen, but he wrote : "*envoyez-moi une partition des trombonnes pour la marche triomphale et de la Basse-tuba, telle qu'elle a été exécutée sous ma direction à Dresde.*"—My particular devotedness I further shewed him by the zeal with which I carried out an entire re-seating of the orchestra, after his own wish. This wish had less to do with system than with habit; and how important it was to him to suffer not the smallest alteration in his habits I clearly saw when he explained to me his method of conducting, for he directed the orchestra—so he said—by a mere glance of his eye: "my left eye is for the first violins, my right for the second violins; wherefore, to work by a glance, one must not wear spectacles as bad conductors do, even if one is short-sighted. I"—he admitted confidentially —"can't see a step before me, and yet I use my eyes in such a way that everything goes as I wish." Certain details in the seating to which he had accidentally accustomed himself, in any case were most irrational; undoubtedly it was from a Paris orchestra of long ago, where some exigency or other had compelled just this arrangement, that the custom dated of placing the two oboe-players immediately behind his back: hereby they had to turn the bell of their instruments away from the public's ear, and our excellent oboist was so enraged at this suggestion that it required a particularly jocular treatment of the incident, on my part, to calm him down for this occasion. Apart from this, Spontini's custom rested at any rate on a very correct system—alas! still totally ignored by the generality of German orchestras—according to which the string-quartett is spread over the whole orchestra; the brass and percussion-instruments, too overwhelming when focused on one point, are divided and disposed on either flank; and the softer 'wind' are fitly drawn together to form a chain between the violins: whereas the division—even now obtaining in the largest and most celebrated orchestras—of the instrumental body into two halves, that of the strings and that of the wind, betrays a positive rawness and want of feeling for the beauty of an intimate blend and equipoise of the orchestral mass of sound. I was most glad of this opportunity to permanently introduce the happy innovation into Dresden, since, started at Spontini's request, it became an easy matter to obtain the King's command for retention

of the change. After Spontini's departure, it only remained
for me to correct and equalise a few accidental eccentricities
in his arrangement, and thus to reach a satisfactory and
very effective disposition of the orchestra.

For all the peculiarities which attended Spontini's direction of the rehearsals, yet the exceptional nature of the
man fascinated players and singers to such a degree, that
a quite unwonted attention was devoted to their carrying-out. Characteristic throughout, was the energy wherewith
he insisted on an often extravagantly acute enunciation of
the rhythmic accents; to this end he had accustomed himself, in his commerce with the Berlin orchestra, to indicate
the to-be-emphasised note by an expression at first incomprehensible to myself, ejaculating "*diese*"; Tichatschek, a
regular genius for the rhythm of song, was particularly delighted by this, since he likewise had the habit of spurring
the choristers to extra precision, at important entries, by
telling them they had only to give due prominence to the
first note and the rest would come of itself. On the whole,
then, there gradually transpired a good and loyal spirit
toward the master; merely the viola-players bore him a
grudge for a long time after, owing to a fright he gave
them: in the accompaniment of Julia's lugubrious cantilena, in the finale of the second Act, the execution of the
eerie figure for the violas did not meet his wish; suddenly
he turned towards them, and cried with a hollow, graveyard
voice: "Is't Death in the violas?" The two wizened, incurably hypochondriac ancients—who, to my distress, still
held grimly on to the first desk of that instrument despite
their right to pensioning-off—stared up with genuine horror
at Spontini, believing they had heard an omen: I had to
try and explain his wish without drastic stage-effects, to
call them slowly back to life.—Upon the boards Herr
Eduard Devrient was most helpful in establishing a
sharply-drawn ensemble; moreover he found means to
satisfy a demand of Spontini's that had placed us all in
great embarrassment. Following the cut accepted at every

German theatre, we had been accustomed to end the opera at the spirited duet of Licinius and Julia, with choral accompaniment, after her rescue; but the master insisted on tacking-on the closing scene with merry chorus and ballet, a tradition of French *opera seria*. It went quite against his grain, to see his brilliant work go-out on a mournful place of burial; the scenery must be shifted, shewing the Rose-grove of Venus in brightest of lights; and midst mirthful dance and song, the sore-tried pair of lovers must be gracefully wedded at the altar by Venus' priests and priestesses, bedecked with roses. And thus it happened—but alas! by no means to the advantage of the success we all so longed for.

On the night of performance, which went with great precision and admirable fire, an ill we none had thought of made its appearance in the casting of the chief-rôle. Our great artist Schröder-Devrient was manifestly no longer of an age, nor was her somewhat matronly figure altogether fitted, to create a good effect as the "youngest" of the Vestals—a term immediately addressed to her—particularly by side of a High-priestess who, as here was the case, was conspicuous for a quite exceptional air of maidenly youth, which nothing could disguise. This was my niece, JOHANNA WAGNER, at that time seventeen years of age, who further by her entrancing voice—especially at just that epoch—and her happy gift for theatric Accent, aroused instinctively in every hearer the wish to see her rôle exchanged with that allotted to the great mistress. This unfavourable circumstance did not escape the keen-eyed Devrient, and seemed to inspire her with the feeling that she must expend every means of effect at her disposal on an attempt to hold successfully her trying ground; a thing that drove her not unfrequently to over-acting, and at one particular climax to a really painful excess. After the great trio in the second Act, when—moving away from her lover, just saved by flight—she steps to the foreground, and in supreme exhaustion the cry "He's saved!" bursts forth from her panting heart, she let herself be betrayed into wholly *speaking* these words in lieu of singing them. What an effect may be produced in moments of supreme passion, by the ejaculation of a crucial word in almost the accent of unembellished speech, she had often before observed in *Fidelio* to the utmost transport of her audience, when, at the passage: "but one step farther and thou liest dead!" she rather spoke the "*dead*" than sang it. This extraordinary effect, which I myself had felt as well, rested on the wonderful terror that overpowered me at seeing myself hurled from the ideal sphere into which Music lifts even the most gruesome situations, and cast suddenly upon the naked soil of most horrible reality, as though by one stroke of the executioner's axe. Here was displayed an immediate knowledge of the utmost acme of the Sublime, which, in memory of this impression, I may call the flash of lightning that illumines for an instant two altogether diverse worlds, at the point where they touch and yet completely part from one another, in suchwise that for just this instant we positively catch a glimpse of both these worlds at once. But what a gigantic issue lies within that instant, and how one must play with its terrors no self-seeking trick, I learnt on this occasion from the total failure of the great artist's aim. The toneless word, forced out with raucous clang, poured like cold water over myself and the whole audience, and we saw nothing in it beyond a missed theatrical effect.—Whether it was that the expectations of the public—who moreover had had to pay double price for the curiosity of seeing Spontini conduct—had been strained to too high a pitch; whether the whole style of the work, with its Frenchified antique subject, had struck people involuntarily as somewhat out of date, despite the pomp and beauty of its music; or whether, in fine, the woefully flat ending may have sobered folk down in much the same manner as the Devrient's missed dramatic effect: in short, no genuine enthusiasm could be got up, and the evening's whole result was a somewhat flabby demonstration of homage to the world-famed master, who, with his enormous armature of orders, presented to my mind a painful picture as he came before the curtain to bow his thanks for the public's short-lived call.

The cold comfort of this success had escaped no one less than Spontini himself. Determined to wrest matters into a better look, he insisted on having recourse to the means he had been accustomed to employ in Berlin, for supplying his operas with constantly full houses and an animated audience. To this end he had always chosen the Sundays, since experience had taught him that of a Sunday the house was always crowded and the public brisk. Now, as it was still some little distance to the next Dresden Sunday—for which he offered to conduct his "*Vestale*" once again—this fresh extension of his stay procured us a renewal of the pleasure and peculiar interest of coming frequently into social intercourse with Spontini. Of the hours passed in converse with him, partly at Frau Devrient's rooms, partly also at mine, I have preserved so exact a recollection, that I gladly make a little of it known.

Unforgettable remains one dinner-party at Schröder-Devrient's, as it brought us into the company of Spontini and his wife (a sister of the famous pianoforte-maker, Erard) for a considerable time, and amid very stirring discourse. His customary share in conversation was a dignified calm while listening to the talk of others, which seemed to say he was waiting to be begged for his opinion. So soon as this happened, he spoke with rhetorical solemnity, in sharp-cut phrases of a categoric tendence, and with an accent that declared all contradiction an affront. However, he waxed in warmth as we drew closer together after dinner. So far as possible to him, he appeared to have really bestowed on me his special favour; he openly declared he had a liking for me, and would prove it by saving me from the misfortune of continuing my career of dramatic composer. True, said he, he would find it hard to convince me of the worth of such a friendly service; as, however, he held it of weight to care for my welfare in this fashion, it would not irk him to spend half a year at Dresden with this object—an opportunity we might also employ for bringing out his other operas, particularly "*Agnes von Hohenstaufen*," under his personal direction.

To characterise the ruinous consequences attending the career of a dramatic composer *as follower after Spontini*, he began with a curious encomium of myself, saying: "*quand j'ai entendu votre Rienzi, j'ai dit, c'est un homme de génie, mais déja il a plus fait qu'il ne peut faire.*" To shew what he meant by this paradox, he came forth with the following: "*après Gluck c'est moi qui ai fait la grande révolution avec la Vestale; j'ai introduit le 'Vorhalt de la sexte'* [the suspension of the sixth] *dans l'harmonie et la grosse caisse* [the big drum] *dans l'orchestre; avec Cortez j'ai fait un pas plus avant; puis j'ai fait trois pas avec Olympie. Nurmahal, Alcidor et tout ce que j'ai fait dans les premiers temps de Berlin, je vous les livre, c'était des œuvres occasionnelles; mais puis j'ai fait cent pas en avant avec Agnès de Hohenstaufen, où j'ai imaginé un emploi de l'orchestre remplaçant parfaitement l'orgue.*" Since that time he had tried to busy himself again with a subject, "*les Athéniennes*"; in fact, he had been pressingly invited by the Crown-prince, the present King of Prussia, to complete this work,—and at the same time, in evidence of his truthfulness, he drew from his pocket-book a few letters of this monarch's, which he gave us all to read. Only after this had been scrupulously carried out by us, did he proceed: that despite this flattering invitation he had given up the musical setting of the subject, for that matter a very good one, because it had come into his mind that he could not possibly surpass his "*Agnes von Hohenstaufen*" and invent something new. The conclusion of his speech was this: "*Or, comment voulez-vous que quiconque puisse inventer quelque chose de nouveau, moi Spontini déclarant ne pouvoir en aucune façon surpasser mes œuvres précédentes, d'autre part étant avisé que depuis la Vestale il n'a point été écrit une note qui ne fut volée de mes partitions?*" That this assertion was no mere phrase, but rested on the most searching scientific investigation, he called upon his wife to witness: this lady had read with him a voluminous treatise by a famous member of the French Academy, whose writing, however, for certain reasons, had not been published in type. In this very thoroughgoing treatise, of the greatest scientific value, it had been proved that without Spontini's invention of the suspended sixth the whole of modern melody would not exist, and that every melodic form which had been made use of since then, was simply taken from his pieces. I was stunned, but hoped to bring the inexorable master to a better opinion, at least of the possibilities still in store for himself. I allowed that everything, to be sure, was just as that Academician had proved; nevertheless I asked him whether he did not think that, if a dramatic poem of a new poetic tendency as yet unknown to him were laid before him, he would not derive from it a stimulus to some further new musical invention. With a pitying smile, he said my question itself contained an error: in what should this New consist? "*Dans la Vestale j'ai composé un sujet romain, dans Fernand Cortez un sujet espagnol-mexicain, dans Olympie un sujet grec-macédonien, enfin dans Agnès de Hohenstaufen un sujet allemand: tout le reste ne vaut rien.*" He certainly hoped I had not the so-called romantic genre "*à la Freischütz*" in mind? With such puerilities no earnest man could concern himself; for Art was an earnest thing, and *he* had exhausted every kind of earnestness. From what nation, finally, should come the composer who could outbid him? Surely not from the Italians, whom he simply dubbed *cochons*; from the French, who had merely imitated them; or from the Germans, who would never leave their swaddling-clothes, and with whom, if there had ever been men of good parts among them, all had now been ruined entirely by the Jews? "*Oh, croyez-moi, il y avait de l'espoir pour l'Allemagne lorsque j'étais empereur de la musique à Berlin; mais depuis que le roi de Prusse a livré sa musique au désordre occasionné par les deux juifs errants qu'il a attirés, tout espoir est perdu."* Our amiable hostess now thought it would be as well to offer the very excited master a little recreation. The theatre lay but a few steps off her dwelling; she therefore invited him to let a friend from among her guests conduct him across to see a scene or two of the "Antigone," which was being performed just then and assuredly would interest him on account of the antique arrangement of the stage, after SEMPER's excellent plans. He wanted to decline the offer, maintaining he knew all this much better from his own "Olympia." However, we managed to persuade him; but he returned after the briefest interval, and declared, with a contemptuous smile, that he had seen and heard enough to confirm him in his opinion. His companion told us that, shortly after he had entered the nearly empty tribune of the amphitheatre with SPONTINI, the latter had turned round to him at the beginning of the Bacchus-chorus: "*C'est de la Berliner Sing-Académie, allons-nous en.*" Through the open door a ray of light had fallen on a solitary figure behind a pillar, unnoticed before; this companion had recognised MENDELSSOHN, and promptly concluded he had overheard Spontini's comment.

From the master's animated utterances during the remainder of the evening, it grew quite plain to us that he had looked for our urging him to stay some time in Dresden, and bring out the whole of his operas there. Frau Schröder-Devrient, however, already deemed wise in Spontini's own interest—as she wished to spare him a sorry disappointment of his cherished expectations regarding the reception of a second performance of the *Vestale*—to hinder even that performance from taking place in his presence. Once again she alleged an indisposition, and I was commissioned by the management to acquaint Spontini with the lengthy delay in view. The prospect of this visit was so painful to me, that I was glad to get myself accompanied by Music-director RÖCKEL, for whom Spontini had likewise formed an affection, and whose French was far more fluent than mine. With true alarm we stepped in, presuming that we were about to have a nasty scene: how astonished were we to find the master, already forewarned by a friendly note of the Devrient's, receive us with a beaming face! He announced to us that he must travel post-haste to Paris, and get on thence as quickly as possible to Rome, whither he had been summoned by the holy Father, who had just bestowed upon him the title of "Count of San Andrea." At like time he shewed us a second document, wherein the King of Denmark "had invested him with the Danish peerage"; this latter was a nomination to Knighthood of the Order of the Elephant, which certainly carries a noble's rank; but he mentioned only the peerage, not the order, since the latter had already become for him too common. His pride and satisfaction found vent in an almost childlike glee; from the narrow circle of the Dresden *Vestale*-operations he was freed as by a spell, and placed in a realm of glory whence he looked down on the opera-worries of this world with an angelic sense of comfort. By Röckel and myself the holy Father and King of Denmark were blessed with all our heart. We took an affecting leave of the singular master, and, to make him quite happy, I gave my promise to ponder anxiously his friendly counsel in that matter of the opera-composing.

Concerning his eventual demise, BERLIOZ—who never left his deathbed—narrated to me how the master had fought his hardest against dying; again and again would he cry: "*je ne veux pas mourir, je ne veux pas mourir!*" When Berlioz consoled him: "*comment pouvez-vous penser mourir, vous, mon maître, qui êtes immortel!*" Spontini angrily waived his remark aside: "*ne faites pas d'esprit!*" —The news of his death, which I received at Zurich, touched me very much indeed, for all my strange experiences and recollections: I gave brief expression to my feelings and judgment of him in the "*Eidgenössische Zeitung,*" laying special stress on the fact that, in contrast to the now ruling Meyerbeer and even the still lingering

Rossini, he had distinguished himself by a sincere belief in himself and his art. That this belief, as I had witnessed wellnigh to my horror, had degenerated into a ghostly superstition—on this I kept silence.

In the mood I was in at Dresden, at the time, I don't remember to have found occasion to ponder a little deeper on the extremely strange impressions I received from this notable encounter with Spontini, and thus to bring them into line with my high esteem for the master—which nevertheless had been raised by just that meeting. Manifestly I had made acquaintance merely with his caricature; yet the seeds of so amazing an exaggeration of self-consciousness may certainly be detected in the character that marked him in his years of vigour. No less demonstrable would seem to me, however, the influence of the intrinsic dry-rot of the whole musical-dramatic tendence of that art-period, which Spontini saw grow old while in occupation of so vague and null a post as the one he held at Berlin. That quite astoundingly he set his chief deserts in minor matters, shewed that his judgment had become childish; this, however, could not therefore diminish in my eyes the uncommon value of his works, even though himself should rate it at a monstrously inflated figure. On the other hand, what had driven him to so immoderate a self-appraisement, namely his comparison with those art-magnates who now dislodged him—this comparison, when I likewise instituted it myself, could no less serve to justify him; for, in his contempt of these magnates, I felt my inmost heart more akin to his than I cared at that time to confess aloud. So it came to pass in a singular way, that this meeting at Dresden, quite laughable as were the almost only traits it offered, yet filled me at bottom with a wellnigh awestruck sympathy for this man whose like I was ne'er to look upon again.

HOMAGE

TO

LUDWIG SPOHR AND
CHORUS-MASTER WILHELM FISCHER.

Nachruf

an

L. Spohr und Chordirektor W. Fischer.

(Brieflich an einen älteren Freund in Dresden.
Paris 1860.)

This Eulogy was originally published in the Neue Zeitschrift *of December 2, 1859, under the title:* " Dem Andenken meines theuren Fischer " (" *to the memory of my beloved Fischer*"), *and with the terminal date* " *Paris, im November* 1859." *As appears from the title in Vol. v of the* Gesammelte Schriften, *it was written as* " *a letter to an old Dresden friend*"—*evidently Ferdinand Heine, one of the recipients of the* " Letters to Uhlig, Fischer, and Heine."

Since its publication in the N.Z. the letter has been considerably retouched by Richard Wagner, but merely as regards its style; the matter and the general run of the sentences remain unaltered.

TRANSLATOR'S NOTE.

EATH has robbed me almost simultaneously of two dear and high-esteemed old friends. The loss of the one has smitten the whole world of music, which mourns the death of LUDWIG SPOHR; to it I leave the appraisement of what rich powers, what noble productivity, have passed from life together with this master. Me it sadly warns that there now has left us the last of that line of noble, earnest musicians, whose youth was still illumined by the immediate rays of Mozart's sun; who nursed with touching loyalty, like Vestal virgins, the sacred flame committed to their charge; and guarded its chaste hearth against the winds and storms of life. This lofty office upheld these men in purity and nobleness, and must I at one breath denote what spake to me with such indelible effect in Spohr, I name it when I say: he was an earnest, upright master of his art; the handle of his life was Faith in his art; his deepest consolation sprang from out the force of that belief. And this earnest Faith made him free from every kind of personal pettiness: what he could not take the measure of, he left aside as foreign to him, without attack or persecution. This was the coldness and abruptness so often cast in his teeth. What was intelligible to him (and a deep and delicate sense of beauty must surely be ascribed to the creator of "Jessonda"), that he loved and warmly prized without reserve so soon as in it he perceived one thing: earnestness, earnest dealing with Art. And here lay the bond which, even in advanced old age, united him to the new art-efforts; he might become a stranger to them, but never hostile. Honour, then, our Spohr: homage to his memory! Faithful following of his example!—

Hardly had the first effects of the tidings of his death given place in me to sadly-joyful recollection of my one-time personal intercourse with Spohr, than this chord of purely human sympathy was touched to painfulest vibration as I learnt the death of our dear FISCHER. Here, esteem for the modest art-comrade must needs be merged in a feeling of mournful reverence for the kind human friend; and yet, as the two decrees of Death so closely brushed each other in point of time, must I also in the natures of the two departed ones perceive so close a kinship that both, for me, were almost welded into one. The memory of the famous, highly-gifted master will be lauded far and wide, and better than in my paltry words; but the eulogy of this grandly vigorous, above all lovable greybeard, of our dear Fischer, I fain would take in mine own hand for the far narrower circle of his associates. How light, indeed, will be the labour; how few words it needs, to praise this excellent man to those who knew him. For, no creator and no author, he made himself not widely known, but merely to the handful who stood within the sphere of his immediate influence, his practical activity, his unsurpassable friendship. Yet gladly do I lend my word to those who would gain full consciousness of what they have lost in Fischer, and no better can I do it than by telling them what I myself have lost in him.

It is wellnigh twenty years ago that, as now I sent my last greeting to him from Paris, from the same place I turned to him with the prayer to take under his shelter my "Rienzi," then lately handed-in at Dresden. Scruples of all kinds were my answer*; in doubt as to the ground of these scruples, I soon set out myself for Dresden; and the origin of Fischer's scruples was soon brought gladly home to me, when he sprang-up in welcome, and embraced with boisterous heartiness a man till then a stranger to him. I shall never forget that first kind deed; it was the first, the very first encouragement that had greeted the helplessly obscure, the want-oppressed young artist on his life's-path. To *thee*, my friend, I well may tell this, since I scarcely need recall to thee what share thou took'dst, thyself, in these encouragements. Then was the footing found whereon

---

* See Wagner's letters to Fischer, of 1841-42, in the *Letters to Uhlig etc.*—TR.

all kinds of "scruples" were one by one securely overcome. The waxing enthusiasm of our TICHATSCHEK for his rôle, for the whole work, soon spread itself, in a measure hardly known in our time, to all concerned in the undertaking; and the Dresden public—predisposed by the marvel of that warm sympathy of all the artists for the work of a totally unknown composer—raised me, on that stirring night of the first performance of my "Rienzi,' to the proud rank of their adopted favourite. Then our Fischer grew more and more at ease, and, as though in the fond knowledge that it was he who first had recognised me and given the impetus to my success, he fixed his dear bright eyes on me in tender silence, as who should say: "Yes! I knew it would turn out so." Thenceforward I was his delight. My efforts and my doings were his pleasure, my Want his toil, and my attainment his success. Full of zeal and loyalty in his duties, as ne'er another, he passed all limit when it became a question of standing by me in exceptionally difficult tasks. If what I had madly asked succeeded, how glad a smile shone from his face! And how he then prevailed, to what a height his achievements as choir-conductor reached, making those achievements a red letter in the chronicles of Art—that we all experienced when he brought about the unbelievable; when, for example, in Bach's Motett: "Sing ye to the Lord!" he schooled the theatre-choir to such a pitch that, relying on the uncommonly correct and certain phrasing of the singers, I felt induced to take the first *allegro*—erewhile interpreted as the most cautious *moderato*, for reason of its hair-bristling difficulty—in its true fiery tempo, notoriously frightening all our critics out of their lives. The possibility of a popular success for Beethoven's Ninth Symphony, in my conception of it, rested on the choruses being delivered with such confident boldness as I indeed proposed, but as only Fischer's—in my opinion—unparalleled excellence as Choir-master could bring to realisement.

These, and many achievements like them, rank the name

of Fischer in Art's history with those who have done true service in spreading an understanding of lofty masterworks. But the more such service has stayed unrecognised, the juster it becomes, once mentioned, to mark it with emphatic token. And therefore would I claim attention that such achievements, for which their real effector is often hardly thanked, are the result of untold labour and anxiety. How often had I to deplore the poor fellow, when he could only answer my reckless demands with his own despair: his good singers were upon the sick list; the best, resigned for refusal of increased salary; the remainder tired out, *hors de combat* from excessive work, or detained to act as supers in the play-rehearsals. Yet he was a man of resource, one who would never break hastily with a thing, but made the best of scanty means and sought from tolerable to bring forth good. Then we two would tread upon each other's heels, and the sturdy one waxed wroth against the stormy one; all the more violently as, after all, he only wished what I wished. Yet the thing succeeded; God knows how! But succeed it did. And then the joy, the revelry, of reconciliation!

Thus were our art-tasks and our friendship one whole thing, ever rounding and re-livening itself, and before all eyes I celebrate the art-companion whilst I praise the friend!—

What a pother, too, the poor fellow had with me! Discreet and sober in his ripe practical estimate of the things of this world, what deep distress, what grief he suffered for me, when Destiny tore me from his side and drove me far away, nevermore—though I cherished other hopes but a few months since—to press his hand again! Could anything have made this rarest man more precious to me, than had our life together, then 'twas our separation. In the very first letter he sent me in my exile, his grief and love burst forth in vivid flame; the brotherly *Thou* I once had proffered him, and the wondrous man had waived in virtue of our outward standing, he thrust it passionately upon me; the father fervently embraced the loved lost son. Erewhile I was his joy, but now his care. And how he cared for me! When the wholly unawaited came miraculously to pass, and my operas, which had scarcely overstepped the walls of Dresden, spread suddenly with rapid stride across all Germany, then his *care* passed over into *careful management*; and where the younger man succumbed the sturdy elder stormed the breach, took all the labour off my shoulders,* packed up, corresponded, urged on, held back—so only *I* might have repose to give myself once more to work and to my art. Again success resulted, and he rejoiced again. But his joy stayed ever troubled; when, when at last would he see me once more? Would he ever? In fine, when all his hope was ebbing, he determined to himself set forth and seek me out beyond the distant Alps. Then he fell ill; he must give up his friend, and spend his savings on a place of cure. So surely had I hoped to see him, but now hear tidings of his mortal sickness and—can only write him. He dies, and never will my letter reach him!

Farewell, dear, precious friend! Now has my native land become more foreign, far, to me; and thou now liv'st quite near, within my heart, whithersoe'er I bear thee with me! †

There live not many on this earth, as was this rare one. If it be allowed the artist to take this man by friendship's hand and draw him under the eyes of the world, it is to shew in him the high-deserving, the rare art-comrade. To his sorrowing heirs he leaves a treasure, which, touching in its origin, offers rich reward to the earnest musician. When Fischer, after all the worries of his office, the labours of his calling and his cares for friends, withdrew for a few hours' peace at home, I often found him there engaged upon the hobby whence he sought his recreation: with deft hand he was copying rare and precious tone-works of all kinds, especially for polyphonic song, by older masters whose

---

* In the *N.Z.* there also appeared: "supervised the copying and arrangements [*Einrichtungen*—? "revision"] of my scores."—TR.

† In the *N.Z.* this sentence was continued by: "where no exile more shall part me from thee!"—TR.

very names were scarcely known to most men. He replied to my astonished smile: that so he pleasantly filled up his time, and learnt uncommon much to boot; for if one could not write such works oneself, he thought, 'twas the next best thing to write them out; thus would one study them through and through. And this man joined the theatre in earliest youth, became an actor, and won in his time the warmest favour of the Leipzig public as *basso buffo*; but this sufficed him not; it spurred him on to ply his art in earnest; he nursed his musical acquirements, and became —beside his post as a comedian—director of the choir. As such, he won himself fresh laurels; but ever did he study on, to keep his gifts in vigour, to take a weighty and decisive share in Art's most earnest and exacting problems, above all to keep a free and open mind for every forward movement, for each improvement of the older order. And thus, after many a scruple and friendly shaking of the head, was he able to stretch an unwavering hand, in frankest greeting, to even such despaired-of and misdoubted * matters as my works; to help in their realisation; and, through his love, to blend himself completely with their author.

'Tis verily a boon, that there should be such men! 'Tis a priceless satisfaction, to have met one such; a lasting sorrow, to see one such depart!—And thus have I ventured to set our dear Fischer by side of the celebrated Spohr: death has joined both men, for me, and melted them into one being. The meaning import of their lives may well present them as alike: the fame and author's rank which place the one man to the fore, full gladly—in obedience to my heart—would I yield the other from mine own, must I not believe I more should please him in his home of bliss by making good the whole with my full gratitude and love.†—

---

* In the *N.Z.*: "by the critics"; whilst the sentence was closed by: "inasmuch as he set his own practical hand to production of the despaired-of works there came to him the understanding of them, he won himself Belief through Love."—Tr.

† In the *N.Z.*: "would I yield the other by making over all the consequence assigned to me, must I not deem my own, as artist, too scanty not to make me liefer pay the difference with my full gratitude and love."—Tr.

GLUCK'S OVERTURE

TO

"IPHIGENIA IN AULIS."

(Eine Mittheilung an den Redakteur der „Neuen Zeitschrift für Musik").

This article appeared in the Neue Zeitschrift *for July 1st, 1854, together with the full score of the new Close, devised by Richard Wagner—and now generally employed for concert purposes,—consisting of thirty-three bars of music.—*
                              TRANSLATOR'S NOTE.

BE not astonished, worthy friend, if I send you something for your journal to-day, despite my recently-repeated statement that I did not feel in a position to occupy myself with literary tasks of any sort or kind. With one large artistic work completed, and on the eve of beginning another,* I'm merely waiting for fine weather: but just to-day it's so grey in the heavens and on earth, that well-nigh naught but theoretic whims will come to form my pastime.† Still, for all this incubus of Grey, I've not yet sunk so low as to meditate a stray polemic with one of my opponents; on the contrary, I am most peaceably disposed by the constant experience that so many, who have made a real acquaintance with my self and works, have given me their hearty friendship—which makes amends enough for the converse experience, that many still pursue their way of bragging to themselves and others that they know a thing or two about me.

No, I have an artistic communication to make to you, which perhaps you'll not take amiss: it concerns a *new Close to Gluck's Overture to " Iphigenia in Aulis."*

As you know, in my great seclusion from all public art-intercourse, to make life bearable I now and then help myself to a rehearsal of one of Beethoven's symphonies, or something similar, with our Zurich Musical Society's little orchestra, recruited every year as chance betides. The immediate stimulus proceeded—and still proceeds—from a handful of friends, to whom I thus afford a pleasure without annoying anyone, unless it may be Town-councillor Hitzschold of Dresden, in whom my readings of these symphonies were so unfortunate as to wake objections.

Now last winter a worthy friend, who neither dabbles in

* *Das Rheingold* and *Die Walküre.*—TR.
† See Vol. ii. p. xi.: "Grey, my friend, is every theory."—TR.

Music nor reads musical journals, expressed to me the wish to hear something of *Gluck's* for once in a way, so as to get an impression of the latter's music, which nowhere had come to his hearing. I found myself in a dilemma, for I could think at first of nothing but the performance of an Act from one of Gluck's operas, and that, too, at a concert. Between ourselves, I can imagine no more hideous travesty of a dramatic, and especially a tragic piece of music, than to have Orestes and Iphigenia, for instance,—in tail-coat and ball-dress, with the big nosegay and the notes between kid-gloves,—proclaiming their death-agonies in front of a concert-orchestra. It must really be set down to the "one-sidedness" of my nature, that, where an artistic illusion is not fully at work on me, I cannot even be half content— a thing which comes so easily to every musician by trade. Wherefore, giving up the recital of a Gluckian opera-scena, for my friend, there remained nothing but the choice of Gluck's most perfect instrumental piece, the Overture to "Iphigenia in Aulis."

Only, here also I lit on a difficulty: the last few bars, as everyone knows, lead straight into the opera's first Scene, and thus the Overture has no ending of its own. Yet I remembered—from concerts in my youth, as also in later years before the performance of "Iphigenia in Tauris" at the Dresden Court-theatre, under my former colleague Reissiger—to have heard this overture given with a Close devised by Mozart: that it had always made a cold, indifferent impression on me, most certainly stayed also in my memory; yet this I fancied I must attribute solely to what I had later seen to be a total misconception of the tempo (now, of course, within my own hands), not also to the Mozartian close itself. I therefore went through the overture according to Mozart's arrangement, in a rehearsal with the orchestra. But when I reached the appendix, it became impossible for me to let the band proceed beyond its first eight bars: I felt at once that, if this Mozartian Close was in and for itself a most unsatisfactory match with the intrinsic thoughts of Gluck's overture, it was absolutely not to be listened-to when performed in the proper tempo of the foregoing composition.—Now, according to my experience, the truth about this *tempo* is as follows.—

The standing pattern for all overtures in the past century, particularly in the case of serious operas, comprised a shorter introduction in slow time, followed by a longer section in more rapid tempo. People were so accustomed to this, that in Germany, where Gluck's "Iphigenia" itself has not been given for ever so long, the overture to this opera—which only got performed at concerts—became instinctively regarded as likewise composed after the usual pattern. It is correct enough that this piece, too, contains two diverse sections of primarily diverse tempo: to wit, a slower one, as far as the 19th bar, and from there onwards a movement exactly twice as fast. But it was Gluck's intention to use the Overture as an introduction to the first Scene, which begins with the very same theme as its commencement; not to outwardly break the tempo, he therefore wrote the Allegro-section in notes just twice as quick as he would have needed if he had marked the change of tempo with an "Allegro." This is quite obvious to anyone who follows up the score and looks into the scene between Calchas and the rebellious Greeks, in the First Act: here we find the identical semiquaver-figure of the Overture, but written down in quavers precisely because the tempo here is signed "Allegro." Over and over again the chorus has to pronounce one syllable to each of these quavers, which exactly fits the temper of the mutineering troops. Now, with trifling modifications necessitated by the character of the remaining themes, Gluck adopted this tempo for the Allegro of his overture; only—as remarked above—with a different signature, so as to keep the outer beat to the first tempo, the "Andante," which returns when the overture is finished. Thus, too, not a trace of change of tempo is indicated in the old Paris edition of the score, but the initial "Andante" goes on unaltered throughout the Overture, and thence into the beginning of the first Scene.

German concert-conductors, however, have overlooked this peculiarity of signature, and where the quicker notes begin, with the upstroke for the twentieth bar, they have also introduced their habitual faster tempo, so that at last the barefaced mark "Allegro" passed into German editions of this overture (and after them, mayhap, into French as well).—How incredibly Gluck's overture has been disfigured by that method of performing it exactly twice too fast, whoever has taste and understanding may judge for himself, if he listens to a rendering of this tone-piece in the proper time as meant by Gluck, and then compares it with the trivial scurry which has formerly been set before him as Gluck's masterwork. That he had not always felt this, that it did not strike him from the first, how there must be something wrong with this much-praised Overture which people even went so far as stupidly and indifferently to play as introduction to a quite other opera (which would have been impossible, had they rightly understood it)—this can then grow explicable to him by nothing but the general meditation, how from youth up we hawl along with us such a ballast of instilled, of inculcated, and finally of will-lessly adopted respect-for-Authority, that when at last the bugbear is scared away by a direct, a determinant impression on our Feeling, we scarce can fathom how we ever held it for a real and genuine Substance. Yet there are many supremely happy beings, to whom neither this impression nor this meditation ever comes at all; people who keep their feelings so well in check, and can so hold at arm's length each involuntary determining thereof by new phenomena, that in face of every fresh experience they plume themselves on staying what they were, or rather what they were made-into in some earlier, some solitary phase of evolution. Of this, too, I will give you an instance, as touching this Gluckian overture.

GLUCK'S OVERTURE TO "IPHIGENIA IN AULIS." 159

In days gone by, when I was adapting "Iphigenia in Aulis"—so rarely given on the stage—for the Dresden theatre,* I procured myself the old Paris edition of the score, so as not to be led astray by certain arrangements of Spontini's in the Berlin score, which had been placed at my disposal. From it I also gained knowledge of Gluck's original intention for the overture, and through this only right conception of the tempo I at once arrived at a sense of the great, the puissant and inimitable beauty of this tone-piece, whereas it had always left me cold before—as already mentioned—though I naturally had never dared to say as much. Thus, too, I came to see the necessity for a totally different conception of the phrasing: I recognised the massive breadth of the adamantine *unisono*, the pomp and energy of the succeeding violin-figures, above the sturdy crotchet-movement for the basses pacing up and down the scale; but chiefly, for the first time did I grasp the meaning of the tender passage:

with its touchingly graceful second half:

which, scrambled through in double-quick time and without expression (as indeed was inevitable), before had always made on me the ridiculous impression of a sheer decorative flourish.—The excellent band, which by then had won full trust in me, quite entered into my conception—although at first with wonder, sprung from rooted habit—and, through their splendid rendering of the overture, thus opened worthily a warm and vivid representation of the whole work, which at Dresden reaped the most popular, i.e. the least affected success of all Gluck's operas.—With the critics, however, I had a strange experience; above all with Herr C. Banck, at that time head reporter of Dresden. What

* The Dresden production took place on February 24, 1847.—TR.

this gentleman had never heard before, namely the opera itself, found in my version of it, and despite my always objectionable conducting, his fairly unstinted approval; but, the altered phrasing of the often-heard overture was an abomination to him. So great a might had custom here: it warded any, even a tentative acceptance of the proffered thing—now given a new appearance by my reading of it; so that I had to reap the marvel of being held for most confused exactly where I had gone the most convincedly and conscientiously to work, for most abandoned where I fancied I had dealt the surest stroke for healthy Feeling. But I had given yet another weapon into my adversary's hand: at certain places where the contrast of the chief-motives rises to the violence of passion, and particularly towards the end, in the eight bars before the last return of the great *unisono*, to me an acceleration of the time seemed indispensable; so that with the last re-entry of the main theme I had, just as necessarily for the character of this theme, to slacken down the tempo to its earlier breadth of flow. Now to the superficially attentive critic, regarding not the 'aim' itself but merely its 'material,' this supplied the proof for my erroneous reading of the main tempo, since I myself had been obliged to give it up again in the end. I saw from this that the Critic must always gain his point, because he sticks to words and syllables, but never is he smitten with the spirit of a thing.

But this incident was likewise to instruct me how it really goes with the Musician proper, the musician by trade. With a noted composer, who then was staying at Dresden, I had also a friendly chat about the incident. That there was no outward change of tempo in the overture he certainly had to concede me, supported as I was by the authentic score: only, he maintained that the schism should be healed by the simple expedient of taking this one and only tempo, and thus the very beginning

in the same quick time as the overture's presumed Allegro

was played by everyone else. I found this back-door excellent for people who don't like seeing themselves or others torn from a habit which, such as the respect for this always falsely-rendered overture, makes out a portion of that basis of Authority whereon they wax big, play music, compose, conduct and—criticise. Only no shaking of this foundation! and that, indeed, for no sake of the professedly beloved master, but—looked at closer—for sheer sake of themselves, of their else quite nugatory existence. For, once admit that one up to now has held as model a work to which one hasn't even paid the justice of a true appraisement, but has let run the racket of most senseless mutilation—and how much besides must tumble out of joint at last!—

You see, my honoured friend, I had much at heart that, "amateur" * musician as I am, I could not help unburdening on this occasion. Let us now return to Mozart, who lately placed me in such great perplexity, through his Close to the Iphigenia-Overture, that I almost despaired of being able to give my Zurich friend an idea of Gluck's music by setting this work before him. All uninitiated in the mysteries of the real, the hall-marked art of Tone, I discovered—as said—that Mozart had only made acquaintance with the overture in that mutilated fashion just denounced; and the plainest proof that a distorted rendering must betray even the most gifted musician into an entirely false conception of another's tone-work—which, to be sure, can still impress one through its other excellences—was afforded me by just Mozart; who certainly would never have written his brilliant, but quite unfitting Close, if he had rightly understood the overture.—Now what was I to do? Make a Close myself! That would

* "*Dilettantischer*"—it is evident that Wagner had heard of Schumann's remark about *Tannhäuser*: "the music, apart from the representation, is weak, often simply amateurish" &c. (in a letter to C. von Bruyck, Vienna, dated May 8, 1853), and we therefore may reasonably connect the above-related incident either with that composer or with Ferdinand Hiller, who was also residing in Dresden at the time.—TR.

have been as easy as A B C for every musician by trade; but not for me, a poor amateur who, as everyone knows, can only trust myself to embark on music when I may hope therein to realise poetic aims.—Was there not a poetic aim at bottom of Gluck's overture? Most certainly there was; but it was of such a kind, that it positively rebuffed any self-willed musical Close.—To me, one-sided layman that I was, the Content of this overture had shewn the following characteristic, highly significant of the whole art-scheme of Overtures in general: in it the chief-motives of the coming drama are happily assigned a most determinant effect upon the Feeling, and mustered side by side. I say: *side by side*; for one can scarcely call them evolved *from out* each other, saving insofar as each unit drives its impression home by having its antithesis placed close beside it, so that the effect of this abrupt juxtaposition, and thus the impression made by the operation of the earlier motive on the specific effect of its successor, is not only of importance, but of quite decisive weight. The whole content of Gluck's overture, then, appeared to me as follows: —(1) a motive of Appeal, from out a gnawing anguish of the heart; (2) a motive of Power, of imperious, overbearing demand; (3) a motive of Grace, of maidenly tenderness; (4) a motive of sorrowing, of agonising Pity. The whole compass of the overture is filled by nothing but the constant interchange of these (last three) chief-motives, linked together by a few subsidiary motives derived from them. In themselves there is nothing altered, beyond the key; merely they are made more and more importunate in their meaning and mutual bearing, through just that characteristic, multifarious interchange; so that when finally the curtain rises, and Agamemnon appeals in the first motive to the dread Goddess who but at price of his gentle daughter will favour the Grecian host, we are placed in fellow-feeling with the lofty tragic conflict whose development from definite dramatic motives we now are to await.

That Gluck gave this overture no Close, thus witnesses not only to a poetic purpose underlying it, but above all to the master's supreme artistic wisdom, which knew exactly *what* alone was representable through an instrumental tone-piece. Happily, also, his object bade him ask nothing from his overture but that which every overture can give at best: incitement (*Anregung*). Had he wanted, as later masters, to round-off the very introductory piece to a Satisfaction (*Befriedigung*), not only would it have estranged him from his higher artistic goal—which lay in just the drama—but that instrumental piece itself could only have been brought to such a fictive rounding-off by burdening it with the most arbitrary demands on the hearer's imagination.

Now to anyone who wished to furnish this overture with a musical Close, for sake of a special concert-performance, there presented itself the difficulty—providing he correctly grasped its contents—of bringing about a 'satisfaction' which not only is absolutely unaimed-at by either the general plan or the character of the motives, but must altogether do away with a correct impression of the work. Was one of these motives to finally obtain precedence, in the sense of ousting the others, or even of triumphing over them? That would be a very easy matter for all the Jubilee-overture-writers of our day; only I felt that I thus should just have not given my friend a notion of Gluck's music—which was really my sole object in the undertaking.

So the best idea seemed one that came to me of a sudden, and helped me out of my Want. I resolved to admit no 'satisfactory ending,' in the wonted overture-sense of to-day; but, by a final resumption of the earliest motive of them all, to simply terminate the changeful play of motives in such a way that we reach at last an armistice, though no full peace. For that matter, what lofty artwork ever gives a full, a satisfying peace? Is it not one of the noblest of Art's functions, to merely kindle in a highest sense?—

My proposal, indeed, was much favoured by the circumstance that the overture, as it passes into the opera's first scene, actually leads us back to that earliest motive; I thus was surely doing the smallest violence to the purely-musical structure by resuming the original thought, just as the master himself had done, and merely bringing it to a simple close on the tonic.—

This Close, in which there fortunately is as good as nothing of my own invention, I forward you herewith; should you so think fit, please make it public.* Perhaps this or that conductor of concert-performances may share my view of an overture which, owing to its celebrity, appears often enough on programmes; perhaps he then may also follow my advice in respect of the tempo, which, taken in my—and as I believe I have proved, the correct—sense, affords quite of itself a guidance to the proper phrasing. For the benefit of my hoped-for comrades in opinion, I merely add that—especially at the last performance in Zurich—I felt impelled by inner need, and in answer to a feeling kindled in me by the subject, to take the first eight bars of the introduction in a gentle, gradual crescendo, and the following eleven bars in a just as unobtrusive decrescendo. Then, after I had got the violinists, in particular, to carry out the semiquaver-figures in the great Forte-theme with as long a sweep of the bow as possible,† I had the tender passage:

rendered in the manner here-denoted, which, to my ear, gave this motive the native charm it can never obtain from a rapid tempo. For the third theme, and the transition thereto, I contrived the following phrasing:

* Note to the 1872 edition (*Ges. Schr.* vol. v.)—"The author reserves the renewal of this publication, for a special edition of the whole Overture."—

† The violinists of the Dresden Kapelle are experts in this mode of bowing.
—R. WAGNER.

A few other nuances in the same sense, particularly with the connecting motives, are obvious of themselves. The passage toward the end, where I felt compelled to momentarily accelerate the time, I have already indicated above. That everything I have advanced, however, must nowhere be carried out glaringly, but always with the greatest delicacy—this is certainly the main thing here, as with all kindred added nuances; wherefore one really can never be too guarded in communications of this sort.— —

From this attempted guide to the concert-room performance of one of Gluck's overtures you may see, my worthy friend, that, although I will have nothing to do with concerts in general, yet I can adapt myself to circumstances; that I do it from no respect for circumstances, however, will become clear to you if you consider, for instance, the aforesaid provocation to perform the Iphigenia-overture. Hardly any otherwise does it stand with the provocation to the present communication, which I address through you to none but those who are glad to receive a communication from me. Perchance, however, you may think it gives me pleasure to chastise those persons who hold me for a troubler of our musical religion, a base denier of the glorious works created by the music-heroes of the past, and deem it their duty to cry me down as such —to punish them right sorely by shaming them into a proper understanding of those heroes and their works. But you thus would credit me with a false motive; for, as to shaming or even instructing these happy beings, it could so little be any affair of mine, both from disgust at the fruitlessness of such endeavour and because it is a matter of total indifference to me to learn what one can put them to, that—to guard myself from such an imputation—I should very much like to conclude at once with the open declaration: *that I hold it the most rational course for us, to perform nothing whatever of Gluck and confrères any more; for this reason, among others, that their creations are mostly performed so unintelligently that their impression, coupled with the respect instilled into us from our youth up, can only make us utterly confused and rob us of our last grain of productivity.*

Let us hope that Herr Fétis or Herr Bischoff will read nothing but the italicised close of this communication, and thus may find occasion for crying Fie! at me anew; which would highly delight me, as I have become very keen for entertainment in my loneliness.—

So!—The grey heavens are clearing; the sky is growing bright and blue. I set you free, then. Make the best of this product of a grey-weather whim, and wish me luck for more congenial labour!

Your

Zurich, 17th June, 1854.
RICHARD WAGNER.

ON THE PERFORMING
OF
"TANNHÄUSER."

Über die Aufführung
des
„Tannhäuser."

Eine Mittheilung
an die Dirigenten und Darsteller dieser Oper.

Considerable portions of this "Address" were printed in the Neue Zeitschrift *for December 3 and 24, 1852, and January 1, 7 and 14, 1853—the extracts being chosen by the editor of that journal and arranged in a sequence other than that of the* Ges. Schr., *vol. v, which latter would appear to have been also the order of the original pamphlet. To the first extract the editor appended a footnote: " This brochure is neither obtainable from the book-trade, nor destined for publication. It lies before us with the author's permission to make a* partial *use of it in this journal." The reasons for the "partial" permission are evident, for all the merely personal and local allusions were omitted in the* Zeitschrift.

In 'Letters to Uhlig' (*Letter 74, August 14, '52) we read: " I am busy working at a concise address. . . . Unfortunately I can only work very slowly, as any work now tries my head extremely. Yet I hope to have done in four or five days at latest"; and in Letter 75 (August 23, '52) " Only to-day have I finished the manuscript of my 'Address on the performance of* Tannhäuser.' *It had to be more detailed than I at first thought, and I am now glad that I hit upon this way of removing a great weight from my mind. I am again much exhausted by the work, and I must now try to thoroughly recover from the effects. After ripe reflection, I found it necessary to give the manuscript at once to be printed here, so as to be able to send as quickly as possible a sufficient quantity of copies to the theatres* (privatim *and* gratis). *I have ordered two hundred, of which I will at once send you a good share, so that you may be able to deliver them to the theatres, together with the scores."—*

TRANSLATOR'S NOTE.

ON THE PERFORMING OF "TANNHÄUSER."

(An Address to the Directors and Performers of this Opera.)

CONSIDERABLE number of theatres are entertaining the idea of producing my "Tannhäuser" before long. This unexpected situation, by no means due to my own initiative, has made me so keenly feel the hurtfulness of my inability to personally attend the preparations for the performances proposed, that for a long time I was in doubt as to whether I ought not to refuse my sanction to those undertakings for the present.—If the artist's work first approaches its actual fulfilment, when it is in course of preparation for direct presentment to the senses; if, therefore, the dramatic poet or composer *there* first begins to exert his definitive influence, where he has to bring his aim to intimate knowledge of the artistic organs for its realisation, and through their perfect understanding to make possible an utmost intelligible re-presentment of it: then this influence is nowhere more indispensable to him, than in the case of works with whose composition he has looked aside from customary methods of performance by the sole artistic organs forthcoming, and for their needful method has kept in eye a hitherto unwonted and un-evolved conception of the nature of the art-genre in question. To none can this have been brought more clearly home, than to myself; and it is among my greatest torments of later years, that I have not been able to be present at the individual attempts already made to perform my dramatic works, so that I might have arranged with those concerned the infinite variety of details by

whose exact observance alone can the executant artists gain a thoroughly correct conception of the whole.

If paramount reasons have now inclined me to place no unconditional obstacles in the way of further performances of my earlier works, it has been in the belief that, so far as lay within my power, I might succeed in making-up for the impossibility of personal and oral intervention, by written communications to the respective managers and performers. But the number of the theatres which have announced themselves for "Tannhäuser" has so very much increased of late, that private correspondence with each several manager and performer would prove a task beyond my strength. Wherefore I seize on the expedient of the present summary, in pamphlet form, which I primarily address to all to whose understanding and good-will I have to entrust my work.

The *Musical Directors* of our theatres have accustomed themselves, almost without exception, to allow the in-scenation, and everything connected with it, to be entirely withdrawn from their concernment; in correspondence herewith, our *Regisseurs* (Stage-managers) confine their attention to the scenery, leaving the orchestra wholly out of count. From this ill state of things results the want of inner harmony, and the dramatic inefficiency, of our operatic representations. In necessary sequence, the performer has lost the habit of observing the slightest connection with a whole, and, in his isolated position toward the public, has gradually evolved to what we see him now—the opera-singer pure and simple. Now, if the musical-director regards the orchestra as a thing entirely for itself, he can only take the measure for its understanding from works of absolute Instrumental-music, such as the Symphony, and everything which departs from the forms of that genre must stay ununderstood by him. But the very thing which departs from the said forms, is just *that* whose own particular form is conditioned by an action or an emotional incident of the play; thus it cannot possibly find its explanation in Absolute Instrumental-music, but solely in that scenic incident. The conductor, therefore, who omits a strict observance of the latter, will detect nothing but caprice in the corresponding musical passages, and by his own capricious, purely-musical interpretation of them, will make them prove as much in execution; for, as he lacks any standard whereby to measure out the purely-musical essence of such passages, he is also sure to go astray in their tempo and expression. This result, again, suffices to so mislead the stage-manager and performers in their part of the business, that, losing the thread of dramatic connection between the stage and orchestra, and at last giving up all continuity of any kind, they feel urged to caprices of another sort in their performance; to caprices which, in their whole wonderful concordance, make out the stereotype conventions of our modern operatic style.

It is manifest that spirited dramatic compositions must in this wise be crippled past all recognition; it is equally certain that even the sickliest of modern Italian operas would gain immeasurably in representation, were due heed paid to that coherence which subsists in even such operas (albeit in merely the grotesquest phase). But I declare that a dramatic composition like my " Tannhäuser," whose sole potentiality of effect rests simply on the said connection between scene and music, must be ruined out and out if Musical and Scenic Directors apply to its performance the methods I have just denounced. I therefore beg that musical-director whom fancy or injunction has assigned the task of producing my work, to read through my score with the very closest attention to the poem, and finally to the countless special indications for the stage performance. When convinced of the necessity for a careful handling of the Scene, it will be for him to acquaint the Regisseur with the full compass of his task. The latter will gain a most inadequate notion of that task by studying the "book" alone; were this otherwise, it would only prove the musical setting unneedful and superfluous. The majority of the stage-instructions are only to be found in the score, against the appropriate musical passages, and the Regisseur has therefore to gain a thorough knowledge of them by aid of the *Kapellmeister* (Conductor).

The Regisseur's next care will be, to come to the precisest agreement with the *Scene-painter*. In ordinary the latter, also, goes to work with no reference whatever to the musical and scenic directors; he has the "book" given him to look through, and he pays no heed to anything in it but what appears to touch himself alone, namely the bracketed passages bearing on his special work. In course of this Address, however, I shall shew how indispensable it is that this companion factor, too, should enter into the inmost intentions of the whole artwork, and how necessarily I must insist upon his reaching the clearest knowledge of those aims from the very outset.

For their dealings with the *Performers*, I have first to point out to the musical-director and stage-manager that the so-called "vocal rehearsals" should not begin until the players have become acquainted with the poem itself, in its whole extent and compass. To this end we must not content ourselves with the book's being sent to each member of the company, for his or her perusal; we desire on their part no critical knowledge of the subject, but a living, an artistic one. I must therefore press for a meeting of the whole body of performers, under conduct of the Regisseur and attended by the Kapellmeister, at which the poem shall be gone through in the fashion usual with a spoken play, each individual performer reading his rôle aloud; the chorus-singers should likewise attend this reading, and their passages are to be recited by either the Chorus-director himself or one of the chorus-leaders. Care should also be taken, that this trial-reading is given with full dramatic

THE PERFORMING OF "TANNHÄUSER."   173

accent; and if, from lack of practice or understanding, the right expression proper to the subject as a poem is not attainable at once, then this rehearsal must be repeated until the needful expression is won from a thorough understanding both of the situations and the inner organism of the plot. Such a demand upon a modern opera-troupe, just as it is in fact a quite unusual one, will certainly be deemed exorbitant, pedantic, and altogether needless; but this very fear of mine throws light enough on the lamentable condition of our Opera affairs. Our singers are wont to busy themselves with the How of execution before they have learnt to know its What: they study the notes of their voice-parts at their own pianos, and, when got by heart, pick up the dramatic by-play in a few stage-rehearsals—too often, only at the dress-rehearsal—in whatever fashion may be dictated by operatic routine and certain fixed suggestions of the Regisseur's for their comings and goings. That they are to be Players in the first place, and only after adequate preparation for their office as such should they venture on concernment with the enhanced, the musical expression of their talk—this, at any rate in the present state of Opera, can by no means fall within their reckoning. Their habit may perhaps seem justified by the products of most opera-composers, yet I must state that my work demands a method of performance directly opposite to the customary. That singer who is not equal to reciting his "part" as a play-rôle, with an expression duly answering to the *poet's* aim, will certainly be neither able to sing it in accordance with the aim of the *composer*, to say nothing of representing the character in its general bearings. By this assertion of mine I stand so firmly, and I hold so definitely to the fulfilment of my stipulation for sufficient reading-rehearsals, that, as against this claim on my side, I once for all express the wish—nay, the will—that, should these reading-rehearsals fail to rouse among those concerned an all-round interest in the subject and its projected exposition, my work shall be laid on the shelf and its production given up.

Upon the results of the reading-rehearsals, and the spirit in which they have been carried out, I therefore make depend the happy outcome of all further study. It is in them that the performers and the ordainers of the performance have to come to an exact and exhaustive agreement upon *everything* which in usual course is left to the helter-skelter of the final stage-rehearsals. More especially will the musical-director have gained a fresh, an essentially heightened view-point for his later labours; led by the first material impression of the whole, as furnished him by the hearing of an expressive lection, in his subsequent rehearsing of the purely-musical detail he will go to work with needful knowledge of the artist's aim—as to which he must otherwise have cherished doubt and error of all kinds, however sincere his zeal for the enterprise.

As concerns the musical study with the Singers, I have the following general remarks to make. In my opera there exists no distinction between so-called "declaimed" phrases and phrases "sung," but my declamation is song withal, and my song declamation. A definite arrest of "song" and definite commencement of the usual "recitative"—whereby, in Opera, the singer's method of delivery is wont to be divided into two completely different kinds—does not take place with me. To the true Italian Recitative, in which the composer leaves the rhythm of the notes almost entirely undefined, and hands over its completion to the singer's good pleasure, I am an utter stranger; no, in passages where the poem drops from a more impassioned lyric flight, to the mere utterance of feeling discourse, I have never made away the right to prescribe the phrasing just as strictly as in the purely lyric measures. Whoever, therefore, confounds these passages with the customary Recitative, and in consequence transforms from pure caprice their stated rhythm, he defaces my music quite as much as though he fathered other notes and harmonies upon my lyric Melody. As in the said recitative-like passages I have throughout laboured to denote their phrasing in exact rhythmic accordance with the 'aim' of my Expression, so I crave of conductors and singers that they first should execute these passages in the strict value both of notes and bars, and in a tempo corresponding to the sense of the words. If I have been so fortunate, however, as to find my indications for the delivery correctly felt, and thereafter definitely adopted, by the singers: then at last I urge an almost entire abandonment of the rigour of the musical beat, which was up to then a mere mechanical aid to agreement between composer and singer, but with the complete attainment of that agreement is to be thrown aside as a worn-out, useless, and thenceforth an irksome tool. From the moment when the singer has taken into his fullest knowledge my intentions for the rendering, let him give the freest play to his natural sensibility, nay, even to the physical necessities of his breath in the more agitated phrases; and the more creative he can become, through the fullest freedom of Feeling, the more will he pledge me to delighted thanks. The conductor will then have only to follow the singer, to keep untorn the bond which binds the vocal rendering with the orchestral accompaniment; on the other hand, this will be possible to him only when the orchestra itself is brought to exactest knowledge of the vocal phrasing—a result only to be brought about, on the one side, by the words and music for the voice being copied into each single orchestral part, and on the other, by sufficiently frequent rehearsals. The surest sign of the conductor's having completely solved his task in this respect would be the ultimate experience, at the production, that his active lead is scarcely noticeable. (I need hardly say that the mode of execution above-denoted—this highest point attainable in artistic phrasing—is not to be confounded with that too customary, where the conductor is held to have acquitted himself most ably when he places his whole intelligence and practised skill at the command of our prima-donnas' wayward whims, as their heedful, cringing lackey: here he is the bounden cloaker of revolting solecisms, but there the co-creative artist.)

I now turn from these general observations on the chief lines of study, to impart my particular wishes as regards the special points in "Tannhäuser"; and here, again, I first shall keep in eye the functions of the Musical Director.

In view of certain circumstances unfavourable to the original production of "Tannhäuser," I saw myself forced at the time into various *omissions*. That most of them, however, were mere concessions wrung from me by utmost Want—concessions, in truth, equivalent to a half surrender of my real artistic aim,—this I would make clear to future conductors and performers of the opera, in order to convince them that, if they regard those concessions as conditions *sine quâ non*, I must necessarily assume withal their surrender of my intrinsic aim in crucial places.—

At Dresden, then, as early as the scene between *Tannhäuser* and *Venus* in the First Act I saw myself compelled (in the above sense) to plan an omission for the later representations: I cut the second verse of Tannhäuser's song and the immediately-preceding speech of Venus. This was by no means because these passages in themselves had proved flat, unpleasing, or ineffective, but the real reason was as follows: the whole scene failed in performance, above all because we had not succeeded in finding a thoroughly suitable representatrix for the difficult rôle of Venus; the rare and unwonted demands of this rôle were doomed to non-fulfilment by one of the greatest artists herself, because inexpugnable circumstances deprived her of the unconstraint required by her task. Thus the portrayal of the whole scene was involved in an embarrassment that became at last a positive torture, to the actress, to the public, and most of all to myself. I therefore resolved to make that torture as short as possible, and consequently shortened the scene by omitting a passage which (if anything was to be cut at all) not only was the best adapted for excision, but was also of such a nature, in itself, that its omission spared the principal male singer no insignificant exertion. This was the sole cause of the abbreviation, and every inducement to continue it would vanish at once where there was no real ground for fear about the success of this scene as a whole. In fact, the very portion of this scene which failed at Dresden, despite the efforts of one of our greatest female artists, succeeded perfectly at Weimar later on, where Venus had a representatrix who certainly could not compare in general with my Dresdener, as artist, yet was so favourably disposed to this particular rôle, and discharged her task with such warmth and freedom from constraint, that this same distressing Dresden scene made the most profound impression here. Under like circumstances the said omission will become nothing less than a senseless mutilation, the verdict whereon I leave to whoever will take the trouble to closely examine the structure of the whole scene, with its gradual growth of mood and situation from their first beginnings to their final outburst; he will bear me witness, I trust, that that cut lops off an organically essential member from the natural body of this scene; and only where the effect of this extremely weighty scene must be given up in advance, could I consent again to its omission—though in such a case I would far rather advise the whole production being given up.

A second omission affects the orchestral postlude of the closing-scene of the First Act. The passage struck-out was intended to accompany a scenic incident (the joyous tumult of the chase, as huntsmen fill the stage from every side) of such animation as I was unable to get enacted upon even the Dresden boards. Owing to the uncommon stiffness and conventionality of our usual stage-supers and such-like, the effect could not be brought to that exuberance of spirits which I had intended, and which should have offered the fitting climax to a mood (*Stimmung*) led over into keenest feeling of life's freshness. Where this effect cannot be brought about, then, the music also must keep to its shortened form. On the other hand, where a combination of favourable circumstances shall enable the regisseur to bring-out the full scenic effect intended by me, there nothing but an undocked rendering of the postlude can realise my whole original aim: namely, through an entirely adequate impression of the scene, to raise to its utmost height the *Stimmung* roused by the previous situation—to a height whereon alone can a bustling passage for the violins, omitted from the prelude to the Second Act, be rightly understood.

In the scores sent to the theatres a third omission will be found marked down in the long closing-scene of the Second Act, from page 326 to 331. This bracketed passage comprises one of the weightiest moments in the drama. In its predecessor we had been shewn the effect of Elisabeth's sacrificial courage, her profoundly moving and assuaging plea for her lover, upon those to whom she had immediately addressed herself—the prince, the knights and minstrels in very act of hounding Tannhäuser to the death: Elisabeth and this surrounding, with their mutual attitude toward one another, took all our interest, which concerned itself but indirectly with Tannhäuser himself. But when this first imperative interest is satiated, our sympathy turns back at last to the chief figure in the whole complex situation, the outlawed knight of Venus; Elisabeth and all the rest become a mere surrounding of the man about whom our urgent Feeling demands to be in so far set at rest, as it shall gain clear knowledge of the impression made by this appalling catastrophe upon its prime originator. After his fanatical defiance of the men's attack, *Tannhäuser*—most terribly affected by Elisabeth's intervention, the expression of her words, the tone of her voice, and the conscience of his hideous blasphemy against her—has fallen to the ground in final outbreak of the shattering sense of utter humiliation, thus plunging from the height of frenzied ecstasy to awful recognition of his present lot: as though unconscious, he has lain with face turned earthwards while we listened breathless to the effect proclaimed by his surrounding. Now Tannhäuser lifts up his head, his features blanched and seared by fearful suffer-

THE PERFORMING OF "TANNHÄUSER." 179

ing; still lying on the ground and staring vacantly before him, he begins with more and more impetuous accents to vent the feelings of his bursting heart: *

> To lead the sinner to salvation,
>   God's messeng'ress to me drew nigh;
> but, ah! that vilest desecration
>   should lift to her its scathing eye!
> O Mary Mother, high above earth's dwelling—
> who sent'st to me the angel of my weal—
> have mercy on me, sunk in sin's compelling,
> who shamed the heavenly grace thou didst reveal!

These words, with the expression lent them by this situation, contain the pith of Tannhäuser's subsequent existence, and form the axis of his whole career; without our having received with absolute certainty the impression meant to be conveyed by them at this particular crisis, we are in no position to maintain any further interest in the hero of the drama. If we have not been here at last attuned to deepest fellow-suffering with Tannhäuser, the drama will run its whole remaining course without consistence, without necessity, and all our hitherto-aroused awaitings will halt unsatisfied. Even Tannhäuser's recital of his sufferings, in the Third Act, can never compensate us for the missed impression; for that recital can only make the full effect intended, when it links itself to our memory of this earlier, this decisory impression.

What could have determined me, then, to omit this very passage from the second, and all later Dresden performances? My answer might well include the history of all the troubles I have had to suffer, both as poet and musician, from our Opera-affairs; but I here will put the matter briefly. The first representative of Tannhäuser—unable, in his capacity of eminently-gifted singer, to grasp anything beyond the "Opera" proper—could not succeed in seizing the characteristic nature of a claim which addressed itself more to his acting powers, than to his vocal talent. In keeping with the situation, the aforesaid passage is accom-

* "*Zum Heil den Sündiger zu führen,*" &c.

panied by whispered phrases for all the singers on the stage, their voices at times, however, threatening to hastily break short Tannhäuser's motif with warnings of their smothered anger: in the eyes of our singers, this gave the passage all the semblance of an ordinary concerted piece, in which no individual thinks himself entitled to take a prominent lead. Now the obstinacy of this error must bear the blame that this passage's true import, the high relief given to Tannhäuser's personality, was completely lost in the performance, and that the whole situation, with its needful breadth of musical treatment, acquired the character of one of those *Adagio-ensembles* which we are wont to hear precede the closing *Stretto* of an opera-Finale. In the light of such an Adagio-section, dragging itself along without a change, the whole thing must necessarily appear too spun-out and fatiguing; and when the question of a cut arose, to stem the manifest displeasure, it was just this passage that —seeing it had been robbed, in performance, of its proper import—appeared to me a tedious 'length,' i.e., a *void*. But I ask any intelligent person to judge my humour toward the external success of my work at Dresden, and whether a twenty-fold performance, with regularly repeated "calls" for the author, could repay me for the gnawing consciousness that a large portion of the received applause was due to nothing but a misunderstanding, or at least a thoroughly defective understanding, of my real artistic aim! If in future my intentions are to be better met, and my aim realised in fact, I must especially insist on a correct rendering of the passage just discussed at length, since it is no longer to be excised. In those days its omission, and the consequent abandonment of its whole import, resulted in all interest in Tannhäuser completely vanishing at the close of the Second Act, and centering simply in his environment and opposites—thus altogether nullifying my intrinsic aim. In the Third Act Tannhäuser was met by this lack of interest to such a point, that people troubled themselves about his subsequent fate merely insofar as the fate of Elisabeth and even Wolfram, now raised into the virtual protagonists, appeared to hang upon it: only the truly marvellous ability and staying-power of the singer of the chief rôle, when in sonorous and energetic accents he told the story of his pilgrimage, could laboriously re-awaken interest in himself. Wherefore my prayer goes out to every future exponent of Tannhäuser, to lay utmost weight on the passage in question; his delivery of it will not succeed till, even in midst of that delivery, he gets full feeling that at this moment he is master of the dramatic, as well as the musical situation, that the audience is listening exclusively to *his* utterance, and that this latter is of such a kind as to instil the deepest sense of awe. The cries: "*Ach! erbarm' dich mein!*" demand so piercing an accent, that he here will not get through as a merely well-trained singer; no, the highest dramatic art must yield him all the energy of grief and desperation, for tones which must seem to break from the very bottom of a heart distraught by fearful suffering, like an outcry for redemption. It must be the conductor's duty, to see to it that the desired effect be made possible to the chief performer through the most discreet accompaniment, on part alike of the other singers and the orchestra.—

Yet another omission was I obliged to make in this closing scene of the Second Act, namely of the passage occupying pages 348 to 356 of the score. It came about for precisely the same reasons as in the case of the passage last referred-to, and was merely a consequence of the prior cut having grown inevitable: i.e., I felt that any interest in Tannhäuser, in this Act, was past praying for. The essence of the present passage is the renewed assumption of supremacy by Elisabeth, and more especially by Tannhäuser, as they approach their surrounding, which hitherto has filled the centre of the stage: here the theme of the men, with its command to Rome, is taken up by Elisabeth in fashion of an ardent prayer for her lover; Tannhäuser adds to the song the impassioned cries of broken-hearted penitence, athirst for action; while the remainder of the men break forth anew with threats and execrations. Whether this passage—which certainly belongs to the strictest sequence of the situation—shall be retained in future representations, I must make dependent on its outcome in the stage-rehearsals. If in the long run it should not entirely succeed, i.e., should it not bring about a heightening of the situation through the animation displayed by the surrounding; above all, if the singer of Tannhäuser should feel himself and his voice too sorely taxed by what has gone before, and especially by that aforesaid passage in *adagio*, to sing this too with fullest energy,—then I myself must strenuously advise that the cut shall here hold good: for only by the amplest force of acting and delivery, will the effect intended here be still attainable. In that event I must console myself that the chief matter, the focusing of the main interest on himself, has been compassed through Tannhäuser's enthralling effect in the Adagio, and must content myself with the further effect reserved for him to produce at the supreme moment of his exit. To that moment I should wish this performer's attention most emphatically directed. The men, affronted and incensed afresh at sight of the hated one's delay, are in act to carry out their threats with hand upon the sword-hilt; an adjuring gesture of Elisabeth's holds them back to the path which *she* has won: then suddenly there rings from out the valley the chant of the Younger Pilgrims, like a voice of promise and atonement; as it enchains the rest, so it falls on Tannhäuser with a summons from the tempest of his blind remorse. Like a flash from heaven, a sudden ray of hope invades his tortured soul; tears of ineffable woe well from his eyes; an irresistible impulse carries him to the feet of Elisabeth; he dares not lift to her his look, but presses the hem of her garment to his lips with passionate ardour. Hastily he leaps to his feet once more; hurls from his breast the cry: "To Rome!" with an expression as though the whole swift-kindled hope of a new life were urged into the sound; and rushes from the stage with burning steps. This action, which must be carried out with greatest sharpness and in briefest time, is of the most determinant weight for the final impression of the whole Act; and it is this impression that is absolutely indispensable, through the mood in which it leaves the public, for making possible the full effect of the difficult Third Act.—

The abridged version of the long instrumental introduction to the Third Act, as contained in the scores revised for the theatres, is the one I now wish kept-to. When first composing this piece, I allowed the subject of expression to betray me into almost recitative-like phrases for the orchestra; at the performance, however, I felt that their meaning might well be intelligible to myself, who carried in my head the fancy-picture of the incidents thus shadowed, but not to others. Nevertheless I must insist on a complete rendering of this tone-piece in its new shape, since I deem it indispensable for establishing the *Stimmung* needed by what follows.

For similar reasons to those given above, after the first representation I saw myself compelled to effect an omission in Elisabeth's Prayer, namely that marked on pages 396 to 398. That the weightiest motivation of Elisabeth's self-offering and death thus went by the board, must be obvious to anyone who will examine carefully the words and music here. Certainly, if the simple outlines of this tone-piece, completely bare of musical embroidery, are to avoid the effect of monotonous length for that of an outflow of sincere emotion, its delivery demands a conception and devotion to the task such as we can seldom hope to meet among our dainty opera-singeresses. Here the mere technical cultivation of even the most brilliant of voices will not suffice us; by no art of absolute-musical execution can this Prayer be made interesting; but *that* actress alone can satisfy my aim, who is able to feel-out Elisabeth's piteous situation, from the first quick budding of her affection for Tannhäuser, through all the phases of its growth, to the final efflorescence of the death-perfumed bloom—as it unfolds itself in this prayer,—and to feel this with the finest organs of a true woman's sensibility. Yet that only the highest dramatic, and particularly the highest *vocal* art, can make it possible to bring this sensibility to outward operation—this is a thing that just *those* lady-singers will be the first to recognise, who have erewhile been clever enough at tricking a feelingless heap of loungers out of their ennui through their own most blinding arts, but cannot help perceiving the utter futility of their juggling-feats when confronted with the present task. —The initial inexperience of my Dresden actress must bear the blame, that I was forced to immolate the passage here referred-to; in course of the later performances I had reason to hope for a successful issue of the *whole* Prayer, were I to restore it to its integrity. But another experience made me hold my hand, and I consider this a most appropriate place for imparting it to the conductors and performers of my opera, in form of the following exhortation.—Whatever characteristic feature of a dramatic work we deem expedient to omit from the first few representations, can never be restored in subsequent performances. The first impression, even when a faulty one, fixes itself alike for public and performers as a definite, a given thing; and any subsequent change, albeit for the better, will always take the light of a derangement. The performers in particular, after once getting over the worry and excitement of the first few nights, soon accustom themselves to holding their achievements, as set and moulded during this incubatory process, for something inviolable by any meddling hand; whilst carelessness and gradual indifference add their share, at last, toward making it impossible to deal afresh with a problem now considered solved. For this reason I entreat directors and performers to come to an agreement, upon everything I here am bringing under their notice, *before* the first production. What they are able to achieve, or not, must be definitely established in the stage-rehearsals, if not earlier; and, saving under utmost stress, one should therefore not decide upon omissions with the sorry hope that what has been neglected may be made good again in later performances: for this it never comes to. In like manner one must not at once feel prompted to lop away this or that passage because of insufficient success at the first public performance, but rather have care that its success shall not be lacking in the next; for where one attempts to make an organically-coherent work more palatable through excisions, one merely bears witness to one's own incapacity, and the enjoyment that seems hereby brought within reach at last is no enjoyment of the work as such, but only a self-deception, inasmuch as the work is taken for something other than it really is.

Now the genuine triumph of the representress of Elisabeth would consist in this: that she not only should give due effect to the Prayer in its entirety, but should further maintain that effect at such a pitch, by the magic of her acting, as to make possible an unabridged performance of its pantomimic postlude. I am well aware that this task is no less difficult than the vocal rendering of the Prayer itself; therefore only where the actress feels quite confident of her effect in this solemn dumb-show, do I wish sanction given to the undocked execution of this scene.

As regards the *revision of the opera's close*, upon whose observance I rigidly insist, I have first to beg all those who do not like this change—owing to impressions harboured from its earlier arrangement,—to consider what I have just said about first performances and repetitions. The revised Close stands towards its first version as the working-out to the sketch, and I soon experienced the pressing need of this working-out; whilst the very fact of my effecting it, may prove to every one that I do not obstinately abide by my first draughts, and therefore, when I press for the reinstatement of passages omitted earlier, that it is not from any blind affection for my works. When I first composed this closing scene I had just as complete an image of it in my brain, as I since have worked-out in its second version;

not an atom here is changed in the intention, but merely that intention is more distinctly realised. The truth is, I had built too much on certain scenic effects, which proved inadequate when brought to actual execution : the mere glowing of the Venusberg, in the farthest background, was not enough to produce the disquieting impression which I meant to lead up to the denouement ; still less could the lighting of the windows of the Wartburg (also in the most distant background) and the far-off strains of the Dirge bring the catastrophic moment, which enters with Elisabeth's death, to instantaneous perception by an unbiased spectator not familiar with the literary and artistic details of the subject. My experiences hereanent were so painfully convincing, that the very non-understanding of this situation afforded me a cogent reason for remodelling the closing-scene ; and in no other way could this be accomplished, than by making Venus herself draw near, with witchcraft sensible to ear and eye, whilst Elisabeth's death is no longer merely hinted at, but the dying Tannhäuser sinks down upon her actual corse. Although the effect of this change was complete and decisive on the unbiased public, yet I can easily imagine how the art-connoisseur, already familiar with the earlier form—and that through his having acquired a clue to the situation by a study of the poem and music apart from representment,—must have found it disconcerting. This I the more readily comprehend, as the new Close could only be represented in a very halting style at Dresden : it had to be carried-out with the existing scenic material from the First Act, and with none of the fresh scenery which it required ; moreover (as I have already mentioned) the rôle of Venus was one of the least satisfactorily rendered in that production, and thus her reappearance in itself could make no favourable impression. These grounds, however, are quite untenable against the validity of the new Close when it is a question, as now, of producing Tannhäuser for the first time on other stages and under quite other conditions, and therefore I cannot grant them the least regard.

Still reserving my discussion of this closing-scene with the regisseur, and especially the scene-painter, I have next to inform the musical-director that I deemed necessary to omit from the second edition the final chorus of the Younger Pilgrims, occurring in the first arrangement; after what has gone before, it is easy for this chorus to appear a length too much, if by the amplest vocal forces, on the one side, and a striking portrayal of the scene on the other, it be not brought to a powerful effect of its own. The chant is sung exclusively by soprano and alto voices: these must be available in considerable number and great beauty of tone; the approach of the singers must be so contrived that, despite the mere gradual arrival of the whole choir upon the stage, yet the chant is sounded from the very first with utmost possible fulness; and finally, the scene must very effectively reproduce the valley's glowing flush at break of dawn,—if the Director is to feel justified in carrying out this Close of the opera in its entirety. Only the largest and amplest-equipped theatres, however, can command the needful means for the effect last-named; but these alone, by supplying the conditions necessary for retaining this Pilgrims'-chant, could also fully meet my aim; for, with its announcement of the miracle, and as forming the counterpart to Tannhäuser's story of his reception in Rome, this chant at any rate rounds off the whole in a thoroughly satisfying manner.*

Before I quite turn my back on the musical-director,† I have a few things to discuss with him as regards the *Orchestra*, and chiefly in reference to the phrasing of the *Overture*.—The theme with which this tone-piece begins,

* The theatres must apply to me for the music of this chorus. — R. WAGNER.

† Touching the vocal parts, I must make one more request to the Kapellmeister: viz., if the singer of *Walther*, whose solos in the "Minstrel's Tourney" are pitched somewhat low (yet in any case are to be maintained in the key prescribed), should find any difficulty with the persistently high register of the concerted pieces,—to effect a change by having the notes assigned to *Heinrich der Schreiber* copied into the music-part of the former, in addition to his own solo-passages, while the higher voice is made over to *Heinrich*.—R. WAGNER.

will at once be correctly grasped by the wind-instrument-
ists, if the conductor insists on their all taking breath
together at the right cæsura in the melody; this invariably
precedes the upstroke leading to the 'good' bar of the
rhythm, and thus occurs in the third, fifth, seventh, &c., of
the melody,—as follows:

In order to gain the effect intended, in imitation of a
chorus sung to words, I further beg an alteration in the
fourth and twelfth bars of the bassoon-parts, resolving the
rhythm ♩. into ♩″♩ . When the trombones later take up
the same theme *forte*, this breathing-mark will not of
course hold good, but, for sake of the needful strength and
duration of tone, the blowers must take breath as often as
they require.—The *fortissimo* passage, from the third bar
of page 5 to the second bar of page 10, should be executed
by the accompanying instruments (i.e., the whole orchestra
except the trombones, tuba, and drums) in such a manner
that, whereas a full *fortissimo* marks the first beat of every
bar, the second and third crotchets are played with decreasing force. Thus:

Only the instruments named above, as directly occupied with
the theme itself, must maintain an even strength.—At the
sixth bar of page 22 the conductor should somewhat restrain
the pace, which had shortly before grown almost too rapid,
yet without causing any conspicuous retardation; the expression of this passage should merely be sharply contrasted
with that of the former, through its obtaining a yearning—
I might almost say, a panting—character, both in phrasing
and in tempo. On page 23, bar 2, the accent is to be removed from the first note of the first violins; similarly in the
first bar of page 24 the *fp* is to be changed to a simple *p*, for
all the instruments. On page 25 the time is to be again taken

THE PERFORMING OF "TANNHÄUSER." 189

somewhat more briskly; only, the conductor must guard against the theme which enters with page 26 being played too fast: for all the fire with which it is to be rendered, a too rapid tempo would give it a certain taint of levity, which I should like kept very far away from it.—In the distribution of the violins into eight groups, from page 34 onwards, it must be seen-to that the six lower groups are of equal strength, while the two upper, from page 35 on, are manned in such a fashion that the second group is stronger than the first; the first part might even be entrusted to one solitary leader, whereas the second must be numerically stronger than all the others.—The clarinetist generally mistakes the 'slur' in the first bar of page 35, and connects the first note of the triplet with the preceding ¾ crotchet; it must, on the contrary, be emphasised apart. On page 36 particular heed should be paid to the clarinet's standing sharply out from all the other instruments; even the first violin must not overshadow it, and the clarinetist must fully realise that, from its first entry on this page down to the fifth bar of page 37, his instrument takes the absolutely leading part.—A moderately brisk accelerando must commence with page 39, and not slacken until the fifth bar of page 41, when it passes into the energetic tempo there required.—From the third bar of page 50 onwards, the conductor must maintain an unbroken body of fullest tone in all the instruments; any abatement in the first eight bars must be strenuously avoided.—It is of the greatest moment for an understanding of the whole closing section of the Overture, that from page 54 onwards the violins be played in utmost *piano*, so that above their wave-like figure—almost merely whispered—the theme of the wind-instruments may be heard with absolute distinctness; for this theme, albeit it is not to be played at all loud, must forthwith rivet the attention of the hearer.—Beginning with the third bar on page 66, the conductor must accelerate the pace—in regular progression, though with marked effect—in such a way that with the entry of the *fortissimo* on page 68 that pitch of rapidity is reached in which alone the trombone-theme, so greatly 'augmented' in rhythm, can be given an intelligible enunciation through its notes losing all appearance of detached and disconnected sounds.—Finally, I scarcely need lay to the heart of the conductor and band that it is only by expenditure of the utmost energy and force, that the intended effect of this unbroken *fortissimo* can be attained. After yet another acceleration of the six preceding them, the last four bars are to be slackened to a solemn breadth of measure.—

As to the "tempi" of the whole work in general, I here can only say that if conductor and singers are to depend for their time-measure on the metronomical marks alone, the spirit of their work must stand indeed in sorry case; only *then* will both discern the proper measure, when an understanding of the dramatic and musical situations, an understanding won by lively sympathy, shall let them find it as a thing that comes quite of itself, without their further seeking.

For what concerns the *manning of the orchestra*—seeing that the body of wind-instruments in this opera exceeds in no essential the usual complement of all good German orchestras—I have only to draw attention to one point, though certainly of great importance to me: I mean, the requisite effective number of *string-instruments*. German orchestras are invariably too poorly manned with 'strings'; upon the grounds of this lack of fine feeling for the truest needs of good orchestral delivery much might be said, and that pretty decisive of any verdict on the state of Music in Germany; but, to be sure, it here would lead us too far afield. Thus much is certain, that the French—however we may cry out against their frivolity—keep their smallest orchestras better manned with 'strings' than we find in Germany, often in quite celebrated bands. Now in the instrumentation of "Tannhäuser" I so deliberately kept in view a particularly strong muster of strings, that I must positively insist on all the theatres increasing their string-instruments beyond the usual tally; and my requirements may be measured by this very simple standard—I declare that an orchestra which cannot muster at least four good viola-players, can bring to hearing but a mutilation of my music.

For the musical equipment of the stage itself I have made still more unwonted demands. If I stand by the exactest observance of my instructions for the stage-music, I am justified by the knowledge that in all the more important cities of Germany there exist large and well-manned music-corps, especially belonging to the military, and from these the stage-music-corps required for "Tannhäuser" can readily be combined. Further, I know that any opposition to the fulfilment of my demand will come chiefly from the parsimony—often alas! most warrantable, as I admit—of the theatrical Directors. I must tell these Directors, however, that they can expect no manner of success from the production of my "Tannhäuser," saving when the representation is prepared with the most exceptional care in every respect; with a care such as needs must give this representation, when contrasted with customary operatic performances, the character of something quite Unwonted. And as this character has to be evinced by the whole thing, under its every aspect, it must be also shewn on the side of its external mounting; for which I count on no mere tinsel pomp and blinding juggleries, but precisely on a supplanting of these trumpery effects by a really rich and thoughtfully-planned artistic treatment of the whole alike with every detail.

I must now devote a few lines to the *Regisseur*, begging him to lay to heart what I hitherto have chiefly addressed to the Musical Director, and thence to derive a measure for my claims on the character of his own collaboration. Nothing I have said about the representation from the musical side can succeed at all, unless the most punctilious carrying-out of every scenic detail makes possible a general prospering of the dramatic whole. The stage-directions in the score, to which I drew his marked attention in my opening statement, will mostly give him an exact idea of my aim; my circumstantial instructions, with reference to certain habitually-omitted passages, may shew him what unusual weight I lay on the precisest motivation of the situations through the dramatic action; and he thence may perceive the value I attach to his solicitous co-operation in the arrangement of even the most trifling scenic incidents. I therefore entreat the regisseur to cast to the winds that indulgence alas! too customarily shewn to operatic favourites, which leaves them almost solely in the hands of the musical-director. Though, in their general belittlement of Opera as a *genre*, people have thought fit to let a singer perpetrate any folly he pleases in his conception of a situation, because "an opera-singer isn't an actor, you know, and one goes to the opera simply to hear the singing, not to see a play,"—yet I declare that if this indulgence is applied to the present case, my work may as well be given up at once for lost. What I ask of the performer, will certainly not be drummed into him by sheer weight of talk; and the whole course of study laid down by me, especially the holding of reading-rehearsals, aims at making the performer a fellow-feeling, a fellow-knowing, and finally, from his own convictions, a fellow-creative partner in the production: but it is just as certain that, under prevailing conditions, this result can only be brought about by the most active co-operation of the regisseur.

So I beg the stage-director to pay special heed to the scenic action's synchronising in the precisest fashion with the various features of the orchestral accompaniment. Often it has happened to me, that a piece of by-play—a gesture, a significant glance—has escaped the attention of the spectator because it came too early or too late, and at any rate did not exactly correspond in tempo or duration with the correlated passage for the orchestra which was influencing that same spectator in his capacity of listener. Not only does this heedlessness damage the effect of the performer's acting, but this inconsequence in the features of the orchestra confuses the spectator to such a pitch, that he can only deem them arbitrary caprices of the composer. What a chain of misunderstandings is hereby given rise to, it is easy enough to see.

I further urge the regisseur to guard against the processions in "Tannhäuser" being carried out by the stage-personnel in the manner of the customary March, now stereotyped in all our operatic productions. Marches, in the ordinary sense, are not to be found in my later operas; therefore if the entry of the guests into the Singers' Hall (Act II. Scene 4) be so effected that the choir and supers march upon the stage in double file, draw the favourite serpentine curve around it, and take possession of the wings like two regiments of well-drilled troops, in wait for further operatic business,—then I merely beg the band to play some march from "Norma" or "Belisario," but not my music. If on the contrary one thinks it as well to retain my music, the entry of the guests must be so ordered as to thoroughly imitate real life, in its noblest, freest forms. Away with that painful regularity of the traditional marching-order! The more varied and unconstrained are the groups of oncomers, divided into separate knots of friends or relatives, the more attractive will be the effect of the whole Entry. Each knight and dame must be greeted with friendly dignity, on arrival, by the Landgrave and Elisabeth; but, naturally, there must be no visible pretence of conversation—a thing that under any circumstances should be strictly prohibited in a musical drama.—A most important task, in this sense, will then be the ordering of the whole Singers'-Tourney, the easy grouping of its audience, and especially the portrayal of their changing and waxing interest in the main action. Here the regisseur must tax the full resources of his art; for only through his most ingenious tactics can this complex scene attain its due effect.

He must treat in a similar fashion the bands of Pilgrims in the First and Third Acts; the freer the play, and the more natural the groupings, the better will my aim be answered. As to the close of the First Act, where (in fact during this whole scene, albeit unobtrusively at first) the stage is gradually occupied by the full hunting retinue; and as to the close of the Third Act, where I have been obliged to make the giving of the Younger Pilgrims' chorus depend in great measure on a skilful handling of the stage—I believe I have already said enough. But one most weighty matter still remains for me to clear up with the regisseur: the execution of the opera's first scene, the *dance*—if so I may call it—in the Venusberg. I need scarcely point out that we here have nothing to do with a dance such as is usual in our operas and ballets; the ballet-master, whom one should ask to arrange such a dance-set for this music, would soon send us to the right-about and declare the music quite unsuitable. No, what I have in mind is an epitome of everything the highest choreographic and pantomimic art can offer: a wild, and yet seductive chaos of movements and groupings, of soft delight, of yearning and burning, carried to the most delirious pitch of frenzied riot. For sure, the problem is not an easy one to solve, and to produce the desired chaotic effect undoubtedly requires most careful and artistic treatment of the smallest details. The 'argument' of this wild scene is plainly set forth in the score, as concerns its essential features, and I must entreat whoever undertakes its carrying out, for all the freedom I concede to his invention, to strictly maintain the prescribed chief-moments; a frequent hearing of the music, rendered by the orchestra, will be the best means of inspiring any person in the least expert with the devices whereby to make the action correspond therewith.—

This scene now brings me into contact with the *Scene-*

painter, whom I shall henceforth figure to myself as in close alliance with the Machinist. Only through an accurate knowledge of the whole poetic subject, and after a careful agreement as to the scheme of its portrayal with the Regisseur—and the Kapellmeister too—will the scene-painter and machinist succeed in giving the stage its needful aspect. In the absence of such an agreement, how often must it happen that, for mere sake of employing work already executed by the scene-painter and machinist after a one-sided acquaintance with the subject, one is forced at the last moment to embark on violent distortions of the intrinsic aim!

The main features of the Venusberg scenery, whose mechanical structure must accurately fit-in with that for the Wartburg valley set in readiness behind it (an arrangement favoured by the mountainous projections common to both), are sufficiently indicated in the score. However, the shrouding of this scene with a veil of rosy mist, to narrow down its space, is a somewhat difficult matter: all the intended witchery would be destroyed, if this were clumsily effected by pushing forward, and dropping down, a massive cloud-piece. After many a careful trial, this veiling was most effectively carried-out at Dresden by gradually lowering a number of vaporous sheets of painted gauze, let slowly fall behind each other; so that not until the contours of the previous scene had become quite unrecognisable, was a massive rose-tinted canvas back-cloth let down behind these veils, thus completely shutting-in the scene. The tempo also was accurately reckoned, so as to coincide with the music.—The main change of scene is then effected at one stroke, as follows: the stage is suddenly plunged in darkness, and first the massive cloud-cloth, and immediately thereafter the veils of gauze, are drawn swiftly up; whereupon the light is instantly turned on again, revealing the new scene, the valley bathed in brilliant sunshine. The effect of this valley-picture—which must be mounted in strict accordance with the directions in the score—should be so overpoweringly fresh, so invitingly serene, that the poet and musician may be allowed to leave the spectator to its impression for a while.

The decorations for the Second Act, shewing the Singers'-Hall in the Wartburg, were so admirably designed for the Dresden production, by an eminent French artist, that I can only advise each theatre to procure a copy and mount this scene in accordance with it. The arrangement of the stage, as regards the tiers of seats for the guests at the Singers'-tourney, was also so happily effected there, that I have only to urge an employment of the plans, which may easily be obtained from Dresden.

Less happily did the scenery for the Third Act turn out at Dresden; not until after the production of the opera did it become evident that a special canvas should have been painted for this Act, whereas I had fancied we could manage with the second back-cloth from the First. But it proved beyond the most ingenious artifice of lighting, to give to the same canvas, previously reckoned for the brightest effect of a spring morning, the autumn-evening aspect so needful to the Third Act. Above all, the magic apparition of the Venusberg could not be effectually rendered with this scenery, so that—as already said —for the second version I had to content myself with somewhat inconsequently letting drop once more the veilings of the First Act; whereby the whole apparition of Venus was driven much too much into the foreground, and thus quite missed its effect of a beckoning from afar. I therefore engage the scene-painter, to whom the mounting of this opera is confided, to insist on a special canvas being provided for the Third Act, and to treat it in such a way that it shall reproduce the last scene of the First Act in the tones of autumn and evening, but with strict observance of the fact that the valley is eventually to be shewn in the glowing flush of dawn.—Then for the spectral apparition of the Venusberg something like the following mode might

THE PERFORMING OF "TANNHÄUSER." 197

be adopted. At the passage indicated in the score the lights should be very much lowered, while half-way up the stage two veils are dropped, one after the other, completely concealing the contours of the valley in the background; immediately afterwards the distant Venusberg, now painted as a transparency, must be lit with a roseate glow. The inventive talent of the scene-painter and machinist should next devise some means whereby the effect may be produced as though the glowing Venusberg were drawing nearer, and stretching wide enough—now that we can see through it—to hold within it groups of dancing figures, whose whirling movements must be plainly visible to the spectator. When the whole hinder stage is occupied by this apparition, Venus herself will then be seen, reclining on a litter. The perspective, however, must still appear as distant as is consistent with the size of actual human figures. The phantom's vanishing will then be brought about by a rapid diminution and final extinction of the rosy lighting of the background, which till then had grown more and more vivid—therefore by the stage being momentarily plunged in total darkness, during which the whole apparatus required by this vision of the Venusberg is to be speedily removed. Next, and while the dirge is being chanted, one perceives through the two still-hanging veils the lights and torches of the funeral train, as it descends from the heights at the back. Then the veils are drawn slowly up, one after the other, and at like time the gradual grey of early morn fills all the scene; to pass at last, as said, into the glowing flush of dawn.

The scene-painter may see, then, how infinitely important to me is his intelligent collaboration—nay, how alone enabling—and that I assign to him a certainly not un-decisive share in the success of the whole; a success only to be won through a clear and instant understanding of the most unwonted situations. But only a close and genuinely artistic acquaintance with my inmost aims, on his part, can secure me that collaboration.

After this somewhat circumstantial disquisition, I must turn at last to the *Actors* in particular. I cannot, however, attempt to discuss with them the minutiæ of their rôles; to gain a full and fitting opportunity for this, I should need to enter on a personal and friendly intercourse with each performer. Therefore I must confine myself to what I have already said about the needful mode of approaching the general study, in the hope that through familiarity with my intentions the performers will of themselves attain the power of executing them. But in all that I have addressed to the Musical Director, in the first place, my claims upon the players are so markedly involved, and in dealing with individual situations I have found occasion to so exactly motivate these claims, that I need only add that my requirements for the conception of those single passages must hold good for every other detail of the performance.—

Yet I deem it as well to go a little deeper into the character of the principal rôles.

Indisputably the hardest rôle is that of *Tannhäuser* himself, and I must admit that it may be one of the hardest problems ever set before an actor. The essentials of this character, in my eyes, are an ever prompt and active, nay, a brimming-over saturation with the emotion woken by the passing incident, and the lively contrasts which the swift changes of situation produce in the utterance of this fill of feeling. Tannhäuser is nowhere and never "a little" anything, but each thing fully and entirely. With fullest transport has he revelled in the arms of Venus; with keenest feeling of the necessity for his breaking from her, does he tear the bonds that bound him to Love's Goddess, without one moment's railing at her. With fullest unreserve he gives himself to the over-powering impression of re-entered homely Nature, to the familiar round of old sensations, and lastly to the tearful outburst of a childlike feeling of religious penitence; the cry: "Almighty, Thine the praise! Great are the wonders of Thy grace!" is the instinctive outpour of an emotion which usurps his heart with might resistless, down to its deepest root. So strong and upright is this emotion, and the felt need of reconciliation with the world—with the World in its widest, grandest sense—that he sullenly draws back from the encounter with his former comrades, and shuns their proffered reconcilement: no turning-back will he hear of, but only thrusting-on towards a thing as great and lofty as his new-won feeling of the World itself. This one, this nameless thing, that alone can satisfy his present longing, is suddenly named for him with the name "Elisabeth": Past and Future stream together, with lightning quickness, at mention of this name; while he listens to the story of Elisabeth's love they melt in one great flood of flame, and light the path that leads him to new life. Wholly and entirely mastered by this latest, this impression never felt before, he shouts for very joy of life, and rushes forth to meet the loved one. The whole Past now lies behind him like a dim and distant dream; scarce can he call it back to mind: one thing alone he knows of, a tender, gracious woman, a sweet maid who loves him; and one thing alone lies bare to him within this love, one thing alone in its rejoinder,—the burning, all-consuming fire of Life.—With this fire, this fervour, he tasted once the love of Venus, and instinctively must he fulfil what he had freely pledged her at his parting: "'gainst all the world, henceforth, her doughty knight to be." This World tarries not in challenging him to the combat. In it—where the Strong brims full the sacrifice demanded of it by the Weak—man finds his only passport to survival in an endless accommodation of his instinctive feelings to the all-ruling mould of use and wont (*Sitte*). Tannhäuser, who is capable of nothing but the most direct expression of his frankest, most instinctive feelings, must find himself in crying contrast with this world; and so strongly must this be driven home upon his Feeling, that for sake of sheer existence, he has to battle with this his opposite in a struggle for life or death. It is this one necessity that absorbs his soul, when matters come to open combat in the "Singers'-tourney"; to content it he forgets his whole surrounding, and casts discretion to the winds: and yet his heart is simply fighting for his love to Elisabeth, when at last he flaunts his colours openly as Venus' knight. Here stands he on the summit of his life-glad ardour, and naught can dash him from the pinnacle of transport whereon he plants his solitary standard 'gainst the whole wide world,—nothing but the one experience whose utter newness, whose variance with all his past, now suddenly usurps the field of his emotions: the woman who *offers up herself* for love of him.—Forth from that excess of bliss on which he fed in Venus' arms, he had yearned for—Sorrow: this profoundly human yearning was to lead him to the woman who *suffers* with him, whilst Venus had but joyed. His claim is now fulfilled, and no longer can he live aloof from griefs as overwhelming as were once his joys. Yet these are no sought-for, no arbitrarily chosen griefs; with irresistible might have they forced an entrance to his heart through fellow-feeling, and it nurtures them with all the energy of his being, even to self-annihilation. It is here that his love for Elisabeth proclaims the vastness of its difference from that for Venus: her whose gaze he can no longer bear, whose words pierce his breast like a sword—to her must he atone, and expiate by fearsome tortures the torture of her love for him, though Death's most bitter pang should only let him distantly forebode that last atonement.—Where is the suffering that he would not gladly bear? Before that world, confronting which he stood but now its jubilant foe, he casts himself with willing fervour in the dust, to let it tread him under foot. No likeness shews he to his fellow-pilgrims, who lay upon themselves convenient penance for healing of their own souls: only "*her* tears to sweeten, the tears she weeps o'er his great sin," seeks he the path of healing, amid the horriblest of torments; for this healing can consist in nothing but the knowledge that those tears are dried. We must believe him, that never did a pilgrim pray for pardon with such ardour. But the more sincere and total his prostration, his remorse and craving for purification, the more terribly must he be overcome with loathing at the heartless lie that reared itself upon his journey's goal. It is just his utter singlemindedness, recking naught of self, of welfare for his individual soul, but solely of his love towards another being, and thus of that beloved being's weal—it is just this feeling that at last must kindle into brightest flame his hate against this world, which must break from off its axis or ever it absolved his love and him; and these are the flames whose embers of despair scorch up his heart. When he returns from Rome, he is nothing but embodied wrath against a world that refuses him the right of Being for simple reason of the wholeness of his feelings; and not from any thirst for joy or pleasure, seeks he once more the Venusberg; but despair and hatred of this world he needs must flout now drive him thither, to hide him from his "angel's" look, whose "tears to sweeten" the wide world could not afford to him the balm.—Thus does he love Elisabeth; and this love it is that she returns. What the whole moral world could not, that could she when, defying all the world, she clothed her lover in her prayer, and in hallowed knowledge of the puissance of her death she dying set the culprit free. And Tannhäuser's last breath goes up to her, in thanks for this supernal gift of Love. Beside his lifeless body stands no man but must envy him; the whole world, and God Himself—must call him blessed.—

Now I declare that not even the most eminent *actor*, of our own or bygone times, could solve the task of a perfect portrayal of Tannhäuser's character on the lines laid down in the above analysis; and I meet the question: "How could I hold it possible for an opera-singer to fulfil it?" by the simple answer that to *Music* alone could the draft of such a task be offered, and only a dramatic *singer*, just through the aid of Music, can be in the position to fulfil it. Where a Player would seek in vain among the means of recitation, for the expression wherewithal to give this character success, to the Singer that expression is self-offered in the music; I therefore merely beg the latter to approach his task with unrestricted warmth, and he may be certain also of achieving it.—But above all, I must ask the singer of Tannhäuser to completely give over and forget his quondam standing as Opera-singer; *as such* he cannot even dream of a possibility of solving this task. To our *tenors*, in particular, there cleaves a downright curse as outcome of their rendering of the usual tenor-rôles—giving them for the most part an unmanly, vapid, and utterly invertebrate appearance. Under the influence, and in consequence, of the positively criminal school of singing now in vogue, during the whole of their theatrical career they are accustomed to so exclusively devote their attention to the paltriest details of vocal trickery, that they seldom attain to anything beyond the care whether that G or A-flat will come out roundly, or the delight that this G-sharp or A has "taken" well. Besides this care and this delight, they generally know nothing but the pleasure of fine clothes, and the toil to make their finery and voice together bring-in as much applause as possible—above all with an eye to higher wages.* I grant, then, that the mere attempt to handle such a task as that of my Tannhäuser will be sufficient in itself to ruffle the composure of the singer, and that this very disquietude will induce him to alter many of his old stage habits; in fact I go so far as to hope that, if the study of Tannhäuser is conducted on the lines laid down by me, so great a change will come over the habits and notions of the singer, in favour of his task, that of itself it will lead him to the right and needful thing. But a thoroughly successful issue of his labours I can only expect when this change shall compass a total revolution in himself and his former methods of conception and portrayal—a revolution such

---

* As I direct these remarks to a whole class, and in such general terms, it naturally is impossible for me to take notice of the manifold varieties which more or less depart from the generic character; wherefore in dealing with crying faults I here must necessarily employ superlatives, which, at any rate, can find no application to many an individual case.—R. WAGNER.

as to make him conscious that for this project he has to become something entirely different from what he has been, the diametric opposite of his earlier self. Let him not reply that already he has had tasks set before him which made unusual demands on his gift for acting: I can prove to him that what he haply has made his own in the so-called dramatic-tenor rôles of latter days will by no means help him out with Tannhäuser; for I could shew him that in the operas of Meyerbeer, for instance, the character for which I have blamed the modern tenor is regarded as unalterable, from top to toe, in means and end, and with the utmost shrewdness. Whoever, then, relying on his previous successes in the said operas, should attempt to play Tannhäuser with merely the same expenditure on the art of portrayal as has sufficed to make those operas both widely given and universally popular, would turn this rôle into the very opposite of what it is. Above all, he would not grasp the energy of Tannhäuser's nature, and thus would turn him into an undecided, vacillating, a weak and unmanly character; since for the *superficial* observer there certainly might exist temptation to such a false conception of the part (lending it somewhat of a resemblance to "Robert the Devil"). But nothing could make the whole drama less intelligible and more disfigure the chief character, than if Tannhäuser were displayed weak, or even by fits and starts "well-meaning," bourgeoisely devout, and at most afflicted with a few reprehensible cravings. This I believe I have substantiated by the foregoing characterisation of his nature; and as I can await no understanding of my work if its chief rôle be not conceived and rendered in consonance with that characterisation, so the singer of Tannhäuser may perceive not only what an unwonted demand I make upon him, but also to what joyful thanks he'll pledge me should he fully realise my aim. I do not hesitate to say that a completely successful impersonation of Tannhäuser will be the highest achievement in the record of his art.—

After this exhaustive talk with the singer of Tannhäuser, I have but little to tell the interpreters of the remaining rôles; the main gist of what I have said to him concerns them all. The hardest tasks, after that of Tannhäuser himself, are certainly those which fall to the two ladies, the exponents of *Venus* and *Elisabeth*. As to Venus, this rôle will only succeed when to a favourable exterior the actress joins a full belief in her part; and this will come to her so soon as she is able to hold Venus completely justified in her every utterance,—so justified that she can yield to no one but the woman who offers up herself for Love. The difficulty in the rôle of Elisabeth, on the other hand, is for the actress to give the impression of the most youthful and virginal unconstraint, without betraying how experienced, how refined a womanly feeling it is, that alone can fit her for the task.—The other male parts are less exacting, and even *Wolfram*—whose rôle I can by no means hold for unconditionally easy—needs little more than to address himself to the sympathy of the finer-feeling section of our public, to be sure of winning its interest. The lesser vehemence of his directly physical instincts has allowed him to make the impressions of Life a matter of meditation; he thus is pre-eminently Poet and Artist, whereas Tannhäuser is before all Man. His standing toward Elisabeth, which a noble manly pride enables him to bear so worthily, no less than his final deep fellow-feeling for Tannhäuser—whom he certainly can never comprehend —will make him one of the most prepossessing figures. Let the singer of this part, however, be on his guard against imagining the music as easy as might at first appear: more particularly his first song in the "Singers'-tourney"—comprising, as it does, the story of the whole evolution of Wolfram's life-views, both as artist and as man — will demand a phrasing (*Vortrag*) thought-out with the most sensitive care, after a minutest pondering of the poetic subject, while it will need the greatest practice to pitch the voice to that variety of expression which alone can give this piece the right effect.—In conclusion I would gladly turn from the "Performers" to the "Singers" in particular, did I not on the one hand fear to weary, and on the other, venture to assume that what I have already said will suffice to make clear my wishes to the representants in their function, too, of vocal artists.—

So I will now close this Address, albeit with a mournful feeling that I have most imperfectly attained my object: namely, to make good by it a thing denied me, and yet the thing I deem so needful—a personal and word-of-mouth address to all concerned.* Amid my deep feeling of the insufficiency of this by-way that I have struck, my only solace is a firm reliance on the good will of my artistic comrades; a good will such as never an artist needed more for making possible his artwork, than I need in my present plight. May all whom I have addressed take thought on my peculiar lot, and above all ascribe to the mood which consequently has grown upon me any stray sentence wherein I may have shewn myself too exacting, too anxious, or even too mistrustful, rigorous and harsh.—In view of the unwontedness of such an Address as the preceding, I certainly must prepare myself for its being wholly or for the most part disregarded—perhaps not even understood—by many of those to whom it is directed. With this knowledge I therefore can only regard it as an experiment, which I cast like a die on the world, uncertain whether it shall win or lose. Yet if merely among a handful of individuals I fully reach my aim, that attainment will richly compensate me for all mischanced besides; and cordially do I grasp in anticipation the hand of those valiant artists who shall not have been ashamed to concern themselves more closely with me, and more familiarly to befriend me, than is wonted in our modern Art-world's intercourse.

* This "Address" was written when Wagner had already spent over three years in exile,—an exile destined to last for nearly ten years more.—TR.

REMARKS ON PERFORMING THE OPERA:
"THE FLYING DUTCHMAN."

Bemerkungen zur Aufführung der Oper:
„Der fliegende Holländer."

The accompanying article was evidently written soon after that on Tannhäuser,—*at any rate either in* 1852 *or early in* 1853. *It does not appear in the* Neue Zeitschrift für Musik.

TRANSLATOR'S NOTE.

N the first place I have to remind the Conductor and Regisseur of what I laid to their heart before, when dealing with the production of "Tannhäuser," as regards the close accord between what passes in the orchestra and what passes on the stage. The ships and sea, in particular, demand from the Regisseur an unusual amount of care: he will find all needful indications at the corresponding places of the pianoforte edition or full score. The opera's first scene has to bring the spectator into that *Stimmung* in which it becomes possible for him to conceive the mysterious figure of the "Flying Dutchman" himself: it must therefore be handled with exceptional kindness; the sea between the headlands must be shewn as boisterous as possible; the treatment of the ship cannot be naturalistic enough: little touches, such as the heeling of the ship when struck by an extra big wave (between the two verses of the Steersman's song) must be very drasticly carried out. Special attention is demanded by the lighting, with its manifold changes: to make the nuances of storm in the First Act effective, a skilful use of painted gauzes, as far as quite the middle distance of the stage, is indispensable. However, as these Remarks are not specially directed to the purely decorative aspect of the performance (for which I must refer to the scenarium of this opera as produced in the Berlin playhouse) I content myself—as said—with pleading for an exact observance of my scattered scenic indications, and leave to the inventive powers of the Scene-painter and Machinist the method of their carrying out.

I therefore turn simply to the performers, and among these more particularly to the representant of the difficult principal rôle, that of the "*Holländer*" (the "Dutchman").

Upon the happy issue of this title rôle depends the *real* success of the whole opera: its exponent must succeed in rousing and maintaining the deepest pity (*Mitleid*); and this he will be able to, if he strictly observes the following chief characteristics.—

His outward appearance is sufficiently notified. His first entry is most solemn and earnest: the measured slowness of his landing should offer a marked contrast with his vessel's weirdly rapid passage through the seas. During the deep trumpet-notes (B-minor) at quite the close of the introductory scene he has come off board, along a plank lowered by one of the crew, to a shelf of rock on the shore; his rolling gait, proper to sea-folk on first treading dry land after a long voyage, is accompanied by a wave-like figure for the violins and 'tenors': with the first crotchet of the third bar he makes his second step—always with folded arms and sunken head; his third and fourth steps coincide with the notes of the eighth and tenth bars. From here on, his movements will follow the dictates of his general delivery, yet the actor must never let himself be betrayed into exaggerated stridings to and fro: a certain terrible repose in his outward demeanour, even amid the most passionate expression of inward anguish and despair, will give the characteristic stamp to this impersonation. The first phrases are to be sung without a trace of passion (almost in strict beat, like the whole of this recitative), as though the man were tired out; at the words, declaimed with bitter ire: "*ha, stolzer Ozean*" etc. ("thou haughty Ocean") he does not break as yet into positive passion: more in terrible scorn, he merely turns his head half-round towards the sea. During the ritornello, after: "*doch ewig meine Qual*" ("but ever lasts my pain"), he bows his head once more, as though in utter weariness; the words: "*euch, des Weltmeers Fluthen*" etc. ("to you, ye waves of earthly sea") he sings in this posture, staring blankly before him. For the mimetic accompaniment of the Allegro: "*wie oft in Meeres tiefsten Grund*" etc. ("how oft in Ocean's deep abysm") I do not wish the singer to cramp too much his outer motion, yet he still must abide by my prime maxim, namely however deep the passion, however agonised the feeling which he has to breathe into the voice-part, he must for the present keep to the utmost calm in his outer bearing: a movement of the arm or hand, but not too sweeping, will suffice to mark the single more emphatic accents. Even the words: "*Niemals der Tod, nirgends ein Grab!*" ("Nor ever death, nowhere a grave!"), which are certainly to be sung with the greatest vehemence, belong rather to the *description* of his sufferings than to a direct, an actual outburst of his despair: the latter he only reaches with what follows, for which the utmost energy of action must therefore be reserved. With the repetition of the words: "*diess der Verdammniss Schreckgebot!*" ("This was my curse's dread decree!") he has somewhat inclined his head and his whole body: so he remains throughout the first four bars of the postlude; with the tremolo of the violins (E-flat) at the fifth bar he raises his face to heaven, his body still bent low; with the entry of the muffled roll of the kettle-drum at the ninth bar of the postlude he begins to shudder, the down-held fists are clenched convulsively, the lips commence to move, and at last (with eyes fixed heavenward throughout) he starts the phrase: "*Dich frage ich*" etc. ("Of thee I ask"). This whole, almost direct address to "God's angel" (*den* "*Engel Gottes*"), for all the terrible expression with which it is to be sung, must yet be delivered in the pose just indicated (without any marked change beyond what the execution necessarily demands at certain places): we must see before us a "fallen angel" himself, whose fearful torment drives him to proclaim his wrath against Eternal Justice. At last, however, with the words: "*Vergeb'ne Hoffnung*" etc. ("Thou vainest hope") the full force of his despair finds vent: furious, he stands erect, his eyes still gazing heavenwards, and with utmost energy of grief he casts all "futile hopes" behind: no more will he hear of promised ransom, and finally (at entry of the kettle-drum and basses) he falls of a heap, as though undone. With the opening of the allegro-ritornel his features kindle to a new, a horrible last hope—the hope of World's-upheaval, in which he too must pass away. This closing Allegro requires the most terrible energy, not only in the vocal phrasing, but also in the mimic action; for everything here is unmasked passion. Yet the singer must do his best to give this whole tempo, despite its vehemence of phrasing, the semblance of a mere gathering of all his force for the final crushing outbreak at the words: "*Ihr Welten! endet euren Lauf!*" etc. ("Ye worlds! now end your last career!"). Here the expression must reach its loftiest pitch. After the closing words: "*ewige Vernichtung, nimm' mich auf!*" ("Eternal Chaos, take me hence!") he remains standing at full height, almost like a statue, throughout the whole *fortissimo* of the postlude: only with the entry of the *piano*, during the muffled chant from the ship's hold, does he gradually relax his attitude; his arms fall down; at the four bars of "*espressivo*" for the first violins he slowly sinks his head, and during the last eight bars of the postlude he totters to the rock-wall at the side: he leans his back against it and remains for long in this position, with arms tight-folded on the breast.—

I have discussed this scene at so much length, in order to shew in what sense I wish the "*Holländer*" to be portrayed, and what weight I place on the most careful adapting of the action to the music. In a like sense should the performer take pains to conceive the whole remainder of his rôle. Moreover, this aria is also the hardest in all the part, and more especially since the public's further understanding of the subject depends upon the issue of this scene: if this monologue, in keeping with its aim, has thoroughly attuned and touched the hearer, the further success of the whole work is for the major part insured—whereas nothing that comes after could possibly make up for anything neglected here.

In the ensuing scene with *Daland* the "Dutchman" retains at first his present posture. Daland's questions, from aboard-ship, he answers with the faintest movement of his head. When Daland comes towards him on dry land, the Dutchman also advances to about the middle of the stage, with stately calm. His whole demeanour here shews quiet, restful dignity; the expression of his voice is noble, equable, without a tinge of stronger accent: he acts and talks as though from ancient habit: so often has he passed through like encounters and transactions; everything, even the seemingly most purposed questions and answers, takes place as if by instinct; he deals as though at bidding of his situation, to which he gives himself mechanically and without interest, like a wearied man. Just as instinctively again, his yearning for "redemption" re-awakes: after his fearful outburst of despair he has grown gentler, softer, and it is with touching sadness that he speaks his yearning after rest. The question: "*hast du eine Tochter?*" ("Hast thou a daughter?") he still throws out with seeming calm; but suddenly the old hope (so often recognised as vain) is roused once more by Daland's enthusiastic answer: "*fürwahr, ein treues Kind*" ("Ay! ay! a *faithful* child"); with spasmodic haste he cries: "*sie sei mein Weib!*" ("be *she* my wife!"). The old longing takes him once again, and in moving accents (though outwardly calm) he draws the picture of his lot: "*ach, ohne Weib, ohne Kind bin ich*" ("Ah! neither wife nor child have I"). The glowing colours in which Daland now paints his daughter still more revive the *Holländer's* old yearning for "redemption through a woman's truth," and in the duet's closing Allegro the battle between hope and despair is driven to the height of passion—wherein already hope appears to wellnigh conquer.—

At his first appearance before *Senta*, in the Second Act, the *Holländer* again is calm and solemn in his outer bearing: all his passionate emotions are strenuously thrust back within his breast. Throughout the lengthy first 'fermata' he stays motionless beside the door; at the commencement of the drum-solo he slowly strides towards the front; with the eighth bar of that solo he halts (the two bars "*accelerando*" for the strings relate to the gestures of

Daland, who still stands wondering in the doorway, awaiting *Senta's* welcome, and impatiently invites it with a movement of his outstretched arms); during the next three bars for the drum the Holländer advances to the extreme side-front, where he now remains without a motion, his eyes bent fixedly on *Senta*. (The recurrence of the figure for the strings relates to the emphatic repetition of *Daland's* gesture: at the *pizzicato* on the next fermata he ceases inviting her, and shakes his head in amazement; with the entry of the basses, after the fermata, he himself comes down to *Senta*).—The postlude of *Daland's* aria must be played in full: during its first four bars he turns to depart without further ado; with the fifth and sixth he pauses, and turns round again; the next seven bars accompany his byplay as he watches now the Holländer, now Senta, half pleased, half curiously expectant; during the subsequent two bars for the double-basses he goes as far as the door, shaking his head; with the theme's resumption by the wind-instruments he thrusts in his head once more, withdraws it vexedly, and shuts the door behind him—so that with the entry of the F-sharp chord for the 'wind' he has disappeared for good. The remainder of the postlude, together with the ritornello of the following duet, is accompanied on the stage by total immobility and silence: *Senta* and the *Holländer*, at opposite extremities of the foreground, are riveted in contemplation of each other. (The performers need not be afraid of wearying by this situation: it is a matter of experience that this is just the one which most powerfully engrosses the spectator, and most fittingly prepares him for the following scene).

The whole succeeding E-major section is to be executed by the *Holländer* with complete repose of outer mien, however stirring the emotion wherewith he delivers his lines; only the hands and arms (and that most sparingly) must he employ to emphasise the stronger accents.—Not until the two bars of the drum solo, before the following E-minor tempo, does he rouse himself, to draw somewhat closer to *Senta*: during the short ritornello he moves a few steps towards the middle of the stage, with a certain constraint and mournful courtesy. (I must here inform the conductor, that experience has shewn me I was mistaken in marking the tempo "*un poco meno sostenuto*": the long preceding tempo, true enough, is somewhat slow at its commencement—particularly in the Holländer's first solo—but little by little it instinctively freshens towards the close, so that with the entry of E-minor the pace must necessarily be somewhat restrained once more, in order to give at least the opening of this section its needful impress of decorous calm. The four-bar phrase, in fact, must be *slackened down* in such a manner that the fourth bar is played in marked "*ritenuto*": the same thing applies to the first phrase now sung by the Holländer). With the ninth and tenth bars, during the solo for the drum, the Holländer again advances one, and two steps nearer to Senta. With the eleventh and twelfth bars, however, the time must be taken somewhat more briskly, so that at the B-minor: "*du könntest dich*" etc., the tempo I really meant—moderato, certainly, but not quite so dragging—at last arrives, and is to be maintained throughout the section. At the *più animato*: "*so unbedingt, wie?*" the *Holländer* betrays the animating effect which *Senta's* first real speech has wrought on him: with this passage he must already begin to shew more visible agitation. But *Senta's* passionate interjection: "*o welche Leiden! Könnt' ich Trost ihm bringen!*" ("What tale of grief! O, could I respite bring him!") stirs him to the depths of his being: filled with astonished admiration, he stammers out the half-hushed words: "*welch' holder Klang im nächtlichen Gewühl!*" ("What gentle strains in Night's most raging storm!"). With the *molto più animato*, he scarce can master himself any longer; he sings with the utmost fire of passion, and at the words: "*Allmächtiger, durch diese sei's!*" ("Almighty, be't through *her*!") he hurls himself upon his knees. With the *agitato* (B-minor) he rises to his feet impetuously: his *love* for Senta displays itself at once in terror of the danger she herself incurs by reaching out a rescuing hand to him. It comes over him as a hideous crime, and in his passionate remonstrance against her sharing in his fate he becomes a human being through and through; whereas he hitherto had often given us but the grim impression of a ghost. Here, then, the actor must give to even his outer bearing the full impress of human passion; as if felled to the ground, he falls before Senta with the last words: "*nennst ew'ge Treue du nicht dein!*" ("if troth of thine lasts not for aye!") so that *Senta* stands high above him, like his angel, as she tells him what *she* means by *troth*.*—During the ritornello of the succeeding *Allegro molto* the *Holländer* lifts himself erect, in solemn exaltation: his voice is stirred to the sublimest height of victory. In all that follows there can be no more room for misunderstanding: at his last entry, in the Third Act, all is passion, pain, despair. Particularly do I exhort the singer not to drag the recitative passages, but to take everything in the most spirited, most stressful *tempo*.—

The rôle of *Senta* will be hard to misread; one warning alone have I to give: let not the *dreamy* side of her nature be conceived in the sense of a modern, sickly sentimentality! Senta, on the contrary, is an altogether robust (*kerniges*) Northern maid, and even in her apparent sentimentality she is thoroughly *naïve*. Only in the heart of an entirely naïve girl, surrounded by the idiosyncrasies of Northern Nature, could impressions such as those of the ballad of the "Flying Dutchman" and the picture of the pallid seaman call forth so wondrous strong a bent, as the impulse to redeem the doomed: with her this takes the outward form of an active monomania (*ein kräftiger Wahnsinn*) such, indeed, as can only be found in quite naïve natures. We have been told of Norwegian maids of such a force of feeling, that death has come upon them through a sudden *rigor* (*Erstarrung*) of the heart. Much in this wise may it go, with the seeming "morbidness" of pallid Senta.—Nor must *Eric* be a sentimental whiner: on the contrary, he is stormy, impulsive and sombre (*düster*), like every man who lives alone (particularly in the Northern highlands).

* "Treue" = "trueness, loyalty," and thus *eternal* "troth."—TR.

Whoever should give a sugary rendering to his "*Cavatina*" in the Third Act, would do me a sorry service, for it ought instead to breathe distress and heart-ache. (Everything that might justify a false conception of this piece, such as its falsetto-passage and final cadenza, I implore may be either altered or struck out).—Further, I beseech the exponent of *Daland* not to drag his rôle into the region of the positively comic: he is a rough-hewn figure from the life of everyday, a sailor who scoffs at storms and danger for sake of gain, and with whom, for instance, the—certainly apparent—sale of his daughter to a rich man ought not to seem at all disgraceful: he thinks and deals, like a hundred thousand others, without the least suspicion that he is doing any wrong.

EXPLANATORY PROGRAMMES.

Programmatische Erläuterungen.

Number 1 *of the following sketches appeared in the* Neue Zeitschrift für Musik *of October* 15, 1852, *forming the third of a series of articles contributed by Theodor Uhlig under the title:* "*On the poetic contents of Beethoven's tone-works.*" *In that series No. 1 was devoted to a general preface by Uhlig himself* (*Sep.* 24), *No. II to Wagner's* Programme of the Ninth Symphony (*Oct.* 1—*see Vol. ii of the* Ges. Schr.), *No. III was the present sketch of the* "*Heroic Symphony,*" *and No. IV the present sketch of the* "*Coriolanus overture.*" *In Letter* 54 (? *end of January or beginning of February,* 1852) *Wagner writes to Uhlig, from Zurich:* "*I may possibly write and sign a notice of the forthcoming performance of the* Coriolanus-*overture here*. . . . *Can you get my article concerning the poetic contents of the* Eroica *from the R.'s?*"—*and in Letter* 56 (*Zurich, Feb.* 26, '52): "*I, too, have only understood Beethoven since I sought for the poetic subject of his tone utterances, and at last found it:* Coriolanus *proves this clearly to me,*" *etc.*

The present No. 3 *appeared in the* Neue Zeitschrift *for August* 5, 1853, *with a note:* "*From the programme of the Zurich Music-Festival*"; *No.* 4 *in the same journal for January* 14, '53, *with a note:* "*Written by the composer on the occasion of the performance of this work at Zurich*"; *and No.* 5 *in the issue for June* 17, '53, *with the same note as that to No.* 3. *In Letter* 56, *above mentioned, Wagner writes:* "*At the first rehearsal of the* Tannhäuser *overture the orchestra begged me to give them an explanation of the contents, after the manner of the* Coriolanus *overture, as it would enable them to 'play better.'*"

TRANSLATOR'S NOTE.

I.

BEETHOVEN'S "HEROIC SYMPHONY."

HIS highly significant tone-poem—the master's Third Symphony, and the first work with which he struck his own peculiar path—is in many respects not so easy to understand as its name might allow one to suppose; and that precisely since the title "Heroic Symphony" instinctively misleads one into trying to see therein a series of heroic episodes, presented in a certain historico-dramatic sense by means of pictures in Tone. Whoever approaches this work with such a notion, and expects to understand it, will find himself at first bewildered and lastly undeceived, without having arrived at any true enjoyment. If therefore I here permit myself to communicate as tersely as possible the view I have gained of the poetic contents of this tone-creation, it is in the sincere belief that to many a hearer of the forthcoming performance of the "Heroic Symphony" I may facilitate an understanding, which he otherwise could only acquire through frequent attendance at particularly lifelike renderings of the work.

In the first place, the designation "heroic" is to be taken in its widest sense, and in nowise to be conceived as relating merely to a military hero. If we broadly connote by "hero" ("*Held*") the whole, the full-fledged *man*, in whom are present all the purely-human feelings—of love, of grief, of force—in their highest fill and strength, then we shall rightly grasp the subject which the artist lets appeal to us in the speaking accents of his tone-work. The artistic space of this work is filled with all the varied, intercrossing feelings of a strong, a consummate Individuality, to which nothing human is a stranger, but which includes within itself all truly Human, and utters it in such a fashion that—after frankly manifesting every noble passion—it reaches a final rounding of its nature, wherein the most feeling softness is wedded with the most energetic force. The heroic tendence of this artwork is the progress toward that rounding off.

The *First Movement* embraces, as in a glowing furnace, all the emotions of a richly-gifted nature in the heyday of unresting youth. Weal and woe, lief and lack, sweetness and sadness, living and longing, riot and revel, daring, defiance, and an ungovernable sense of Self,* make place for one another so directly, and interlace so closely that, however much we mate each feeling with our own, we can single none of them from out the rest, but our whole interest is given merely to this one, this human being who shews himself brimful of every feeling. Yet all these feelings spring from one main faculty—and that is *Force*. This Force, immeasurably enhanced by each emotional impression and driven to vent its overfill, is the mainspring of the tone-piece: it clinches—toward the middle of the Movement —to the violence of the destroyer, and in its braggart strength we think we see a Wrecker of the World before us, a Titan wrestling with the Gods.

This shattering Force, that filled us half with ecstasy and half with horror, was rushing toward a tragic crisis, whose serious import is set before our Feeling in the *Second Movement*. The tone-poet clothes its proclamation in the musical apparel of a Funeral-march. Emotion tamed by deep grief, moving in solemn sorrow, tells us its tale in stirring tones: an earnest, manly sadness goes from lamentation to thrills of softness, to memories, to tears of love, to

---

* "Wonne und Wehe, Lust und Leid, Anmuth und Wehmuth, Sinnen und Sehnen, Schmachten und Schwelgen, Kühnheit, Trotz und ein unbändiges Selbstgefühl"—I add the German, as the *Stabreims* are so significant of the epoch in Wagner's life (1850-52) at which the above was written.—TR.

searchings of the heart, to cries of transport. Out of grief there springs new Force, that fills us with a warmth sublime: instinctively we seek again this force's fountain-head in Grief; we give ourselves to it, till sighing we swoon away; but here we rouse ourselves once more to fullest Force: we will not succumb, but endure. We battle no more against mourning, but bear it now ourselves on the mighty billows of a man's courageous heart. To whom were it possible to paint in words the endless play of quite unspeakable emotions, passing from Grief to highest Exaltation, and thence again to softest Melancholy, till they mount at last to endless Recollection? The Tone-poet alone could do it, in this wondrous piece.

Force robbed of its destructive arrogance — by the chastening of its own deep sorrow—the *Third Movement* shows in all its buoyant gaiety. Its wild unruliness has shaped itself to fresh, to blithe activity; we have before us now the lovable glad man, who paces hale and hearty through the fields of Nature, looks laughingly across the meadows, and winds his merry hunting-horn from woodland heights; and what he feels amid it all, the master tells us in the vigorous, healthy tints of his tone-painting; he gives it lastly to the horns themselves to say—those horns which musically express the radiant, frolicsome, yet tender-hearted exultation of the man. In this Third Movement the tone-poet shews us the man-of-feeling from the side directly opposite to that from which he shewed him in its immediate predecessor: there the deeply, stoutly suffering, —here the gladly, blithely doing man.

These two sides the master now combines in the *Fourth* —the last—*Movement,* to shew us finally the man entire, harmoniously at one with self, in those emotions where the memory of Sorrow becomes itself the shaping-force of noble Deeds. This closing section is the harvest, the lucid counterpart and commentary, of the First. Just as there we saw all human feelings in infinitely varied utterance, now permeating one another, now each in haste repelling each: so here this manifold variety unites to one harmonious close, embracing all these feelings in itself and taking on a grateful plasticness of shape. This shape the master binds at first within one utmost simple theme, which sets itself before us in sure distinctness, and yet is capable of infinite development, from gentlest delicacy to grandest strength. Around this theme, which we may regard as the firm-set Manly individuality, there wind and cling all tenderer and softer feelings, from the very onset of the movement, evolving to a proclamation of the purely Womanly element; and to the manlike principal theme—striding sturdily through all the tone-piece—this Womanly at last reveals itself in ever more intense, more many-sided sympathy, as the overwhelming power of *Love*. At the close of the movement this power breaks itself a highway straight into the heart. The restless motion pauses, and in noble, feeling calm this Love speaks out; beginning tenderly and softly, then waxing to the rapture of elation, it takes at last the inmost fortress of the man's whole heart. Here it is, that once again this heart recalls the memory of its life-pang: high swells the breast filled full by Love,—that breast which harbours woe within its weal; for woe and weal, as purely-human Feeling, are one thing and the same.* Once more the heart-strings quiver, and tears of pure Humanity well forth; yet from out the very quick of sadness there bursts the jubilant cry of Force,—that Force which lately wed itself to Love, and nerved wherewith *the whole, the total Man* now shouts to us the avowal of his Godhood.

But only in the master's tone-speech was the unspeakable to be proclaimed—the thing that words could here but darkly hint at.

---

* From this, and one or two other indications, it is evident that the "Programme" was written contemporaneously with Part III of *Oper und Drama*—see Vol. ii. pp. 291-292.—TR.

2.

BEETHOVEN'S OVERTURE TO "CORIOLANUS."

THIS comparatively little-known work of the great tone-poet is certainly one of his most significant creations, and nobody, who has a close acquaintance with the subject of portrayal, can hear a good performance of it without being profoundly moved. I therefore permit myself to sketch that subject as I have found it expressed in the tone-poet's own presentment of it, so as to prepare, for those who feel like me, the same sublime enjoyment as I myself have reaped.

Coriolanus, the man of Force untamable, unfitted for a hypocrite's humility, banished therefore from his father-city and, with its foes for allies, combating that city to extermination; *Coriolanus*, moved by mother, wife and child, at last abandoning vengeance, and condemned to death by his confederates for this treason wrought against them—this *Coriolanus* I may presuppose as known to most men. From all this great political canvas, so rich in bearings and 'relations' whose setting forth, how allowable soever to the Poet, was quite forbidden the Musician—since *he* can express moods, feelings, passions and their opposites, but no sort or manner of political relations—*Beethoven* seized for his presentment one unique scene, the most decisive of them all, as though to snatch at its very focus the true, the purely human emotional-content of the whole wide-stretching stuff, and transmit it in the most enthralling fashion to the likewise purely-human Feeling. This is the scene between Coriolanus, his mother, and wife, in the enemy's camp before the gates of his native city.—If, without fear of any error, we may conceive the plastic subject of all the master's symphonic works as representing scenes between man and woman, and if we may find the archetype of all such scenes in genuine Dance itself, whence the Symphony in truth derived its musical form: then we here have such a scene before us in utmost possible sublimity and thrillingness of content. The whole tone-piece might well be taken for the musical accompaniment of a pantomimic show—only in the sense that, whereas we must imagine the subject itself as set before the eye in pantomime, this accompaniment makes known to us the *entire* language seizable by the ear.

The first few bars present us with the figure of the *man* himself: gigantic force, indomitable sense-of-self (*Selbstgefühl*) and passionate defiance, express themselves as fury, hate, revenge, determination to destroy. It only needs the name of "Coriolanus," to conjure up his form before us at one stroke, to make us feel instinctively the feelings of his clamorous heart. Close beside him stands the *woman*: mother, wife, and child. Grace, gentleness and manners mild confront the headstrong male with childlike pleas, with wifely prayers and mother's admonition, to turn the stubborn heart from its fell purpose.—Coriolanus knows the danger menacing his scorn*: his birthplace has sent out to him the most insidious of advocates. Upon all the sleek and crafty politicians, there at home, he had felt the power to turn his back in cold contempt; their embassies addressed his political Understanding, his civic prudence: a scathing word anent their baseness had kept them at his arm's length. But here the fatherland addressed his *heart*, his involuntary, his purely-human Feeling; for *this* assault he had no other armour—than to ward his eyes, his ears, against the irresistible.—Thus at the pleaders' earliest plaint he hastily averts his gaze, his hearing; we see the turbulent gesture with which he breaks the woman's prayer and shuts his eyes,—yet cannot hush the sorrowful lament that echoes after him.—In the inmost chamber of his heart the worm of ruth begins to gnaw the giant's scorn. But terribly this scorn defends itself; stung by the worm's first bite, it breaks out in fuming anguish; his storm of rage, his dreadful throes,

---

* "Trotz" = "scorn" in the sense of proud, unbending *defiance*, inspired by a feeling of the justice of one's own cause.—TR.

lay bare the foaming grandeur of this vengeful Scorn itself, and alike the burning violence of the pain inflicted by remorse's tooth. Deep-moved by this appalling spectacle, we see the woman falter and break down in sobs; scarce dares her plea now issue longer from her breast, racked as it is with fellow-feeling for the man's tempestuous grief. Fearsomely the war of Feeling wages to and fro: where the woman looked for naught but rugged arrogance, she now must see in the very force of Scorn its cruelest of sufferings.—But this Scorn has now become the only life-force of the man: Coriolanus without his vengeance, without his annihilating anger, is no more Coriolanus, and he must cease to live if he give up his scorn. This is the bond that holds his power of life together; the outlawed rebel, the ally of his country's foes, cannot become again what once he was: to let go his vengeance, means to cast away his being—to forego the annihilation of his birthplace, to annihilate himself. He faces the woman with the announcement of this awful choice, this only choice now left him. He cries to her: "*Rome* or *I!* For one must fall!" Here once again he shews himself in the full sublimeness of his shattering ire. And here again the woman wins the power to plead: Mercy! Reconciliation! Peace!—she prays him. Ah! she little understands him, she cannot see that: Peace with Rome—means his undoing! Yet the woman's wailing tears his heart asunder; once more he turns away, to fight the fearful fight between his Scorn and his necessity of self-destruction. Then with a sudden effort he pauses in the torturing strife, and—seeks himself the gaze of the beloved woman, to read with agony of bliss his own death-warrant in her pleading mien. His bosom heaves in presence of this sight; all inward storms and struggles rush together to one great resolution; the offering of self is sealed:—Peace and Reconcilement!—The whole Force the hero heretofore had turned on the destruction of his fatherland, the thousand swords and arrows of his hate and unslaked vengeance, with violent hand he girds them to *one* point, and—plunges it into his heart.

Felled by his own death-thrust, the colossus crashes down: at foot of the woman who besought for Peace, he breathes out his dying breath.

Thus Beethoven's tone-poem of Coriolanus.

3.
OVERTURE TO THE "*FLIEGENDE HOLLÄNDER.*"

THE "Flying Dutchman's" dreaded ship is scudding before the tempest; it reaches the coast and puts to land, where its captain has been promised healing and redemption; we hear the pitying strains of that foretoken of salvation, which sound like wailings blent with prayer: sullen and bereft of hope, the doomed man listens to them; weary and athirst for Death, he comes ashore; while the crew, faint-hearted and their lives outlived (*lebensübernächtig*), in silence bring the ship to rest.—How often has the unhappy one passed through the selfsame thing! How often has he steered his ship athwart the breakers to the shores of Man, where once in every seven years 'twas granted him to land; how often has he dreamt the end of all his trials reached, and ah!—how often, direly undeceived, has he set sail again upon his raving voyage! To force his own undoing, he has called on flood and storm to arm themselves against him: into the yawning whirlpool has he plunged his ship, —but the gulf refused to swallow it; against the beetling headland has he urged it,—but the rocks have never wrecked it. All the fearsome perils of the deep, at which he erst had laughed in madcap lust of venture, they now but laugh at him—they harm him not: he's curst to all eternity to hunt the desert seas for spoils that yield him no delight, but ne'er to find the only thing that could redeem him!—A stately ship sweeps proudly by; he hears the merry, happy songs of men rejoicing at the near approach of home: anger takes him at this sound of gladness; raging he rushes onward through the storm, affrights and silences the singers, and puts the joyous crew to flight. Then from the bottom of his misery he cries aloud for ransom: in the aching void of his un-mated being—none but a *wife* can bring him weal! Where, in what distant land may dwell the rescuer? Where beats a feeling heart for sufferings so great as his? Where is she, she who will not flee in horror from him, like these coward men who shuddering cross themselves at his approach?—A ray divides the gloom of night; like a lightning-flash it pierces through his tortured soul. It fades, and leaps to life once more: the seaman keeps the lodestar firm in eye, and stoutly steers through waves and billows toward it. What draws him with such might—it is a woman's look, which, full of sad sublimity and godlike fellow-feeling, thrusts through to him! A heart has opened its unending depths to the unmeasured sorrows of the damned: for him must it make offering, to end alike his sorrows and its life. At this divinest sight the fated man breaks down at last, as breaks his ship to atoms; the ocean's trough engulfs it: but he, from out the waves he rises whole and hallowed, led by the victress' rescuing hand to the daybreak of sublimest Love.

4.

OVERTURE TO "TANNHAÜSER."

To begin with, the orchestra leads before us the Pilgrims' Chant alone*; it draws near, then swells into a mighty outpour, and passes finally away.—Evenfall: last echo of

* In the *N. Z.* the opening sentence ran thus: "A band of pilgrims marches past us; their chant—of faith, remorse and penitence, mounting to hope and confident assurance of salvation—draws near at the commencement, swells louder, as if close beside us," etc.—TR.

the chant.—As night breaks, magic sights and sounds appear: a rosy mist floats up, exultant shouts assail our ear; the whirlings of a fearsomely voluptuous dance are seen. These are the "Venusberg's" seductive spells, that shew themselves at dead of night to those whose breast is fired by daring of the senses.—Attracted by the tempting show, a shapely human form draws nigh: 'tis *Tannhaüser*, Love's minstrel. He sounds his jubilant Song of Love in joyous challenge, as though to force the wanton witchery to do his bidding.—Wild cries of riot answer him: the rosy cloud grows denser round him, entrancing perfumes hem him in and steal away his senses. In the most seductive of half-lights, his wonder-seeing eye beholds a female form indicible; he hears a voice that sweetly murmurs out the siren-call, which promises contentment of the darer's wildest wishes. *Venus* herself it is, this woman who appears to him.—Then heart and senses burn within him; a fierce, devouring passion fires the blood in all his veins: with irresistible constraint it thrusts him nearer; before the Goddess' self he steps with that canticle of love triumphant, and now he sings it in ecstatic praise of *her*.—As though at wizard spell of his, the wonders of the Venusberg unroll their brightest fill before him: tumultuous shouts and savage cries of joy mount up on every hand; in drunken glee Bacchantes drive their raging dance and drag Tannhaüser to the warm caresses of Love's Goddess, who throws her glowing arms around the mortal drowned with bliss, and bears him where no step dare tread, to the realm of Being-no-more (*Nichtmehrseins*). A scurry, like the sound of the Wild Hunt, and speedily the storm is laid. Merely a wanton whir still pulses in the breeze, a wave of weird voluptuousness, like the sensuous breath of unblest love, still soughs above the spot where impious charms had shed their raptures, and over which the night now broods once more.—But dawn begins to break already: from afar is heard again the Pilgrims' Chant. As this chant draws closer yet and closer, as the day drives farther back the night, that whir and soughing of the air—which had ere-

while sounded like the eerie cries of souls condemned—
now rises, too, to ever gladder waves; so that when the sun
ascends at last in splendour, and the Pilgrims' Chant
proclaims in ecstasy to all the world, to all that lives and
moves thereon, Salvation won, this wave itself swells out
the tidings of sublimest joy. 'Tis the carol of the Venusberg itself, redeemed from curse of impiousness, this cry
we hear amid the hymn of God. So wells and leaps
each pulse of Life in chorus of Redemption; and both dissevered elements, both soul and senses, God and Nature,
unite in the atoning kiss of hallowed Love.

5.

PRELUDE TO "LOHENGRIN."*

FROM out a world of hate and haggling, Love seemed
to have vanished clean away: in no community of men
did it longer shew itself as lawgiver. Yet midst the
empty care for gain and owning, the only orderer of
world-intercourse, the unslayable love-longing of the human
heart began at last to yearn again for stilling of a need
which, the more it chafed and burned beneath the weight
of actuality, the less was able to be satisfied within that
actuality itself. Devout imagination therefore set both
source and bourne of this unfathomable love-stress outside
the actual world, and, longing for the solace of its senses
by a symbol of the Suprasensual, it gave to it a wondrous
shape; under the name of the "Holy Grail" this symbol
soon was yearned and sought for, as a reality existing
somewhere, yet far beyond approach. 'Twas the precious
vase from which the Saviour once had pledged his farewell
to his people, the vessel whereinto his blood had poured

---

* "*Vorspiel*"—in the *N. Z.* (June 17, 1853) our author had called it "*die
Instrumental-Einleitung*," i.e. "the Instrumental Introduction."—TR.

when he suffered crucifixion for his brethren, the cup in which that blood had been preserved in living warmth, a fountain of imperishable Love. Already had this cup of healing been reft from worthless Man, when once a flight of angels brought it back from Heaven's height, to lonely men athirst for Love; committed it to keeping of these men, miraculously blest and strengthened by its presence; and hallowed thus the pure to fight on earth for Love Eternal.—

This wonder-working Coming of the Grail in escort of an angel-host, its committal to the care of chosen men, the tone-poet of "Lohengrin"—a Grail's-knight—selected for the subject of a sketch in Tone, as introduction to his drama, and here he haply may be let depict it to the fancy's eye.—At the beginning, the clear blue air of Heaven seems to condense to a mysterious vision, scarce traceable by the eye of over-earthly yearning, yet holding the enraptured gaze with magic spell; in infinitely soft, but gradually distincter outline, appears the wonder-bringing host of angels, descending slowly from ethereal heights, and bearing in its midst the sacred vessel. As the vision waxes plainer still and plainer, and hovers down towards this vale of Earth, the sweetest fragrance wells from out its wings: entrancing vapours stream from it in clouds of gold, usurping every sense with hallowed awe, and thrust into the throbbing heart's profoundest depth. Now blissful pain, now shuddering delight, transfix the breast; with power resistless all its downtrod seeds of Love swell out to wondrous growth, awakened by the quickening charm: widen as it may, it seems that it must burst at last for vehemence of its desire, its self-surrender, its ardour to dissolve away, as never heart of man had felt before. But this feeling wakes again to highest, happiest bliss, as the holy sight draws ever nearer to the kindled senses; and when at last the Cup itself is bared in all the marvel of reality, and plainly set before the gaze of the elect, when the godlike fluid held within the "Grail" sends forth the sunbeams of sublimest Love, like the shining of a heavenly

fire, and every heart is set a-quivering with its radiance:
then swoon away the seer's senses; to his knees he sinks,
in worship and annihilation. Yet o'er the man thus lost in
Love's delight the Grail now sheds its blessing, and consecrates him to its knightly service: the dazzling flames
are softened down to gentler glory; like a breath of joy
and ecstasy ineffable, it spreads across the earthly vale, and
fills the suppliant's breast with happiness ne'er dreamt
before. Then, smiling as it looks below, the angel-host
wings back its flight to Heaven in tender gladness: the
fount of Love, run dry on Earth, it has brought unto the
world anew; it has left the "Grail" in keeping of pure
mortals, whose hearts Its very Content now has drenched
with blessing. In the clearest light of Heaven's æther
the radiant host melts into distance as it came before.

ON FRANZ LISZT'S SYMPHONIC POEMS.

Über Franz Liszt's Symphonische Dichtungen.

(Brief an M.W.)

This Letter on Liszt's Symphonic Poems, *originally written to the daughter of Princess Wittgenstein on February 15, 1857, from Zurich, was published in the* Neue Zeitschrift *for April 10th of that year. On April 19th Liszt writes to Wagner:* "*Receive my most cordial thanks, and may it be to you a joy to have given me so much and such heartfelt joy. . . . The essential is, that you love me and deem worthy of your sympathy my honest efforts as musician. This you have said in a way which no one else could say it in.*" *On May 8, 1859, Wagner writes to Liszt:* "*Concerning that letter I have recently had a brand-new experience. K[arl] R[itter] had not yet read it; luckily I found it among my papers at Venice, and gave it to him. Afterwards he came to me, and told me he had heard from certain people, not very far away from you, that I had expressed myself evasively in this letter, and taken pains to say nothing really definite about you. He himself had been worried by this, and now, after reading it, was highly delighted to find the enormous importance I had attached to you. So—astonished at the possibility of a misinterpretation—I also read my letter through again, and certainly had to chime-in with K.'s hearty indignation at the incredible stupidity, superficiality and triviality, of those who had found it possible to misunderstand this letter. But I now have taken an oath: not another word will I publish. What we are to one another, we know well enough . . . but the Devil take what we are to the world!*" *To this Liszt replies (May 14, '59):* "*I told you at the time how* sincerely *your letter to M. about the Symphonic Poems had delighted me—as to the twaddle which dulness, triviality and spite have talked about it, it's not worth noticing.*"

Translator's Note.

I ALMOST owe you a somewhat longer chat about our friend and his new orchestral compositions; by word of mouth one can only do this sort of thing in broken sentences, and even for that I am not likely to have another opportunity for some time to come. On several occasions you have expressed the wish to hear my candid, definite estimate of LISZT: to fulfil that wish ought really to place me in a dilemma, since you know that only enemies tell the truth, and the judgment of a friend, especially a friend who owes so much to another as I to *Liszt*, must necessarily appear so tainted with party-feeling as scarcely to rank of any value. Yet I shall not trouble much on that account; for it seems to me that this is one of those prudent maxims wherewith the envious world of mediocrity—or, as you have so wittily called it, "*Mediokratie*"—has girt itself as with an unscalable rampart, whence it may cry to each man of significance: Halt, till I, thy natural foe, have recognised thee! No, I will hold by the experience that whoever waits for recognition by his foes, before he can make up his mind about himself, must have indeed his share of patience, but little ground for self-reliance. Please take what I shall tell you, then, as the testimony of a man whom nothing but a full heart can bring to speech, and who therefore speaks as confidently as though there either were no maxims in the world at all, or all were on his side.

But something else perplexes me: namely, whatever is there for me to write you? You were a witness to my wonderful uplifting by Liszt's production and performance of his new works. You saw how I was thrilled with joy, that at last a thing like this should have been created and set before me. No doubt you also noticed how chary I often was with words, and you surely held this for nothing but the hush of deep emotion? And such, at first, it really was; yet I must tell you, this hush of mine is now maintained with consciousness, through my having come to a more and more fixed conviction that the own-est essence of our thoughts * is unconveyable in direct ratio as they gain in depth and compass and thus withdraw beyond the bounds of Speech—of Speech, which does not belong to our own real selves, but is given us second-hand to help our converse with an outer world that, at bottom, can only understand us clearly when we place ourselves entirely on the level of life's vulgar needs. The more our thoughts * depart from that level, the more laborious becomes the effort to express them: until at last the philosopher, at risk of being not understood at all, uses language merely in its inverse sense, or the artist takes refuge in the wondrous workshop of his art, quite useless for the life of everyday, to forge himself an expression for what even then—and in the best of cases—can be understood by none but those who already share with him his thought. Now Music is indisputably the fittest medium for the thought (*Anschauung*) that cannot be conveyed by Speech, and one well might call the inmost essence of all Beholding (*Anschauung*) Music. If, then, when Liszt placed his works before me I received that message which Music alone can convey, the circuit was completed; and to me it must appear not only foolish, but impossible, to try to speak about That which had become music for very reason that it could *not* be spoken out. Who has not already attempted to describe

---

* "Anschauungen"—the dictionary (Flügel's) gives us "contemplation; view; inspection; intuitive vision; intuition" (to which I may add "beholdings") as the English equivalents of this word; none of them is satisfactory when taken alone, and therefore, while provisionally adopting "thoughts," I reserve the right to use the German term wherever expedient.—TR.

musical impressions by means of words? Only those who have absolutely not received the true impression, can imagine they have succeeded; but whoever has been so full of that impression as Liszt, for instance, when he wrote about music, has had to battle with the same huge difficulties as he, and, after seeking to achieve the impossible through an art of verbal composition (*sprachbildlichen Ausdruckes*) such as could stand at behest of none but the musical genius, has had to recognise that he has really made himself intelligible to none but the like-minded musician, and least of all to the purely literary reader; for the latter has rewarded Liszt, of all men, by rejecting his words and phrases as unintelligible, distasteful, extravagant, and so forth.

What, then, am I to say to you? The whole upshot of the matter will haply have to be a somewhat detailed exposition of the impossibility of *saying* anything. Yet this will rather apply to the inner kernel of the thing; as for the formal portion of an artwork, the side it turns towards the outer world, our connoisseurs and æsthetes have indeed collected so rich a store of terms and epithets, that one does not get truly embarrassed until asked to describe the thing which all these gentlemen have never clapped their eyes on. So I will talk to you about that side of Liszt's works which brings them into possible contact with that world's perceptive faculties. With this, however, you must be content; for all the rest, I refer you —to the profoundness of my silence at the hearing.

I will begin with the outmost thing of all, with what the world sees when it looks at Liszt. It knows him as a Virtuoso, in all the glamour of the most brilliant and successful of careers as such; and that's enough for it, to shew it how to take him. But one fine day Liszt upsets all its reckonings, by quitting that career and making his definite appearance as Composer: what on earth is it to think? The most inconvenient thing of all is, that such a thing had never occurred before, particularly with a musician

who had become quite classical. It had happened, indeed,
that after making a heap of money, for instance, a virtuoso
had finally yielded to the ambitious wish to play a little at
composing; one had forgiven it as an amiable weakness,
and so one decides to pardon the celebrated pianoforte-hero
in this case, too, for his latest whim, but naturally with a
regret that he should not rather go on playing the piano.
In this sweet frame of mind one kindly passes over his new
great compositions in total silence, and only the most em-
bittered sentinels of classic music so far forget themselves
as to give rein to their ill humour. Let us not be surprised
at this; it would really be suspicious if things had suddenly
turned out otherwise. Which of ourselves was not tongue-
tied also, at the first? And yet we must therefore tax
ourselves with not having gone deep enough into Liszt's
nature before, or at least with not having come to a clear
enough conception of it. Whoever had frequent occasion
to hear Liszt play Beethoven, for instance—particularly in
a friendly circle—must surely have always been struck with
the fact that there was no question here of re-production,
but of genuine production. To accurately lay down the
line that parts both functions, is much harder than one
commonly assumes; thus much, however, has grown clear
to me, that to be able to reproduce Beethoven one must oneself be also able to produce. True, it might be impossible
to make those people understand this, who never in their
lives have heard anything but our ordinary concert-performances and virtuoso-renderings of Beethovenian works;
into the nature and worth whereof I have gained in time so
sad an insight, that I prefer to wound no one by pursuing
the topic farther. On the other hand I ask all who have
heard, for instance, Opus 106 or 111 of Beethoven's (the
two great sonatas in B and C) played by Liszt in a private
circle, what they previously knew of these creations and
what they then discovered in them? If this was a mere
reproduction, it was at least of infinitely greater worth than
all the sonatas, reproducing Beethoven, which have been
"produced" by our pianoforte-composers in imitation of

those still badly-understood works. For this was the peculiarity of Liszt's procedure, that what the others trumped up with pen and paper *he* made the piano speak for him. Yet who will deny that even the greatest and most original master was but a reproducer in his earliest period? Only, we must remember that so long as even the greatest genius merely reproduces, his compositions can never gain the value and importance of the works reproduced and the masters who wrote them, but full worth and full significance enter first with definite exhibition of originality. But Liszt's doings in his first, his reproductive period, surpassed all previous achievements of the kind, in that he was the first to place the worth and significance of the works of his forerunners in their fullest light, and thus soared up to nearly the same height as the composer whom he reproduced. This peculiarity of his has been wellnigh overlooked, for reason of its novelty; and here we have the secret of the present surprise at Liszt's new appearance, which in truth is nothing but the announcement of the maturing of this artist's productivity.

I tell you all this, since only through the above reflections have I myself at last gained clearness on the subject and the surprising problem it involves. Perhaps, however, it is unnecessary for me to tell this to precisely *you*; for, with the same instinct that guided Liszt in his development, you will surely also have divined the secret, whereas we men—having always so much to do with ourselves, though there is really nothing to be done with us—often stand abashed before you women in such cases. Nevertheless you may think it not unworth the while to share the man's advantage, too, insofar as there is any advantage in his bringing to the consciousness of himself and others, though often very late, what the women have long since felt unconsciously. This, in fact, is the only meaning my whole letter can have for you.

So, upon his own, uncustomary path, Liszt seems to me to have come within the last ten years to the full ripeness of his creative-force, through his productivity as composer proper. If very few can comprehend that path itself, equally few are in a position to grasp the phenomenon which suddenly presents itself at its goal. As said above, it would be suspicious and perplexing, were this otherwise. But now there comes another point: supposing one has been irresistibly driven to see the worth of this phenomenon, the uncommon richness of inventive power which at once confronts us in these great tone-works brought before us as by a stroke of the magician's wand, then one might at first be bewildered again by their *form*; and, after one's first head-shaking had been devoted to the possibility of our friend's true calling as composer, one's second might arise from a comparison with the things we have been accustomed to.—You see, obedient to my motto, I am approaching my subject entirely from without, from the direction whence the world will have to approach it; I thus am touching merely what permits of being expressed in words, and keep for my conclusion the point on which it's probable that nothing will let itself be said. Onward, then—to " Form " !—

Ah! * * *, were there no Form, there would certainly be no artworks, but quite certainly no art-judges either; and this is so obvious to these latter that the anguish of their soul cries out for Form, whereas the easy-going artist—though neither could he, as just said, exist without Form in the long run—troubles his head mighty little about it when at work. And how comes this about? Apparently because the artist, without his knowing it, is always creating forms, whereas these gentlemen create neither forms nor anything else. So that their cry looks very much as though they expected the artist, beyond his creation of the whole thing, to prepare a little tidbit for the gentlemen, who otherwise would have nothing at all for themselves. Indeed this polite attention has always been shewn them by those who never could turn out anything for *themselves*, and therefore helped themselves along with — forms; and what that means we know well enough, don't you think? Swords without blades! But when there comes a man who can forge him blades (I have just been in the smithy of my young Siegfried, you see!) the boobies cut their fingers by fumbling at them in the same way as they clutched the proffered empty hilts before; then they naturally grow cross because the spiteful smith retains the hilt within his hand, as is necessary for bearing arms, and they cannot even get a sight of the only thing the others had reached out to them. Look you, that's the whole history of this outcry about absence of Form! But has anybody ever seen a sabre borne without a hilt? Does not its swift and steady slash bear witness, on the contrary, that it is mounted in a good strong hilt? No doubt, this hilt does not become visible and tangible for others, until the sword has been laid down; when the master is dead and his weapon has been hung up in the armoury, at last one perceives the handle (*Griff*) too, and haply plucks it from the blade—as an abstraction ("*Begriff*")—yet can't imagine that the next man who sallies forth to fight must necessarily bear his sword-blade also in a hilt. So blind are people, and that's about it:—let's wash our hands of them!

Yes, * * *, 'tis true enough: Liszt has indeed no Form. But let us rejoice thereat; for if folk saw the "hilt," we should have to fear that at least he was bearing his sword reversed, and in this evil, hostile world that would be a little too much gallantry, since one must give people a taste of the edge to make them believe there really is a blade stuck firmly in the hilt. Yet enough of jesting, though we still will dwell a little on this "Form."

After hearing one of Liszt's new orchestral works, I was involuntarily struck with admiration at its happy designation as a "symphonic poem." And indeed the invention of this term has more to say for itself than one might think; for it could only have arisen with the invention of the new art-form itself. Perhaps this may sound strange to you; wherefore I will relate my definite views about the thing.

In the first place, the general compass and specific titles of the separate works recall the "overtures" of previous masters, which had already thriven to a considerable length. What an unhappy name this "Overture" was, especially for tone-works suited for almost any other place than the opening of a dramatic representation, everyone must have already felt who saw himself obliged to keep on giving it to his music-pieces, particularly since Beethoven's great example. But this usage was not the only fetter on his freedom; a far deeper coercion lay within the form itself, the form he was employing. Whoever wishes to rightly account for the speciality of this form, must study the history of the Overture from its earliest origin; he will be astonished to find that it arose from nothing but a dance, which was played in the orchestra as introduction to a scenic piece; and he will be filled with marvel at what has come of it in course of time and through the inventive genius of great masters.—Not only the Overture, however, but every other independent instrumental tone-piece owes its form to the Dance or March; and a series of such pieces, as also a piece in which several dance-forms were combined, was called a "Symphony." The Symphony's formal germ survives till this day in its third movement, the Menuet or Scherzo, where it suddenly appears in utmost naïvety, as though to tell the secret of the Form of all the movements. Now I have no wish to depreciate this form, especially as one owes to it so many marvellous products; I will merely observe that it is a very definite form and easy to be made irrecognisable if liberties are taken with it, and therefore demands a strict attention from those who would fain express themselves therein—pretty much as Dance itself requires a strict attention from the dancers. What it was possible to express in this form, we see to our utmost delight in the Symphony of Beethoven, and expressed the most beautifully and satisfyingly just where he governed his expression entirely by that form. On the other hand it was always disturbing, the instant it was employed—as in the Overture—to accommodate an Idea whose enunciation rebelled against the stricter rule of Dance. In place of *development*, such as is necessary for a dramatic subject, this rule demands that *change* (Wechsel) inherent in all forms arisen from the March or Dance: namely the following of a softer, quieter period after the livelier motion of the commencement, and finally the repetition of that livelier motion; and that for reasons deeply seated in the nature of the thing. Without such a change and such a repetition a Symphonic movement, in the hitherto-accepted meaning of the term, is not so much as thinkable; and what is openly shewn in the third movement of a symphony, as Menuet, Trio, and repetition of the Menuet, may be proved to exist—though in greater disguise, and particularly in the second movement inclining more to the variation-form—as the backbone of the form of all the other movements. Now it will be obvious that, in the conflict of a dramatic idea with this form, the necessity must at once arise to either sacrifice the development (the idea) to the alternation (the form), or the latter to the former. As you may remember, I once set up Gluck's Overture to Iphigenia in Aulis as a model, because the master, with surest feeling of the nature of the problem now before us, had here so admirably understood to open his drama with a play of moods and their opposites, in keeping with the Overture-form, and not with a development impossible in that form. That the great masters who came after him felt this to be a limitation, however, we may see distinctly by the overtures of Beethoven; the composer knew of what an infinitely richer portraiture his music was capable, he felt equal to carrying out the idea of Development; and nowhere do we find this more plainly evidenced, than in the great Overture to Leonora. But he who has eyes, may see precisely by this overture how detrimental to the master the maintenance of the traditional form was bound to be. For who, at all capable of understanding such a work, will not agree with me when I assert that the repetition of the first part, after the middle section, is a weakness which distorts the idea of the work almost past all understanding; and that the more, as everywhere else, and particularly in the coda, the master is obviously governed by nothing but the dramatic development? But whoso has brains and lack of prejudice enough to see this, will have to admit that the evil could only have been avoided by entirely giving up that repetition; an abandonment, however, which would have done away with the overture-form—i.e. the original, merely suggestive (*nur motivirte*), symphonic dance-form—and have constituted the departure-point for creating a new form.

What, now, would that new form be?—Of necessity a form dictated by the subject of portrayal and its logical development. And what would be this subject?—A poetic motive. So!—prepare to be shocked!—" Programme-music."

That looks a perilous conclusion; and whoever chanced to hear it, might raise an outcry about the suggested abolition of music's independence. Heigho! let us examine a little closer what this cry, this alarm may have to say for itself.—This most superb, incomparable, most independent and peculiar of all the arts,—the art of Music,—were it possible for it ever to be injured, save by bunglers never consecrated in its sanctuary? Do they mean to tell us that Liszt, the most musical of all musicians to me conceivable, could be that sort of bungler? Hear my creed: *Music can never and in no possible alliance cease to be the highest, the redeeming art.* It is of her nature, that what all the other arts but hint at, through her and in her becomes the most undoubtable of certainties, the most direct and definite of truths. Look at the very coarsest dance, listen to the vilest doggerel: its Music (if only she has taken it seriously, and not intentionally caricatured it) ennobles even that; for, just by reason of her own peculiar earnestness, she is of so chaste and wonderful a nature that she transfigures everything she touches. But it is equally manifest, equally sure, that Music will only let herself be seen in forms erst borrowed from an aspect or utterance of Life, which, originally strangers to Music, obtain through her their deepest meaning as if through revelation of the music latent in them. Nothing is less absolute (as to its appearance in Life, of course) than Music, and the champions of an Absolute Music evidently don't know what they're talking about; to utterly confound them, one would only have to bid them shew us a music without the form which it has borrowed from either bodily motion or spoken verse (as regards the causal connexion).*—Now we have recognised the march- and dance-form as the irremovable foundation of pure Instrumental-music, and we have seen this form lay down the rules of construction for even the most complex tone-works of every kind so rigorously, that any departure from them, such as the non-repetition of the first period, was considered a transgression into formlessness and had therefore to be avoided by the daring Beethoven himself—to his otherwise great detriment. On this point, then, we are at one, and admit that in this human world it was necessary to afford divine Music a point of attachment, nay—as we have seen—a 'conditioning moment,' before ever she could come to an appearance. I ask now, whether March or Dance, with all the mental pictures of those acts, can supply a worthier motive of Form than, for instance, a mental picture (*Vorstellung*) of the main and characteristic features in the deeds and sufferings of an Orpheus, a Prometheus, and so forth? I further ask: if Music's manifestation is so governed in advance by Form, as I have already proved to you, whether it is not nobler and less trammelling for her to take this Form from an imagined Orpheus or Prometheus motive, than from an imagined march or dance motive?—Surely no one will have an instant's doubt about it, but rather allege the difficulty of obtaining an intelligible musical form from these higher, more individualised concepts (*Vorstellungen*), since it has hitherto appeared impossible to group them for the ordinary understanding (I don't know whether I am expressing myself correctly) without employing those lower, more general motives of form.

The ground of this apprehension consists herein: un-

* "(dem causalen Zusammenhange nach)."

qualified or fantastic musicians, denied that higher consecration, have set before us tone-works departing to such an extent from the customary Symphonic (dance-) form, of which they simply had not gained the mastery, that the composer's aim stayed absolutely unintelligible if his bizarre dance-forms were not followed step by step with an explanatory programme. Hereby we felt that Music had been openly degraded, though solely because on the one hand an unworthy idea had been given her to express, on the other, this idea itself had not come to clear expression ; which mostly arose from all its scanty stock of intelligibility having been derived from the traditional, but arbitrarily mangled dance-form, and bungled in the application. But let us not trouble our head with these caricatures, which are to be found in every art you choose to name ; let us keep to the infinitely richer, more developed powers of Expression which Music has reaped from the efforts of great geniuses, down to our own times. We must place our doubt, then, less in Music's capability (for things undreamt have been already compassed in the older cramping forms) than in the artist's possession of the needful poetico-musical attribute, the gift of beholding the poetic subject in such a way as to serve the musician for moulding his intelligible musical forms. And here in very deed resides the secret, and the problem ; its solution could be reserved for none but a highly-gifted chosen man, who, whilst out and out musician, is at like time out and out a seer (*anschauender Dichter*). What I mean, it is difficult to make clear ; I leave to our daily increasing body of great æsthetes, to puzzle out its dialectic term.* Thus much I know, however, that everyone endowed with head and heart will understand me when he hears Franz Liszt's " Symphonic Poems," his " Faust," his " Dante " ; for it is these, that were the first to clear my notions of the problem itself.

I pardon everybody who has hitherto doubted the benefit of a new art-form for instrumental music, for I must own to having so fully shared that doubt as to join

* Hanslick is meant, of course.—TR.

with those who saw in our Programme-music a most unedifying spectacle—whereby I felt the drollness of my situation, as I myself was classed among just the programme-musicians, and cast into one pot with them. Whilst listening to the best of this sort, nay, often even works of genius, it had always happened that I so completely lost the musical thread that by no manner of exertion could I re-find and knit it up again. This occurred to me quite recently with the love-scene, so entrancing in its principal motives, of our friend Berlioz' "Romeo and Juliet" symphony: the great fascination which had come over me during the development of the chief-motive, was dispelled in the further course of the movement, and sobered down to an undeniable malaise; I discovered at once that, while I had lost the musical thread (i.e. the logical and lucid play of definite motives), I now had to hold on to scenic motives not present before my eye, nor even so much as indicated in the programme. Indisputably these motives existed in the famous balcony-scene of Shakespeare's; but in that they had all been faithfully retained, and in the exact order given them by the dramatist, lay the great mistake of the composer. The latter, if he wished to use this scene as the motive of a symphonic poem, ought to have felt that, for expressing pretty much the same idea, the Dramatist must lay hands on quite other means than the Musician; he stands much nearer to the life of everyday, and is intelligible solely when the idea with which he presents us is clothed in an Action whose various component 'moments' so closely resemble some incident of that life, that each spectator fancies he is also living through it. The Musician, on the contrary, looks quite away from the incidents of ordinary life, entirely upheaves its details and its accidentals, and sublimates whatever lies within it to its quintessence of emotional-content— to which alone can Music give a voice, and Music only. A true musical poet, therefore, would have presented Berlioz with this scene in a thoroughly compact *ideal* form; and in any case a Shakespeare, had he meant to hand it over to a Berlioz for musical reproduction, would have written it just as differently as Berlioz' composition should now be different, to make it understandable *per se*. We have been speaking of one of the gifted musician's happiest inspirations, however, and my opinion of his less happy ones might easily set me dead against this line of work if, on the other hand, it had not brought to light such perfect things as the smaller pictures of his "*Scène aux champs*," his "*Marche des pèlerins*" etc., which shew us to our amazement what may be accomplished in this mode.

Why I adduced this instance from the "love-scene," was merely to give you a notion of the extreme difficulty of solving the problem, and to shew you that in reality it involves a *secret*—comparable to that invisible "hilt" of which I spoke above, but which, in view of the blade's effects, I assume as held securely in Liszt's hand, and indeed so peculiarly fitted to just *his* hand that it is altogether hidden from our eyes therein. But this secret is withal the essence of the Individuality and its way of looking at things (*der ihr eigenen Anschauung*), which would forever remain a mystery to us, did it not reveal itself in the gifted individual's artworks. Farther than this artwork and its impression on ourselves—at bottom, again, a matter of our individuality—we cannot go; the amount of generally-applicable artistic rules to be drawn therefrom is precious little, and those who think to make much capital out of it, have simply missed the main affair. Thus much, however, is certain: Liszt's way of looking at a poetic subject must needs be fundamentally different from that of Berlioz, and indeed must be of that kind which, in speaking of the Romeo scene, I attributed to the Poet who meant to hand his subject over to the Musician for carrying out.

You see, I now have got so near the heart of the matter, that I cannot wisely say much more; we have reached the point where the one individuality imparts its secret to the other, and he who could expatiate aloud thereon, must have taken very little up, as one certainly can blab no secrets save those one has not understood. If, then, I am silent as to *what* Liszt imparted to me through his Symphonic Poems, I will merely conclude by telling you something about the formal side of their message.—In this regard I was above all struck by the great, the speaking plainness with which the subject (*der Gegenstand*) proclaimed itself to me: naturally this was no longer the subject as described by the Poet in words, but that quite other aspect of it, unreachable by any manner of description, whose intangible and vaporous quality makes us wonder how it can display itself so uniquely clear, distinct, compact and unmistakable, to our Feeling. With Liszt, this masterly grip in the musical conception speaks out with such a puissance at the very outset of the piece, that after the first sixteen bars I often could not restrain the astonished cry: "Enough, I have it all!" This I deem so prominent a feature in the works of Liszt that, despite the aversion shewn by a certain party to recognise Liszt's prowess on this field, I haven't the slightest fear as to their finding a very speedy entrance to the affections of the Public proper. The difficulties which stand in the way of dramatic compositions, due to the far greater complexity of their media of expression, are smaller in the case of more purely orchestral works; our bands are mostly good, and where Liszt himself—or one of his more familiar pupils—can conduct the performances, the same success will always follow as Liszt found, for instance, with our simple-hearted people of St Gall, who so touchingly expressed their astonishment that compositions which they had been warned against as formless and chaotic, should have struck them as so swift and easy of understanding. As you know, this confirmed my good opinion of the Public — though nothing but a sudden shock can avail to lift it above its wonted view-point, and the effect can neither be lasting nor react upon the life of everyday, for very reason of its violence.* Nevertheless the evidence of such an uplifting remains the artist's solitary guerdon from without, and in any case he must guard against expecting it from every person, after the event, for he might find the individual sobered down and only too prone to criticise. Thus on the next day, even after being carried away by the performance, it perhaps will occur to many a musician to pounce upon this or that "peculiarity," "harshness," or "abruptness"; and particularly the rare, unwonted harmonic progressions may *then* give many people ground for hesitation. One might inquire how it came to pass then, that they found nothing to offend them during the performance itself, but simply abandoned themselves to the fascination of a new and unwonted impression, which we may well opine could not have been produced without the aid of those "peculiarities" and so forth? As a matter of fact, it is the characteristic of every new, unwonted and determinant impression, that it has about it something strange to us, something which rouses our mistrust; and this, again, must reside in that secret of the Individuality. In respect of what we are, we are surely all alike, and the race (*die Gattung*) may be the only true thing here; but in respect of how we look at things we are so unlike that, taken strictly, we remain forever strangers to each other. But in this consists the Individuality, and however objective may have been its path of evolution— i.e. however wide-embracing our field of vision (*Anschauung*) may have grown, however filled by nothing but the Object —there will always cleave to that *Anschauung* a something which remains peculiar to the special individuality. Yet only through this one thing of its own, does the personal *Anschauung* impart itself to others; whosoever would make the one his own, can do so only by taking up the other;

---

* "Sie wissen, dass diess meine gute Meinung über das Publikum bestätigte, von dem wir allerdings nichts Anderes, als eine plötzliche Erhebung aus seinem gewohnten Anschauungswesen verlangen dürfen, welche eben desshalb nicht nachhaltig und auf das gemeine Leben rückwirkend sein kann, weil sie im Grunde eine sehr gewaltsame ist."

to see what another individual sees, we must see it with his eyes—and this takes place through Love alone. Wherefore by our very love for a great artist we as good as say that, in taking his creation to our heart, we adopt withal those individual peculiarities of view which made that creation possible to him.*—Now, as I have nowhere more distinctly felt this love's enriching and informing power, than in my love for Liszt, in consciousness thereof I fain would bid those doubters: Only trust, and ye will marvel at the gain your trust will bring you! Should you falter, should you fear betrayal, then look a little closer *who* he is for whom I ask your trust. Know ye a musician more musical than Liszt? who holds within his breast the powers of Music in richer, deeper store than he? who feels more finely and more delicately, who knows and 'cans' more, whom Nature has more highly gifted and who has cultivated more untiringly those gifts, than he? Can ye name to me no second, oh! trust ye then this only one (who, moreover, is far too noble a man to dupe you) and rest assured that through that trust ye there will be the most enriched where now, for lack of trust, ye fear contamination!

I can say nothing further to you, * * *, and even the last few lines I have no longer addressed to yourself, but to quite another sort of folk, so that you will hardly know what to do with them, unless it should come into your head to make them public.—Indeed, upon glancing through my letter again, I find I have spoken less to you than to those I felt so eager to address some years ago. When I think of the confusion I gave rise to at the time, I cannot but regard myself as fallen back into an old offence, and, seeing how badly I came off before, I really ought to be more careful. So I have earned a punishment for my imprudence, and, if you fancy that by so doing you will damage no one

---

* "Wenn wir einen grossen Künstler lieben, so sagen wir daher hiermit, dass wir dieselben individuellen Eigenthümlichkeiten, die ihm jene schöpferische Anschauung ermöglichten, in die Aneignung der Anschauung selbst mit einschliessen."

but myself, I suppose I must submit to your handing this letter to the printer. Should you feel too friendly toward me to wish to do me any harm, and prefer to have me punished incognito, then you might name some other person as its author—perhaps Herr *Fétis*; people will believe anything of him, you know.

But above all greet my *Franz* for me, and tell him the old, old story, that I love him!

Your

RICHARD WAGNER.

EPILOGUE

TO THE

"NIBELUNG'S RING."

Epilogischer Bericht

über die

Umstände und Schicksale,

welche die Ausführung des Bühnenfestspieles „Der Ring des Nibelungen" bis zur Veröffentlichung der Dichtung desselben begleiteten.

This article was originally dated " Luzern, 7. Dezember 1871," and published in pamphlet form (E. W. Fritzsch, Leipzig, 1872) under the title : " Bericht an den Deutschen Wagner-Verein über die Umstände und Schicksale, welche die Ausführung des Bühnenfestspieles '*Der Ring des Nibelungen*' begleiteten" — *i.e.* "*Report to the German Wagner Union on the circumstances and fates which have attended the execution of the* 'Ring des Nibelungen.'" *It will be observed that the title in the* Gesammelte Schriften *(vol. vi, p.* 365), *as given overleaf, differs inasmuch as it omits the reference to the* " *Wagner-Verein," limits the report to the period terminating with the poem's publication* (1863), *and becomes an* "*epilogue." These changes are explained, partly by the fact that the article is immediately preceded by the* Ring *poem itself, partly by Wagner's having reserved its closing section for republication in vol. ix* Ges. Schr. *together with other matters more directly pertaining to the concrete "Bayreuth idea." As one or two sentences point to a conclusion not forthcoming in the article as it stands at present, I may add that the other section deals with King Ludwig's coming to the author's rescue; with the opposition encountered at Munich; with the temporary abandonment of the* Ring *in favour of* Die Meistersinger ; *with the performance of portions of the work* (Das Rheingold *and* Die Walküre, *at Munich), against his inclination; and finally with the Wagner Verein, which had just been started by Emil Heckel, of Mannheim, in response to a slightly earlier pamphlet of Wagner's* (April, 1871), *likewise incorporated in vol. ix* Ges. Schr. *The closing apostrophe, however, has not been reprinted in either volume ; I have therefore appended it as a footnote to page* 260, *to which it more immediately refers.*

TRANSLATOR'S NOTE.

HOW I fell upon the extravagant idea of planning and working out the Bühnenfestspiel* "*der Ring des Nibelungen*," I have already intimated at the close of an earlier "Communication to my Friends." † As regards the subject itself, that idea had sprung from a more and more earnest consideration of the extraordinary fertility of the 'stuff,' and had shaped itself into the wish to possess myself entirely of it. As regards the character of the consideration which I devoted to the stuff, that also will become plain enough to anybody who will honour the second section, in particular, of my lengthy treatise on "Opera and Drama" with a serious inspection.

Harder would it be for me, to explain the somewhat presumptuous mood that prompted the task and fortified me in the straining of my whole productive forces, through a long series of years, to the prosecution of a work which every man of practical experience was bound to deem inexecutable at any of our opera-houses. Everyone was astounded that I, of all people, after my eminently practical experience, should be deluded into so monstrous an undertaking. True, I replied that with *this* work I was completely turning my back on the modern opera-house, and that it was just my repugnance against any further commerce with our Opera-house that had played no insignificant part in inspiring me with that extravagant idea. People thought it unnecessary to take my reply in sober earnest. Was I the man to give up all notion of a live performance of such a work, when I was doing my utmost to put life into its smallest feature? No: one felt bound to suppose that, seeing the endless pains I was taking to prepare my work for drastic execu-

---

* Stage-festival-play.—TR.
† See volume iv of these *Gesammelte Schriften und Dichtungen*. — R. WAGNER.—Volume i of "Richard Wagner's Prose Works" (Eng.).—TR.

tion, I must inwardly be counting on a quite excellent production and its consequent success. To this I might very well assent, yet still persist that I had no thought of a performance at our theatres. On the contrary, I already informed my closer friends of the plan I made public later in the Preface to the poem of my Bühnenfestspiel; they listened to me, but didn't know what to make of it. Whoever was actively disposed towards me, thought needful to suggest a compromise with the existing Theatre and its belongings. I was told that new actors and singers, such as I demanded, could not be conjured out of the ground or clouds; that even if some rich man, for example, were found to offer himself as patron for the execution of my idea, I still should have to put up with the existing means of representation; why, then, should I not go to work first-hand at a place where they existed? —So we were back at once in the old, old groove, and only my head was full of mad chimeras!

From time to time since then, I have given myself no little trouble to point out the black spot in the organisation of our theatres, to expose its causes, and prove its demoralising consequences on every hand. But everything stays as it was. For that's the German all over, so soon as it is a question of Art, and particularly the Theatre—fields whereon he loses all that sturdy earnestness for which he is so famous. Appeal to his sense of honour, and he will smile benignly: for really, now, you can't be meaning "honour"; assail his common sense, shew him by rule of three that our Theatre is squandering in the most disgraceful manner, not only the artistic, but also the financial means at stake—he will smile again, this time a roguish smile, and tell you it's no affair of his. Out-argue him, spread your facts before him, nay—shock him : he's braver even than his soldiers; they fall, when they are shot; but he, one first must push him over like the Russians.—

This and much else kept rising afresh in my mind. That plan I had imparted to my friends; but in the depths of my heart I fed my obstinacy on a still more

EPILOGUE TO THE "NIBELUNG'S RING." 259

desperate idea. Time seemed nothing to me, and true Being lay beyond the province of its laws. Among all my acquaintances it was I who possessed the largest practical experience on the field of musical dramaturgy, as also the most unquestioned skill in applying that experience. In a large measure it was the aptitude acquired hereby, that had enabled me to conceive my sweeping project. So I would carry out my work and notify each smallest detail, to hold it ready for the right day coming, perhaps long after I was dead. Since I had no kind of pleasure in the Existing, and felt myself in nowise pledged to its continuance, I thought of the possibility that some day—perchance at dead of night—a state of things might supervene that would put an end to many fine affairs, and among them to our excellent German theatres. In my own way, I pictured this regrettable event not undivertingly: the lot reserved for our Theatre-Intendants and Directors troubled me little, for at any rate they must understand something or other better than the Theatre, and so they would not lack for further and more suitable employment. Neither did the generality of our play-actors and singers demand my too great sympathy; they could be most admirably provided for, as tailors, hairdressers, counterjumpers, or even bookkeepers and cashiers. But least of all did I bewail our wild comedians and musicians proper*; wherever I had found a vestige of some consolation for the stage, it had been among these lost children of our modern social system: degraded to a human caricature by the utterly stupid management of our theatres, midst them alone had I met true talent and genuine calling to the wondrous mysteries of theatric art. One had only to lift them into consciousness of the dignity of their avocation; and nothing else was needed for this, but setting them on the right road to discharge a worthy task: when lo! the riddle of their mission in life, of their so problematic being,

---

* "Musiker"—probably here used in its sense of "bandsmen"; "wild" being employed as in the case of "wild flowers."—TR.

was solved at once. And for these—whom I saw roving like gipsies through the chaos of a new commercial order of the world—I now would plant my banner. Upon it should be written somewhat this: " Shew the world what ye poor useless waifs can be to it, if only ye hold yourselves before it as its faithful mirror!"

Many years have elapsed since the time when, in such a mood, I began to carry out my work, and I cannot say that my views with regard to its some-day representation have altered in any essential; even that banner, in a weightiest sense, will have to remain.* However, I will give a hasty review on the one hand, of the fortunes of my work itself, on the other, of the new experiences and lights which have brought me kindlier, more hopeful prospects of arriving safely at my journey's goal.

It was impossible for me to keep the secret of my monstrous scheme entirely to myself; if I forewent the public, the acquiescence of the Folk, at least I could not dispense with the confederacy of more familiar friends. I had the completed poem printed at my own expense, in a very small edition, and sent out copies to my nearer and more distant acquaintances. My disinclination to having it regarded and judged as a literary product was so pronounced, that I expressly safeguarded myself against this in a short preface, in view of the chance that one of the copies given to my friends might fall into the hands of

* As mentioned in my introductory note, the original article ended with the following paragraph :—

" In this sense [of the " German spirit "] I greet the ' German Wagner Union,' which I hear has just been formed at the free instigation of devoted friends of my art and the idea I champion. If once, in my despair, I thought I should have to plant my banner on the ruins of a general cataclysm—to assemble the nobler remnant rescued from a Culture at enmity with Art : to my unspeakable satisfaction I now have only to assemble the healthy elements of the art I had descried, under that selfsame banner which floats above the so auspiciously resuscitated German Empire, in order from the noblest factors of a long neglected truly-German Culture to build up forthwith, nay, merely to unveil the building long prepared-for unbeknown within the German Spirit, by drawing off its last false wrappage—which, like a tattered garment, soon shall moulder into dust, and its threadbare rags dissolve into the aura of a new and purer atmosphere of Art."—Tr.

some person unacquainted and unconnected with me—whom I thus desired to consider himself warned from dragging my poem before the tribunal of the public press. The said abstinence has been observed in the most literal sense down to the present day, though I have since found reason to change my mind in this particular.

As, however, I shall have to return to this point in the further course of my report, for the present I will recount the experiences which taught me that my poem had after all not stayed quite unregarded in remoter circles. While people held themselves committed by myself to ignore this certainly remarkable phenomenon, of a cycle of Nibelungen-dramas from the pen of a musician, they felt perfectly justified in going farther, and *secreting* it at all costs. Before my Nibelungen-poem was printed and distributed, at the beginning of the year 1853, the 'stuff' of the medieval Nibelungenlied, so far as I can ascertain, had only once been turned into a stage-piece; that was a long time ago, by Raupach in his prosy fashion,* and it had been performed in Berlin, as such, without success. However, some time before its private publication, certain portions of my poem, as also my plans with regard to this Nibelungen-stuff, had reached the notice and mostly the ridicule of the journals, apropos of my negotiations on the point with *Franz Liszt*, at that time officially engaged at Weimar. It soon transpired that I had made a particularly "lucky find" with the choice of my stuff, a "find" which others might feel the more disposed to appropriate as my undertaking must at any rate be considered, and above all declared, a quite unworkable chimera. A first symptom of the notice bestowed on my lucky find was the speedy appearance of a grand opera "die Nibelungen," by the Berlin Kapellmeister *H. Dorn*,† in which a popular prima donna

---

* "*Der Nibelungen Hort*," 1834. Previously to this there had been Fouqué's trilogy, "*Der Held des Norden*," published in Berlin, 1808-10. —Tr.

† Performed for the first time, at Weimar, on Jan. 22, 1854; the libretto, in five acts, was written by E. Gerber.—Tr.

is said to have made a great effect by springing upon the stage on horseback. Soon after, the "Nibelungen" began to stir among our Literary-poets, who suddenly found themselves prompted to adapt this so obviously national stuff for the stage, for which it hitherto had seemed so little fitted; till at last there actually appeared a rhapsodist * among them, to go about the country giving very lively readings of whole cycles of Nibelungen-epics, clad completely in the primal garment of the Edda—as I learn from the newspapers.

It would be more than presumptuous, because totally incorrect and as good as impossible, were I to flatter myself that I had exercised the smallest influence on the labours of my rivals in this Nibelungen business : so far as I know, those theatrical poets had not felt called to imitate my exhaustive studies of the myth in question—studies which had been the first to set its figures before me in a light at all profitable for Drama. As it would evince a very superficial notice of my work on their part, it would rather be a matter of regret to me that I had not been able to rouse these gentlemen—by far more closely concerned with literary research—to a profounder consideration of their subject, had I not more reason to conclude that they had passed it by in cold contempt. So it would seem that my project's mere name † had determined them, out of sheer respect for the admittedly important stuff, to save it from the shame of being set before the German public by a musician. In this sense one appears to have made the best job one could of it, and hastened to give the theatre-public something from the Nibelungenlied about "grim Hagen" and "vengeful Grimmhilde," in the old-accustomed, though not particularly effective manner.

* Wilhelm Jordan, who began his peripatetic recitals in 1865 ; his epic, "*Nibelunge*," was in two portions, "*Sigfriedsage*" (pub. Frankfort, 1869) and "Hildebrand's Heimkehr" (ibid. 1874).—TR.

† In F. Hebbel's trilogy "*Die Nibelungen*" the second part is called "*Siegfried's Tod*," which was also the name of Wagner's first version of *Die Götterdämmerung*. Hebbel lived at Vienna (where Wagner was residing at the time he wrote the Preface to the *Ring*) and his work, "crowned with a prize of 1,000 Thalers," was published in 1862.—TR.

Nevertheless the specific garment of my poem, too, was noticed at the last. The songs of the *Edda*, which Simrock since had made so easily accessible, seemed to positively invite everyone to try his hand on the old-northern source in just the way that I appeared to have done. True, the Literary-historian *Julian Schmidt* had found occasion to label it "old-Frankish gear," reminding us of the three-cornered hats and other trappings of our peasants; but people didn't allow themselves to be put off by this *quid pro quo*, and we soon were deluged with the most jaw-breaking names of gods and heroes from the old Norräna. They bristled in the text-books, written actually in Stabreim here and there, which many a musician got vamped up for him; nay, they thronged the independent poems of our well-printed poets.—Here again I had one thing to regret, namely that my work had not been able to arouse, as well, the only feeling in which those relics of antiquity should be brought before us—the feeling for their purely-human element, so close to our own hearts, instead of mere regard for their value as curiosities. On the contrary, it was evident that their curiousness had been their sole attraction; from this, the absolutely outlandish, one expected a good effect. The effect was a failure, however; and, in view of the singular moral and intellectual attributes of modern Criticism, it was only to be anticipated that this aberration would be raised into a standard for judging *my* work too, whenever people—though carefully abstaining from any serious discussion of it—thought fit to give it a side-thrust in the dark. And so it happened when, under circumstances which I still reserve for closer mention, I had resolved on making my poem completely public. Among the grounds which moved me to this action I certainly must rank the overcoming of my earlier repugnance, and in fact my present inclination, to submit my poem even to a literary verdict. It was just my observation of the manifest, though hitherto unavowed influence of an acquaintance with my work upon other people's schemes for literary and dramatic products, that induced me to expose my own idea, so far as it was to be seen in my conception and manipulation of the *poetic* stuff, and leave it to sound judgment to estimate the considerable difference between my treatment and that of the others.

Now it certainly would have been something novel in the history of modern German Journalism, if the poetic efforts of an "opera-composer" had been seriously compared with the elaborations of literary poets by profession. Surely decency itself forbade, and the whole relations of the gentry of "poetic diction" to one another and in particular to their publishers. The most remarkable thing was, that expressions of the most significant approval of even this my poem were actually brought me from that camp at times, through private channels; but where they would have been of use to my great project, namely under the eye of the public—which might have had its attention drawn by a commendatory, or at all events intelligent review of my poem, and thus have been moved to render me the aid so indispensable for that project's carrying out —*there* every such expression was studiously held back. Nothing did I meet with, but bad jokes of the theatrical reporters and chartered musical jesters; farther than this even the editoriate of the "*Allgemeine Zeitung*" could not get, though its singular consortium of Augsburg bellelettrists has to introduce to the German public a couple of brand-new poets of the very highest rank on an average once a year. No, people stuck to giving me out as an opera-maker, the poverty of whose musical capacity might be judged from the mere fact that he was obliged to eke it out with eccentric text-concoctions of his own; an opinion heartily subscribed by the musical reviewers of the same consortium.

Remembering the spirit of our Art-criticism, as published, it would be indiscreet to ask for an explanation of such behaviour in the face of more and more salient and unpreventable facts—as which one needs must style the successes of even my most despaired-of works. Should awkward questions like this be asked, that spirit, let it never so loudly call itself the spirit of publicity (at least of *Publizistik* *), has always a curious refuge at hand, in its native obscurantism; so that in cases such as mine, one ought rather to ask the man who thinks he needs its help, what he expects from that quarter toward the attainment of really artistic ends, seeing how manifest it is that no expenditure of pains, however great, can enable it to impose upon the nation the rubbishy for the good, the consumptive for the strong and healthy? On the contrary, one well might suppose that a pressing recommendation from this side would rather cast suspicion on an important artistic enterprise like mine; for everyone must have learnt to his cost at some time, how he threw away his money when he allowed a most exciting puff in the famous supplement to the "*Allgemeine Zeitung*," for instance, to influence him to buy the newly-published drama of this or that of its famous poets.

Accordingly one could only ask oneself in despair, what on earth was to be done to make the German public fairly acquainted with the existence of some new thing of significance, something which could not first be brought within the accustomed categories? The nearest category into which the execution of my magnum opus (*meiner grossen Arbeit*) would have had to fit itself, was that of *Opera*; but it was the knowledge of the utter havoc our operatic system would wreak upon my project, were I to entrust the latter to its care, that had been my starting-point; and it was my repugnance against any immediate contact therewith, that finally became my chief incentive to come forward with my poem as a literary product—as it were to ascertain whether my work, regarded from this side, could rouse sufficient attention to wake among the educated of the nation a fancy for entertaining the wider-reaching plan or execution which I coupled with it. The state of our literary Journalism, to which I have just alluded, resulted in my being left in total ignorance whether I had arrived

---

* A debased-German term for "journalism" in general.—TR.

at any such effect. On the contrary—as lay indeed in the nature of the thing, since driven every day more deeply home upon me—I was constantly referred back to the category of "Opera" as my right departure-point, the proper mother-womb of my conceptive force; and now, as it seems, it is from thence alone that the incubative forces, not only for my artwork, but also for its future stage-performance, will have to be supplied me. So the Literary-drama may form a pretty good idea of how things stand with it.—

Before I proceed to the plan for the production of my work, as given by way of preface to the public issue of my poem, I will briefly sketch my attitude towards this poem during the lengthy period when its musical composition was under way, and finally during its long-continued interruption.

After five years' arrest of my musical productiveness, it was with great alacrity that I set to work on the [musical] composition of my poem, in the winter of 1853 to 1854. With the "Rheingold" I was starting on the new path, where I had first to find the plastic nature-motives which, in ever more individual evolution, were to shape themselves into exponents of the various forms of Passion in the many-membered Action and its characters.* The peculiar nature-freshness that seemed to breathe from hence upon me, like the higher mountain air, bore me untired over all the exertions of my work; by the spring of 1857 I had completed the music of the "Rheingold," the "Walküre," and a large portion of the "Siegfried." But now there came the reaction against this lasting strain, which had been brought no tonic from without. Since eight long years no performance of a dramatic work of mine had exercised its quickening influence on my senses, and through them on my powers of conception; only

---

* "Mit dem 'Rheingold' beschritt ich sofort die neue Bahn, auf welcher ich zunächst die plastischen Natur-Motive zu finden hatte, welche in immer individuellerer Entwickelung zu den Trägern der Leidenschafts-Tendenzen der weitgegliederten Handlung und der in ihr sich aussprechenden Charaktere sich zu gestalten hatten."

under the greatest difficulty had it been possible for me, from time to time, to hear even the sound of an orchestra. Germany, where people were giving my *Lohengrin* which I myself had never heard, remained shut against me. The state to which I was reduced by such deprivations seems to have been realised by none of my German friends; it was reserved for the tender feeling of a French writer Herr *Champfleury*,* to subsequently hold up before me the moving picture of my mental condition at that time. Practical friends in Germany, on the contrary, appeared rather to take the fatal fact of my long debarment from active intercourse with the Theatre as arguing that I must have lost my earlier advantages, have fallen into the unpractical, unstageable, unsingable, and thus have made my newer works not worth the being produced. This fear became at last a settled notion, nay, with all who thought they had reasons for giving up any further concern with me, a hopeful consolation. One needed to follow me no farther, and that had its agreeable side for those who felt a call to fulfil upon their own account the expectations kindled by my earlier works. Our most renowned reviewers of theatrical music regarded me as no longer in the land of the living.

Unfortunately it seemed as if even persons who previously had felt disposed to help forward my great plan, were not altogether averse to letting that daily more generally-held opinion determine them to prudently stand back; and thus when I laid one silent score on top of the other, never to dip into its leaves again, even to myself at times I appeared like one who walks in sleep, unconscious of his actions. Yes, and if I looked up from these dumb scores into the surrounding glare of day—that terrible day of our German Opera with its Kapellmeisters, tenors, prima donnas and alarms about the repertoire—I couldn't but burst out laugh-

---

* The *nom de plume* of Jules Fleury, who published in 1860 a delightful brochure upon "Richard Wagner" (Paris), which he slightly expanded in 1861, including it in a book entitled, "*Grandes Figures d'Hier et d'Aujourd'hui.*"—Tʀ.

ing at myself and the "stupid stuff" I was grinding out down there!

As it were a cordial against this growing disheartenment, there sprang up within me the fancy to carry out a long-conceived dramatic subject, for a work which, by not exceeding the dimensions of my earlier ones, might afford me the prospect of getting it performed at once.

With the sketch of "Tristan und Isolde" I felt that I was really not quitting the mythic circle opened-out to me by my Nibelungen labours (*dem Kreise der durch meine Nibelungenarbeit mir erweckten dichterischen und mythischen Anschauungen*). For the grand concordance of all sterling Myths, as thrust upon me by my studies, had sharpened my eyesight for the wondrous variations standing out amid this harmony. Such a one confronted me with fascinating clearness in the relation of *Tristan* to *Isolde*, as compared with that of *Siegfried* to *Brünnhilde*. Just as in languages the transmutation of a single sound * forms two apparently quite diverse words from one and the same original, so here, by a similar transmutation or shifting of the Time-motive, two seemingly unlike relations had sprung from the one original mythic factor. Their intrinsic parity consists in this: both Tristan and Siegfried, in bondage to an illusion which makes this deed of theirs unfree, woo for another their own eternally-predestined bride, and in the false relation hence-arising find their doom. Whereas the poet of *Siegfried*, however, before all else abiding by the grand coherence of the whole Nibelungen-myth, could only take in eye the hero's downfall through the vengeance of the wife who at like time offers up herself and him: the poet of *Tristan* finds his staple matter in setting forth the love-pangs to which the pair of lovers, awakened to their true relation, have fallen victims till their death. Merely the thing is here more fully, clearly treated, which even there was spoken out beyond mistake: death through stress

---

* "Lautverschiebung,"—according to *Flügel*, this is "the transition, or progressive transmutation, of the mute consonants which is traceable in identical words of the Indo-Germanic family of languages; Grimm's law."—TR.

of love (*Liebesnoth*)—an idea which finds expression in Brünnhilde, for her part conscious of the true relation. What in the one work could only come to rapid utterance at the climax, in the other becomes an entire Content, of infinite variety; and this it was, that attracted me to treat the stuff at just that time, namely as a supplementary Act of the great Nibelungen-myth, a mythos compassing the whole relations of a world.

As, apart from this attraction, it was of moment to me to see my new work alive before me forthwith, and as Germany still remained closed against me, it will not be inexplicable that a very curious offer from without—whose mention would more properly belong to my biography—should have somewhat actively influenced me in the conception of this new work. An agent—genuine or pretended—of the Emperor of Brazil informed me of his sovereign's leaning toward myself and German art in general, and desired me to accept an invitation to Rio de Janeiro, as also the commission to write a new work for the excellent Italian opera-company there. So far as I am concerned, the incident never passed beyond my surprise at its extraordinary nature; and the only after-effect it had, was to make me consider the possibility of getting a work of mine performed for once in a way by Italian singers.* What frightened everyone into fits of laughter, when I told them of my not unfavourable views hereon,

---

* "Es blieb meinerseits bei dem Erstaunen über das Wunderliche dieses Begegnisses, und nur der eine Erfolg davon wirkte in mir nach, welcher mir aus der Erwägung der Möglichkeit, für die Ausführung eines Werkes mich einmal mit italienischen Sängern zu befassen, erwuchs." Literally this would be "the possibility of once concerning myself with Italian singers for the carrying-out of a work"; the ambiguity resides in the word "*Ausführung*" ("carrying-out" *or* "execution") as—although the term generally used by Wagner for a theatrical performance is "*Aufführung*"—in this particular article he frequently employs the former word both for his own part of the "carrying-out" (i.e. the composition) and for the part to be taken by *all* concerned in a production such as he proposes. This is a little unfortunate, since the terms "*Konzeption*" and "*konzipirt*" (employed at the end of the first and last sentences, respectively, of this paragraph) admit of a similar doubt in the interpretation, whilst the point itself is of considerable interest in the history of the *Tristan* music.—TR.

was the consideration of the very low status of purely-musical culture among these singers, which necessarily must incapacitate them for making themselves in any degree conversant with music such as mine. To this I replied that it was merely a question of overcoming an intellectual difficulty with these singers, which perhaps might be more easily accomplished than people thought, and less by means of an abstract course of Universal Music than by giving them a thorough, concrete training in one specific rôle, devoting one's whole instructions to the *pathos* of its rendering. My friends gave ear to me, but made me join in their laughter at last, when, after going through with them the finished score of "Tristan," they reminded me that I fancied I had conceived precisely *this* work as an opera for the Italians.*

Yet there after all remained with me a hazy feeling as though there were still another element to be sought out, for the life-conditions of my art, than that to which alone I hitherto had been directed, and which had furnished those conditions in such uncommonly scanty measure. My endeavour to obtain a hearing in Paris—determined not a little by this feeling, and consequent upon the fortunes just recounted—was chiefly prompted by the ineluctable need to come into some stimulating contact with the organic media of my art. What I first thought of, was to bring my works to performance there (I admit: for *myself* in especial) with a picked troop of German artists. But the soon-recognised impossibility of carrying out this plan, on the one hand, and on the other the aforesaid dream of fraternising with a hitherto remote and foreign element, and thus gaining my needed means of art-expression, kept me

---

* Recent experiences will probably have turned that laughter into the silence of amazement. "Lohengrin"—the reports on whose production and initial reception at *Leipzig* and *Berlin*, for instance, might prove not uninstructive reading—was produced at *Bologna* in this year of 1871 and received with such lasting and profound success that *Tristan* involuntarily rises vividly to my mind again; and, after the past fortunes of that work in the great fatherland of solid earnestness, I ponder on the question: "*was ist deutsch?*" ["What is German?"].—R. WAGNER.

in a state of constant fluctuation—easily accountable under the circumstances, and only put to an end by my acceptance of the tolerably well-known invitation, which astonished no one more than myself, to produce my "Tannhäuser" at the French Opéra.—

The fortunes of this undertaking, unpleasant enough in their public aspect, have left almost nothing in my mind but memories of an elevating nature. Although that enterprise was outwardly a thorough blunder from the first, yet its inner movement brought me into very important relations with the most amiable and estimable element in the French character. But I soon had to learn that the great, nay extravagant hopes which people over there were building upon my eventual influence on the spirit of French Art itself, could only have a prospect of fulfilment if I kept entirely free from any sort of coercion by current French artistic taste, and remained within my own-est element. What had dawned upon my friends in France, and what to my German art-comrades and art-critics stayed nothing but a preposterous chimera, was in reality an Artwork which, thoroughly as it differed from both Opera and Modern Drama, yet should rise above them simply by carrying to their end the choicest tendencies of either, and uniting them in one ideal and unencumbered whole. Now, this work could be moulded only on a soil whereon the modern Form had not shaped itself to such a sharpness of outline as in France—thereby helping French art-wares, on the other hand, into so general a vogue; on the contrary, this selfsame Form, which had been hung upon the body of German Art in slack and almost slovenly folds, needed but to be drawn off it as an unseemly disfigurement, to reveal the Artwork long prepared beneath its pall, and thriven at last to native, purely-human form. Thus it was my very perception of the unparalleled disorder and confusion of its *surface* art-affairs, that sharpened my sight anew for the secret lying deep beneath, and so with most determined purpose (*mit bestimmtester Tendenz*) drew me back to Germany.

Ever since my return, I here have met the one sole care, to hold me off at arm's length; in particular it seemed to be the fondest wish of the theatrical authorities, to bring me into no sort of contact with performances of my works. Only once did I pluck up heart to actually express a desire to exercise some influence on the representation of one of my operas. My visit had taken *Vienna* by surprise; the intoxicating impression of a first hearing of my "Lohengrin" was granted me: overcome thereby, and by a truly moving reception on the part of the public, I fancied I must forthwith make an effort to mingle in the art-doings of the theatre. It would not fall within the purview of the present report, to discuss the circumstances and influences (for that matter, already notified elsewhere) which finally stultified the most promising preparations for a first performance of "Tristan und Isolde," and hindered my work's appearance. As characteristic, however, I may state that all my exertions were in vain, to get a few stage-rehearsals placed at my disposal so as to correct certain serious misunderstandings, and consequent blunders, in the otherwise very distinguished representation of "Lohengrin." And when I finally offered the management to write a new work for Vienna, with special regard to the means and personnel of their theatre, I was handed a written answer to the effect that, after due consideration, they believed they had paid sufficient heed to the name "Wagner" for the present, and thought it well to let another composer have a chance of speaking. This other was *Jacques Offenbach*, who, in fact, at like time received the order for a new work, to be expressly written for Vienna.

And yet, my treatment in Vienna was the humanest: at *Berlin* the Intendant simply refused to receive me, should I think of calling.

This behaviour might be explained in part by the diligently circulated charge, that I was insatiable in my demands. Yet at the Frankfort theatre, where my sole and most fatiguing efforts brought about a performance of

"Lohengrin" with the most exiguous of means,* I furnished proof that my only care was for *correctness*, and accordingly non-mutilation, but in nowise for any sort of lavish splendour. This evidence remained without a shred of notice. Merely the *Hamburg* theatre once invited me to attend a fiftieth representation of my "Tannhäuser," for the purpose of receiving the same ovations as one had just bestowed upon Herr *Gounod* for his "Faust," and now held ready for me as well, out of sheer impartiality: I declined with thanks, saying that I would regard the honour paid to my Paris friend as received by him for both of us.

So once more, in midst of the best-regulated world, I was shouldered back to Chaos; and in this mood it was, that I resolved on overtly publishing my poem of the "Ring des Nibelungen"—partly with the aforesaid view to obtaining it some literary notice, partly also to give that wished-for notice the only serviceable trend for me, by directing it towards an actual production of my work. With that object I set down my plan in black on white, in a Preface which I now append as supplement to the foregoing report.†

---

* September 12, 1862.—TR.

† In the pamphlet a couple of sentences here explain that part of the Preface had already been reprinted in an earlier pamphlet: "*Ueber die Aufführung des Bühnenfestspieles: Der Ring des Nibelungen*" (April, 1871—incorporated later in the "*Schlussbericht*" of vol. ix *Ges. Schr.*), and that only the portion omitted *there* was now reproduced. In vol. vi, however, the whole Preface is given, just as it stood in the first public edition of the *Ring* poem; merely the *date* in that volume is an obvious misprint—"Wien, 1862"—seeing that the said edition was issued in 1863 and bore the date of "April, 1863."
—TR.

PREFACE TO THE
PUBLIC ISSUE OF THE POEM OF THE BÜHNENFESTSPIEL
"DER RING DES NIBELUNGEN."

My nearer friends to whom I imparted the poem of my Bühnenfestspiel, some long while back, were at like time made acquainted with the notion I had formed of the possibility of a complete musico-dramatic representation thereof. As I still hold by that notion, and have not yet learnt to despair of a real success for the undertaking, whenever adequate material support can be brought into play, my plan shall now be imparted to wider circles, together with the poem's publication.—

It was my foremost thought, that such a representation should be free from all the influences of the daily repertory of our standing theatres. For this I had to premise one of the smaller towns of Germany, favourably situate, and suitable for the accommodation of an unusual influx of visitors; a town in which there would be no collision with any of our larger standing theatres, and where one would thus not be faced with the regular theatre-public of our great cities and all its habitudes. Here a provisional theatre was to be erected, as simple as possible, perchance of mere timber, and calculated solely for the artistic fitness of its interior; a plan for this, with an amphitheatric auditorium and the great advantage of an invisible orchestra, I had discussed with an eminent and experienced architect.*—Hither, about the first months of spring, should be summoned a company of first-rate dramatic singers, chosen from the

* Gottfried Semper.—TR.

personnel of the German opera-houses, to practise without let or hindrance the serial stage-work composed by me.—The performances, reckoned by myself at three whole sets, were to be given on fixed days in the middle of summer; to these the German public was to be invited, for—as in the case of our great music-festivals already—they should not be offered to the local public of a city, but to all the friends of Art, both near and far. A complete performance of the accompanying dramatic poem was to comprise: on a fore-evening the "Rheingold," on the three ensuing evenings the principal pieces, "Walküre," "Siegfried," and "Götterdämmerung."

The advantages, which would accrue from such an arrangement, to me appeared to be the following.

Firstly for the production itself:—From the standpoint of a practical artist, a truly successful performance seemed *possible* in no other way. With our German Opera's utter want of style, and the almost grotesque incorrectness of its doings, one can never hope to find at any single theatre a whole body of artistic material trained for higher tasks: the author who thinks of entrusting a higher, earnest-meaning task to this neglected department of public art, finds nothing to rely on but the real talent of *individual* singers, instructed in no school, trained in no style of representation, strewn here a few and there a few—for the German's talent in this respect is scanty—and entirely left to their own devices. What no one theatre can offer, could only be furnished—fortune favouring—by a combination of scattered forces, called together for a certain time, to one definite meeting-point.—In the next place it would be of benefit to these artists that for a time they should busy themselves with the study of one sole task, whose characteristics they would grasp the more speedily and definitely, as their attention would not be distracted by the exercise of their ordinary operatic functions. The result of this concentration of their whole mental powers upon one style and one task is in itself not easy to over-rate, when we consider how little success could be expected if the selfsame singer who last night had sung in a badly-translated modern Italian opera, for instance, had to-day to study the "Wotan" or "Siegfried." Moreover this method would have the practical effect, that the training would occupy a relatively far shorter time than could be possible in the common groove of repertory duties: which, again, would much conduce to fluency of study.

If in this way alone could the pick of talent give an earnest, characteristic rendering of the rôles in my drama, on the other hand the isolation of the production would be the only means of securing a good and fit presentment of the scenic setting. If we reflect upon the consummate achievements in this line at the Paris and London theatres, we must chiefly, and wellnigh solely explain them by the favouring circumstance, that for each piece the painters and machinists have the run of the stage for some considerable time beforehand; they thus are able to devise arrangements of a certain complicated nature, quite impossible where the pieces vary day by day, with the result that none can be mounted in a manner even approaching artistic decency. The scenery contemplated for my "Rheingold," for instance, is perfectly unthinkable at a theatre of so constantly changing a repertoire as the German; whereas, under the favourable conditions just described, it offers to the scene-painter and machinist precisely the most welcome opportunity of proving their art to be an art indeed.

To complete the impression of a performance prepared in such a manner, I next should lay especial stress on the invisibility of the orchestra—to be effected by an architectural illusion quite feasible with an amphitheatric plan of auditorium. The importance of this will be manifest to anybody who attends our opera-performances with the notion of getting the true impression of a work of dramatic art; through the inevitable sight of the mechanical movements of the band and its conductor, he is made an unwilling witness of technical evolutions which should be almost as carefully concealed from him as the cords, ropes, laths and scaffoldings of the stage decorations—which, seen from the wings, as everyone knows, destroy all vestige of illusion. If one has ever experienced what a pure, transfigured sound, freed from all admixture of the non-musical noise inseparable from the production of instrumental tone, is offered by an orchestra which one hears through an acoustic sounding-board; if one then imagines what an advantageous position the singer must occupy with regard to the hearer, when he stands almost directly facing him: we should only have to argue further to the easier understanding of the singer's words, to arrive at a most promising opinion of the success of the acoustic-architectonic plan proposed by me. But only in the supposed case of a provisional theatre, specially constructed for the purpose, would such a contrivance be feasible.

Now just as important as for the performance itself, in my way of thinking, would be the effect of these arrangements upon the Public.—Accustomed hitherto, as member of the standing Opera-public of a city, to seek nothing but distraction in the very dubious products of that equivocal art-genre, and peremptorily to reject whatever did him not this service, the listener at our Festival-performance would suddenly enter a quite different relation with what is set before him. Clearly and definitely apprised of what it here and this time had to expect, our public would consist of openly invited guests from far and near, assembled at the place of entertainment for sole sake of receiving the impression of our performance. In the heart of summer this visit would include the advantage of a recreative excursion, on which the first duty of everyone would be to rid himself of the cares of workaday existence. Instead of hunting for distraction at the close of a worrying day at the counter, the office, the desk, or any other professional toil—when the evening is to relax the one-sided strain of fagged-out nerves, and therefore to every man, according to his taste, some form of superficial amusement must needs seem grateful—this time he will take his distraction in the day, so as to collect himself when twilight nears: and the signal for the beginning of the festival-performance will bid him in for this. So, with all his powers refreshed and readily responsive, the first mystic sound of the unseen orchestra will attune him to that devotional feeling without which no genuine art-impression is so much as possible. Drawn by his own desire, he willingly will follow; and quickly will he reach an understanding of things which hitherto were bound to remain strangers to him, nay impossible. Where he erst arrived with weary brain, in search of dissipation, and found nothing but a new exertion and thus a painful overstrain; where he therefore had to complain of too great length, of too much seriousness, or finally of complete un-understandableness: he now will revel in the easy exercise of a hitherto unknown faculty of Beholding (*Anschauungsvermögen*), filling him with a new sense of warmth, and kindling a light in which he grows aware of things whereof he never dreamt before.—Moreover as we are here assembled for a feast, and it is a stage-feast to-day, not a feast of eating and drinking: so, just as music and speeches are there employed to whet the appetite between the courses, here in the easily protracted entr'actes one might employ any reasonable kind of refreshment—as I assume, in the open air of a summer evening—to brace the intellectual faculties.—

Now that I have indicated the essential differences between the Festival-performances, as meant by me, and the ordinary Opera-performances of our great cities; and having given a rapid glimpse of the surprising advantages offered by the arrangements which I propose, for the conspicuous success of such a performance: I will further permit myself to point out the ulterior effects that would inevitably ensue, both in general and upon musico-theatric art in particular.

Just as *Faust* ultimately proposes to replace the Evangelist's "In the beginning was the *word*" by "In the beginning was the *deed*," so the valid solution of an artistic problem seems feasible upon no other path than this of

Deed. We cannot rate high enough the impression of a Bühnenfestspiel performed in the manner just denoted, if we draw our inference from effects already experienced with other signal achievements. I myself have often been assured that the hearing of an excellent performance of my "Lohengrin," for instance, has caused a total revolution in the taste and likings of individuals; and certain it is, that a former art-loving Director of the Viennese Court-Opera,* who only with the greatest trouble had managed to get this opera performed at all, saw himself encouraged by its happy results to revive certain older works of a more serious and solid type of Opera, which had long been banished by the effeminacy of the public's taste.—Now, without losing ourselves in extravagant dreams of the effect intended (which I here conceive as solely due to the correctness and general excellence of the performance), let us take this thing alone in eye: in what kind of mood would the artists, and the audience accompanying them, return to judge their former doings? Though I am not disposed, as a rule, to cherish too great expectations of the lastingness of moods inspired by means unwonted, yet it surely is presumable that our performers could not fall back completely into their old habitual groove; and that the less, if they have seen their unaccustomed doings accepted in an unaccustomed fashion, and above all if we have held by the general principle of choosing none but really rising talents, merely in need of just the helpful hand and practice. But we also may presume that our festival-performances will have been attended by the administrative chiefs, and many an artist, of the other German theatres, if only out of curiosity: all now have *seen* with their eyes, and *heard* with their ears, what no manner of abstract demonstration could ever have made plain to them; they have received the direct impression of a stage-portrayal in which Music and poetic Action, in every smallest particle,

---

* Karl Eckert, Director from 1857 to 1860. *Lohengrin* was performed at Vienna, for the first time, on August 18, 1858, with Heinrich Esser as conductor.—TR.

had become one unitarian whole. They have also witnessed its effect upon the public, as its effect upon themselves. 'Twere impossible that such an experience should be entirely without influence on their own future operations. Here and there, in particular at the more well-to-do theatres, people would probably soon attempt to repeat for themselves, at first portions, and finally the whole of those performances: with the understanding reaped from those Grand Original-performances, even the less finished reproduction would stand out advantageously as compared with wonted doings at the selfsame theatres. This in itself might give the impetus to a truly German style of musico-dramatic execution—a style whereof no single trace exists at present.

Then the surest way to fortify these happy, yet probably at first but weak and often blurred effects, and to preserve them from gradually vanishing quite away, would be to arrange for repetitions of the Grand Original-performances themselves. In the first place they would have to be repeated once a year, or once in every two or three years, according as there had been written some new original work of kindred style, or worthy in general of the distinction afforded by such a performance.—This would involve the founding of a prize for the best work of musico-dramatic art, and the prize itself would consist in nothing but the work's selection for performance at the Festival. The work's form would constitute the sliding-scale for its production: a work that could be performed in one evening would suffice for annual Festivals, let us say, on account of its smaller cost of staging; whereas the more extensive ones, such as my present Bühnenfestspiel, would be reserved for rarer intervals.

The German nation prides itself on being so deep, original and earnest, that on this one side of Music and Poetry—where it really has placed itself at the head of all the European nations—it only seems necessary to furnish it with a form-giving institution, to discover if it verily deserves that praise. Again, an institution such as

I have in mind for keeping up the said musical performances, would completely answer to the German nature, which delights in splitting into its component parts so as to procure itself the periodic pride and pleasure of re-union. Better than unfruitful, entirely un-German academic institutions, it could very well go hand in hand with the Existing; merely it would feed upon the latter's choicest forces, to lastingly ennoble them and steel them to a genuine sense of self-reliance.

We thus at last should have the prospect of seeing the German Spirit's most characteristic excellences brought yearly forward in a new work—if possible—of a special class essentially belonging to ourselves; and thus at last would come the time when, at least in one highly significant branch of art, the German would begin to be *national* through first becoming *original*—a quality in which alas! the Italian and the Frenchman are long ahead of him.—

So important and eventful a consequence as this I truly have in mind, in devoting my immediate thoughts to the provision of the means for a first performance of the accompanying "Bühnenfestspiel." As I possess experience and aptitude enough to carry to success the executive side of such a performance, it would merely be a question of providing the *material* means.

Two ways present themselves to me.

An association of well-to-do, art-loving men and women, with the immediate object of collecting the needful funds for a first performance of my work.—When I remember how pettily the Germans are accustomed to proceed in such affairs, I have not the courage to promise myself success from any circular directed to this end.

On the other hand the thing would come quite easy to a German Prince, who would need to lay no novel precept on his budget, but simply to divert the sums he had hitherto devoted to maintaining the worst of public art-institutes—so profoundly compromising and ruining the German's ear for music—his opera-house. Should the nightly theatre-goers of his capital insist on retaining the soothing dissipation of a modern opera-performance, the Prince I dream of might gladly allow them that entertainment, only, not at his expense: for, let him think what he likes of his munificence to Opera, he has therewith patronised neither Music nor the Drama, but just the very thing which grievously offends all German sense of music as of drama—the Opera.

But now that I have shewn him what a quite uncommon effect upon the morality of a hitherto degrading art-genre, what a distinctively German field of action must be hereby brought within his power, he would only have to set aside the yearly sum allotted to the maintenance of Opera in his capital, and devote it, if sufficient, to annual, if insufficient, to biennial or triennial Festival-performances of the kind described: and thus would he found an institution that needs must give him an incalculable influence upon German art-taste, on the development of German artistic genius, on the cultivation of a genuine, not arrogated national spirit, and win his name a fame imperishable.—

Will this Prince be found?—

"In the beginning was the Deed."

In waiting for this Deed, the author feels constrained to make a faint beginning through the "word"—and very literally through the word, without tone, nay, without sound, the word just merely given forth in type—inasmuch as he resolves on handing over his poem, as such, to the larger Public. Though I thus am falling foul of my earlier wish, to come out with nothing but the finished whole, whereto its music and its scenic show are indispensable, I readily admit that patience and long-suffering have worn me out at last. I *no longer* hope to live out the production of my Bühnenfestspiel: ay, scarce dare I hope to find the lief and leisure to finish its musical composition. So I verily make over to the reading-public a bare dramatic poem, a literary product. Even to see it noticed by that public may not be such an easy matter, for it has no market of its own. The literarian lays it on one side, as an "opera-text" concerning none but the musician; the musician, because he fails to see how such an opera-text could ever get composed. The Public proper, which so willingly and gladly has decided in my favour, demands the "Deed."

Alas! that stands outside my power!

VIENNA. April, 1863.

# A LETTER TO HECTOR BERLIOZ.

Ein Brief an Hector Berlioz.

The Letter to Berlioz *originally appeared in the* Presse Théatrale *of February* 26, 1860, *in reply to Berlioz' feuilleton in the* Journal des Débats *of February* 9, 1860—*subsequently reprinted in that composer's* " À travers chants."

A German translation of Wagner's "Letter" *was published in the* Neue Zeitschrift *of March* 2 *and* 9, 1860, *with a footnote:* "*As our readers are aware, the German press has hastened to reproduce Berlioz' criticism of Wagner's Paris concerts, so that it will be unnecessary for us to say anything here about the substance of that criticism. On the other hand we deem it our duty to furnish a literal translation of Wagner's reply, which has just appeared in the* Presse Théatrale *of February* 26." *The translation in the N.Z. is obviously not from Wagner's hand, but, with the exception of one or two clauses (to be noted later on), its general sense is identical with that supplied by our author in vol. vii of his* Gesammelte Schriften—*upon which the present English rendering is based.*

Champfleury, in his work already mentioned on page 267, *makes the following significant remarks:* "*Il est bon de noter que M. Berlioz, contrairement aux usages du journalisme, ne publia son feuilleton qu'un mois après le premier concert, craignant avec juste raison d'appeler l'attention sur un adversaire redoutable. Ce feuilleton, rempli de misères et de facéties de vaudevilliste, comme en emploie trop souvent le membre de l'Institut, lui valut une lettre de Wagner, digne, calme et pleine de conviction, qui restera comme un modèle de convenance vis-à-vis d'ironies impuissantes.*"

TRANSLATOR'S NOTE.

Paris.—February, 1860.

EAR BERLIOZ,
Five years ago in London, when a common fate had brought us into closer contact with each other, I boasted of one advantage over you: the advantage of being in a position to completely understand and appreciate your works, whereas my own, in one very essential point, would always remain strangers and unintelligible to you. I was mainly thinking of the instrumental character of your works, and—taught by experience how perfectly an orchestral piece may be brought into performance, under favouring conditions, whilst works of dramatic music, once they quit the traditional pattern of the frivolous genre of Opera proper, can at best be merely dimly shadowed by our opera-personnel *—I had almost lost sight of the chief hindrance in the way of your understanding my intentions: to wit, your ignorance of the German language, with which my dramatic conceptions are so intimately bound. My present fate, however, compels me to make the attempt to surrender that advantage; for eleven years I have been debarred from any possibility of bringing my own works before me, and I shudder at the thought of remaining any longer the solitary German, perchance, who has not yet heard my "Lohengrin." It will therefore be neither ambition nor love of advertisement, that leads me to seek the hospitality of France for my dramatic works withal; by means of good translations I shall try to make my works performable here, and should anybody take compassion on the unheard lot of an author who is tor-

* The clause between the dashes does not appear in the *Neue Zeitschrift*'s translation.—TR.

menting himself to get a hearing of his own creations on such a toilsome by-way, then I haply may dare to hope, dear Berlioz, to some day make myself entirely and completely known to you as well.

Through your last article,* however, devoted to my concerts and containing so much flattering recognition of myself, you have ceded me yet another coign of vantage, of which I will at once avail myself to shed a little light, both for you and for the public, on the wonders you have set before it in solemn earnest with the question of a "*musique de l'avenir.*" Since even you appear to fancy that it is a question of a "school" which arrogates that title to itself and whereof I am the master, I perceive that even you belong to those who have no hesitation in believing that at some time or other I allowed myself to set up certain theses which you divide into two categories, declaring yourself quite ready to accept the first, as of old and recognised validity, whereas you think necessary to protest against the second as utter nonsense. You do not express yourself very definitely as to whether you are inclined to merely credit me with the foolish vanity of giving out old and well-worn saws as something new, or with the insane attempt to make out a case for something downright idiotic. In view of your friendly feelings toward me, I cannot but think it will gratify you to be promptly snatched from this dilemma. Learn, then, that not I am the inventor of the "*musique de l'avenir,*" but a German music-reviewer, Herr Professor Bischoff of Cologne, a friend of Ferdinand Hiller's—who will be known to you, in turn, as a friend of Rossini's. The pretext for inventing such a ridiculous name, however, seems to have been lent him by a stupid and malicious misunderstanding of a literary work which I published ten years since, under the title of "The Art-work of the Future." I wrote that essay at a time when a violent crisis in my life had for a while withdrawn me from the practice of my art; at a time when, after many and ripe experiences, my mind was

* In the *N.Z.* : "in the *Journal des Débats.*"—TR.

settling to a more radical examination of problems in Art and Life which until then had been for me enigmas. I had passed through the Revolution,* and seen with what incredible contempt it viewed our public art and its institutes; so that a complete triumph of the Social Revolution, in particular, appeared likely to involve the total demolition of those institutes. I looked into the grounds of that contempt and, to my amazement, had to recognise wellnigh the same as have determined yourself, for instance, dear Berlioz, to unbosom your disgust at the spirit of those public art-institutes on every opportunity; namely the consciousness that in their relation with the public those institutes, especially the Theatre and above all the Opera-house, are pursuing tendencies which have not one jot in common with those of true Art and sterling artists, but merely don a cloak of good pretence the better to serve the most frivolous leanings of a metropolitan public. Going farther, I asked myself what position Art should occupy towards the Public, so as to inspire it with a reverence that could never be profaned; and, not to be merely building castles in the air, I took my stand on the position erewhile occupied by Art to the public Life of the Greeks. Here I lit forthwith upon that *art-work* which throughout all time must rank as the most perfect, to wit, the *drama*; because therein the highest and deepest artistic aim can manifest itself in the most distinct and universally understandable fashion. As we marvel still to-day that 30,000 Greeks could once assemble to listen with the utmost interest to tragedies like those of Æschylus, I also asked what could have been the means of bringing forth effects so extraordinary; and I discovered that they lay precisely in the association of *all the arts* to form the one, the true great Artwork. This led me to inquire into the relation of the separate arts to one another, and after fathoming that of Plastic-art to the actually represented Drama, I probed the mutual references of Poetry and Music; and here I

* In the *N. Z.*: "In the year 1848 I was dismayed by the incredible," &c. —Tr.

found new lights, which cleared up much that heretofore had troubled me. For I recognised that exactly where the barriers of the one art are found to be insuperable, there begins, with definition past a doubt, the field of action of the other: therefore, that through an intimate conjunction of both arts, the thing impossible to express by either of them singly may be expressed with most persuasive clearness; whereas the attempt to express by one sole branch of art what is possible only to the two, must lead to a monstrosity, to an excursion into the purely unintelligible, to the ruin of the separate art itself. Thus my object was to shew the possibility of an artwork in which the highest and profoundest, that the human mind can grasp, should be imparted to purely human fellow-Feeling in a way the most intelligible to its simplest faculties of reception, and so plainly and convincingly as to need no reflective Criticism to play the go-between. This work I called: "*the Artwork of the Future.*"

Judge then, dear Berlioz, what my feelings must be, when, after ten long years of contumely from the pens of obscure scribblers, from the herd of half or wholly silly wit-purveyors, from the chatter of the blind and ever merely sheep-like masses, I find a man so earnest, an artist so uncommonly gifted, so honest a critic and so sincerely prized a friend, casting in my teeth that stupidest of all misunderstandings of an idea which, even if erroneous, was at least deep-going in intention—with this catchword of a "*musique de l'avenir*"; and that upon assumptions which, had I really any share in the authorship of the theories wherewith you credit me, would simply rank me among the most ridiculous of men. As my book will probably remain a stranger to you, please take my word that there was not a syllable in it about the special art of Music, under its grammatic aspect, nor on the expediency of writing nonsense or folly therein; in view of the magnitude of my design, and as I am no theorist by trade, I rightly felt bound to leave that task to others. For myself, I heartily regret having ever published the ideas I then traced out: for when the artist is so hardly understood by even the artist, as lately has happened again to me; when even the most cultivated critic is often so entangled in the prejudices of the half-educated amateur that, when a work of art is set before him, he hears and sees things which as a matter of fact do not occur therein, and on the other hand does not catch sight of its essentials—how ever is the art-philosopher to be understood by the public, save pretty much as my essay was understood by Professor Bischoff of Cologne ?—

But more than enough of this. I have now made away with my last advantage over you, that of knowing the right side of this question about a "Music of the Future." Let us hope for the time when, as artists favoured quite alike, we mutually may commune with each other; grant you to my dramas an asylum upon France's hospitable soil, and be assured of the heartfelt longing with which I look forward to the first, and let us hope the thoroughly successful, performance of your "Trojans." *

---

* In the *N. Z.* the letter ended as follows: "with an impatience three-fold justified : firstly, by the affection which I cherish for you ; secondly, by the important position which your work will undoubtedly take in the present world of music ; finally, and most of all, by the special weight I lay upon it in connection with the ideas and principles which have always guided myself."—Tr.

„Zukunftsmusik."

An einen französischen Freund
(Fr. Villot)
als
Vorwort zu einer Prosa-Übersetzung
meiner Operndichtungen.

The "Zukunftsmusik" ("*Music of the Future*") essay was written—as the title over-leaf records—as a letter " to a French friend, Fr. Villot, as preface to a prose-translation," in French, of Wagner's "opera-poems." The "*poems*" consisted of The Flying Dutchman, Tannhäuser, Lohengrin *and* Tristan und Isolde.

Mons. *Villot was, at the time, Conservator of the Picture Museums at the Louvre in Paris, and made his salon a meeting-point for the literary and artistic world of the day; he subsequently became General Secretary of the Louvre, as* "*Ch. Nuitter*" *tells us in the* 1893 *reprint of the* "*Quatre Poèmes*" *&c. From this reprint it would appear, though it is not definitely stated, that* " *Nuitter* " (*the nom de plume of Charles Louis Etienne Truinet*) *was the French translator, both of Preface and Poems.*

The German version of this "*preface*" *was originally published by J. J. Weber, Leipzig, in* 1861.

TRANSLATOR'S NOTE.

HONOURED FRIEND,
                      You wished to receive from myself a clear account of the ideas I published some years ago in Germany, in a series of art-writings—ideas which excited both notice and opposition enough, to prepare me an open-mouthed reception in France itself. You held this of weight in my own interest, to boot, as you were good enough to believe that a lucid exposition of my thoughts would dispel much prejudice and error; and thus that many an embarrassed critic, at the coming performance of one of my dramatic music-works in Paris,* would feel relieved at having to merely judge the work of art itself, and not a dubious theory into the bargain.

I must admit that it would have been extremely hard for me to accept your friendly invitation, if the wish you expressed to me, to at like time lay before the public a translation of my opera-poems, had not suggested the only way on which I think possible to answer it. For I should have deemed it clean impossible, had I been obliged once more to thread the labyrinth of theoretic speculation in a purely abstract form; whilst the great repugnance I now experience against so much as reading through my theoretic essays, teaches me that I was in a thoroughly abnormal state of mind when I wrote them—a state such as well may arise for once in an artist's life, but cannot fitly be repeated. Allow me first of all to point you out the characteristic features of that mental state, in the light they now appear in to me. If you grant me a little space for this, by starting with the description of a subjective mood I may hope to lay before you the concrete substance of artistic theories which it would be impossible for me to now reiterate in abstract form—

    * *Tannhäuser*, at the Grand Opéra.—TR.

let alone the hindrance to the object of my communication.

If we may broadly denote the whole range of Nature as an evolutionary march from unconsciousness to consciousness, and if this march is shewn the most conspicuously in the human individual, we may take its observation in the life of the Artist as one of the most interesting, because in him and his creations the World itself displays itself and comes to consciousness. But in the Artist, too, the bent to re-present is by its nature thoroughly unconscious, instinctive; and even where he needs deliberation (*Besonnenheit*), to shape the picture of his intuition to an objective work of art by aid of his own familiar technique, the decisive choice of his expressional means will not be settled by Reflection proper, but rather by an instinctive bent that makes out the very character of his specific gift. The necessity for a lengthy bout of reflection will only come upon him where he stumbles on some great obstacle to the application of the expressional means he needs; thus where the means of realising his artistic aim are persistently made hard of access for him, or finally debarred. In the last-named case will be found, in a progressive ratio, the artist who requires not merely lifeless tools, but a living combination of artistic forces, to realise his aim. Such a combination is needed by the dramatic poet in the most emphatic sense, to bring his poem to its most intelligible expression; for this he is directed to the Theatre, which, as the epitome of the arts of re-presenting (*als Inbegriff der darstellenden Kunst*), itself makes out a definite branch of art, with laws peculiar to itself. The dramatic poet approaches this Theatre as a ready-made art-medium; with it, with all its idiosyncrasies, has he to blend himself, to see a realisation of his artistic aim. If the poet's tendencies entirely concur with those of the Theatre, there can be no question of the aforesaid conflict; and one has merely to weigh the character of that concurrence, to ascertain the value of the work of art thus brought to light of day. If on the contrary those tendencies are radically divergent, it is easy to imagine the distress (*Noth*) of the artist who, for expressing his artistic aim, sees himself constrained to employ an art-organ which primarily belongs to quite another aim than his.

The enforced perception that I myself was in such a plight, compelled me at a certain epoch of my life to halt upon the road of more or less unconscious artistic production, and devote a lengthy period of reflection to bringing the problem of this situation to my personal consciousness, through an investigation of its causes. I may assume that the problem in question had never yet thrust itself so obtrusively upon an artist, as now upon me, since the artistic elements involved had surely never been so diverse and peculiar; seeing that on the one side Poetry and Music, on the other the modern Lyric Stage, the most dubious and equivocal institute of public art in latter days —the Opera-house—were to strike up an alliance.

Let me first of all point out to you a salient difference, very weighty in my eyes, between the position held by operatic authors in Italy and France towards the Opera-house, and that which they hold in Germany; this difference is so considerable, that its characteristics will suffice to make you comprehend how the problem could have presented itself so glaringly to none but just a German author.

In Italy, where the operatic genre first took its rise, no other task has ever been set before the musician than the writing of a number of arias for definite singing individuals, with whom dramatic talent was quite a secondary matter; and these arias were simply meant to give those virtuosi the opportunity of shewing off their quite specific vocal skill. Poem and scenery merely furnished this exhibition of virtuosity with a decent pretence of Time and Space; the prima donna made way for the ballerina, who danced the selfsame thing as she had sung; and the composer had no other office, than to cater for variations of one given type of aria. So everything was in thorough concord, down to the smallest detail; especially as the composer composed for quite definite singers, and their individual gifts laid down the character of the particular variation he had to supply. Italian Opera thus became an art-genre quite apart, and, having nothing in common with genuine Drama, it virtually remained a stranger to Music too; for the rise of Opera in Italy marks the downfall of Italian music—an assertion whose truth will be obvious to anyone who has acquired an adequate notion of the sublimity, the wealth and ineffably expressive depth of Italian church-music in the previous century, and after hearing the "*Stabat mater*" of Palestrina, for instance, can never honestly maintain that Italian Opera is a legitimate daughter of that wondrous mother.—This by the way: for our immediate object let us merely recollect the one thing, that in Italy down to our day there reigns a perfect concord between the tendencies of the opera-house and those of the composer.

Neither did this relation alter upon its arrival in France: merely the task of both singer and composer was made severer; for here the dramatic poet intervened to far greater purpose than in Italy. In keeping with the nation's character and an immediately-antecedent notable development of dramatic poetry and the impersonating art, the canons of that art were raised into a standard for Opera also. At the institute of the "Grand Opéra" there matured a settled style, borrowed as to its leading features from the rules of the Théâtre Français, and including all the conventions of a dramatic representation. Without going into details now, let us merely remember that it was a definite model-theatre at which this style was moulded, and that it was equally incumbent on performers as on author; that the author found to hand the sharp-drawn frame he had to fill with plot and music, with his eye upon definite, well-drilled singers and performers, with whom he found himself in full accord as to his legitimate aim.

Now Opera reached Germany as a thoroughly elaborated foreign product, fundamentally alien to the nation's character. German princes at first called Italian opera-companies, with their own composers, to their courts; German composers must travel into Italy, to learn the art of operatic composition there. Later on, the theatres began to set translations of French operas, in particular, before their public. Attempts at German Opera consisted in nothing but an imitation of the foreign operas, only in the German tongue. A central model-theatre was never founded. Everything stood cheek by jowl in utmost anarchy, the Italian style, the French style, and German copies of both; item, attempts to obtain an independent, popular genre from the primitive and never higher-developed German *Singspiel*, for the most part thrust back again and again by the formal superiority of the finished wares imported from abroad.

One obvious evil, that sprang from such confusing influences, was the utter style-lessness of operatic execution. To keep the repertoire attractive through variety, in towns whose scantier population afforded but a small and seldom-changing audience, Italian, French, and German operas copied from them both or grafted on the humblest *Singspiel*, of tragic or of comic content, were pitchforked on to the stage and rendered by one and the selfsame singers. What had been calculated for the most eminent Italian vocal virtuosi, with special regard for their individual aptitudes, was sung into tatters by singers without any schooling, without any throat-dexterity, in a language diametrically opposed in character to the Italian, and mostly in a laughable disfigurement. Add hereto French operas, designed for a pathetic declamation of polished rhetorical phrases, presented in translations scrambled-up by literary hodmen at the lowest price, mostly disregarding all declamatory connection between the words and music, crammed full of the most hair-bristling faults of prosody; a circumstance in itself sufficient to prevent any formation of a sound style of delivery, to make singers and public alike indifferent to the text. Hence a want of finish on every hand; nowhere a model opera-house, conducted on reasonable principles, to set the tone; faulty, if not altogether lacking, cultivation of even the vocal organs at disposal; everywhere artistic anarchy.

You feel that for the true, the earnest musician, this Opera-house was virtually non-existent. If natural bent or training turned his steps towards the theatre, he could not but prefer to write in Italy for the Italian, in France for the French Opera; and while Gluck and Mozart were composing French and Italian operas, there was being built in Germany a national music proper, on foundations quite other than that of the operatic genre. Entirely shunning Opera, from that music-branch whence the Italians broke loose at the rise of Opera there evolved in Germany a Music proper, from Bach to Beethoven, and reached that height of wealth and wonder which has conferred on German music its admittedly universal importance.

Thus to the German musician, who from his native field of instrumental and choral music looked out upon dramatic music, the opera-genre presented no finished and imposing Form, whose relative perfection might have served him as a model akin to what he found, on the other hand, in his own varieties of music. Whereas in Oratorio, and above all in the Symphony, there lay before him a noble, perfect form: the Opera proffered him an inconsequent tangle of petty, undeveloped forms, to which there clove a convention quite incomprehensible to himself, and nocuous to all freedom of development. To fully grasp my meaning, compare the broad and amply developed forms of a symphony of Beethoven's with the music-pieces of his opera "Fidelio": you feel at once how cramped and hindered the master must have felt, almost nowhere able to reach the full unfolding of his power; wherefore, as if to launch forth all his fill of force for once, he threw himself with wellnigh desperate weight upon the overture, and made of it a music-piece of theretofore unheard significance and breadth. From this solitary experiment with Opera he retired in dudgeon, without giving up the wish, however, to find a poem that should enable him to unfold the fulness of his musical power. The *ideal* was hovering before him.

And verily an *ideal* must needs arise in the mind of the German musician for this enigmatic art-genre, with its everlasting attraction and repulsion of him—for this Opera, whose *reality* of current form he deemed so utterly unsatisfactory; and herein lies the peculiar drift of German art-endeavours, not merely on this, but on every field of art. Let me characterise that drift a little more precisely for you.

Indisputably the Romanic nations of Europe arrived betimes at one great advantage over the Germanic, namely in the development of *form*. While Italy, Spain and France were moulding that agreeable native form which speedily obtained a general and legitimate application to every utterance of Life and Art, on this side Germany remained in a state of undeniable anarchy—scarce mantled, but rather aggravated, by the attempts to press into its service those ready-made forms of the foreigners' own. The obvious disadvantage into which the German nation thus fell, for everything that touches Form (and how widely this extends!), very naturally delayed the evolution of German Art and Literature so long, that only since the second half of the eighteenth century was there engendered a movement akin to that which the Romanic nations had experienced from the beginning of the period of the Renaissance. This German movement could at first take wellnigh nothing but the character of a reaction against the foreign, disfigured, and therefore disfiguring form; seeing that this reaction could not take place in favour of a haply smothered German form, however, but rather of a form in truth not extant anywhere, the movement made resolutely for the discovery of an ideal, a purely human form, belonging exclusively to no single nationality. The thoroughly characteristic, novel, and in the history of Art unmatched, exertions of the two greatest German poets, Goethe and Schiller, are distinguished by this one feature: they for the first time made that problem of an ideal, a purely-human art-form, in its widest reach, the object of research; and the search for this form is wellnigh the main essential content even of their creative work. Rebellious against the coercion of that form which the Romanic nations still obeyed as law, they arrived at viewing it from an objective standpoint, at perceiving the defects inherent in its qualities, at following it back to the archetype of European art-form, in that of the Greeks; in needful freedom there to gain full understanding of the antique form, and thence to set out for an ideal art-form, which, purely human and delivered from the cramp of narrower national customs, should mould those very customs into purely-human ones, obeying none but everlasting laws.

The disadvantage under which the German had laboured hitherto, as compared with the Romanic peoples, would thus be turned to an advantage. Whereas the Frenchman, for instance—confronted with a fully developed, entirely self-contained and congruent form, and yielding a willing obedience to its seemingly unalterable laws—feels himself committed to a perpetual reproduction of that form, and thus (in a higher sense) to a certain stagnation of his inner productivity: the German, recognising all the advantages of such an attitude, would perceive withal its serious mischiefs; its lack of freedom would not escape him, and there would open up the outlook on an ideal art-form, embracing each eternal truth of every single art-form, but liberated from the fetters of the accidental and untrue. The immeasurable importance of this art-form would then consist herein: purged of the cramping element of narrower nationality, it would be a universally understandable form, accessible to every nation. Though as regards Literature the diversity of European tongues presents an obstacle, yet in Music, that language understandable by all the world alike, there would be supplied the great conforming force, which, resolving the language of abstractions into that of feelings, would transmute the inmost secret of the artist's thought (*Anschauung*) into a universal message;

particularly when its plastic expression, as furnished by the dramatic show, should raise that message to a plainness hitherto claimed by the art of Painting as her unique and peculiar province.

You have here a bird's-eye sketch of that Artwork which became for me an ever more distinct ideal, and whose theoretic traits I once felt driven to outline more minutely; at a time when a more and more intense dislike of that art-genre, which bore to the ideal I mean the repellent likeness of the monkey to the man, usurped my being to such a pitch that I felt impelled to flee before it, far, far away, into the most complete seclusion.

To make this period of my life intelligible to you without wearying you with biographic details, let me merely lay my finger on the peculiar conflict into which a German musician must nowadays feel plunged, who, with the Symphony of Beethoven in his heart, sees himself thrust into dealings with modern Opera such as I have described to you as functioning in Germany.

Despite a serious education, from earliest youth I was in close and constant contact with the Theatre. My childhood fell within the last years of Karl Maria von Weber, who periodically conducted his operas in the same city, Dresden. My first musical impressions were derived from this master, whose strains inspired me with a dreamy earnestness, whose person fascinated me with a strange enthusiasm. His death in a distant country filled my childish heart with dread. Of Beethoven I first heard when I was also told of his death, which followed shortly after Weber's; I then made the acquaintance of *his* music too, as though attracted to it by the enigmatic news of his decease. Kindled by impressions so earnest as these, the passion for music grew ever stronger within me. Yet it was only later, after my other studies had introduced me to classical antiquity, in particular, and woken a wish to try my hand at poetry, that I arrived at a more systematic study of music. I wanted to write some music for a tragedy which I had already penned. Rossini is said to have once asked his teacher whether he needed to learn counterpoint, for composing operas? As the teacher, with his eye on modern Italian Opera, replied in the negative, the pupil gladly abstained. After my instructor had taught me the hardest contrapuntal arts, he said to me: "You probably will never require to write a *fugue*; only, the ability to write one will give you technical self-reliance, and make everything else quite easy." Thus schooled, I entered the practical career of a Music-director at the theatre,* and began to compose operas to texts of my own writing.

This little biographic notice must suffice you. After what I have said about the state of Opera in Germany, you will have no difficulty in drawing inferences as to my further course of evolution. The peculiar feeling of gnawing pain, that seized me when conducting our ordinary operas, was often interrupted by an enthusiastic sense of ineffable wellbeing when here and there, at the very moment of performance of nobler works, I came by an inner consciousness of the quite unparalleled effect of certain combinations in dramatic music; an effect of such depth, such inwardness, and yet so direct a vividness, as no other art is able to produce. That such impressions, revealing undreamt possibilities as it were by a lightning-flash, could ever and anon present themselves to me—this it was that chained me ever and again to the theatre, intense as was the disgust with which I was filled, on the other hand, by the typical spirit of our opera-performances. Among these impressions of a particularly vivid nature, I remember my hearing of an opera of Spontini's at Berlin, under the master's own direction; I felt quite uplifted and ennobled for a while, when rehearsing Méhul's glorious "Joseph" with a minor opera-company.† When twenty years back I stayed in Paris for a considerable time, the

---

* At Wurzburg, 1833, where he wrote *Die Feen*. The "*Musikdirektor*" is generally the second in command, after the Conductor (*Kapellmeister*); Wagner's first post was that of Chorus-master.—TR.

† At Riga, in July 1838.—TR.

consummateness of musical and plastic *mise en scène* at the performances of the Grand Opéra could not fail to produce a most dazzling and stimulating impression on me. The highest grade of influence, however, had already been exerted on me in my earlier youth by the achievements of a dramatic singer of—for me—quite unmatched worth, the Schröder-Devrient. Paris, too, perhaps yourself, made the acquaintance of this great artist in her day. The quite incomparable dramatic talent of this lady, the quite inimitable harmony and individual *characteristique* of her impersonations, which I actually beheld with living eyes and ears, cast a spell over me that gave the bent to my whole future artistic course. The possibility of such achievements had opened out before me; and, with her in eye, there matured in me a standard not only for the musico-dramatic representation, but also for the poetico-musical conception, of an artwork to which I scarce could any longer give the name of "opera." I was distressed to see this artist compelled to digest the least significant products on all the field of operatic composition, to gain the matter for her talent of portrayal; and again, astounded at the sincerity and entrancing beauty which she infused into her impersonation of Romeo in Bellini's feeble work, I said to myself withal: what an incomparable artwork must that be, which in all its parts should be fully worthy of the talent of such an executant artist, and still more, of an association of artists like her.

Now the higher my idea of what could be done in the opera-genre was raised by such impressions, and the more I conceived that idea to be truly realisable by turning into the channel of this musical drama the whole rich stream of German music, swelled full by Beethoven, the more depressing and repellent must be my daily intercourse with actual Opera, which lay so infinitely distant from the ideal I harboured within my heart. Spare me a description of the inner chagrin, at last beyond all bearing, that filled the soul of an artist who, descrying each day more plainly the possibilities of an incomparably perfect artwork's realisement, yet saw himself bound fast within the unbreakable circle of a daily commerce with that very art-genre whose customary mechanical practice betrayed the absolute antithesis of his ideal. All my attempts to bring reform into the operatic institute itself, my proposals to give that institute a settled tendency and trend towards the realisement of my ideal wishes, by making the rare and seldom visits of the excellent a standard for the accomplishments of everyday — all these endeavours were shipwrecked. With plainest certainty I had to learn at last the kind of culture made-for by the modern Theatre, and in particular by the Opera; and this indisputable knowledge inspired me with so much loathing and despair that, abandoning every attempt at reform, I withdrew from any further dealings with that frivolous institution.

I had received the most urgent personal provocation to seek an explanation of the modern Theatre's unalterable character in its social situation. 'Twere a mad attempt, undoubtedly, to take an institute whose public function was almost exclusively directed to the distraction and amusement of people bored to death by pleasure—and further, to earning money to cover the cost of exhibitions reckoned for that end—and employ it for a diametrically opposite object, namely the snatching of a populace from out its vulgar interests of everyday, to attune it to a reverent reception of the highest and sincerest things the human mind can grasp. I had time enough to think out the reasons for that attitude of our Theatre towards the Public, and on the other hand to ponder the bases of those social relations which themselves should form the conditions for the appearance of the Theatre I had in mind, with the same necessity as that Theatre of ours had issued from our modern relations. Just as I had won a solid anchorage for the character of my dramatico-musical ideal in the rare and isolated doings of brilliant artists, so history supplied me with a typic model for that ideal relation, dreamt by me, of Theatre and Public. I found it in the theatre of ancient Athens, where its walls were thrown open on none but special, sacred feast-days, where the taste of Art was coupled with the celebration of a religious rite in which the most illustrious members of the State themselves took part as poets and performers, to appear like priests before the assembled populace of field and city; a populace filled with such high awaitings from the sublimeness of the art-work to be set before it, that a Sophocles, an Æschylus could set before the Folk the deepest-meaning of all poems, assured of their understanding.

The reasons for the downfall of this matchless Artwork, after which I needs must ask in sorrow, full soon displayed themselves to me. My first attention was riveted by the social causes of that fall, and I believed I found them in the causes of the downfall of the antique State itself. In consequence I tried to argue out the social basis of that organisation of the human race which, improving on the antique State's defects, might found a system in which the relation of Art to public Life, such as once obtained in Athens, should be re-established on an if possible still nobler, and at any rate more durable footing. My thoughts hereon I wrote down in a little essay, entitled "Art and Revolution"; my original wish, to publish it as a series of articles in a French political journal, I gave up on being informed that the period (it was in the year 1849) was not suitable for drawing the attention of the Parisian public to such a subject. At present it is I, myself, who should deem it too far-reaching, to make you better acquainted with the contents of that pamphlet, and you certainly will thank me for sparing you the attempt. Enough, that I have indicated into what apparently out-of-the-way meditations I was led by my desire to win for my artistic ideal a foothold in reality, how ideal soever in its turn.

Longer was I detained by the inquiry into the character of that regretted dissolution of the great Greek Artwork. Here I beheld the surprising phenomenon of a disbandment and disseverance of the single art-branches erewhile united in the perfect Drama. From the all-powerful union

—where, working in common for one common end, they had made it possible to set before the assembled Folk the loftiest and deepest aims of manhood in a universally intelligible form—the separate component parts of Art fell loose, no more to be the inspiring mentors of the public, but to become the otiose pastime of the private connoisseur; so that whilst the crowd was treated to public gladiator-combats and fights of beasts, the man of culture sought his lonely solace in literature and painting. Now it was above all weight for me, that I fancied I must recognise how the single, separately prosecuted art-varieties, however much their power of expression was eventually developed and intensified by mighty geniuses, yet without falling into unnaturalness and positive abnormity, could never and by no manner of means replace that all-enabled Artwork, which had been possible to nothing but their combination. With the sayings of the most eminent art-critics at my hand—with the investigations of a Lessing, for instance, anent the boundaries of Poetry and Painting—I believed I had reached the insight that each single art-branch evolves along a line of force which finally brings it to its limit, and that it cannot overstep this limit without danger of losing itself in the unintelligible and absolute-fantastic, nay, absurd. At this point I thought I plainly saw in it a longing to reach out its hand to the other, the correlated art-variety—from this point on, the only capable one; and though, in regard of my ideal, it must actively interest me to follow these tendencies in each particular art-variety, I finally believed I could prove such a tendency to exist the plainest and most strikingly (especially in view of the uncommon significance of the newer music) in the relation of Poetry to Music. Whilst trying in this wise to picture to myself that Artwork in which all the single art varieties should combine for their own highest completion, I lit upon a conscious glimpse of that very ideal which had unconsciously been forming in my mind and hovering before the longing artist. Since I could not assume the possibility of a complete appearance of this ideal Artwork in the

Present—particularly when I remembered the thoroughly false position of the Theatre, as regards our public life—I called my ideal the "Artwork of the Future." Under that title I published an already more exhaustive essay, in which I set forth at some length the thoughts just sketched for you; to that title (as I may mention in passing) we owe the invention of the spectral "Music of the Future" which plays its so popular pranks in even French reports on art, and you now will readily guess through what a misunderstanding, and for what an object, it has been invented.

From a closer account of the details of that essay, too, I will exempt you, my honoured friend! I myself attach no further value to it, than it may have for those who would be interested to hear how, and in what manner of speech, a productive artist was once at the pains of throwing light—above all for himself—on problems which are generally left to the critic by trade to puzzle out, but which can hardly thrust themselves upon the latter with the same peculiar urgency as on the former. Similarly I will give you merely a general outline of the contents of a third and more elaborate art-writing which I published soon after the appearance of the last-named, under the title: "Opera and Drama"; for I cannot but think that its expositions of my main idea, going into almost the finest detail, must have been of greater interest to myself than they can be to others, either now or in the future. They were private meditations, to which, pricked on by lively interest in the subject, I partly gave a polemical tinge. That subject was a minuter inquiry into the relations of Poetry and Music to each other, this time with a quite definite view to the Dramatic Artwork.

Here I thought necessary, before all else, to refute the mistaken notion of those who deemed the ideal, if not already reached, yet immediately prepared-for in the actual genre of Opera. Already in Italy, but still more in France and Germany, this problem had exercised the most prominent minds of Literature. The battle of the Gluckists and Piccinists in Paris was nothing but a controversy, by its nature undecidable, as to whether the ideal of Drama was to be attained, or not, in Opera; those who maintained the affirmative side of this thesis were held in serious check, despite their seeming victory, so soon as their opponents pointed out that Music was so predominant in Opera that to her alone, and not to Poetry, was to be attributed its success. Voltaire, though theoretically inclined to side with the former party, yet saw himself compelled by the concrete case to pronounce that crushing verdict of his: "*Ce qui est trop sot pour être dit, on le chante.*" In Germany—where a similar problem, started first by Lessing, was discussed between Schiller and Goethe with a decided leaning to the most favourable expectations from Opera—the last-named, Goethe, though in crying contrast with his theoretical opinion, involuntarily confirmed the verdict of Voltaire; for he himself wrote sundry opera-texts, and, to place himself on the *niveau* of the genre, thought good to keep them as trivial as possible both in invention and execution; so that only with regret can we see these utterly vapid pieces enrolled among his poems.

That this favourable opinion had so often been taken up again by men of intellect, but never could come to fruit, shewed me on the one hand the apparently near possibility of reaching the supreme height of Drama by a thorough union of Poetry and Music, on the other the fundamental faultiness of just the Opera-genre itself; a constitutional defect which could not come to the consciousness of the musician first of all, by the nature of the thing, and yet must necessarily escape the notice of the literary poet too. The poet, not being himself a musician, found in Opera a clamped and bolted scaffolding of musical forms, which imposed upon him in advance quite settled laws for the invention and execution of the dramatic groundwork he was expected to supply. Not he, but only the musician, could alter an iota of these forms; and of what a kind their substance was, the poet—called in to lend a helping hand—disclosed involuntarily by the obvious way in which he felt compelled to lower the tone of his inventive powers, sinking both plot and verses to that flagrant triviality for which he was scourged by Voltaire. In sooth 'twill not be necessary to expose the abortiveness and platitude, nay the absurdity, of the whole genre of opera-libretto; even in France the best attempts of this class have consisted more in covering up the evil, than in removing it. So the intrinsic framework of the opera remained for the poet an alien and unassailable affair, to which he merely paid a forced obedience; and thus it is that truly great poets, with few and unfavourable exceptions, have never had aught to do with Opera.

The only further question is, how the Musician could possibly have given to Opera an ideal stamp, when the Poet, in his practical concern therewith, could not so much as keep erect the claims we make on every reasonable Play? The Musician, who, eternally preoccupied with the maturing of those purely musical forms, saw nothing before him but a field for the exercise of his specific musical talent? In the first part of my last-named writing: "Opera and Drama," I believe I have proved the contradictoriness and perversity of the expectations cherished of the musician in this matter. Seeing that I expressed my highest admiration of the beautiful and entrancing things achieved by great masters on this domain, I had no need to belittle their acknowledged art-fame when exposing weaknesses in their achievements, since I was able to trace these weaknesses to the root-defect of the genre itself. No, my real object, in that at any rate ungratifying exhibition, was to furnish proof that the ideal perfectionment of Opera, which had hovered before so many leading minds, must first of all be based on a total alteration in the character of the *poet's* share in the artwork.

To convince myself that this effectual participation of the Poet's would be a free-willed act, and one desired by himself, I took count of the aforesaid hopes and wishes, repeatedly and significantly uttered by great poets, to see an ideal art-genre reached in Opera. I tried to fathom the meaning of this bias, and fancied I found it in that natural longing which leads the poet, for conception as for form, to employ the material of abstract thought, namely Speech, in a mode to work upon the Feeling itself. Just as this tendency is predominant even in the invention of the poetic 'stuff,' and only that picture of man's life is called poetical in which all motives merely explicable to abstract reason have been transformed into motives of purely-human Feeling, so is it beyond a doubt the sole prescriber of form and expression in the poem's working-out, in his diction the poet seeks to replace the abstract, conventional meaning of words by their original sensuous meaning, and through a rhythmic arrangement of his verse, as finally through the already wellnigh musical adornment of rhyme, to ensure for his phrase an effect that shall take the Feeling captive and control it as if by a spell. In this tendency of the poet, essential to his very being, we see him arrive at last at the limit of his art-branch, where he comes already into immediate contact with Music; and thus that work of the poet's must rank as the most excellent, which in its final consummation should become entirely music.

I therefore believed I must term the "mythos" the poet's ideal Stuff—that native, nameless poem of the Folk, which throughout the ages we ever meet new-handled by the great poets of periods of consummate culture; for in it there almost vanishes the conventional form of man's relations, merely explicable to abstract reason, to shew instead the eternally intelligible, the purely human, but in just that inimitable concrete form which lends to every sterling myth an individual shape so swiftly cognisable. To investigations connected herewith I devoted the second portion of my book, concluding it with the question: What must be the most perfect Form, wherein to display this ideal poetic Stuff?

In the third part I plunged into an examination of the technical possibilities of such a Form, with the end-result

"ZUKUNFTSMUSIK." 313

that *only the extraordinarily rich development—entirely unknown to former centuries—attained by Music in our times* could bring about the baring of those possibilities.

I feel the importance of this assertion too keenly, not to regret that this is not the place for allowing myself a more exhaustive recapitulation of its grounds. In the said third part I believe I have supplied them, at least sufficiently for my own conviction; therefore if here I offer you but a scanty outline of my views on this matter, I pray you to take my word for it, that whatever may to you appear paradoxical, will there be found at least more closely argued.

Since the rebirth of the fine arts among the Christian nations of Europe, two art-varieties have undeniably obtained an altogether new development, perfect beyond anything they had reached in classical antiquity; I speak of Painting and Music. The wonderfully ideal stamp received by Painting as early as the first century of the Renaissance, stands so beyond all doubt, and its characteristics have been so well expounded, that we here need only note the novelty of this phenomenon in the general history of Art, as also the fact that it is a phenomenon belonging in a quite peculiar manner to the newer art. In a still higher and—I believe—still more important measure, have we to make the same assertion regarding Modern Music. Harmony, entirely unknown to the ancients, its inconceivable expansion and aggrandisement through Polyphony, are the invention and the most peculiar work of latter centuries.

With the Greeks we know Music only as an attendant upon Dance; the dance's movements gave to her, as also to the poem chanted to the dance-tune, the laws of Rhythm; and these rhythmic laws so strictly governed verse and melody, that Greek Music (a term which almost always included Poetry) may be regarded merely as Dance expressing itself in tones and words. It was these dance-tunes, still living in the Folk, originally pertaining to the rites of heathen gods, and making out the whole of antique music, that were adopted by the earliest Christian congregations, to celebrate their gradually maturing Service of God. This rite, entirely excluding Dance as worldly and ungodly, most naturally let drop as well the essential part of antique melody, its uncommonly animated and changeful rhythm; whereby this melody took on the rhythmically quite un-accented character of the Chorale, as still prevailing in our churches. But manifestly, with the loss of its rhythmic elasticity, this melody was robbed of its own peculiar motive of expression; and even to-day, to convince ourselves of the uncommonly slight expression of antique melody when deprived of just this ornament of Rhythm, we have only to think of it as also without the harmony now laid beneath it. To raise the melody's expression—in the inmost sense of the term—however, the Christian spirit invented many-voiced Harmony, on the basis of the four-part chord; and the characteristic changes of this chord at once supplied the melody with an expressional motive such as had previously been furnished it by Rhythm. What a wonderfully inward expression, not so much as dreamt of theretofore, the melodic phrase hereby attained, we see with ever fresh amazement in the quite incomparable master-works of Italian Church-music. Here the different voices, originally destined for nothing but bringing the harmonic chord to simultaneous hearing with the melodic note, at last themselves obtained a free and increasingly expressive development, so that, with aid of so-called Counterpoint, each of these subordinate voices (the melody being called the *canto fermo*) now moved with an independent expression of its own; whereby in the works of the most exalted masters the rendering of such a sacred chant produced so deep a searching of the heart, that no kindred effect of any other art can possibly be compared therewith.

The downfall of this art in Italy, and the contemporaneous rise of opera-melody among the Italians, I can call nothing but a relapse into Paganism. When, with the downfall of the Church, the worldly longing gained the upper hand in Italy for application to Music too, people took the shortest route, gave back to melody its pristine rhythmic attribute, and employed it for Song in just the same manner as it had earlier been employed for Dance. I will forego any special proof of the astounding incongruences between modern verse—developed on the lines of Christian melody—and this dance-melody now laid above it, merely begging you to remark that this melody treated that verse with an almost complete indifference, and finally allowed the singing virtuoso to be the sole dictator of its movements and its variations. Our chief reason, however, for calling this melody a relapse in evolution, and not an advance, is that it indisputably did not know how to take advantage of the uncommonly weighty invention made by Christian music, of Harmony and its embodiment as Polyphony. Upon a harmonic basis of such scantiness that it can dispense at a pinch with all accompaniment, Italian opera-melody has contented itself with so exiguous a periodic structure, even as regards the ordering and linking of its parts, that the educated musician of our times stands sorrowfully aghast before this threadbare, wellnigh childish art-form, whose narrow confines doom even the most talented composer, should he occupy himself therewith, to an utter standstill in respect of Form.

In Germany, on the contrary, this selfsame bent to secularise the Christian music acquired a new, peculiar import. German masters, too, went back to the original rhythmic melody, which, side by side with the music of the Church, had survived among the Folk as national Dance-tune. But in lieu of casting away the Christian Church's wealth of harmony, these masters rather sought to renovate it by a union with the livelier motion of rhythmic melody, and in such a way that harmony and rhythm should take equal shares in the expression of the melody. Herewith the independent motion of Polyphony was not only retained, but brought to such a pitch of contrapuntal art, that each voice took an independent part in delivering the rhythmic melody; so that the melody was no longer restricted to the original *canto fermo*, but appeared in each of the accompanying voices also. How immensely varied and enthralling an effect, of a potency all Music's own, may thus be attained in ecclesiastic song itself, wherever the lyric swing thrusts on to rhythmic melody—this anyone may learn at once, who is lucky enough to hear a fine performance of Bach's vocal compositions; and among others I may make special mention of an eight-part motett by Sebastian Bach: " Sing to the Lord a new song! " in which the lyric swing of rhythmic melody seems to be dashing through an ocean of harmonic waves.

But in Instrumental-music this development of rhythmic melody upon the base of Christian harmony was finally to take a still freer course, to gain a still more manifold and finely-traced expression. Without touching at present on the 'intensive' import of the orchestra, allow me to draw your first attention to the mere enlargement of Dance-melody's original *form*. Through the formation of the string-instrument quartet, the polyphonic line of treatment was extended also to the orchestra, its different voices being handled in the same independent fashion as the singing voices in Church-music; thus the orchestra was emancipated from the subordinate position it theretofore had occupied, and occupies in Italian Opera till this very day, as a mere rhythmic-harmonic accompaniment. Now it is highly interesting, and our only means of enlightenment as to the essence of all musical Form, to note how every effort of the German masters was directed to giving the simple dance-melody, delivered independently by instruments, a gradually richer and broader evolution. This melody originally consisted of a very brief 'period,' essentially composed of only four bars, though that number became doubled or even quadrupled; our masters' main aim seems to have been to give it a greater extension, and thus to reach a broader, ampler form wherein to deploy their harmony. The art-form peculiar to Fugue, when applied to Dance-melody, gave occasion for also lengthening the duration of the whole piece, as follows: this melody was delivered by each 'voice' in turn, now in diminution, now in augmentation; shewn in changing lights, through harmonic modulation, and its motion kept in constant interest, through contrapuntal figures and counter-themes. A second procedure consisted in this: one fitted several dance-melodies to each other, allowing them to alternate in accordance with the character of their expression, and linking them by transitional passages, in which the art of Counterpoint was of particular assistance. Upon this simple groundplan was built the peculiar artwork of the *Symphony*. HAYDN was the genius who first developed this form to a broader compass, and gave it power of deep expression through an exhaustless play of motives, as also of their transitional links and workings-out. Though the Italian operatic melody had kept to its threadbare formal build, it had received in the mouth of talented and feeling singers, and borne on the breath of the noblest musical organ, a graceful sensuous colouring as yet unknown to German musicians—a colouring whose sweet euphony was absent from their instrumental melodies. It was MOZART who became aware of this charm, and, while he brought to Italian Opera the richer *development* of the German mode of instrumental composition, he imparted in turn to the orchestral melody the full *euphony* of the Italian mode of song. The ample heritage and promise of both these masters was taken up by BEETHOVEN; he matured the Symphonic artwork to so engrossing a breadth of form, and filled that form with so manifold and enthralling a melodic content, that we stand to-day before the Beethovenian Symphony as before the landmark of an entirely new period in the history of universal Art; for through it there came into the world a phenomenon not even remotely approached by anything the art of any age or any people has to shew us.

In this Symphony instruments speak a language whereof

the world at no previous time had any knowledge: for here, with a hitherto unknown persistence, the purely-musical Expression enchains the hearer in an inconceivably varied mesh of nuances; rouses his inmost being, to a degree unreachable by any other art; and in all its changefulness reveals an ordering principle so free and bold, that we can but deem it more forcible than any logic, yet without the laws of logic entering into it in the slightest—nay rather, the reasoning march of Thought, with its track of causes and effects, here finds no sort o foothold. So that this Symphony must positively appear to us a revelation from another world; and in truth it opens out a scheme (*Zusammenhang*) of the world's phenomena quite different from the ordinary logical scheme, and whereof one foremost thing is undeniable :—that it thrusts home with the most overwhelming conviction, and guides our Feeling with such a sureness that the logic-mongering Reason is completely routed and disarmed thereby.

The metaphysical necessity for the discovery of this quite new faculty of speech precisely in our times, appears to me to lie in the daily more conventional drift of modern word-languages. If we look closer at the evolutionary history of these languages, even to-day we meet in their so-called word-roots a rudiment that plainly shews us how at the first beginning the formation of the mental concept of an object ran almost completely parallel with the subjective feeling of it; and the supposition that the earliest Speech of man must have borne a great analogy with Song, might not perhaps seem quite ridiculous. Starting with a physical meaning for his words, in any case quite subjectively felt, the speech of man evolved along a more and more abstract line; so that at last there remained nothing but a conventional meaning, depriving the Feeling of any share in understanding the words, just as their syntax was made entirely dependent on rules to be acquired by learning. In necessary agreement with the moral evolution of mankind, there grew up equally in speech and manners a Convention, whose laws were no longer intelligible to natural Feeling, but were drilled in to youth by maxims comprehensible to nothing but Reflection. Now ever since the modern European languages — divided into different stocks, to boot — have followed their conventional drift with a more and more obvious tendency, Music, on the other hand, has been developing a power of expression unknown to the world before. 'Tis as though the purely-human Feeling, intensified by the pressure of a conventional civilisation, had been seeking an outlet for the operation of its own peculiar laws of speech; an outlet through which, unfettered by the laws of logical Thought, it might express itself intelligibly to itself. The uncommon popularity of Music in our times; the constantly increasing interest, spreading through every stratum of society, in the products of the deepest-meaning class of music; the ever growing eagerness to make musical training an integral part of education: all this, so manifest and undeniable in itself, at like time proves the correctness of the postulate, that Music's modern evolution has answered to a profoundly inward need of mankind's, and that, however unintelligible her tongue when judged by the laws of Logic, she must possess a more persuasive title to our comprehension than anything contained within those laws.

In face of this irrefutable conclusion, there would henceforth stand only two ways open to Poetry. Either a complete removal into the field of Abstraction, a sheer combining of mental concepts and portrayal of the world by expounding the logical laws of Thought. And this office she fulfils as Philosophy. Or an inner blending with Music, with that Music whose infinite faculty has been disclosed to us by the Symphony of Beethoven.

Poetry will lightly find the path hereto, and perceive her final ascension into Music to be her own, her inmost longing, so soon as she grows aware of a need in Music, herself, which Poetry alone can still. To explain this need, let us first attest that ineradicable attribute of all human apperception which spurs it to find out the laws of

Causality, and in presence of every impressive phenomenon to ask itself instinctively the question "Why?" Even the hearing of a Symphonic tone-piece does not entirely silence this question; rather, since it cannot give the answer, it brings the hearer's inductive faculty* into a confusion which not only is liable to disquiet him, but also becomes the ground of a totally false judgment. To answer this disturbing, and yet so irremissible question, so that in a manner of speaking it is circumvented from the first, can only be the poet's work. But it can succeed in the hands of none but that poet who is fully alive to Music's tendence and exhaustless faculty of Expression, and therefore drafts his poem in such a fashion that it may penetrate the finest fibres of the musical tissue, and the spoken *thought* entirely dissolve into the *feeling*. Obviously, no other form of poetry can help us here, save that in which the poet no longer describes, but brings his subject into actual and convincing representment to the senses; and this sole form is Drama. Drama, at the moment of its actual scenic representation, arouses in the beholder such an intimate and instant interest in an action borrowed faithfully from life itself, at least in its possibilities, that man's sympathetic Feeling already passes into that ecstatic state where it clean forgets the fateful question "Why?" and willingly yields itself, in utmost excitation, to the guidance of those new laws whereby Music makes herself so wondrously intelligible and—in a profounder sense—supplies withal the only fitting answer to that "Why?"

In that third part of the last-named book I tried to outline more precisely the technical laws for bringing about this intimate blend of music and poetry in Drama. You surely will not expect me to here attempt their recapitulation, since the preceding sketch must already have fatigued you no less than myself; and by my own fatigue I see that, quite against my will, I am again approaching that state of mind which obsessed me when at work on those

---

* "Das kausale Vorstellungsvermögen"—literally "the faculty of imagining causes," i.e. for any given effect.—Tr.

theoretic writings some years ago, and so strangely weighed upon my brain that I have called it an abnormal state—into which I entertain a lively horror of falling back.—

I called that state of mind abnormal, because it drove me to treat as a theorem a thing which had become quite positive and certain to me in my artistic intuition (*Anschauung*) and production, so as to make it equally clear to my reflective consciousness, and for this I needed abstract meditation. But nothing can be more alien and distressful to the artist's nature than such a course of thought, so thoroughly opposed to his customary method. He therefore does not surrender himself to it with the needful coolness, the property of the theorist by profession; rather is he thrust on by a passionate impatience, which prevents him from devoting the requisite time to a careful handling of style; he fain would give entire in every sentence the view (*Anschauung*) that embraces the whole picture of his subject; doubt, as to whether he has succeeded in this, drives him to a constant repetition of the attempt—which fills him at last with a heat and irritation that should be absolute strangers to the theorist. Then he grows alive to all these faults and evils, and freshly harassed by his feeling of them, he hurriedly ends his work with a sigh, that after all he will probably be understood by none but those who already share with him the same artistic view.

Thus my mental state was like a brain-cramp; I was trying to speak out theoretically what the aforesaid disparity between my artistic tendencies and the tendencies of our public art, and especially the Opera-house, seemed to preclude me from conveying on the inerrably convincing path of direct artistic production. For refuge from this torturing state, I felt driven back to the normal exercise of my artistic powers. I sketched and carried out a dramatic plan of such considerable dimensions that, in mere obedience to the claims of my subject, I deliberately removed myself from all possibility of grafting this work upon our Opera-repertoire, as it now is. This musical

III.   X

drama, embracing a whole elaborate tetralogy, was to be performable in public only under the most unusual circumstances. That ideal possibility, remote from every influence of Modern Opera, both flattered my fancy and raised my spirits to such a pitch that, chasing away all theoretic crotchets and devoting myself thenceforward to unbroken artistic production, I could drop back into my own true nature as though recovering from a serious illness. The work of which I speak, and the greater part of whose musical composition I have since already finished, is called "*Der Ring des Nibelungen.*" If the present attempt to lay other of my opera-poems before you in prose translation should not displease you, you perhaps might find me ready to have something similar undertaken with that cycle of dramas.

Whilst, thus completely resigned as to any further artistic contact with publicity, I was refreshing myself from the aches and pains of my trip into the realm of speculative Theory by working out my new artistic plans; whilst no inducement, nor in particular the idiotic misunderstandings which mostly fell to the lot of my theoretic works, could turn my steps again to that domain: from the other side there came about a change in my relations to publicity, upon which I had not reckoned in the slightest.—

My operas—one of which ("Lohengrin") I had never conducted at all, and the others only at the theatre where I was personally engaged before—had spread with growing success over an ever larger number, and finally over all the theatres of Germany, and were there arriving at a permanent, indisputable popularity. Through this phenomenon, at bottom most surprising to myself, I renewed experiences such as I had often made during my former practical career, and which, however much the Opera-house repelled me on the one side, on the other side had chained me to it again and again; inasmuch as they shewed me single exceptions, whose uncommonly fine doings and effects opened my eyes to possibilities which, as I have already told you, determined me to harbour ideal plans.

I was present at not one of these performances of my operas, and it therefore was only from the reports of intelligent friends, as also from the character of their public success, that I could argue to their spirit. The picture to be drawn from my friends' reports is not of a kind to inspire me with a more favourable opinion of those performances in general, than I had been forced to form about the character of our operatic representations in the bulk. But, whilst confirmed in my pessimistic views as a whole, I now enjoyed the pessimist's advantage, namely of the more rejoicing at the good, nay excellent, which cropped up here and there, as I had not held myself justified in expecting or demanding it; whereas before, as optimist, because the good and excellent was possible, I had erected it into a standard for everything else, and had thus been driven to intolerance and ingratitude. The single first-rate achievements, of which I heard thus unexpectedly, filled me with new warmth and moved me to the thankfulest acknowledgment; whilst I had hitherto connected the possibility of competent art-doings with a general state of thorough soundness, that possibility presented itself as even now attainable by way of exception.

Almost still more deeply was I stirred by my observation of the extraordinarily warm impression produced upon the Public by my operas, even in the case of very dubious, and often most disfiguring performances. When I think how hostilely the critics behaved, especially at first—the critics to whom my art-writings were an abomination, and who obstinately averred of my operas, though really written at an earlier period, that they were deliberately and "reflectively" composed according to those theories—I can see nothing less than a most weighty and encouraging sign, in the outspoken liking of the public for works of such a tendency as mine. It was intelligible enough that the larger public should not let Criticism confound its liking, when the critics cried, as once in Germany: "Turn your back upon Rossini's siren strains; shut your ears against his tempting knack of melody!" and the public went on hearing with delight. But here was a case where the critics warned the public without cease, against paying its money for things which by no possible chance could please it; for what alone it seeks in Opera, its melodies, forever melodies—were right-down not forthcoming in my operas; no, nothing but the most wearisome recitatives, the most un-understandable musical gallimathias; in short—" Music of the Future"!

You may imagine then what an impression it must have made upon me, to receive not only the most irrefragable proofs of a really popular success of my operas with the German public in the aggregate, but also personal evidence of a total change of taste and judgment on the part of individuals who theretofore had found pleasure in nothing but the most lascivious tendencies of opera and ballet, had waived with contumely each suggestion to bestow their notice on a more earnest tendency of musico-dramatic art! Such experiences have fallen pretty often to my lot, and what encouraging, profoundly comforting conclusions I felt justified in drawing from them, I will here allow myself to notify in brief.

Manifestly it was no question of the greater or lesser measure of my talent, since even my most vindictive critics did not take the field against that, but against the tendencies pursued by me, and sought to explain my eventual successes by my talent's being better than my maxims. Thus, unmoved by the somewhat flattering recognition of my aptitudes, I had only to rejoice that I had set out with a right instinct when I deemed it possible for an equal interpenetration of Poesy and Music to bring about an artwork that should produce an irresistibly convincing impression at the moment of its stage-performance, an impression such as to resolve all arbitrary Reflection into purely-human Feeling. That I saw this effect attained in part, notwithstanding many great flaws in the performance—upon whose absolute correctness, on the other hand, I needs must set so great a store—inspired me with even bolder views of Music's all-enabling efficacy;

and these I finally will endeavour to explain to you at greater length.

I can only hope to make myself clear to you on this difficult, and yet extremely weighty point, if I take nothing but *form* in eye. In my theoretic works I tried to lay down not only form, but also content; seeing, however, that Theory is necessarily an abstract definition, and not a concrete demonstration, I exposed myself to great danger of not being understood, or even of being mis-understood. Therefore, as said above, at no price would I willingly engage again in such a course. Yet I recognise the inconvenience of discussing a form without in some way or other denoting its content. Thus, as I told you at first, it was only your wish to receive at like time a translation of my opera-poems, that could at all decide me to make the attempt to give you an authentic statement of my theoretic procedure, so far as it has become conscious to myself. Let me therefore say a little to you about those poems; this, I hope, will enable me to speak thereafter of nothing but the musical form—upon which there hinges so much here, and as to which so many erroneous notions have spread abroad.

Before all else, however, I must crave your indulgence for laying these opera-poems before you in nothing but a prose translation. The endless difficulties experienced by us in the verse translation of "Tannhäuser"—which opera will soon be introduced to the Parisian public through a full stage-performance—have shewn that labours of this kind demand an expenditure of time such as could not be applied just now to the translation of my other pieces. I must therefore quite forego any impression to be made upon you by their poetic form, and content myself with shewing you the character of their subject-matter, their dramatic treatment and its tendency, so as to give you an inkling of the share taken in their conception and configuration by the spirit of Music. May the present translation suffice for that, though it pretends to nothing beyond rendering the original text as literally as possible.

The first three of these poems: "Der fliegende Holländer," "Tannhäuser" and "Lohengrin" were written, composed and, with the exception of "Lohengrin," produced upon the stage before I commenced my theoretic writings. By them (if that were fully possible at mere hand of the subject-matter) I might therefore demonstrate the evolutionary march of my artistic productivity, up to the point where I saw myself prompted to take theoretical stock of my own procedure. This I mention, however, merely to draw your attention to the great mistake which people make, when they think needful to suppose that these three works were written with conscious purpose after abstract rules imposed upon myself. Let me rather tell you that even my boldest conclusions as to the attainable dramatico-musical form were thrust upon me through my at like time carrying in my head the plan for my great Nibelungen drama, a portion of which I had even turned into verse already; * and there [in my head] I was maturing it in such a fashion, that my theories were wellnigh nothing but an abstract expression of the productive process going on within me. Hence my system proper, if so you choose to call it, finds in those first three poems but a most conditional application.

It is otherwise with the last of the poems I place before you, with "Tristan und Isolde." This I drafted and carried out after I had already completed the musical setting of the greater portion of my Nibelungen pieces.† The outer motive for this break in that great labour, was the desire to furnish a work whose stage requirements and smaller compass should make it sooner and more easily performable; a wish inspired on the one hand by the need to at last hear something of my own once more, while on the

---

* *Siegfried's Tod*, the first version of *Die Götterdämmerung*, written in 1848.—Tr.

† As far as the middle of the second Act of *Siegfried*, which was laid aside in the spring of 1857.—Tr.

other, the aforesaid encouraging accounts of performances of my older works in Germany now gave it a semblance of possible fulfilment. Upon that work I consent to your making the severest claims deducible from my theoretic premises: not because I formed it on my system, for every theory was clean forgotten by me; but since here I moved with fullest freedom and the most utter disregard of every theoretic scruple, to such an extent that during the working-out I myself was aware how far I had outstripped my system. Believe me, there is no greater sense of wellbeing, than this complete inhesitancy of the artist when producing, as felt by me whilst working out my "Tristan." It perhaps was only possible because a previous period of reflection had strengthened me in much the way my master once said he had done by a course of the hardest contrapuntal exercises, namely, not for writing fugues, but for that which a man can only make his own by rigorous practice: self-reliance, sureness!

Let me devote a word or two to an opera which preceded even the "Flying Dutchman": "Rienzi," a work full of youthful fire, a work which procured me my first success in Germany, and which is continually given beside my other operas, not only at the theatre where I first produced it, Dresden, but since at many another. Upon this work, which owes its conception and ultimate form to the desire of emulation woken by my earliest impressions of the Heroic Opera of Spontini, as also of the dazzling genre of Grand Opera which took its rise in Paris, the Opera of Auber, Meyerbeer and Halévy—upon this work, I say, I lay to-day, and in your regard, no special stress; for there is not yet traceable in it any essential feature of my later-evolving art-views, and I have no particular object in posing as a successful opera-composer, but only in enlightening you anent an enigmatic aspect of my tendencies. This "Rienzi" was completed during my first stay in Paris; I had the glittering Grand Opéra before me, and was insane enough to flatter myself with the wish to see my work produced there. Should this youthful wish still come to pass, you surely will join me in marvelling at the decrees of Fate, which permit so long an interval of time, and experiences so wholly alienating, to step between wish and fulfilment.

This five-act opera, executed on the very broadest scale, was directly followed by the "Flying Dutchman," which I originally meant to be performed in one sole Act. You see, the glamour of the Paris ideal was fading before my eyes, and I had begun to draw my laws of Form from other waters than the sea of use and wont spread wide before me. The substance of my mood now lies before you: the poem speaks it plainly out. What degree of poetic value may be assigned it, I know not; but I do know that even while writing down that poem I already felt differently to when throwing off the libretto for "Rienzi, where I had nothing in mind but just an "opera-text," to crowd as full as possible with all the existing and incumbent forms of sheer Grand Opera: namely Introductions, Finales, Choruses, Arias, Duets, Trios, and so forth.

With this and all my following sketches I once for all forsook the realm of *history*, even in my choice of stuff, for that of *legend* (*Sage*). I may here dispense with pointing out to you the inner tendencies which guided that decision, and lay stress upon the influence exerted by this choice of Stuff on the moulding of the poetic and, in particular, the musical Form.

All that detailed description and exhibition of the Historico-conventional which is requisite for making us clearly understand the events of a given, remote historical epoch, and which the historical novelist or dramatist of our times has therefore to set forth at such exhaustive length—all this I could pass over. And thus not only for the poem, but in particular for the music, there was removed any compulsion to adopt a mode of treatment quite foreign to them, and above all quite impossible to Music. The legend, in whatever age or nation it occurs, has the merit of seizing nothing but the purely-human Content of that age and nation, and of giving forth that content in a form peculiar to itself, of sharpest outline, and therefore swiftly understandable. A ballad, a refrain of the Folk, suffices to acquaint us with this telling character in the twinkling of an eye. This legendary colouring, for the display of a purely-human event, has in particular the real advantage of uncommonly facilitating the task I assigned to the poet above, the task of silencing the question "Why?" Just as through the characteristic scene, so also through the legendary tone, the mind is forthwith placed in that dream-like state wherein it presently shall come to full clairvoyance, and thus perceive a new coherence in the world's phenomena; a coherence it could not detect with the waking eye of everyday, wherefore it had ever asked about the Why as though to conquer its abashedness in presence of the world's Incomprehensible, of that world which now becomes to it so clear and vividly intelligible. How Music is at last to fully round this quickening spell, you now will lightly comprehend.—

But even for the poet's manipulation of the stuff, its legendary character affords the essential advantage that whereas the simple sequence of the plot, so easily surveyable in all its outward bearings, renders it needless to linger by any outer explanation of its course, on the other hand the poem's far largest space can be devoted to exhibiting the inner springs of action, those inner soul-motives which are finally and alone to stamp the Action as a 'necessary' one—and that through the sympathetic interest taken in those motives by our own inmost hearts.

In looking through the poems now placed before you, you will readily notice that I but very gradually grew conscious of the advantage just referred to, and but gradually learned to profit by it. Even the outward volumen, increasing with each poem, will afford you evidence of this. You will soon perceive that my initial bias against giving the poem a broader reach sprang chiefly from my keeping at first too much in eye the traditional Form of opera-music, which had hitherto made a poem impossible that did not allow of numberless word-repetitions. In the

"Flying Dutchman" my only care, in general, was to keep the plot to its simplest features, to exclude all useless detail such as the intrigues one borrows from common life, and in return to more fully develop those traits which were to set in its proper light the characteristic colouring of the legendary stuff, since here they seemed to me to altogether coincide with the idiosyncrasy of the inner motives of action; and to do this in such a way, that that Colour itself should be turned into Action.

You perhaps will find the plot of "Tannhäuser" already far more markedly evolving from its inner motives. Here the decisive catastrophe proceeds without the least constraint from a lyric tournament of bards, in which no other power save the most hidden inner workings of the soul drives onward the decisive blow, and in such a manner that even this denouement's *form* belongs purely to the lyric element.

The whole interest of "Lohengrin" consists in an inner working within the heart of Elsa, involving every secret of the soul: the endurance of a spell of wondrous power for blessing, that fills her whole surrounding with the most persuasive sense of truth, hangs solely on her refraining from the question as to its *Whence*. Like a cry from the inmost want (*Noth*) of woman's heart, this question struggles loose—and the spell has vanished. You may guess how singularly this tragic "Whence?" concurs with that aforesaid theoretic "Why?"

I too, as I have told you, felt driven to this "Whence and Wherefore?" and for long it banned me from the magic of my art. But my time of penance taught me to overcome the question. All doubt at last was taken from me, when I gave myself up to the "Tristan." Here, in perfect trustulness, I plunged into the inner depths of soul-events, and from out this inmost centre of the world I fearlessly built up its outer form. A glance at the volumen of this poem will shew you at once that the exhaustive detail-work which an historical poet is obliged to devote to clearing up the outward bearings of his plot, to the detriment of a lucid exposition of its inner motives, I now trusted myself to apply to these latter alone. Life and death, the whole import and existence of the outer world, here hang on nothing but the inner movements of the soul. The whole affecting Action comes about for reason only that the inmost soul demands it, and steps to light with the very shape foretokened in the inner shrine.

Perhaps in the execution of this poem much will strike you as going too far into subtle (*intime*) detail; and even should you concede this tendency as permissible to the poet, you yet might wonder how he could dare hand over to the musician all this refinement of minutiæ, for carrying out. In this you would be possessed by the same bias as led myself, when drafting the "Flying Dutchman," to give its poem nothing but the most general of contours, destined merely to play into the hands of an absolute-musical working-out. But in this regard let me at once make one reply to you: whereas the verses were there intended as an underlay for Operatic melody, to be stretched to the length demanded by that melody through countless repetitions of words and phrases, in the musical setting of "Tristan" not a trace of word-repetition is any longer found, but the weft of words and verses foreordains the whole dimensions of the melody, i.e. the structure of that melody is already erected by the *poet*.

Should its present application have turned out thoroughly successfully, from that alone you might bear me witness that this procedure of mine must effect a far more intimate amalgamation of poem and music, than could the earlier one; and if I may venture at like time to hope that you will set a greater value on my execution of the "Tristan" poem in itself, than on kindred efforts with my earlier works, this very circumstance would lead you to conclude that its full foreshadowing of the musical form must at least have been of profit to the poetic workmanship itself. If, then, the complete foreshadowing of the musical form is able to lend a special value to the very poem, and that in entire accordance with the poet's will, the only further question would be: whether the melody's musical form does not thereby suffer harm itself, through forfeiting its freedom of movement and development?

On this, please take your answer from the *musician*; with the deepest feeling of its rightness, he boldly makes assertion that melody and its form, by this procedure, are brought a wealth and inexhaustibility such as one could not so much as form a notion of without it.

I fancy I shall do best by closing my communication to you with the theoretic argument for this assertion. I will attempt it by henceforth confining myself to just the musical form, the *melody*.—

In the shrill and frequent outcry of our shallow musical dilettanti for "Melody, Melody!" I find evidence that they take their idea of Melody from musical works in which, by side of the melody, there stretches an expanse of unmelodiousness, setting the melody they mean in the light they love so dearly. In the Opera-house of Italy there gathered an audience which passed its evenings in amusement; part of this amusement was formed by the music sung upon the stage, to which one listened from time to time in pauses of the conversation; during the conversation and visits paid from box to box the music still went on, and with the same office as one assigns to table-music at grand dinners, namely to encourage by its noise the otherwise timid talk. The music which is played with this object, and during this conversation, fills out the virtual bulk of an Italian operatic score; whereas the music which one really listens to, makes out perhaps a twelfth part thereof. An Italian opera must contain at least *one* aria to which one is glad to listen; if it is to have a success, the conversation must be broken, and the music listened-to with interest, at least six times; whilst the composer who is clever enough to attract the audience's attention a whole twelve times, is lauded as an inexhaustible melodic genius. Now how are we to blame this public if, suddenly confronted with a work which claims a like attention throughout its whole extent and for each of its parts, it sees itself torn from all its habits at musical performances, and cannot possibly take as identical with its beloved melody a thing which in the luckiest event may pass for a mere refinement of that musical noise—that noise whose naïve use before had facilitated the most agreeable interchange of small talk, whereas it now obtrudes the upstart claim of being really heard? It must cry out again and again for its six to twelve melodies, if only to gain the stimulating and protective intervals for conversation, the main end and object of the opera-evening.

To tell the truth, what a curious bias takes for wealth, to the better-educated mind can only appear as penury. The loud requirements founded on this error, one may forgive to the great Public proper, but not to the Art-critic. Let us therefore try to get to the bottom of this error, so far as that is possible.

We will start with the axiom that *music's only form is melody*, that it is not even thinkable apart from melody, that music and melody are absolutely indisseverable. Therefore, taken in a higher sense, to say that any music has no melody, can only mean: the musician has not arrived at the full construction of a form such as to seize and definitely impress the Feeling; a statement which simply announces the composer's lack of talent, his want of originality, compelling him to cobble up his piece from melodic phrases often heard before, and therefore leaving the ear indifferent. In the mouth of the less-educated friend of Opera, however, and as touching any specimen of genuine music, this remark stands self-confessed as meaning merely a given narrow form of melody which, as we have already seen, belongs to the childhood of musical art; wherefore the delight in nothing else but it, must likewise seem to us truly childish. Here, then, it is less a question of Melody, than of its first restricted *dance-form*.

Now I do not really wish to say anything depreciatory about this earliest rudiment of melodic form. I believe I have already proved that it is the basis of the finished

art-form of the Beethovenian Symphony, and upon that
assumption we have to thank it for something quite
astounding. But one thing has to be borne in mind:
namely that this form, which Italian Opera has preserved
in all its pristine undevelopedness, has received in the
Symphony a maturing and expansion such as to give it,
in comparison with that earlier form, the relation of the
flower-crowned plant to the sucker. I therefore fully
endorse the significance of that original melodic form, the
dance-form, and—true to the maxim that, let a form be
never so developed, it needs must bear its origin still
stamped upon it—I claim to trace that dance-form in the
Beethovenian Symphony; nay, I hold that this Symphony,
as a melodic aggregate (*Komplex*), should be looked upon
as nothing other than the idealised Dance-form itself.

Let us next remark, however, that this form extends to
every portion of the Symphony, which is thus the opposite
of Italian Opera, where the melody stands entirely isolated
and the intervals between the separate melodies are occupied by a manner of music we can only term absolutely
unmelodic, since it scarcely quits the character of downright noise. With Beethoven's forerunners we see these
nasty gaps still stretching between the melodic chief-
motives even in Symphonic movements: though HAYDN,
indeed, was mostly able to give these interspaces a very
interesting stamp, MOZART—who here approached much
nearer to the Italian notion of melodic form—had often,
nay almost habitually relapsed into that banal build of
phrases which constantly shews his Symphonic movements
in the light of so-called table-music, i.e. a music which, between attractive melodies, offers also an attractive hubbub
for conversation's sake: on myself at least, the perpetually
recurring and noisily garrulous half-closes of the Mozartian
Symphony make the impression as if I were hearing the
clatter of a prince's plates and dishes set to music. The
distinctive and masterly procedure of Beethoven, on the
contrary, was directed to entirely banishing those fatal
interspaces, and giving to the connecting-links between

the chief melodies the full character of Melody themselves.

To throw more light on this procedure, uncommonly interesting as it might be, would lead us here too far. Yet I cannot refrain from drawing your attention to the construction of the first movement of a Beethovenian Symphony. Here we have the actual dance-melody divided into its smallest component parts, each of which, often consisting of nothing but two notes, is made expressive and interesting by the predominance of now a rhythmic, now a harmonic character. These parts, again, arrange themselves in ever novel combinations, now swelling to a stream of sequences, now scattered in a whirlpool, yet always so absorbing in their plastic motion that the hearer cannot tear himself from their influence for a single instant, but, on the tiptoe of excitement, must accord to each harmonic tone, nay to every rhythmic pause, a meaning in the melody. The quite new result of this procedure, then, was to stretch out the melody, through richest evolution of all the motives lying in it, to one vast, one solid piece of music, which in itself is nothing but one sole continuous melody.

Now it is surprising that this procedure, acquired upon the field of Instrumental-music, should have been fairly approximately applied to mixed Choral and Orchestral music, but never properly as yet to Opera. In his great Mass Beethoven has employed the choir and orchestra almost exactly as in the Symphony: this Symphonic mode of treatment was possible because in the generally known, and now almost purely symbolical text-words of the Church a form was given him which he could divide, reduplicate and re-unite almost in the same way as with Dance-melody itself. But no sensible musician could possibly think of treating the text-words of a dramatic poem in this fashion, since it is their duty to contain, no mere symbolic import, but a definite logical train of thought. It could only have been done with those very text-words which, on the other hand, were planned for the mere traditional forms of Opera. Yet there must remain open the possibility of obtaining in the dramatic poem itself a poetic counterpart to the Symphonic form, which, while completely filling out that ample form, should at like time answer best the inmost statutes of *dramatic* form.

As the problem just touched-on is extremely hard to handle theoretically, I think I can best explain myself in metaphoric form.

I called the Symphony the attained ideal of melodic Dance-form. As a matter of fact, the Beethovenian Symphony contains in that part called "Menuetto" or "Scherzo" a quite primitive piece of real dance-music, which could very well be danced to. An instinctive need seems to have led the composer into quite immediate contact with the material basis of his work, for once in its course, as though his foot were feeling for the ground that was to carry him. In the remaining movements he sets an ever greater distance between himself and the possibility of a genuine dance being executed to his melody—unless, indeed, it were so ideal a dance as to bear the same relation to the primitive dance as the Symphony to the original Dance-tune. Hence, too, a certain reluctance to overstep certain bounds of musical expression, and in particular to pitch too high the passionate, tragic tendency, since it would rouse emotions and awaitings in his hearer such as to wake that troubling question of the "Why?"—which the Musician was not the person to answer satisfactorily.

But the dance to throughly carry out this music, that ideal form of Dance, is in truth the *dramatic action*. It really bears precisely the same relation to the primitive dance, as the Symphony to the simple Dance-tune. Even the primal folk-dance already expresses an action, for the most part the mutual wooing of a pair of lovers; this simple story—purely physical in its bearings—when ripened to an exposition of the inmost motives of the soul, becomes nothing other than the Dramatic Action. You will spare me,

I trust, from proving that this is not adequately represented by our *Ballet*. The Ballet is own brother to the Opera, offspring of the same mistakes as she; wherefore we see them going hand in hand for choice, as if to cloak their facing nakedness.

Not a Programme, which rather prompts the troublous question " Why ? " than stills it—not a Programme, then, can speak the meaning of the Symphony ; no, nothing but a stage-performance of the Dramatic Action itself.

I have already supplied the proofs for this assertion, and have only further to point out in its regard what a quickening, amplifying influence a thoroughly appropriate poem may bring to bear on even this melodic form. The poet who is fully alive to the inexhaustibly expressive power of Symphonic Melody, which with one harmonic turn can change the tone of its expression in the thrillingest of manners, will be moved to meet its finest, rarest nuances half-way; no longer will he be tortured by the older narrow form, of Opera-melody, into furnishing a mere dry canvas bare of contents ; rather will he eavesdrop from the musician the secret hidden from the latter's self, the secret that Melodic Form is capable of infinitely richer evolution than the musician had as yet deemed possible within the Symphony itself; and, presaging this evolution, he will already strike the fetters from his poem's freedom.

Thus where the Symphonist still timidly groped back to the original dance-form—never daring, even for his expression, to quite transgress the bounds which held him in communication with that form—the Poet now will cry to him : " Launch without a fear into the full flood of Music's sea ; hand in hand with me, you can never lose touch of the thing most seizable of all by every human being ; for through me you stand on the solid ground of the Dramatic Action, and that Action, at the moment of its scenic show, is the most directly understandable of all poems. Stretch boldly out your melody, that like a ceaseless river it may pour throughout the work : in it say you what I keep silent, since you alone can say it; and silent shall I utter all, since my hand it is that guides you."

Of a verity the poet's greatness is mostly to be measured by what he leaves unsaid, letting us breathe in silence to ourselves the thing unspeakable; the musician it is who brings this untold mystery to clarion tongue, and the impeccable form of his sounding silence is *endless melody*.

Necessarily, the Symphonist will not be able to shape this melody without his own peculiar implement; that implement is the *orchestra*. That he will employ it in a sense quite other than the Italian Opera-composer, in whose hands the orchestra is nothing but a huge guitar for accompanying the Aria, I scarcely need impress upon you.

It will enter much the same relation to the drama meant by me, as the Tragic Chorus of the Greeks to theirs. This Chorus was always in attendance; to it were bared the motives of the dramatic action going-on before its eyes; these motives it sought to penetrate, and thence to form a judgment on the action. Only, this interest of the Chorus's was more of a reflective kind, throughout; itself had neither part nor lot in action or in motives. The orchestra of the modern Symphonist, on the contrary, will take so intimate an interest in the motives of the plot, that whilst, as embodied harmony, it alone confers on the melody its definite expression, on the other hand it will keep the melody in the requisite unceasing flow, and thus convincingly impress those motives on the Feeling. If we must regard as the ideal art-form that which can be grasped without a shadow of reflection, and through which the artist's Beholding (*Anschauung*) is conveyed the clearest to the unimpeded Feeling; if, subject to the above provisoes, we mean to recognise the Musical Drama as that ideal art-form: then the Symphonist's orchestra is the wondrous instrument for the only possible presentment of that form. Faced with it and its significance, it is obvious that the Chorus—which in Opera has climbed the stage itself already—will entirely lose the meaning of its antique prototype. The Chorus now can only be included as an active personage; and where its presence as such is not required, in future it must seem to us superfluous and disturbing, since its ideal interest in the action will have passed completely to the Orchestra, and there be manifested in continual, but never troubling presence.

I have recourse to metaphor once more, to give you finally a picture of the melody I mean, the melody encompassing the whole dramatic tone-piece; and for this I will keep to the impression which it is to produce. Its endless wealth of detail is in nowise to reveal itself merely to the connoisseur, but also to the most naïve layman, if only he has come to the needful collectedness of spirit. First of all, then, it should exert on him somewhat the effect produced by a noble forest, of a summer evening, on the lonely visitant who has just left the city's din behind; the peculiar stamp of this impression—which I leave the reader to elaborate in all its psychological effects—is that of a silence growing more and more alive.* For the general object of the artwork it may be quite sufficient to have produced this root-impression, and by it to lead the hearer unawares and attune him to the further aim; he therewith takes the higher tendence unconsciously into himself. But when, overwhelmed by this first general impression, the forest's visitor sits down to ponder; when, the last burden of the city's hubbub cast aside, he girds the forces of his soul to a new power of observing; when, as if hearing with new senses, he listens more and more intently—he perceives with ever greater plainness the infinite diversity of voices waking in the wood. Ever and ever a new, a different voice peers forth, a voice he thinks he has never heard as yet; as they wax in number, they grow in strange distinctness; louder and louder rings the wood; and many though the voices be, the individual strains he hears, the glinting, overbrimming stream of sound seems again to him but just the one great forest-melody: that melody which from the very first had chained him to devotion, as once the deep-blue firmament of night had chained his eye when brighter and ever clearer he beheld its countless multitude of stars, the longer he had plunged his gaze into the spectacle.

* Cf. the opening of *Das Rheingold.*—TR.

This melody will echo ever in him, but hum it he cannot; to hear it whole once more, he must go into the wood again, and on a summer evening. How foolish, if he tried to trap one of the sweet wood-warblers, perchance to have it trained at home to chirp a morsel of that great wood-melody! What else would he hear for his pains, but—say now!—which particular melody?—

What an infinitude of technical details I have passed over in this cursory, yet perhaps itself too circumstantial statement, you may easily imagine; particularly if you reflect how inexhaustibly varied is their nature, even in a theoretic exposition. To clearly set forth all the single features of Melodic Form, in the sense which I assign to it; to plainly denote its relations with Opera-melody proper, and its possibilities of extension, not only in respect of periodic structure, but with special regard to its harmony —would straightway throw me back on my fruitless attempt of days gone by. I therefore confine myself to giving the indulgent reader the veriest general indications; for in truth we now are drawing near the point, even in this address itself, where the artwork alone can say the final word.

You would be mistaken, if you thought this last clause referred to the coming performance of my "Tannhäuser." You know the score of my "Tristan," and though it does not occur to me to set it up as a model of the ideal, you will grant that from "Tannhäuser" to "Tristan" I took a wider step than from my first standpoint, that of Modern Opera, to "Tannhäuser." Whoever, then, should regard this communication to you as a mere preparative for the performance of "Tannhäuser," would in part be nursing most erroneous expectations.

Should the pleasure be in store for me, of seeing my "Tannhäuser" received with favour by the Paris public too, I am certain to owe a large portion of that success to this opera's very visible connection with the operas of my predecessors; among whom I refer you to Weber in especial. Yet allow me briefly to point out what may to some extent distinguish even this work from the works of my forerunners.

Manifestly, what I have here depicted as the strictest consequence of idealistic principles, had lain at the heart of our great masters from all time. Neither did these conclusions as to the possibility of an ideal Artwork occur to myself as the result of abstract Reflection, but I was led to them, most assuredly, by what I observed in the works of our masters. Though there stood before great GLUCK himself merely the narrowness and buckram of the operatic forms he found to hand, and in nowise radically enlarged —forms mostly standing quite disjointed side by side— yet his followers already knew to enlarge them step by step and link them with each other, to such a degree that, whenever an important dramatic situation gave occasion, they were fully sufficient for the highest end. No one is more enchanted than I, to recognise the great, the powerful and beautiful dramatic music we find in many works of honoured masters: to me it seems unnecessary to give you here a list of specimens. Nor do I conceal from myself that even in the feebler works of frivolous composers [*] I have met with isolated effects that made me marvel at the incomparable might of Music, as mentioned to you once before; for, in virtue of her invulnerable definiteness of melodic expression, she raises even the least talented singer so high above the level of his personal attainments, that he produces a dramatic effect forever unapproachable by even the grandest artist of the spoken Play. But what disheartened me the more, was this: in Opera I could never meet all these inimitable excellences of Dramatic Music developed to one pure style, embracing equally each portion of the work. In the most important works, immediately beside the noblest and most perfect, I found the incomprehensibly senseless, the inexpressively conventional, nay, the frivolous.

Though the hideous juxtaposition of absolute Recitative and absolute Aria is retained almost everywhere, prevent-

---

[*] Meyerbeer—a similar allusion occurs on p. 100 of vol. ii.—TR.

ing any finished style, and everlastingly breaking and barring the musical flow (through the fundamental error of a faulty poem), yet in our great masters' finest Scenas we often find this evil quite overcome; to the Recitative itself there has been given already the stamp of rhythmic melody, and it opens imperceptibly into the broader structure of the melody proper. With our eyes now alive to the grand effect of this procedure, how painfully must it affect us when the banal chord makes sudden entry without so much as by-your-leave, telling us: "the *recitativo secco* will now be taken up again." And just as suddenly thereafter the full orchestra strikes in, with its inevitable *ritornello* for announcing the Aria; that same ritornello which the selfsame master had elsewhere employed for a connecting or modulatory passage of such deep suggestiveness, that we had seen in it a speaking beauty all its own, giving us the most interesting insight into the situation's very heart. But how if a 'number' positively reckoned for nothing but a sop to the lowest art-taste should immediately follow one of those gems of art? Nay, how if a noble, a thrillingly beautiful phrase should suddenly end in the stereotyped *cadenza* with the customary brace of runs and a forced last note, whilst the singer unexpectedly quits the person to whom the phrase was addressed, comes down to the footlights, turns his face to the claque, and gives the signal for applause?

True enough, these last-named solecisms do not exactly occur with our really great masters; rather with certain composers who make us wonder the more, how they could also have come by those superlative beauties. But the worst feature of the whole thing is this: that after all the noble, perfect work already achieved by great masters, bringing Opera so near the consummation of a purer style, these relapses could happen again and again; nay, that Un-nature herself could sally forth more brazenly than ever.

Indisputably, the taproot of the evil is a humiliating regard on the artist's part for the temper of the average

Opera-public, which always gains the upper hand at last in weaker natures. Even of WEBER—that noble, pure and 'inward' spirit—I have heard that, shrinking ever and anon from the consequences of his own refined procedure, he accorded his wife the "rights of the Gallery," as he called it, and got her to raise objections destined to influence him here and there to refrain from taking his style too strictly, to make prudent concessions to the Gallery's wants.

These "concessions" which my first beloved model, Weber, still thought needful to make to the Opera-public —I may pride myself, I believe, that you will find none of them in "Tannhäuser"; and, as regards the *form* of my opera, perhaps this constitutes its most essential difference from the works of my forerunners. For this I really needed no remarkable courage; for, precisely through my observation of the effect of the best class of operatic work upon the public, I have learnt to form the most favourable opinion of this public. The artist who addresses himself, not to the abstract, but to the intuitive apperception, of rooted purpose sets his work before the Public, and not before the Art-judge. The only thing that can trouble the Artist, is the question how far this public has become infected by the critical element, thereby losing the ingenuousness of purely-human insight (*Anschauung*). Now I deem the hitherto prevalent Opera-genre—just because of its lapful of concessions, leaving the audience in complete uncertainty what to look for—precisely fitted for bewildering the public to such a pitch as to drive it against its will into a false and untimely train of reflection, while its embarrassment must needs be seriously increased by the chatter of all those in its own midst who pose as judges. If on the contrary we note the public's infinitely greater certainty in presence of the spoken Play, and how nothing in the world can here induce it to hold a foolish plot for sensible, an inappropriate speech for fitting, a wrong emphasis for telling: this fact alone will give us the solid fulcrum for bringing Opera, as well, into a sound relation with the Public, a relation favourable to a thorough understanding.

As the second point, where even my "Tannhäuser" might differ from Opera proper, I therefore name you the *dramatic poem* on which it rests. Without the slightest intention of assigning any value to this poem in a stricter sense, I believe I may emphasise the fact that it contains a logical dramatic 'argument' (*Entwickelung*), even though based upon legend and marvel—a story in whose draft and execution there was likewise made no sort of concession to the banal requirements of an opera-libretto. My aim here, then, is to engross the public in the dramatic action before all else; and in such a manner that not for an instant may it be compelled to lose sight of that action, but, on the contrary, the whole musical adornment may seem to it a mere means for displaying that action. It therefore was the refusal of concessions in the subject-matter, that enabled me also to reject every concession in its musical setting; and in these two points together you might find the most valid definition of my "innovations," but by no means in an absolute-musical caprice such as people have thought fit to foist upon me under the name of "Music of the Future."

In conclusion let me say that, despite the great difficulty which has stood in the way of a perfectly satisfactory verse-translation of my "Tannhäuser," I lay my work with confidence before even the Paris public. A thing which I should only have resolved-on with great anxiety a few years since, I now approach with the assurance of one who looks upon his project less in the light of a speculation, than as an affair of the heart. This change of mood I chiefly owe to individual experiences that have fallen to my share since my last migration to Paris. Among these was one that quickly filled me with a glad surprise. You, my honoured friend, allowed me to approach you as a man already both acquainted and familiar with me. Without having ever attended a performance of my operas in Germany, you had long ago made friends with my scores,

as you yourself assured me, through a careful study. This
acquaintance with my works had woken in you the wish
to see them given here, nay, had brought you to the opinion
that such performances offered promise of a favourable,
and not unmeaning influence upon the susceptibilities of
the Paris public. As you have thus contributed in so
large a measure to inspiring me with confidence in my
undertaking, may you not be vexed with me for paying
you a first instalment of my thanks with this perhaps too
circumstantial and fatiguing letter; on the contrary, may
you set down my perchance too zealous compliance with
your wish to my inner longing to at like time afford the
Parisian friends of my art a somewhat clearer survey of
my ideas, than I could willingly counsel anyone to derive
at first hand from my earlier art-writings.

RICHARD WAGNER.

PARIS, September 15, 1860.

A REPORT ON THE PRODUCTION OF "TANNHÄUSER" IN PARIS.

Bericht über die Aufführung des „Tannhäuser" in Paris.

(Brieflich.)

The letter on "Tannhäuser" in Paris *was originally published in the supplement to the* Deutsche Allgemeine Zeitung *for April* 7, 1861, *and reprinted in the* Neue Zeitschrift *five days later.*

TRANSLATOR'S NOTE.

Paris, 27th March, 1861.

I PROMISED to give you a full report, some day, of my Tannhäuser affairs in Paris; now that they have reached a climax, and can be surveyed in their whole extent, it is some satisfaction to myself to come to a final settlement by a calm review of their leading features—as it were for my own behoof. But none of you can rightly grasp the nature of this business, unless I also touch upon the true motive of my coming to Paris at all. Let me therefore begin with that.

After wellnigh ten years' preclusion from all possibility of reinvigorating myself by assisting at good performances of my dramatic compositions—if only periodically—I felt driven at last to contemplate removal to a spot which might bring this needful living contact with my art within my reach, in time. I hoped to be able to find that spot in some modest nook of Germany itself. The Grand Duke of Baden had already promised me, with most touching kindness, the production of my latest work at Carlsruhe under my personal direction; in the summer of 1859 I pressed him most importunately, in lieu of the projected temporary sojourn, to use his influence to forthwith procure me a permanent domicile in his country,* as there would otherwise be nothing for me to do but settle down in Paris for good. My plea's fulfilment was—impossible.

However, when I removed to Paris in the autumn of that same year, I still kept in sight the production of my "Tristan," for which I hoped to be summoned to Carlsruhe for the 3rd December. Once brought to performance under

---

* Referring to his exile; for the first, the partial, amnesty was not granted until the summer of 1860.—TR.

my own supervision, I believed I then could entrust the work to the other theatres of Germany. The prospect of dealing in the same way with the rest of my works, in future, sufficed me; and on this assumption Paris offered me the solitary interest of hearing an excellent quartet, an admirable orchestra, from time to time, and thus keeping myself in refreshing touch with at least the living organs of my art. All this was changed at a blow when I received notice from Carlsruhe that it had turned out impossible to produce my "Tristan" there. My sorry plight at once inspired me with the notion of inviting certain firstrate singers of my acquaintance to Paris for the following spring, so as to bring about the desired model-performance of my new work, with their assistance, on the boards of the "Italian Opera"; to this I also meant to invite the Directors and Regisseurs of friendly German theatres, in order to compass the same result as I had had in eye with the Carlsruhe production. Since the execution of my plan was impossible without the assistance of the larger Paris public, I was bound to bespeak its interest for my music, and to that end I undertook the well-known three concerts in the Théâtre des Italiens. The highly encouraging result of these concerts, in the matter of applause and interest, unfortunately could not help forward the main enterprise I had in view; for it was just these concerts that plainly shewed me the difficulties of any such undertaking, whilst the impossibility of gathering at one time in Paris the singers I had chosen was sufficient in itself to make me abandon the plan.

Hemmed in on every hand, and once more casting a longing look on Germany, I learnt to my intense surprise that my lot had become the subject of animated discussion and advocacy at the court of the Tuileries. It was to the extraordinarily friendly interest—almost unknown to myself before—of several members of the German embassies here, that I had to thank this propitious turn of affairs. It went so far that the Emperor, having also heard the most flattering account of my "Tannhäuser" (the work most spoken of) from a German princess for whom he entertained a particular esteem,* at once gave orders for the performance of that opera in the Académie impériale de musique. Now I don't deny that, though highly delighted at first by this quite unexpected evidence of my works' success in social circles from which I personally had stood so distant, I soon could think with naught but grave misgivings of a performance of "Tannhäuser" at that particular theatre. To whom was it clearer, that this great opera-house had long estranged itself from every earnest artistic tendence; that in it quite other claims, than those of Dramatic Music, had brought themselves to currency; that Opera itself had there become a mere excuse for Ballet? In fact, when of late years I had received repeated invitations to think about the performance of one of my works in Paris, I had never dreamt of the *Grand Opéra*, but rather—for a trial—of the unassuming *Théâtre Lyrique*. And for two definite reasons: firstly, that here no special class of the audience prescribes the tone; secondly, that—thanks to the poverty of its exchequer—the Ballet pure and simple has not as yet become the focus of its whole art-doings. But, after many times returning to the idea, of his own accord, the Director of this theatre had been obliged to renounce a performance of "Tannhäuser," mainly because he could find no tenor competent to fill the difficult chief rôle.

As a matter of fact, my first conference with the Director of the Grand Opéra shewed me that the introduction of a ballet into "Tannhäuser," and indeed in the second act, was considered a sine quâ non of its successful performance. I couldn't fathom the meaning of this requirement, until I had declared that I could not possibly disturb the course of just this second act by a ballet, which must here be senseless from every point of view; while on the other hand I thought the first act, at the voluptuous court of Venus, would afford the most apposite occasion for a choreographic scene of amplest meaning, since I myself

* Princess Metternich, née Countess Pauline Sandór, wife of the Austrian ambassador.—TR.

had not deemed possible to dispense with dance in my first arrangement of that scene. Indeed I was quite charmed with the idea of strengthening an undoubtedly weak point in my earlier score, and I drafted an exhaustive plan for raising this scene in the Venusberg to one of great importance. This plan the Director most emphatically rejected, telling me frankly that in the production of an opera it was not merely a question of a ballet, but of a ballet to be danced in the middle of the evening's entertainment; for it was only at about this time that the subscribers to whom the ballet almost exclusively belonged, appeared in their boxes, as they were in the habit of dining very late; a ballet in the opening scene would therefore be of no use to them, since they were never by any chance present for the first act. These and similar admissions were subsequently repeated to me by the Cabinet-minister himself, and all possibility of a good result was made so definitely dependent on the said conditions being fulfilled, that I began to believe I should have to renounce the whole undertaking.

But while I thus was thinking again, more actively than ever, of my return to Germany, and spying out for a foothold to be granted me for the performance of my new works, I was now to discover the full value of the Emperor's command; for he placed the whole institute of the Grand Opéra at my disposal, without conditions or reserve, and allowed me carte blanche for whatever engagements I deemed needful. Every acquisition desired by me was forthwith carried out, without the slightest counting of the cost; to the mise-en-scène a care was devoted such as I had never conceived before. Under circumstances so entirely novel to me, I soon was more and more persuaded of the possibility of seeing a thoroughly complete, nay, an ideal performance. The vision of such a performance, wellnigh no matter of which of my works, had long occupied my mind since my withdrawal from our Operahouse; what nowhere and never had stood within my power, was unexpectedly to greet me here in Paris, and at a time when no efforts had availed to procure me an even remotely similar privilege on German soil. I openly admit that this thought inspired me with a warmth unknown for many a day, a warmth only intensified, perhaps, by a bitter feeling mixed therewith. I soon had eyes for nothing but the possibility of a splendid performance, and in the absorbing care to realise that possibility I allowed no other sort of consideration to influence me: if I attain what I may dare hold possible—said I to myself—what care I for the Jockey Club and its ballet?

Henceforth my every thought was for the performance. There was no French tenor to be had, so the Director told me, for the rôle of Tannhäuser. Informed of the brilliant talents of the youthful singer *Niemann*, though I had never heard him myself, I cast him for the title-rôle; after the most careful preliminaries, his engagement was concluded at great expense, especially as he was master of a very fluent French pronunciation. Several other artists, and in particular the barytone *Morelli*, owed their engagement to nothing but my wish to acquire them for my work. Moreover, instead of certain first singers already popular here, whose too settled method alarmed me, I gave the preference to youthful talents whom I might hope to mould more easily to my style. I was surprised by the carefulness, quite unknown among ourselves, with which the voice-and-pianoforte rehearsals are here conducted; under the intelligent and sensitive guidance of the *chef du chant*, Vauthrot, I soon found our studies progressing at a rapid pace. In particular was I rejoiced to see how the younger French artists arrived at a better and better understanding of the thing, and caught a genuine liking for their task.

Thus I myself was taken with a new liking for this earlier work of mine: I most carefully revised the score afresh, entirely re-wrote the scene of Venus and the ballet-scene preceding it, and everywhere sought to bring the vocal parts into closest agreement with the translated text.

Now, as I had made the performance my unique aim,

and left every other consideration out of count, so my real trouble at last began with the perception that this performance itself would not attain the height expected by me. It would be hard for me, to tell you exactly on what points I had finally to see myself undeceived. The most serious, however, was that the singer of the difficult chief rôle fell into greater and greater disheartenment the nearer we approached the actual production, in consequence of interviews it had been thought necessary for him to hold with the reporters, who assured him of the inevitable failure of my opera.* The most promising hopes, which I had harboured in the course of the pianoforte-rehearsals, sank deeper and deeper the more we came in contact with the stage and orchestra. I saw that we were getting back to the dead level of ordinary Operatic performances, that all the requirements meant to bear us far above it were doomed to stay unmet. Yet in this sense, which I naturally had disallowed from the first, we lacked the only thing that could confer distinction on such an Operatic show: some noted 'talent' or other, some tried and trusted favourite of the public; whereas I was making my début with almost absolute novices. Finally what most distressed me, was that I had not been able to wrest the orchestral conductorship, through which I might still have exercised a great influence on the spirit of performance, from the hands of the official *chef d'orchestre*; and my being thus compelled to mournfully resign myself to a dull and spiritless rendering of my work (for my wish to withdraw the score was not acceded to) is what makes out my genuine trouble even to this day.

Under such circumstances it became almost a matter of indifference to me, what kind of reception my opera would meet at the hands of the public: the most brilliant could not have moved me to personally attend a longer series of performances, for I found far too little satisfaction in the thing. But hitherto you have been diligently kept in

---

* The clause about the reviewers was omitted in the *Deutsche Allgemeine Zeitung*, and therefore in the *Neue Zeitschrift*.—TR.

ignorance of the true character of that reception, as it seems to me, and you would do very wrong if you based thereon a judgment of the Paris public in general, however flattering to the German, yet in reality incorrect. On the contrary, I abide by my opinion that the Paris public has very agreeable qualities, in particular those of a quick appreciation and a truly magnanimous sense of justice. A public, I say: a whole audience to which I am a total stranger, which day by day has heard from the journals and idle chatterers the most preposterous things about me, and has been deliberately set against me with wellnigh unexampled care—to see such a public repeatedly taking up the cudgels in my behalf against a clique, with demonstrations of applause a quarter of an hour long, must fill me with a warmth of heart towards it, were I even the most indifferent of men. But, through the admirable foresight of those who have the sole distribution of seats on first nights, and had made it almost impossible for me to gain admission for my handful of personal friends, there was assembled on that evening in the Grand Opera-house an audience which every dispassionate person could see at once was prejudiced in the extreme against my work; add to this the whole Parisian Press, which is always invited officially on such occasions, and whose hostile attitude towards me you have simply to read its reports to discover: and you may well believe that I have a right to speak of a great victory, when I tell you in all sober earnest that this by no means exquisite performance of my work met with louder and more unanimous applause than ever I experienced personally in Germany. The actual leaders of an opposition perhaps almost universal at first—several, nay, very likely all of the musical reporters here—who up to then had done their utmost to distract the attention of the public, were seized towards the end of the second act by manifest terror of having to witness a complete and brilliant success of "Tannhäuser"; and now they fell on the expedient of breaking into roars of laughter after certain cues, pre-arranged among themselves at the general-rehearsals, whereby they created a diversion sufficiently disturbing to damp a considerable manifestation of applause at the curtain's second fall. These selfsame gentlemen, however, had observed at the stage-rehearsals, which I had also not been able to hinder them from attending, that the opera's real success lay guaranteed in the execution of its third act. At the rehearsals an admirable 'set' by Mons. Despléchin, representing the Wartburg valley in the light of an autumn evening, had already exerted on everyone present a charm which irresistibly gave birth to the *Stimmung* requisite for taking-in the following scenes; on the part of the performers these scenes were the bright spot in the whole day's work; quite insurpassably was the Pilgrims' Chorus sung and managed; the Prayer of Elisabeth, delivered in its entirety by Fräulein *Sax* with affecting expression, the 'fantasie' to the Evening-star, rendered by *Morelli* with perfect elegiac tenderness, so happily prepared the way for the best part of *Niemann's* performance, his narration of the Pilgrimage—which has always won this artist the liveliest commendation—that a quite exceptional success seemed assured for just this third act, even in the eyes of my most determined adversaries. So this was the act the aforesaid leaders fastened on, trying to hinder any onset of the needful mood of absorption (*Sammlung*) by outbursts of violent laughter, for which the most trivial occasion had to afford the childish pretext. Undeterred by these adverse demonstrations, neither did my singers allow themselves to be put out, nor the public refrain from devoting its sympathetic attention, and often its profuse applause, to their valiant exertions; and at the end, when the performers were vociferously called before the curtain, the opposition was at last entirely beaten down.

That I had made no mistake in viewing this evening's outcome as a complete victory, was proved to me by the public's demeanour on the night of the second performance; for here it became manifest with *what* opposition alone I should have to do in the future, to wit, with that of the

Paris Jockey Club—whose name I need not scruple to give you, as the public itself, with its cry "*à la porte les Jockeys*," both openly and loudly denounced my chief opponents. The members of this club—whose right to consider themselves the rulers of the Grand Opéra I need not here explain to you—feeling their interests deeply compromised by the absence of the usual ballet at the hour of their arrival, i.e. towards the middle of the representation, were horrified to discover that "Tannhäuser" had *not* made a fiasco, but an actual triumph at its first performance. Henceforth it was their business to prevent this ballet-less opera from being given night after night; to this end, on their way from dinner they had bought a number of dog-calls and such-like instruments, with which they manœuvred against "Tannhäuser" in the most unblushing manner directly they had entered the opera-house. Until then, that is to say from the beginning of the first to about the middle of the second act, not a single trace of the first night's opposition had been shewn, and the most prolonged applause had undisturbedly accompanied those passages of my opera which had become the speediest favourites. But from now on, no acclamation was of the least avail: in vain did the Emperor himself, with his Consort, demonstrate for a second time in favour of my work; by those who considered themselves masters of the house, and all of whom belong to France's highest aristocracy, the condemnation of "Tannhäuser" was irrevocably pronounced. Whistles and flageolets accompanied every plaudit of the audience, down to the very close.

In view of the management's utter impotence against this powerful club, in view of even the State-minister's obvious dread of making serious enemies of its members, I recognised that I had no right to expect my proved and faithful artists of the stage to expose themselves any longer to the abominable agitation put upon them by unscrupulous persons (naturally with the intention of forcing them to throw up their engagements). I told the management that I must withdraw my opera, and consented to a third performance only upon condition that it should take place on a Sunday: that is to say, on a night outside the subscription, and thus under circumstances which would not incur the subscribers' wrath, while on the other hand the house would be left completely clear for the public proper. My wish to have this performance announced on the posters as "the last" was not allowed, and all I could do was to personally inform my acquaintances of the fact. These precautionary measures, however, were powerless to dissipate the Jockey Club's alarm; on the contrary, it fancied that it detected in this Sunday performance a bold stratagem against its dearest interests, after which—the opera once brought to an unqualified success—the hated work might be forced quite easily down its throat. In the sincerity of my assurance, that in case of such a success I should still more certainly withdraw my work, people hadn't the courage to believe. So the gentlemen forsook their other pleasures for this evening, returned to the Opéra in full battle-array, and renewed the scenes of the second night. This time the public's exasperation, at the attempt to downright hinder it from following the opera at all, reached a pitch unknown before, as people have assured me; and it was only the, as it would seem, unassailable social standing of Messieurs Disturbers-of-the-peace, that saved them from positive rough handling. To put the matter briefly: astonished as I am at the outrageous behaviour of those gentlemen, I am equally touched and moved by the real public's heroic exertions to procure me justice; and nothing can be more distant from my mind, than to entertain the smallest doubt of the Paris Public whenever it shall find itself on a neutral terrain of its own.

My withdrawal of the score, at last announced officially, has placed the Directors of the Opéra in great and genuine perplexity. They frankly and openly confess to regarding my opera as one of their greatest successes, for they cannot remember having ever seen the public side so actively in favour of a contested work. The most abundant receipts appear to them assured with "Tannhäuser," the house being already sold-out for several performances in advance. They are informed of a growing irritation on the part of the public, which sees its rights of hearing and judging a new, much-talked-of work in peace and quietness, denied it by an infinitely small minority. I learn that the Emperor remains thoroughly well-disposed, that the Empress would gladly take upon herself the protection of my opera, and demand guarantees against further disturbances of the peace. At this moment there is circulating among the musicians, painters, artists and authors of Paris a protest against the unseemly occurrences in the Opera-house: a protest addressed to the Minister of State and, as I am told, already numerously signed. Under such circumstances folk think I might well feel encouraged to let my opera proceed. But a weighty artistic consideration holds me back. Hitherto my work has had no quiet, no collected hearing; its intrinsic character—lying in its intentional appeal to a *Stimmung* foreign to the customary opera-public, a *Stimmung* compassing the whole—has not dawned as yet upon the audience; up to the present they have only been able to catch at certain glittering points which served me, strictly speaking, merely as a garnish (*Staffage*), and to single these out for ready sympathy. But should they once arrive at a calm, attentive hearing of my opera, then, after what I have hinted to you about the character of the performance here, I fear they would soon unearth the latter's inner feebleness and want of verve—for these evils are no secret to those who really know my work, though I have been debarred from intervening personally for their removal; so that I could not dream for this time of a radical, not merely an external, success for my opera. Wherefore let all the inadequacies of this production lie buried decently beneath the dust of those three evenings' warfare, and may many a one, who bitterly deceived my hopes reposed in him, save his honour for the nonce with the belief that he fell fighting for a good cause!

So let us hold the Parisian "Tannhäuser" as played-out

for the present. Should the wish of earnest friends of my art be fulfilled ; should a project, seriously entertained of late by people who know their business, and aiming at nothing less than the speedy foundation of a new opera-house for the realisement of reforms which I have mooted here, as well as elsewhere—should this be carried out, then perhaps you may hear from Paris itself yet once again of "Tannhäuser."

As to what has been done with my work in Paris till to-day, rest assured that you now have heard the strictest truth. One simple thing may be your warranty : that it is impossible for me to content myself with a semblance, when my inmost wish stays unfulfilled ; and that wish is only to be stilled by the consciousness of having evoked a really intelligent impression.

Hearty greetings from yours,

RICHARD WAGNER.

THE VIENNA OPERA-HOUSE.

Das Wiener Hof-Operntheater.

This article arose from a conversation between Richard Wagner and Friedrich Uhl, editor of the Viennese "Botschafter," *upon the subject of the new Opera-house then in course of construction. It was published as a separate pamphlet at the end of October,* 1863, *after having appeared in the* "Botschafter" *towards the middle of the same month. As there exist no copies of that journal in the British Museum, I have not been able to collate the reprint in the* Ges. Schr. *with the original, but it is improbable that the texts would be found to differ, save as regards, perhaps, the opening sentence.*

It will be of interest to remember that the author had just seen a great deal of the inside working of the Grand Opéra at Paris, 1860-61, *and of the Imperial Opera-house at Vienna,* 1862-3, *with the performance of* Tannhäuser *at the former, and the abortive rehearsals of* Tristan und Isolde *at the latter place.*

TRANSLATOR'S NOTE.

Vienna, 1863.

Y friend the Editor of the "*Botschafter*" had long been aware how much I busied my brain with plans of theatric reform in general, when recently a private conversation brought up the special subject of the possibilities of permanently good work being done by the Imperial Court-Opera-house: to my friend my views and suggestions seemed so practical and easy of understanding, that he begged me to expand what I had said, and send it to the "*Botschafter*." This I promised to do; but since then, again, a fair amount of time has passed.—It is always distasteful to the expert to have to speak, not to official authorities who may happen to have asked for his opinion on a given case, but at random in the papers, about things which—since they lie so perilously open to the pleasure or displeasure of all the world—every twopenny scribe, every fifth-rate musician or other practitioner considers he understands as well and better than himself. However, it remains the only way to bring his opinion before the tribune of those few who have accustomed themselves to devoting a serious examination to even a seemingly frivolous topic; for these few, as things too often go, are found the fewest in the ranks of official authorities, particularly in affairs theatric, and therefore are only to be caught by casting one's net into the broader waters of the general reading public.

In this sorry case for the earnest artist or friend of Art there lies, if one looks a little closer, the total condemnation of our Opera-theatre's time-honoured course of action. The keeping watch on this latter, the verdict on it, are abandoned to persons who have no actual knowledge and experience of the matter: to give proof and explanation of which statement, I have only to instance the fact that, whereas the editors of our great journals treat their Political columns with a scrupulous regard for definite party-principles, they mostly leave the Theatre, and Music above all, to the tender mercies of the veriest idle chatterer and wag, for choice, without the least consideration of the paper's general tendency. Beyond this person, strictly speaking, no one troubles his head about the theatre's efficiency; and it is more especially surprising, that people never dream of attaching genuine experts to the supreme controlling boards of subventioned theatres, experts whose duty it should be to watch the theatre's administration in the only sense to make subventions warrantable.

For first of all, it seems to me, there is a great difference between what one ought to demand of a subventioned, and of an un-subventioned theatre. All that the earnest friend of Art deplores when looking at the Theatre, if he is a man of common-sense, should be confined to matters of the theatre subventioned in high quarters. An unsubventioned theatre, on the contrary, is mainly an industrial concern, whose exploiters—provided the police have nothing to say against their ways—are at bottom answerable to no one but their customers: the coming or staying-away of the theatre-goer is the criterion of their doings, and the work turned out by the ordinary theatrical reporter stands in a thoroughly fit relation to the manifestations of their public's taste; both parties here are perfectly matched, for here no claims of Art prevail, but solely those of personal good-pleasure. But that matters should stand on precisely the same footing at the subventioned theatre, is the really mournful thing; still more mournful is it, that here they should even be worse: for the subvention merely serves to dull the edge of speculative energy and initiative—so indispensable at the other place —since the necessity of money-making does not step in to whet it.

Obviously, then, we have here a grave omission: to wit,

together with the allotment of the subvention, it should be clearly and definitely laid down in *what* respect the functions of this theatre are to differ from those of unsubventioned theatres; it should be the sole duty of the higher boards of control, however, to see that these conditions are rigorously observed. Real intelligence and true art-understanding being rare commodities, and it therefore being impossible to reckon on always finding men who purely through their own good judgment could exercise that higher supervision, those higher requirements themselves should be all the more carefully concerted, and established in the form of clear and easily-intelligible regulations. Now if, in the measure of my knowledge and experience, I here propose to suggest such regulations for the "Royal Imperial Court-Opera-house," for the foremost principle I luckily need counsel nothing but a restitution of that which an illustrious Austrian friend of Art, the *Kaiser Joseph II.*, once laid down for the conduct of the theatre. It would be impossible to express this principle more comprehensively, and yet concisely, than did the noble founder of the two Imperial Court-theatres when he fixed the function required of them as follows:—

"To contribute to the ennobling of the nation's manners and taste." *

This fundamental principle once re-established in all earnest, even for the opera-house, the next thing would be to frame a constitution for its maintenance throughout all time; and if I here propose to sketch out such a constitution, I fancy I first must throw a little light upon the state into which this opera-house has fallen through abandoning that foremost principle: in fact I may hope that the mere upheaval of the bad maxims by which it now is guided, will of itself result in the establishment of the healthy constitution I have in mind.

* "See Ed. Devrient's *Geschichte der deutschen Schauspielkunst* (History of the German Stage)."—RICHARD WAGNER.—It should be remembered that "*Sitten*" is a very comprehensive term, including not only "manners and customs," but also "morals."—TR.

If we view the operations of one of the chief musico-dramatic institutes in all Germany, the Imperial Opera-house, from *without*, we are faced with a piebald medley of the most diverse products from the most contrasted realms of style; the only thing that clearly comes to sight at first, is that not one of these performances bears the stamp of correctness in any respect, and therefore each appears to take the reason for its existence, by no means from anything within itself, but from a fatal outer necessitation. It would be impossible to name a single performance in which end and means had been in thorough harmony: thus in which the lack of talent, the faulty training, or the unfit employment of individual singers; insufficient preparation, and consequent uncertainty of others; raw and spiritless delivery of the choruses, gross blunders in the inscenation; an almost total want of balance in the dramatic action, clumsy and senseless by-play on the part of individuals; and finally, grave faults and negligences in the reading and rendering of the music itself, carelessness in its nuancing, want of harmony between the phrasing of the orchestra and that of the singers,—had not made themselves felt somewhere or other in a more or less disturbing, and even an offensive manner. Most of these performances bear the character of a heedless devil-may-care, against which, as background, the efforts of single singers to force themselves out of the artistic frame, in order to gain particular applause for patches of their execution, seem all the more repulsive and give the whole a something of the downright laughable. If the public has grown too used to the nature of those performances to be aware of anything amiss, so that the faults I complain of may be denied by habitual opera-goers: then we should only have to ask the singers and bandsmen of the theatre themselves, to hear them admit with one consent how demoralised they feel, how well they know the ill character of their work in common, and with what disheartenment they mostly embark on such performances—aware that, insufficiently prepared, they are doomed to turn out full of faults.

For if we view this theatre from *within*, where we had anticipated laziness and leisure we are suddenly amazed to find a factory-like excess of labour, overwork, and often an altogether wonderful endurance beneath the utmost burden of fatigue.—I believe that the abuses practised on artistic forces at such an opera-house are comparable with no other kind; and among the most grievous memories of my life I number the experiences reaped in my own person, and especially in that of the members of the orchestra, under similar circumstances. Just reflect that the personnel of a first-class band consists, for no little part, of the only truly musically-cultured members of an opera-company; bear in mind again what this means with *German* musicians, familiar as they are with the flower of all musical art, in the works of our great German Masters; note that *these* are the people employed for the lowest uses of art-industry, for hundred-fold rehearsals of the musically-emptiest operas, simply for the toilsome underpropping of unmusical and ill-trained singers! For my part I avow that in such enforced activity in my time, both suffering in myself and suffering with others, I have often learnt to mock the torments of the damned in Dante.

Firstrate members of the singing-personnel, no doubt, often find themselves exposed to similar tortures: but they have already grown so used to placing themselves outside the general frame, that they are less affected by these common griefs. As a rule with them the personal craving for approbation swallows up everything else; and even the better of them at last accustom themselves, amid the general confusion, to shake off any sense of how the singing and acting is going on around them, and pay sole heed to playing their own hand as best they can. In this they are supported by the public, which, consciously or unconsciously, turns its attention away from the ensemble, and devotes it purely to the doings of this or that chief favourite. The first result is, that the public losing more and more its feeling for the artwork placed before it, and regarding nothing but the performance of the individual virtuoso, the whole remaining apparatus of an operatic representation is degraded to the level of a superfluous adjunct. The further evil consequence, however, is that the individual singer, now regarded to the exclusion of the whole, arrives at that overbearing attitude towards the institute and its directors which has been known in every age as prima-donna-tyranny and such-like. The exactions of the Virtuoso (and with us it suffices to have an endurable voice, to pass as such!) now enter as a fresh destructive element into the theatre's organism. With the German's scanty talent for singing, and particularly with the great dearth of voices, the management's trouble in itself is greater here than anywhere else, especially as there are too many German theatres of first rank (as far as rich endowments go) for each to find a fair supply of vocal forces.—Incompetent to make the general product of his artistic factors the point of attraction for his public, the Director sees himself obliged to stake everything on the engagement of 'stars'; the difficulty of eking out the necessary sums for this, again, compels him to set full sail for the worst of tastes, and above all to filch the money thus squandered from any careful nursing of the ensemble. But the chief evil of the ensuing disorganisation is the loss of all *esprit de corps* among the members of the opera-company: no one has any feeling for the whole, because no one has the least respect for its doings. Each sees how things are going, how everything is dictated by the laws of vulgar daily want, that wellnigh each performance is nothing but a makeshift in a strait; and to diligently exploit these straits for his own profit, to wit to increase them by making his assistance all the dearer, becomes at last the only rule for each man's conduct toward the management. The management, having lost all hold upon the feeling of artistic fellowship, now finds itself compelled in turn to check this tendency of individuals, by material means of discipline. The Director keeps his singers to their work by monetary regulations, and should any of them have retained a vestige of artistic conscience, it vanishes at last before the reckoning of sheer financial interests; so that purely from dread of a money fine, the singer takes up tasks which he knows he is unfit for, either in general or under prevailing circumstances, or that they will be ruined through an ill-prepared ensemble.

The deduction from all this is, that it is absurd to ask a management, whose daily worry is the smoothing of these difficulties, to take higher artistic ends in eye—an absurdity such as could occur to none but people who have never had a clear idea of the only basis on which artistic ends can be taken in eye at all. As affairs have shaped themselves at present, it must be palpable to any thinking man that the fault does not lie in the person of the Director, nor in the question whether he is a German Kapellmeister, an Italian singing-teacher, a French ballet-master, or whatever else you please, but mainly in a vice inherent in the organisation of the institute itself. This vice rests plainly and principally herein: no sort of higher artistic end is set before the opera-house; and that negative vice is expressed quite simply in the positive requirement which insists upon this theatre's *giving representations day by day.*—

From the highest functionary down to the last subordinate, the whole personnel of the opera-house knows that the root of all the troubles, confusions and defects in its representations lies almost solely in the obligation to play each day; and everyone can see at once that by far the largest part of these calamities would disappear, if the representations were *lessened by about a half.*

Manifestly a better efficiency of the opera-house is under no circumstances so much as thinkable, if a great reduction be not effected in this requirement. If the Théâtre Français in Paris and the Royal Burgh-theatre (*Hofburgtheater*) in Vienna are able decently to comply with this requirement of playing daily, and without any too notable damage to their style of execution, the reason lies in this: (1) that an infinitely larger number of pieces, even good and firstrate pieces, stands at the disposal of the Recited Drama, than at that of the Opera-house; (2) that these pieces fall easily into well-marked categories, for which definite groups of actors can be appointed when the financial means suffice, as they do at both these theatres; and (3) that the performances of an acting company depend in large part on the private study of individuals, the greater simplicity of operations in a spoken play demanding a relatively smaller number of ensemble-rehearsals. — But things are quite different with an opera-house, particularly where one means to represent the so-called "grand" genre, and therefore the Grand Opéra at Paris (as also the Berlin Opera-house) has very properly limited itself to playing three times, and quite exceptionally four times a-week; added to which, the singing personnel is replaced by the ballet personnel for whole performances. For (1) the existing number of good operas is out of all proportion smaller than that of good plays; (2) the genre of Comedy, so helpful to the Play, has scarcely any parallel in Comic Opera, especially as regards the German repertory, and it therefore is not at all easy to form different groups of singers; (3) the musical study, as also the more complex stage arrangements for an opera, demand a disproportionately larger number of rehearsals in common.

Thus a fault has been committed in the present constitution of the Imperial Opera-house, which might have been avoided if the very ably drafted statutes of the Paris Grand Opéra had been taken as model. I have already adduced the evil results, even from a business point of view—results which spring to the eyes of all the world, and are known to every member of this theatre. Their disastrous influence on the public's artistic taste I will outline more precisely after I have shewn the advantages of a marked reduction in the representations at the opera-house, with maintenance of the root-principle laid down by Kaiser *Joseph II.*, namely to work for the ennobling of the public art-taste.

This I can reach through nothing better than a scrutiny of the requirements contained in that chief object set before the Imperial theatres by their illustrious founder.

"The Theatre should contribute to the ennobling of the nation's manners and taste."

For practical purposes this maxim ought perhaps to be formulated still more definitely, as follows :—its aim should be to work for the raising of the nation's manners [or morals—"*Sitten*"] through ennobling its taste. For it is manifest that Art cannot work on Morals (*Sittlichkeit*) directly, but only through the medium of an improvement in taste. Therefore we have first, and almost solely, to keep in sight the effect of theatric doings on the public's *taste*; for any attempt to bring an opera-house into a directly favourable relation to public morals, particularly in view of its operations hitherto, might in itself seem more than problematic to many an earnest friend of the nation. In fact we may admit at once that Opera, by its origin as in its whole nature, is a truly doubtful genre of art; and that, in any measures for its advancement, sufficient care can never be taken to cleanse it from this dubious character and develop with quite peculiar energy the good and beauteous seeds it holds within.

Not to lose myself just now in a harangue upon this knotty subject, still most unclear to many, and to keep to the practical scope of my suggestions, I will indicate as the only instant means for reaching the goal last-mentioned the means of *good performances*.

The Public holds, and rightly, by nothing but the performance, the theatrical transaction, for that it is which speaks directly to its Feeling; and only through the manner *how* the performance speaks to it, does it understand *what* is spoken. The public knows neither Poetry nor Music, but simply the Theatric Representation; and what the poet and musician mean to say, it learns through nothing but the medium of what is set immediately before it. This must therefore be *distinct and understandable*: each blurring puts the public in perplexity, and this bewilderment is the cause of all the warped and crooked strands of taste we meet-with in the public's judgment. We therefore can never so much as talk about a cultivation of taste, until the thing whereon this taste has to exercise itself, to come to a decision, is represented seizably and clearly. Opera's highest problem undoubtedly lies in a complete agreement between its dramatic and its musical tendence; but where there is no glimmering of such agreement, the whole becomes a senseless chaos of the most bewildering kind, precisely through its heaping-up of different artistic means. For Music's very inability to work purely as such in Opera, when the Dramatic Action stays unclear, is proof sufficient that this art-genre's sole artistic efficacy can be ensured by nothing but the agreement of them both. This agreement must therefore be established as the opera's *style*.

Let us settle then, *that the Opera-house should be an art-institute whose duty it is to contribute to the ennobling of public taste through constantly good and correct performances of musico-dramatic works. Since, owing to the very complex nature of such performances, a greater expenditure of time is needed for their preparation than with the performances of Spoken Drama, the number of representations at the Imperial Court-Opera-house should be reduced to the half of that hitherto obtaining; and even of these a part alone should fall to Opera, the other part to Ballet.*

Naturally, steps would have to be taken to ensure the attainment of the true object of this reduction. We don't deny that the mere *possibility* of always having excellent performances does not amount to their *warranty*. It certainly would already be a great thing to have in the foremost precept of Kaiser Joseph II., to be graven upon the theatre in letters of gold, a shelter and defence against all contrary demands; yet additional guarantees must be supplied, and in the constitution of the theatre itself. It is obvious that they could not be mere mandatory or inhibitive statutes; for we here are dealing with artistic taste and feeling, and these can never be obtained by force of edicts. But there are such things as measures for appeal to conscientiousness, for spurring emulation; and these can be simply founded *on the relation of the artistic officers to one another.*

It is surprising how little to the purpose have been arrangements of a similar kind in German theatres. The whole burden of artistic responsibility for the immediate doings of an opera-house is virtually allotted to the so-called *Kapellmeister*, i.e. to that official who ultimately conducts the musical accompaniment in the orchestra, and has to keep it in harmony with the performance of the soloists and chorus. True, the public has long forgotten to make the Kapellmeister answerable for blunders in the casting of the rôles, as also for the singers' lapses; whilst *he* has grown accustomed to regarding himself as wholly devoid of influence over the singers, to limiting his power over them to that of a mere prompter (*Einhelfer*).—German Kapellmeisters are unfortunately chosen from a class of musicians who have gained a specific musical training entirely aloof from the Theatre, people who can read their scores, play the piano a little and give the orchestra its beat, and therefore are competent to render excellent service in ecclesiastical institutes, singing-academies, musical unions and such like—but haven't the remotest idea of music's application to a dramatic representation. How far this department lies from the German musician in general, is proved simply enough by his astounding incapacity for dramatic composition, and is shewn in the prejudice commonly entertained against so-called Kapellmeister-operas. Now, that the whole musical conduct of an operatic institute is left to the mercies of musicians such as these, as everywhere in Germany, is no small ground of the great shortcomings of German Opera. In France however, though the French musician is well known to possess more skill and feeling for dramatic music, despite his admittedly less thorough knowledge of specific music,—in France, of all places, they have hit upon the expedient of dividing the functions exclusively assigned to the Kapellmeister in Germany, and distributing them between two different persons. A carefully selected *Vocal conductor* (chef du chant) practises the singers in their parts: for the correctness of their conception, their purity of intonation, the clearness of their accent and the fitness of their declamation, as in general for their proper rendering, he is clothed with a responsibility empowering him to exert an earnest supervision over their studies. At the Paris Grand Opéra this post is deemed so honourable, that I found it occupied in days gone-by by *Halévy*, already famous through his best works. This chief's especial merit, and his peculiar ambition too, consist in bringing the vocal parts to faultless practice and reproduction: his voice-rehearsals, which he conducts at the pianoforte, are attended by the *Orchestral conductor* (chef d'orchestre) and finally by the *Régisseur*; here the work to-be-performed is discussed in common from every point of view, needful alterations or adaptations are decided on, the tempo regulated, and the whole technical side of the performance planned out; after which, the conduct of the rehearsals passes over to the Regisseur for thorough drilling in the stage-business and dramatic situations, upon whose finished reproduction this Regisseur sets *his* whole merit and ambition. Whilst the Vocal-conductor watches over these rehearsals in his own sense, and exercises the right, for instance, of interrupting their course by fresh voice-rehearsals in remedy of faults that may have crept into the singing, the Orchestral-conductor —who likewise follows these rehearsals with the score— finds full occasion for making himself acquainted with the opera's dramatic and scenic character, even to its finest nuances, and for learning his score in such a sense that it shall mainly be nothing but a faithful counterpart and constant ally of the dramatic action. Equipped with this knowledge, he now practises his orchestra in the music, in his turn; herewith he gains full opportunity of proving his special knowledge and ability as pure musician, but is also placed in the only position for making them tell in the sense of a real dramatic performance.

Unquestionably it is to this constitution that the Paris Grand Opéra owes the great excellence and correctness of its representations, and even works of very doubtful value acquire here a seeming importance simply because they afford the basis for a fascinating performance which speaks entirely for itself. Such is the result of *a judiciously devised co-operation of judiciously divided functions.*

I can hear the German Kapellmeister's protest: apart from the slur upon his personal authority, he thinks the needful unity of conception, and thus the possibility of his answering in the last instance for the success of the whole, are placed in question. Perfectly true, the most eminent achievement in this line would issue from that man who should combine in his own person the knowledge and abilities of the Vocal-conductor, the Regisseur and the Orchestral-conductor: but since an individual equally trained and qualified for all these duties would be extremely rare to meet with, for an institute which cannot count upon the continual ownership of geniuses we must devise arrangements to replace his services as far as possible. For where such arrangements are absent, there happens what occurs at every German opera-house, in pretty much the following way. The absolute musician, Kapellmeister by name, who indeed is regarded as a genius at every theatre (particularly if he has been there a good long time) and therefore is commonly called "*unser genialer*" so and so, but doesn't know a jot about the spirit of dramatic singing,—this gentleman plays-through the singers' notes at the pianoforte-rehearsals, until at last they hit them and learn them by heart; but he mostly finds that this very subordinate office might just as well be handed over to an ordinary 'coach' (*Korrepetitor*), wherefore it often happens that really quite subordinate musicians are actually appointed thereto. When the singers have got so far, the Regisseur—who in his turn knows nothing of music at all—holds one or two managing-rehearsals (*Arrangirproben*), in which he has no other guidance than the text-book; his functions are of a *quite* subordinate kind, and mostly directed to the mere comings and goings of the actors and chorus, to which latter in particular he metes by standing operatic conventions its favourite, inalienable positions—a thing which is found so clear and simple, that one sometimes altogether dispenses with the Regisseur too, and does just as well with a so-called inspector (*Inspizient*). The functions of the Regisseur are therefore viewed with such contempt by the Kapellmeister that he simply takes no notice of them at all, and looks upon the interruptions caused by the former's orders as a downright impertinent disturbance of the so-called orchestral rehearsals; for the Kapellmeister, to tell the truth, sets his peculiar and unique ambition in the orchestra's playing fairly well together, with the common result that he never sees what is going-on upon the stage until the evening of performance, when, glancing up from his score to help the singers over a stile, it suddenly flashes across him like a stroke of lightning.

This is the normal course of operatic rehearsals at German theatres, and from it one may infer the character of performance of an opera thus prepared—an opera whose effect was calculated for the result of thoroughly well-drilled study, such as is provided by the Paris regulations. The blind may see that even the purely musical portion must very frequently remain quite unintelligible to the Kapellmeister, who knows nothing of the music's connection with the scene: a thing sufficiently and loudly proved by the often quite incomprehensible mistakes in tempo.

Should this fundamental blunder in the organisation of all German opera-houses have been admitted, and a betterment be deemed imperative in the future interest of the Imperial Court Opera-house, one might simply recommend an adoption of the aforesaid Paris constitution. The traditional "Kapellmeisters" [lit. "Chapel-masters"], whose very name is senseless now, at a theatre too! and whose plurality is in itself an evidence of the aimless overwork at this theatre,—would vanish in the future: they would be replaced by a *Vocal-director* and an *Orchestral-director*, each with a substitute; whilst a care entirely unknown as yet would have to be devoted to the appointment of a Regisseur, or *Stage-director,* so that we might have in time an official of equal standing with the two other directors, a man able and authorised to act in common with them in the manner specified above.

To test the result of their joint labours, as to whether it met the high requirement thus set before the theatre, would then be the duty of the *Director-in-chief.* This officer would find his opportunity in a careful following of the performances themselves, and as for that purpose he must possess a ripe and expert judgment, for this weighty post a man should always be chosen who has already filled one or other of the three main offices of the working opera-directors, and has also proved that in principle and essence he is well acquainted with the functions of the other two, —thus a man of truly practical art-experience and cultured taste. Keeping constantly in view the technical qualifications just named, the choice of this Director could be made with all the greater freedom, as, in consequence of the proposed reduction in the number of performances, the actual business arrangements would be so far simplified that there would only remain for his decision mere measures whose preparation could be easily seen-to by a practical business-agent, upon whom one naturally would make no sort of artistic claims.

Refraining from entering upon any further details, I believe that with these simple regulations for the artistic conduct of the opera-house I have at like time suggested the only possible warranty for the requirements contained in Kaiser Joseph the Second's dictum being carried out, since it is of no use drawing up a list of specific rules until one can provide for their being followed. In any case these latter must be left to the taste and conscience of the appointed experts, whereas nothing but a judiciously ordered relation of the functionaries to one another, in general, can afford the smallest hope of good.

However, not to leave my subject incomplete, I must at once reply to possible objections, all the more likely to be raised as the Theatre, and in particular the Opera-house, is commonly a prey to those routine notions which regard it as before all else a half-industrial concern. In the first place, then, it might be asked: how is one to cover the deficit in the box-office receipts, arising from a reduction in the number of performances?

In my opinion the financial authorities would find this deficit very much lessened, for one thing, by the far larger seating-accommodation of the future new opera-house. The auditorium, though calculated to hold almost double the number of spectators, would be better filled at each of the fewer performances, than the present smaller house with its nightly representations. But in any case the suggested reduction in the number of performances would remove the necessity for maintaining a double company, such as has been found requisite to supply the needs of a nightly repertoire. Just as the gain of time will tend to excellence in the representations, so, and to the same end, a saving of money may be effected by simplifying the costs of administration. Should the deficit prove not completely covered in this way, however, we must bear in mind that here would be the very chance for putting to its proper use, to a use in keeping with the dignity of the institute, the rich subvention granted by the munificence of His Majesty the Kaiser. That subvention can surely be only meant for maintaining at this theatre a higher tendency than the commercial tendency of unsubventioned theatres: it therefore would be for the experts to decide by *what* costly measure, beyond the power of an industrial undertaking, that aim was to be attained; and in the case supposed, it is obvious that the *time* needful for ensuring constantly firstrate performances is that costly thing, to purchase which one must make sacrifices beyond the means of an unsubventioned theatre. On the other hand it would rest with the objector, to prove that the often very large subvention of Royal theatres—with its wonted employment for the expensive mounting of representations bad in themselves, for the enormous salaries of soloists who would sing just as well for half their pay, and for the support of a crowd of useless officials who merely increase the difficulties of the management by their bureaucratic priggishness — had hitherto been a furtherance to theatric art.

But another objection might perhaps be raised—this time not from an artistic, but a social view-point—namely that the Imperial subvention really ought to enable the opera-house to play each night, because these nightly entertainments have become a positive necessity for the Society of so large and populous a city as Vienna.— Against this it certainly would be labour lost, to remonstrate simply from the standpoint of Art's purity and dignity; for it is one of the evil results of the prevailing ministrations of Opera-theatres, in particular, that their mishmash of art-delights and shallow amusement has found no honour as a genuine artistic rite. I must therefore bethink me how to offer my objectors a compensation for their stolen opera-evenings, and I propose to them—none of your singing academies or orchestral concerts, but just the thing that most attracts them to the theatre, namely— *Italian Opera*. Through this compromise an undoubtedly serious burden would at like time be removed, and in the most becoming manner, from the Court Opera-house as constituted according to my proposals. For I think we really do not need Italian Opera. Even though the existing stock of good musico-dramatic works is by no means large, and though the future management would therefore be obliged to give many an opera composed by foreigners (as I hope, however, in unimpeachable translation), yet this could scarcely come from anywhere but the repertoire of French, and indeed so-called Grand Opera, since that lies incomparably nearer to the German's line of thought, and in particular to the speciality of German vocal talent, than the Italian, and above all the modern Italian Opera. Let us by no means therefore be unappreciative of the alluring sweetness of Italian song; let us recognise the natural fulness of the Italian voice, and be just towards the diligence applied by Italian singers to its training, the zeal and care devoted to the practice of their solos, to the harmony of their ensembles : only, let us own that, especially through our loss of support from the supremely sonorous Italian tongue, all these effective attributes of Italian operatic music are thrown overboard so soon as ever this Italian music is executed by German singers, and in the German tongue.

Even from the standpoint of good taste, then, the friends of Italian Opera should be requested to get its works performed exclusively by Italian singers, and in the Italian tongue. For the unquestionably purer joy they thus would reap from this genre, they would shew us their gratitude by the Italian virtuoso (1) being removed from the German opera-house, and (2) being housed in Vienna at their, the Italian-Opera-friends' expense.—I am so afraid of being taken for a mere fantastical chimerist if I make proposals purely from my own experience, that I am glad to be able to support this wish again by the long-assured example of other places, and to refer this question also to the Parisian arrangement : for the French Grand Opéra is extraordinarily well endowed, but their Italian Opera not at all,—wherein we surely have to recognise no national one-sidedness, but simply a matter of common justice, since Italian Opera has been found so great a favourite with the upper and richer classes of society, that every impresario may always reckon on the best of business through simply speculating on this weakness, and therefore never needs a farthing of subvention. To throw light upon this enduring and for ourselves, for instance, most discouraging phenomenon, would lead us here too far ; let us therefore content ourselves with noting it, and with observing that, not merely in Paris and London, but even here in Vienna, theatrical managers think they can make no better speculation than by engaging and bringing out Italian troupes,—one of which is already promised by a Viennese surburban theatre for appearance in the coming spring.

Whereas then it seems utterly unnecessary to specially

subvention an Italian Opera for Vienna, but expedient and indispensable to concentrate the whole strength of the subvention upon an institute which has before it a higher, nay, a highest task, in the sense of its illustrious founder—and an institute which, owing to its past neglect of that task, has to make special exertions to approach a goal already quite forgotten and therefore without a single advocate — we nevertheless might shew an intelligent regard for the interests of all sections of the public of this great metropolis by judiciously conceding to the future purveyors of Italian Opera one of the independent theatres of Vienna, of suitable site and structure, but with the stipulation that *good* Italian Opera should be given there. This condition might perhaps be made applicable merely to that season of the year which is found most favourable for attendance at the Italian Opera; then the Italian troop might perhaps change places with a French company, for *lighter French Comedy-opera*; and since one cannot well impose obligations without shewing oneself obliging too, the Director of this theatre might be allotted as a binding pledge a certain moderate sum, to be taken from the subvention of the Court Opera-house.—In this way one would at any rate have judiciously provided both for the Public and for Art itself. Those classes of Opera which can only be disfigured, and never properly rendered, by German singers, would be removed from the artists of the Court Opera-house; and thus their task of acquiring and developing a true artistic style for the only genre that suits them, would be made considerably lighter, nay, first made possible. For that section of the public which prefers Italian or lighter French Opera, however, these genres would be represented in the only fit and truly representative manner; so that even on this side-issue too, at least correctness of taste would be insured. But it would depend entirely on the inclination of that section of the public whether performances in these genres should be maintained; the higher interests of Art, which we are here pursuing in the sense of Kaiser Joseph's noble maxim, know no further, no particular obligations towards this quarter.

The *Ballet*, in my suggested plan, would be retained in its entirety at the Court Opera-house.*—To the taste of the public of a modern capital one must willingly concede, not only a more earnest and stimulating, but also a suave and pleasantly distracting entertainment at the theatre: indeed, it is chiefly due to this propensity, that we owe the theatre's continuance and support. In my reform-proposals I consequently have not opposed this tendence, but have simply taken thought for its being met in a way to cultivate the public taste. I have exposed the imperfection, incorrectness, unfitness, and thus the taste-destructive element in the doings of the opera-house; I have laid bare its causes, and pointed out its remedies: but I have left entirely untouched the genre of art to be performed, so far as concerns its inner æsthetic content, for my present inquiry has not been directed to dramatic or musical literature, but solely to theatric art, the moment of actual stage-portrayal. Whether what is given shall be given well or badly, is all that I have taken into consideration, and I fancy I have done wisely, and even most beneficially for the heartily-desired improvement of that branch of literature itself, in placing all my accent on the manner of performance; not only because I thus confine myself to things intelligible to everyone, but also because I am conscious that upon this path, of insuring correct and good-styled performances, I am *ipso facto* preparing the ground, in the only resultful fashion, for the ennoblement of dramatic-musical production itself. In this sense, that is to say in merely criticising the manner of performance, I can the less present a hostile front to Ballet as I must uphold its performances, and in particular at the Vienna opera-house, as a perfect model of correctness, sureness, precision and spirit, for imitation by the Opera. Certainly

---

* It may perhaps be necessary to inform the untravelled English reader that at most foreign opera-houses whole nights are often devoted to the *Ballet d'action*.—TR.

the task set before every dramatic representation is easier of attainment by the Ballet, as it stands on an undeniably lower level than Opera: the very fact of every order having to proceed from one sole technical director, the Balletmaster, is here of decisive benefit. The result is a general harmony, end and means completely fit each other, and good performances of Ballet, such as we may see at the Court Opera-house of this city, never leave us in uncertainty as to the character of the artwork placed before us; one has simply to determine for oneself as to whether one is in the humour for this graceful kind of dissipation, or whether our mood demands a deeper content and a more manifold form,—in which latter case we should of course not find ourselves in the proper place.—

In consciousness of having spoken so humanely for the Ballet, and having gladly accepted its continued services as ally of the Opera, I now feel in the cheerful position of being able to say farewell to a very important section of my hoped-for readers with some prospect of their favourable reception of my plans of reform. In truth I may flatter myself with having suggested nothing but thoroughly practical and executable reforms, in nowise any overthrow, and therefore that my footing is identical with the tendencies of new Austria and its enlightened government. Wherefore I carefully avoid divulging my private estimate of the ulterior results to be expected from the simple ameliorations in management proposed above, since it certainly might appear too bold and utopian to many people, and content myself with leaving my purely practical suggestions to speak for themselves.

While I thus deny myself a picture of the significant results I hope to see arising from a thorough betterment in the relations of the Viennese Court Opera-house—results for the good of musico-dramatic art, and in step with the best endeavours of the German spirit—I cannot abstain from throwing a last ray of light on the *actual* result of this Opera's faulty management, as here denounced by me.

For it is conceivable, perhaps even to be foreseen, that

everything I have advanced will be met by the simple answer: "What you want, we none of us want at all; we don't want to have the opera-house given any other work to do, than just what it does at present; we can't see any fault in it; its promiscuous jumble is exactly what we like; good or bad business is simply a matter of chance, which may be unfavourable to-day, and favourable again to-morrow: but taking things all round, we are perfectly happy, thank you; and in any case, radical reforms won't do an atom of good."

Now I myself am truly of opinion that, with the position assigned it in our social system, the Theatre is altogether in a critical plight, and that it is better for a man, who has anything earnest in view, not to concern himself therewith at all. And as for the Viennese Court Opera-house in particular, it certainly is not to be denied that it has been favoured at times by happy circumstances, which, just when no one could any longer expect anything good from it, quite suddenly brought the most hopeful things again to light of day. Such was the case when a cultured German musician, Herr Eckert namely,* was called for a brief period to its direction, and favourable circumstances, eagerly seized on, placed at his disposal a number of quite admirable singers in the flower of their prime—singers through whose harmonious working he brought about performances quite epoch-making for Vienna. But unfortunately it is obvious enough how quickly this all was lost again, and we thence may see how little *sheer luck* avails to keep a complex institution going.—On the other hand we may see what an excellent bulwark against untoward fortune is afforded by *judicious constitutions*, if we apply a little common-sense to a consideration of the Grand Opéra in Paris. The artistic tendence of this theatre has long been shamefully distorted, to meet the most frivolous interests of its fashionable frequenters: in short it lacks, as guiding principle, the splendid maxim of Kaiser Joseph II.! Nevertheless its still-surviving practical con-

* See page 279.—TR.

stitution, while assuring to the shallowest works an execution that blinds one to their intrinsic value, yet at all times affords to him who would concern himself in noble earnest with this theatre the immediately effective fulcrum for fitly carrying out his aim; and if the French Opera is a soil at present barren in regard of noble productions, it is simply because no producers of noble tendence are forthcoming. The bringing forth creative artists of this tendence is certainly, and always must be, a rare good fortune of the times. But supposing it were to occur to ourselves; supposing a musico-dramatic author of noble, earnest endeavour, were to wish to get his intentions realised at our opera-house: nowhere would he find there an even tolerable support; people would strive their utmost to stave him off, would willingly expose him to derision, or with ignominious modesty would own that they had neither time nor means to place at the disposal of his claims. No, under the rule of Quandary (*Verlegenheit*), the only veritable director of the present opera-house— that Quandary which clouds all sense for even honour —things have come to such a pass that *Vienna*, which erewhile sent its *Gluck* to Paris, at present helps itself along with all the cast-off operatic trash of the country and abroad; so that French visitors who come to the home of that German music they prize so highly, expecting to find a high artistic recompense for the modern sickliness of Parisian dramatic music, are astonished to re-encounter in the immediate neighbourhood of Gluck, Mozart and Beethoven, the very emptiest products of the vulgarest Paris routine.

If the peculiar disgrace arising from the first lyric theatre in Germany, which ought to be the fountain-head of noblest German art-production—if the disgrace arising from this theatre's having to help itself along in such a fashion is not felt by the Viennese public, we may be quite sure that it is felt all the more keenly by the artists of this theatre, by its bandsmen and conductors. But without a fostering of the feeling of honour in the artistic body itself, to every thinking man it must remain a riddle how artistic ends, such as merely to somewhat justify the expenditure of so richly subventioned a theatre, are ever to be attained. Most certainly the high administrators of the Imperial subsidy will not wish to take the responsibility for such an abuse; wherefore, if a thorough reform be not approved, it decidedly would be advisable to withdraw *all* subsidy from the Opera-house. What Vienna quite of itself can do for even Art, on the path of a purely speculative, an un-subventioned commerce with an imaginative, gay and genial public, is proved by two of the most original and delightful products in all the realm of public art: the *Magic-dramas of Raymund* and the *Waltzes of Strauss*. If you don't wish for *higher things*, then be content with this: indeed its intrinsic worth is nothing to be made light of, and in respect of grace, refinement and genuine musical substance, one single Straussian waltz looms as far above the most of the often toilsomely imported foreign factory-products, as the Stephen's-tower above the dubious hollow pillars at the side of the Parisian boulevards.

All this, as I have said, is felt with shame by the true artistic members of the Court Opera-house; and the discouragement, the loss of heart among them has already gone so far, that a genuine fellow-feeling for their sufferings was the motive which finally decided me to publish my ideas on this theatre's reform, as I here have done in spite of many an inward feeling of reluctance.—May at least this humanistic tendence of my essay be vouchsafed some measure of respect; for, however prepared I am for feather-brained rejoinders, I yet am confident that an appeal to the honour of my readers will not die out without an echo of response.

SUMMARY.

AUTHOR'S INTRODUCTION.

The 'occasional' character of this volume's contents; abstract lines replaced by concrete cases. Modern Journalism and personal animosity. *Judaism in Music* and its critics. Fate of the pamphlets on performing of *Tannhäuser* and *Holländer*. Variations of one great theme (4).

ON THE GOETHE-INSTITUTE.

The fire and beauty of Liszt's proposals *re* the Goethe-Stiftung, but "you desire a union where the most absolute disunion is inevitable." Poetic literature, painting, and sculpture; a Goethe "art-lottery." Position of the plastic artist toward the public and toward his 'organs of realisement,' his raw material (10). The poet and *his* organs, living artists. Do our theatres afford a reliable art-material? Goethe did not find so. Poets forced into Literature, cast back on pen and paper, or printer's ink. How would the painter or sculptor like to be confined to shop-signs and tombstones? The present mis-placement of Poetry should be remedied (14). The absolute musician and concert-institutes; but the dramatic musician as badly off as the poet (15).—The duty of the Goethe-Stiftung, according to Liszt's aim, "to consist in a furtherance of Art." How? Realist and idealist. A *prize* cannot have this ideal effect; he who does not feel within himself the *necessity* of art-creation, will never bring forth a genuine artwork. The artist must be given the possibility of bringing his thought-out work to show, and obstacles must be removed from new departures. The faulty means of representation have brought about decay in the nation's dramatic genius. Nervelessness of younger poet-world. Folk and Deed, in genuine Drama (18). —The Goethe-Stiftung should found a Theatre in the noblest spirit of the nation's poetry; then only, could one rightly challenge the plastic arts to compete with poetry; and they would have to range themselves under the *architect's* guidance. But this must be an *original* theatre. Quadrennial festivals. Art-scholars who know everything already; "let them follow example of Weimar theatre" (22).

A THEATRE AT ZURICH.

A winter season just over; its results, money-loss for the Director; yet he had a good company and gave the public what it wished. No inducement offered him to continue the experiment. How will his successor proceed, (1) follow his example, (2) lower his salary list, and speculate with novelties, (3) trust to sheer luck, till the police give him marching orders? (27). Complete

SUMMARY.

indifference to the fate of the Theatre, arising from an unconscious dissatisfaction with its doings; this feeling is conscious, however, with Zurichers who have travelled and seen performances e.g. at Paris or Naples. *There is no original Theatre but that of Paris* and the best Italian opera-houses. At each theatre in Paris the pieces written for special class of performers and audience; copied in the provinces and finally in Germany. Italian audience *v.* German; the German honourably receives with like interest the stopgaps and the arias (31). German playwrights have tried to localise the foreign substance of Parisian pieces while borrowing their form; result an utter caricature. Frau Birchpfeiffer's *Hundred-thousand Thalers* compared with Paris adaptation of Victor Hugo's *Nôtre Dame.* But this rubbish is sent on to places like Zurich, and loses all interest, save for its coarsest features. However, on this debased foundation *some* harmony is still preserved; but the higher the task, the less can Zurich fulfil it, since it was calculated for quite other forces (34). This winter the public dissuaded the director from giving higher-class plays, but insisted on "Grand Opera"! Thereby one confesses lower dramatic standing of Opera as art-genre; a Play can only enthral through being understood, but Opera depends on mere externals; thus the public shews its profound contempt for theatric art in general (35).

Gold-bedecked Grand Opera in Paris, for amusement of the ennuyed rich; its pretext of a dramatic aim. But this is cut to pieces at small theatres; the singers don't know what they are singing about, become demoralised, and "The public will never notice it" (38). This indifference carried into works of a higher aim, and *here* so intolerable that the public prefers the flatter products. Love of change and consequent overwork of the performers. A reciprocal contempt between Public and Theatre. Applause and its absence; if the public could only witness the performer's indignation when a stock-device hangs fire! The beggar and alms; no respect or love forthcoming, no public spirit, no Board of Control. Though the Theatre can never be made an *educational* institute, those who feel a need in common should bestir themselves for its improvement (42). Public-minded men have neglected it; yet the often numerous attendance, and pleasure taken in occasional good performances, prove that it is a 'moment' of public life demanding public thought and cultivation. For this, our *will* alone is needed, and the public should appoint a Managing Committee to carry it out (44). *No theatre can be of real use unless its doings are original.* The scantiest means are equal to realising an artistic aim, if it is ruled for expression thereby, bringing them to highest expression whereof they are capable. Transitional stage to be gone through; seek out young artists, not soaked with routine. Not till performer can effectively interpret a good play, can he adequately render a musical drama; voice not to be strained in recited play. Then lighter opera to be first taken up, but in *good* translations (47). Existing number of suitable works being limited, we must advance to creation of dramatic works ourselves. Dearth of artistic productivity explained by *centralisation*; crumbs from Paris board; the literary, and the musical lyric; a public art-institute needed to incite and develop *native* talent (50).

A cry must go forth to poets and musicians, to furnish works specially for our Zurich theatre. Then one-sided player-caste must gradually be replaced

SUMMARY. 389

by cultured citizens (52). Gymnastics, singing-unions, pageants and Folk-plays shew dramatic bent in nation; guide these to one common goal. The maturer artists to train the native youth; inspiring effect of Theatre on the young. Industrial aspect would vanish, and Theatre become highest artistic rallying-point of civic life (54). Plan for Managing Committee; circular appeal to friends of dramatic art; finances; reduce performances to 2, or at most 3 a-week. Train company in summer; State-support; at last the personnel the "flower of a native burgher-artisthood." If this impossible, our civilisation incapable of *humanising*. Artistic Deed and common Will. The Future a reasonable preservation and advancement of the Existing (57).

ON MUSICAL CRITICISM.

What *I* would do, if circumstances and moods imposed on me the publication of a Journal for Music.—Happiest time of my life, in some respects, when I never opened a musical paper, and conducted works of musical art; but public taste and uncritical criticism forced me at last to take arms against the critics, and appeal to *men of culture;* hence my art-writings, intended to wake a conscious Will in friends of Art. We need a healthy, revolutionary Criticism, to annul present bad conditions in Life and Art (64). How far can a Journal for Music effect this?—Must not imitate the æsthetic journals, which never soar higher than "Literature in general" and a paradise of criticism, but must help Music on to where she shall no longer need a literary intervention; turn away from music-wares and music-thrummers, as you already propose, and give Music back to her proper meaning, "the art of poetry and tone" (68). Education of Athenian youth = Music and Gymnastic, arts of inner and outer man. The Journal must address itself also to the Poet who is longing to quit the rut of literature-poetics, and therefore must rid him of his dread of tone-jugglery (70). Alliance of poet and composer will open out a boundless field for fruitful discussion; but the *knowledge* thus gained must thrust on to actual realisation of the *living artwork*, and we then must admit "Gymnastic," the art of bodily portrayal, the Performer. Our literarians flitting in their garb of printer's black; the will of God and the Directors. We must resolutely buckle to; then, when the Artwork lives, you can close your Journal for Music.—Foreshadowment of the *Ring* (74).

JUDAISM IN MUSIC.

Reasons for publication of pamphlet (1869): implacable hostility of Press, as governed by the new national-religious element in European society (78).

(Article of 1850.—" Hebraic art-taste"; the matter lying at bottom; national dislike of Jews. Religion and Politics may here be passed over; the Liberals and emancipation of the Jews. Herr v. Rothschild now the "Jew of the Kings" and "King of Creeds"; the Jew is more than emancipate—his Money rules, and even our art-taste has come between his busy fingers (82).

Inquiry into causes of repugnance.—Outward appearance, foreign to European nations—its relations with Stage; speech, learnt, but not a mother-tongue—language comes from bond of community; pronunciation, no heart-felt passion—but Song is Talk aroused to highest passion. The Jews, plastic art, and music (86). Our modern Culture accessible only to well-to-do ; the Jew could buy it, but stands isolated in Society; thus we have had Jewish thinkers—the Thinker the backward-looking poet, but the true Poet the foretelling Prophet. Our modern arts a portion of this Culture, particularly music, the *easiest* to learn ; but what the Jew, thus cut off, had to say, could only be the trivial and coldly indifferent : the *how*, not the *what*; parrot-like talking without saying any real thing (89). Thrust back with contumely by our Folk, the Jew has to seek in his native stem the food-stuff for his art ; but here he only finds a *how*, for the Jews have never had an art. No import, only an expression : music of the Synagogue, its characteristics usurp his fancy and form his method (91). In listening to our naïve or artistic music he takes the barest surface, not its inner organism that has no likeness to *his* musical nature ; thus he hurls together the diverse forms and styles of every age and master. True, noble Calm is nothing but Passion mollified by resignation ; but the Jew has only sluggishness and prickling unrest. The Judaic period of modern music is final unproductivity, stability gone to ruin (93).—Mendelssohn, endowed by Nature with specific musical gifts as few before him, finest and most varied culture, highest and tenderest sense of honour ; yet never could call forth in us that heart-searching effect we have felt whenever one of our art-heroes has but opened his mouth. Kaleidoscope of forms and colours ; Bach his special model ; Bach's musical language contrasted with Mozart's and Beethoven's. Mendelssohn's endeavour to speak out a vague and almost nugatory content as interestingly as possible ; tragedy of his situation (96). Meyerbeer and a public of boredom ; sips of art, the jargon made modern-piquant, thrilling situations ; duping pushed to self-deception. Writes operas for Paris and sends them touring round the world —surest means of winning renown. Wounded vanity and tragi-comedy. *Ineptitude of present musical epoch ;* inner death and a swarming colony of insect-life (99). Heine and the remorseless demon of denial : the conscience of Judaism, as Judaism the evil conscience of modern civilisation. Börne seeking redemption among us ; only to be won with *our* redemption into *genuine manhood*, through anguish, want, suffering and sorrow (100).

(APPENDIX, 1869).

How Brendel dared the 1850 publication ! Leipzig had received a Jewish baptism of music, and *blond* musicians become a rarity; the storm almost drove B. from his post at the Conservatoire. Reasons for pseudonym ; the disguise soon fathomed ; clumsier artillery and abusive girdings; the article soon prudently smothered-up by Jews, and systematic defamation commenced. *Lohengrin* and praise from Stahr and Franz ; then silence. Prof. Bischoff distorts *Art-work of the Future* into "Music of the Future"; this ridiculous calumny now circulates throughout the European Press (104). My music "must be as abominable as my theory" : this was the point to lay stress on; Hanslick and his "Musically-Beautiful" essay ; elegant dialectic paint, to cover trivialest commonplaces. It surely was no mighty feat, to make the "Beautiful" Music's chief postulate ; but to Beethoven etc. he tacked on Mendelssohn, to some extent as their superior, enthroning

Schumann by his side. Having made his name, H. now became a reviewer in the papers and set the fashion of a depreciatory tone about myself. How Liszt fared with these gentry. Falling-off of Joachim. Our friends barred-out from the Press, whose Liberal side has been cast by the Ultramontanes into the Jews' hands (108). The "curious discipline" of the Press an open secret in Paris; the tiniest cranny stopped, if only by a visiting-card in a garret keyhole. In London more frankness: the *Times*, Mendelssohn-worship, and Old Testament. In Russia alone had the Jews overlooked this terrain (110). My earlier works began their popularity *before* this agitation had made any headway, but the Directors are scared from giving my later ones by the papers' cry of their being composed on lines of my "senseless" theories. "*German Art and German Politics*": did I make myself a favourite thereby? France asks why my works should be imported there, when my artistic rank is disallowed in my native land? (112).

In Music-Jewdom I included the sickly mannerists of our day, of whatever nationality; these take refuge under wing of Hanslick's "Beautiful." Kant and Schiller's Æsthetics replaced by a dreary jumble of dialectic nothings; Vischer's 'system'; one might think one heard the soldiers wrangling at foot of the Cross. But this party *produce* nothing, and let Offenbach rain down his 'calamities.' My endeavours to lead given artistic forces to energetic action, greeted with hubbub enough to daunt my patrons [in Munich]. Can anything like this occur to a native musician in France or Italy? (115).—A period of concentration had set in, for Literature and Music, when the legacies of matchless masters were to be realised for good of the nation, the whole world; Music's roots were to be followed back from Beethoven, through Bach, to Palestrina. Schumann and his two periods: when he was editor of *Neue Zeitschrift* you may see with what a mind I should have had to commune, another dialect than this New-æsthetic Jewish jargon; but the German's self-reliance, when without the needful fire, leads on to *passiveness*; Schumann borne in triumph by the music-Jews (117). Our Union of German Musicians, its poverty and powerlessness; biennial festivals and one small music-sheet (118).

Victory of Judaism on every hand. Why then did I stir up the agitation? After lapse of eighteen years my views unchanged: an inner necessity compelled me to trace causes of our musical downfall, also to appeal to nobler-minded Jews; but their *internal* tyranny is of *utmost* rigour; example of Auerbach, not permitted to publish his views of *Ring* and *Tristan* poems. Yet a hope remains, that *open* exposure may strike off the fetters (122).

MEMENTOES OF SPONTINI.

(Notice of Spontini's death, from *Eidgenössische Zeitung*, 1851).—Spontini contrasted with Rossini and Meyerbeer; his earnest artistic aim and lofty attitude towards the public; his disgust at present doings. With him closes a noble art-period (127).

(From Wagner's Autobiography—?)—The *Vestale* revival at Dresden Court-theatre, 1847; Spontini's late indignities at Berlin; invited to conduct Dresden performance. Majestic answer, and instrumental demands; Frau

Schröder-Devrient to the rescue, but S. arrives in a fluster; baton requirements (129). Rehearsal and difficulties with drill of "Roman army"; imperfect knowledge of German, and short sight; fervid oration to carpenters, lamp-cleaners etc.; saved from the undignified mistake. Fresh series of rehearsals decided on; uncommon energy in pursuit of a goal forgotten by most (132). His instructions to singers: horror at sound of "*Braut*"; the Pontifex, priestly trickery and miracle. Asks me to introduce trombones and bass-tuba into Triumphal March—letter from Paris thereon. Conducting by "a mere glance of his eye"; re-seating of orchestra, a great improvement on usual German plan; insists on precision of accent in choruses. "Is't Death in the violas?" A merry ending, after rule of French *opera seria* (136). The performance: Johanna Wagner and Frau Devrient better fitted for one another's rôles; the Devrient's missed theatrical effect, and the lightning-flash illumining two worlds at once. The opera, with its Frenchified antique subject, seemed out of date, and the composer received but a cold homage; as at Berlin, he chooses Sunday for a second performance and fuller house (138). A dinner at Frau Devrient's: S., as mark of special favour, advises me to discontinue career of dramatic composer, "With your *Rienzi* you have already done more than you can"; his own works and the impossibility of surpassing *Agnes von Hohenstaufen*; invention of the 'suspended sixth,' and piratings of his melody by others—confirmed by unpublished treatise of "a French Academician"; "in what should the New consist?" I have composed a Roman, Mexican, Greek, and a German subject"; opinion of French, Italian, German, and Jewish composers. Visit to *Antigone* and remark: "It's Berlin singing-academy," overheard by Mendelssohn (141). Frau Devrient's scheme to stop a second performance of *Vestale*, in S.'s interest; Roeckel and I find him overjoyed by new titles and orders, and off for Paris and Rome. Deathbed and Berlioz: "I *won't* die!" His immoderate self-appraisement and love of minor matters could not reduce my estimate of the uncommon value of his works; awestruck sympathy for one whose like I have never seen again (143).

HOMAGE TO SPOHR AND FISCHER.

Death has robbed me of two esteemed old friends: Spohr the last of the noble, earnest musicians whose youth was lit by Mozart's sun; the handle of his life was faith in his art; a deep and delicate sense of beauty; never hostile to the new art-efforts. Fischer's nature akin to Spohr's; F.'s practical activity and unsurpassable friendship. *Rienzi* at Dresden; his was the first kind deed to a helplessly obscure young artist: "Yes! I knew it would turn out so." His achievements, with the Dresden choir, for spread of understanding of lofty masterworks a red letter in Art's annals (149). Made the best of scanty means; how we stormed, and joy of reconciliation. His sympathy for my exile; the brotherly *Thou*, and how he cared for me! Took all the labour of correspondence with the theatres, that I might have leisure for my work. His promised visit, illness and death; never will my letter reach him. A rich legacy of noble work; old masters' scores copied out in hours of recreation. Career; a constant, earnest study; unwavering hand held out to works so misdoubted as mine. 'Tis verily a boon that there should be such men (152).

GLUCK'S OVERTURE TO "IPHIGENIA IN AULIS."

A grey-weather whim. I now and then refresh myself by a rehearsal with our little Zurich orchestra ; how to give a Zurich friend an idea of Gluck's music? An operatic scena impossible at a concert, for where artistic illusion is not *complete* I cannot be even half content; so I chose Gluck's overture. Inadequacy of Mozart's added Close, still more when played in Gluck's own tempo. The standing time-pattern for overtures. Gluck meant the overture simply as introduction to first scene, hence used but *one* time-signature; universal mistake herefrom. German conductors, respect-for-authority, and happy beings with arrested development who check their feelings (158). Old Paris edition used by me at Dresden, when giving the rarely-given opera itself ; the superficial critic's horror at my tempo—sticking at syllables, but never smitten with the spirit ; a noted musician-by-trade, and his suggested compromise ; the imminent disaster of acknowledging that one has been praising a work quite wrongly rendered ! (161). "Amateur" musician that I am, what was I to do for a Close? Here there is no development, but a constant contrast of three chief motives ; Gluck's poetic aim was not to give a 'satisfactory ending,' so I resume the motive that ushers-in these three. What lofty artwork ever gives a full, a satisfying peace? (163). Additional hints for phrasing, but nothing must be done glaringly ; one can never be too guarded with such suggestions.—Though I will have nothing to do with concerts in general, I can adapt myself to circumstances.—Do I wish to shame those who call me a denier of past music-heroes ? *Let us leave Gluck & Co. alone, if we can't perform them better.* Fétis and Bischoff will again cry Fie !—The heavens are clearing (166).

ON THE PERFORMING OF "TANNHÄUSER."

Unexpectedly a number of theatres now (1852) applying for its performing-rights; one of my greatest torments that I cannot be present, but must convey instructions by pen ; personal correspondence being beyond my strength, I print this pamphlet.

Anarchy among Conductors, Regisseurs and Scene-painters, each working independently at German theatres. Even the sickliest Italian opera would gain immensely by heed paid to dramatic coherence ; a work like "Tannhäuser" must be ruined out and out by present methods of performance (172). —The poem to be first read aloud by the assembled performers, in presence of chorus, with full dramatic accent ; singers generally pick up their rôles at their own pianos, but until they can *recite* their parts they can never sing them in accord with even the *composer's* aim. If this not complied with, I withdraw my work. Advantage of the Conductor's attending these rehearsals. In *Tann.* no real Recitative ; strict tempo to be observed by singers in the recitative-like phrases till they have mastered my aim, *then* they should give free play to natural feeling ; for full agreement, words should be written out in each *orchestral* part.—Caution against misunderstanding—(175). The cuts (to be restored) necessitated at Dresden: 1, second strophe of T.'s song to Venus, because Fr. Devrient unsuited for rôle of Venus, and thus to shorten scene—this entire scene at Weimar, however, made a good effect; 2, orchestral postlude to act i, because of stiffness of supers; 3, bustling violin-passage in prelude to act ii, consequent thereon (178). Cut 4, *Adagio* in act ii: this situation forms the axis of T.'s career, nothing can compensate us for missing its due impression; omitted because singers treated it as an ordinary ensemble, instead of simply accompanying in whispers; could a twenty-times-repeated performance at Dresden, with regular calls for author, repay me for the gnawing consciousness that my aim was misunderstood? T. must here feel that he is master of the *dramatic* situation, that the audience is listening to him alone: "*Ach! erbarm dich mein!*" (181). Cut 5, in closing ensemble of act ii, because all interest in T. past praying for—if this passage too sorely tries singer etc. cut must be maintained, and trust to supreme effect of exit, which is indispensable for the mood in which public approaches act iii; 6, abridged version of prelude to act iii—to remain; 7, in Elisabeth's Prayer, because of Johanna Wagner's inexperience, and could not be restored later at Dresden since first impressions fix themselves on public and performers as a definite unalterable thing—the dumb-show after Prayer difficult, but vital (185). Revision of opera's close: first version contains same idea, but merely sketched and thus not understood; public *v* art-connois-seurs. Younger Pilgrims' Chant only to be given where scenery quite satisfactory and voices good, full and ample in number; this chant at any rate rounds off the whole in a satisfactory manner (187). Tempi and dynamics of overture; in general an artistic understanding *v* metronomical marks. Manning of orchestra, usual deficiency of strings in German theatres compared with French; 'stage-music' to be recruited from military bands. Avoid parsimony, for performance must be unwonted, in character with work (191).

Duties of the Régisseur: "an opera-singer isn't an actor"; discard deference to operatic favourites, and make the performer a partner in the artist's creation from his own convictions; gesture and by-play to synchronise with orchestra. Freedom of grouping in the 'Processions': Entry of Guests and a march from *Norma*; usual serpentine curve, double file, and stage-conversation, prohibited; Minstrels' Tourney; entries and exits of Pilgrims; Dance in Venusberg, a wild and yet seductive chaos—freedom of invention to Regisseur, but must follow chief indications and strictly observe the music (194). *Scene-painter and Machinist:* necessity of intelligent acquaintance with subject, and agreement thereon with Conductor and Regisseur. The cloud-veilings in Venusberg scene; lighting of stage; Wartburg valley to be so fresh that spectator may be left a while to its impression. French designs for Dresden mounting of act ii. Necessity of separate canvas for Wartburg valley in act iii; arrangements for making glowing Venusberg seem to draw nearer; funeral train and flush of dawn (197).

The rôles. That of Tannhäuser himself may be one of the hardest problems ever set before an actor: his saturation with the passing incident, and the dramatic contrasts hence arising. Never "a little" anything; naming of the nameless, 'Elisabeth;' the whole Past now lies behind him like a dream;

SUMMARY. 395

one thing alone in this love, the all-consuming fire of Life. The moral world and how it treats the strong; a struggle for life or death; his colours flaunted openly; only one thing can daunt him—the woman who *offers up herself* for love of him. Sorrow, once yearned for, now drunk deep, "her tears to sweeten"; unlike his self-saving fellow-pilgrims. The heartless lie at his journey's end; in despair and hatred of this self-righteous world, he seeks again the Venusberg, to hide him from his "angel's" look. Her love-death sets the culprit free; the world, and God Himself, must call him blessed (201). To Music alone could such a task be proposed, and only a dramatic *singer* could fulfil it, but not as *opera*-singer. Curse that cleaves to tenors, through present criminal school of singing; vocal trickery, fine clothes, applause and high wages. This rôle will ruffle singer's composure, and force him to change his habits; but a *total* revolution needed. Not a bit like Meyerbeer's so popular "dramatic-tenor" rôles, neither vapid and unmanly like *Robert*, nor "well-meaning" with a few reprehensible cravings. A completely successful impersonation will be the highest triumph of his art (203). Venus must have a full *belief* in her part; so justified, that she can yield to none but the *self-offering* woman. Elisabeth needs virginal unconstraint, without betraying how much experience that requires. Wolfram addresses sympathy of more refined section of audience; pre-eminently Poet and Artist—Tannhäuser being before all Man. Performers as singers also.— Valediction: a die cast on the world, unknowing whether it shall win or lose; cordially do I grasp the hands of valiant artists who shall not be ashamed to realise my aim (205).

REMARKS ON THE FLYING DUTCHMAN.

Scenic requirements for act i (210). The Holländer's rôle; its exponent must succeed in rousing and maintaining the deepest sympathy. Hints for by-play and vocal expression of his first scene; terrible repose passing into terrible energy; the success of the whole work depends on issue of this scene (212). Scene with Daland; everything takes place as if by instinct, H. deals mechanically and without interest, like a wearied man; the old longing wakes again; battle between hope and despair (213). Scene with Senta in act ii: calm, solemn and motionless; Senta and H. are riveted in contemplation of each other—the performers need not fear to weary the audience. Gradual rise of passion, till at last his *love* converts H. to a *human* being, whereas he before had often seemed a ghost. Performer never to drag the recitative passages (216). Characters of Senta, Eric and Daland—the sale of his daughter to a wealthy man, without suspicion that he is doing any wrong (217).

EXPLANATORY PROGRAMMES.

(1) BEETHOVEN'S EROICA.—Title misleading, if one regards it as merely relating to a military hero; the hero is the *man* in whom are present all the purely human feelings in highest fill and strength; its heroic tendence the progress toward his nature's rounding off. *First Movement:* force, clinching to violence of the destroyer, a wrecker of the world (222). *Second Movement:* an earnest, manly sadness: we give ourselves to it, till sighing we swoon

away; yet we will not succumb, but endure. *Third Movement:* force in all its buoyant gaiety, the lovable glad man winding his hunting-horn from woodland heights. *Fourth Movement:* sorrow become the shaping-force of noble deeds; the counterpart and commentary of first; the Womanly clinging to the Manly, Force wed to Love; the total Man now shouts to us the avowal of his Godhood (224).

(2) BEETHOVEN'S OVERTURE TO CORIOLANUS.—A comparatively little-known work of this great tone-poet. Coriolanus, the man of Force untamable, unfitted for a hypocrite's humility; one unique scene chosen by Beethoven from this great political canvas, the scene between C. his mother, wife and child, in the enemy's camp before his native city. His scorn assailed by Woman's pleading; the war of Feeling; "Rome or I, must fall." Woman pleads for "Peace." A torturing strife and sudden resolution; the offering of self is sealed; felled by his own death-thrust, the colossus crashes down; peace at Woman's foot (228).

(3) OVERTURE TO FLYING DUTCHMAN.—His ship scudding before the tempest; promise of salvation; how often has he dreamt the end of all his trials reached! A passing vessel, he puts the joyous crew to flight. Where dwells the woman's heart to rescue his unmated being? A ray divides the gloom; a woman's offering; he breaks down at last, as breaks his ship to atoms; from out the waves he rises, led to Love's daybreak by the victress' hand (229).

(4) OVERTURE TO TANNHÄUSER.—Pilgrim's Chant; night falls; magic sights and sounds appear to those whose heart is fired by daring of the senses. Love's minstrel and the siren call of Venus; to *her* he sings the canticle of love triumphant; wonders of the Venusberg; he treads the realm of Being-no-more. A scurry, like the sound of the Wild Hunt; the storm is laid, merely a wanton whir remains; as dawn begins, it blends with the sacred chant. The sun rises in splendour on a world redeemed; soul and senses, God and Nature, united by the kiss of Love (231).

(5) PRELUDE TO LOHENGRIN.—Love had vanished from the world; the human heart began to long again for stilling of its need, and made for itself a symbol in the Holy Grail.—A flight of angels brings back the holy Cup—once reft from worthless Man; the seeds of Love swell out to wondrous growth, the Cup is bared, and left in guardianship of pure knights. Smiling as it looks below, the angel-host wings back its way to Heaven (233).

ON LISZT'S SYMPHONIC POEMS.

The judgment of a friend who owes so much, as I to Liszt, must needs seem biased; but this is a maxim of the world of mediocrities: "Halt! till I, thy natural foe, have recognised thee." Nothing but a full heart can bring me to speech (237). But what is there to say? You saw my joy when Liszt produced and performed his new compositions, and you witnessed my silence. The more our thoughts depart from the level of life's vulgar needs, the less can they be expressed in words, and words can never convey the deeper impressions made by music. Yet the outer side one can talk of. The world's surprise at a virtuoso appearing as composer—so inconvenient for its mental

SUMMARY. 397

habit ; but Liszt's reproduction [playing] of Beethoven's sonatas should have
forewarned it that he must also have the productive gift—this I scarce need
tell a *woman* (241). Within last ten years [written in 1857] Liszt has come to
full ripeness of his creative force. If one has perceived the uncommon
richness of inventive power in these great tone-works, one might perhaps
be bewildered by their *form*. Outcry for Form : tidbits for the critics, who
else would have nothing for themselves; they prefer bladeless swords, for
they can't see a master's hilt till he is dead and his sword hung up in the
armoury (243). " Symphonic Poems " a better title here than " Overtures " ;
the new form required a new name. Overture's origin in a dance played
before the drama ; then separate march or dance-forms strung together into
the Symphony, as openly shewn by its Third Movement. Change and
repetition, instead of Development—how they clash in Leonora-overture
(245). " Programme-music "—how shocking ! But could Liszt, the most
musical of all musicians, really desecrate Music? Hear my creed : *Music can
in no alliance cease to be the redeeming art* (246). But music cannot manifest
herself save in a form borrowed from either bodily motion or spoken verse,
in the first instance ; in this human world it was necessary to afford divine
Music a point of attachment, a conditioning moment. Are dance and march
motives higher than a poetic, an Orpheus or Prometheus motive ? Our doubt
arose, not from Music's incapacity, but from musicians attempting to draw
a *detailed* picture, from their not possessing the needful poetic gift of condens-
ation—e.g. Berlioz' love-scene in *Romeo and Juliet* symphony. (I myself
was classed among these programme-musicians, drolly enough). Dramatist
stands much nearer to everyday life, but Musician must upheave life's
accidentals and sublimate its emotional content. An idealistic form ; Shakespeare would have written his love-scene differently, for Berlioz to reproduce
(250). Essence of the Individuality revealed in the gifted individual's artworks ; Liszt's way of looking at a poetic subject must needs be fundamentally
different from Berlioz' ; here we have the secret ; " Enough, I have it all ! "
These works must find speedy favour with Public proper, for all the critics'
cry of "harshness" etc. ; the " singularity " must reside in that secret of the
individuality : in what we *are* we are surely all alike, in how we *look at*
things we all are wellnigh strangers ; by our love for a great artist we shew
that we adopt his individualities of view. And will Liszt dupe our trust?
Name a second Liszt ! (253).
Ascribe this letter to Fétis if you please, but tell my Franz I love him (254).

EPILOGUE TO THE NIBELUNG'S RING.

Straining my whole productive forces, through a long series of years, to the
prosecution of a work which every practical man declared inexecutable at any
of our opera-houses. Plan for its performance ; to my friends my head seemed
filled with mad chimeras. In matters theatric the German loses all his
earnestness. I found no pleasure in the Existing, and dreamt of the day,
after my death perhaps, when all our theatres and their fine doings would be
swept away ; for the ' wild comedians and musicians proper ' would I plant my
banner (260).

Private publication of the poem, but secret leaked out ; our literary-poets soon flooded us with " Nibelungen " ; Dorn's opera and Jordan's rhapsody. 'Twere presumptuous to suppose I had exerted any influence on my rivals' labours, for they don't seem to have imitated the exhaustiveness of my preliminary studies ; the mere name must have prompted them to save the national myth from the shame of poetic treatment by a musician. The *Eddas*, now so easily accessible through Simrock's modern version, positively invited people to try their hand on this " old-Frankish gear " ; deluged with jaw-breaking names of gods and heroes from the old Norräna, in text-books and well-printed poets ; their curiousness had been their sole attraction. I thought it time to challenge comparison ; met with nothing but bad jokes, even from *Allg. Ztg.* which has to introduce a brace of brand-new poets every year ; musical reviewers endorsed the condemnation (264). Yet a pressing recommendation from this side might rather cast suspicion on an important artistic enterprise like mine, now the public has so often been misled by the puffs of this press. Dilemma—as the Opera-house would have played utter havoc with my work ; I merely wished to rouse attention of the educated, and thus gain adherents to my plan of performance, but the press left me in total ignorance whether I had or not (266).

The musical composition begun with alacrity in winter of 1853-54, carried to midway in *Siegfried* by spring of 1857, then put aside from reaction against the lasting strain : one dumb score laid above another, while I could not even hear my earlier works in Germany. So I drafted a work that might be performable at once, *Tristan und Isolde* : virtually a supplementary Act of the great Nibelungen-myth. Offer, spurious or genuine, of Emperor of Brazil made me think of writing it for Italian singers ; their musical status, need of instruction in *pathos* (270). Paris and idea of fraternising with a foreign element. Invitation to produce *Tannhäuser* at Grand Opéra. The fortunes of that undertaking, outwardly unpleasant enough, have left pleasant memories of amiable traits in French character ; but I soon learnt that I must keep to my *own* element, free from coercion by current French taste ; with most determined purpose I returned to Germany. Here all the theatres have kept me at arm's length ; cry of "exorbitant demands" though I ask no lavish splendour, but correctness and non-mutilation of performances. Vienna, Berlin, Hamburg and its "impartiality" (273).

PREFACE TO THE "RING" POEM.

Its representation to be free from all the influences of the daily repertoire of our standing theatres ; a smallish town, but fit for receiving influx of visitors ; provisional theatre, mayhap of wood, amphitheatric, with invisible orchestra. Picked troop of German singers ; the number and time of performances ; guests invited from far and near. Characteristics of German Opera and singers ; benefit of studying *one* task—not to-night an Italian Opera and to-morrow Wotan. Advantages for proper mounting, as at Paris and London theatres. Artistic and acoustic effect of sunk orchestra ; also singer will thus stand almost directly facing spectator, making words easier to catch (277). The Public : instead of a distraction for the fagged-out brain, this will come in middle of a pleasure-trip; the hearer revelling in easy exercise of new-won faculty of Beholding; drawn by his own desire, he willingly will follow. Entr'actes for refreshment, in the open air of a summer evening, to brace the intellectual faculties (278).

Ulterior effects: "in the beginning was the *deed*"; our performers could scarcely fall completely back into their old groove, on return to their theatres, especially if we have chosen young talents merely in need of helpful training; directors of German theatres will probably have attended out of curiosity and, witnessing the impression on the public, would soon attempt to copy the performances at home; this might give impetus to a truly German *style* of execution. Repetition of original performances at stated intervals, with new works of kindred or other earnest aim (280). German nation, standing at head of Europe in Music and Poetry, only needs a form-giving institution to unite its artistic efforts; this could very well go hand in hand with the Existing, feeding on its choicest forces to lastingly ennoble them. Through becoming *original*, the German would begin to be *national*—a quality in which French and Italians are far ahead (281).

The *material* means: either an association for collecting funds, or a German sovereign. The latter would need only to divert the subsidy from his opera-house—let those who need this soothing dissipation procure it at their own expense; a distinctively German field of action thus brought within his power; by cultivation of a genuine national spirit he would win his name imperishable fame. Will this Prince be found?

A faint beginning through the printed "word." I *no longer* hope to live to see the performance, and even the literary product will find no ready market, as it falls into no class. The Public demands the "deed." Alas! that lies beyond my power (283).

A LETTER TO BERLIOZ.

In London 1855 I boasted of an advantage over you, that I could understand your works while you could not mine, owing to different degree of performability and your ignorance of German. Good translations and performances will rob me of that coign of vantage, I hope, but you offer me another with your somewhat indefinite charges anent a "music of the future"; origin of the term (288). My "Art-work of the Future" written at a crisis in my life; its attempts to foreshadow a work that should stand toward present Life as Greek Drama to public life of Greeks, to shew the possibility of an artwork in which the highest and profoundest thought should be imparted to the naïvest purely-human Feeling, without need of reflective Criticism. My surprise that so earnest a man, gifted an artist, and honest a critic should cast in my teeth the vulgarest miscomprehensions of a book he has never read.—Let us hope for the time when our dramatic works may make us know each other better (291).

"ZUKUNFTSMUSIK" ("MUSIC OF THE FUTURE").

Your [Fr. Villot's] wish to have a clear account of my ideas; through the accompanying translation of four of my opera-poems my course is made easier.

SUMMARY.

Abnormal state of mind when writing my theoretic essays; let me first describe the general current of my thoughts at the time (295). In Nature, Man and Artist, the evolutionary march is from unconsciousness to consciousness; but the artist will not need to *reflect* until he finds difficulties in his path. The problem can never before have been thrust so strongly on an artist, as the artistic factors had never been so diverse and peculiar; a *German* artist was still more strangely placed (297). Opera in Italy was for the singer and dancer; the composer wrote for definite, given singers, neither Music nor Drama; Italian Opera no legitimate daughter of Palestrina. In France the dramatic poet intervened to greater purpose; a definite model-theatre, the Théâtre Français, set the style for performers as for author. Opera reached Germany as a finished foreign product, alien to the nation's spirit; tragedy and comedy sung by same singer; Italian and French operas, and German copies, cheek by jowl; artistic anarchy; for the earnest musician the Opera-house was virtually non-existent—e.g. Beethoven and his *only* opera (300). An *ideal* hovering in the air. Advantage of the Romanic nations in having an accepted *form*; only since middle of 18th century have German authors striven for its like. Goethe and Schiller seeking for a purely-human form; thus would the German's disadvantage be reversed, as this art-form would be purged of the cramping element of narrower nationality, universally intelligible, and accessible to every nation. Music its fittest medium, her language being understood by all the world, particularly when joined with dramatic show. A German musician, with Beethoven's symphonies in his head, thrust into dealings with modern Opera, as it is in Germany (303).

Childhood's impressions; Weber's and Beethoven's death and music; I wanted to write music for a tragedy I had penned; exercises in counterpoint and teacher's dictum. Practical career begun at Opera-house; alternate delight and disgust at operatic doings; Paris stimulating. Schröder-Devrient's talent cast a spell over me that gave the bent to my whole artistic course; an ideal possibility had opened before me—what an incomparable artwork must that be whose every part should be worthy of such an artist, of a company of such (305). My attempts to reform the operatic institute itself all shipwrecked; this brought me to consider the Theatre's standing in our social system, compared with Greek, and to forecast a society which should re-establish the Athenian relation of Art to Public Life on a more lasting basis: "Art and Revolution"; I was told my essay was unsuitable for the Paris public at such a time (307). Dissolution of the great Greek Artwork; the crowd treated to gladiator-fights while the man of culture consoled himself with literature and painting. Lessing and the boundaries of poetry and painting: I believed that each art-branch evolves along a line of force till it reaches a limit where it needs must join hands with the next, thenceforth the only capable art, and I pictured to myself an artwork that should combine all the single arts; not daring to think it completely possible in the Present, I called it "Artwork of the Future." That essay's only value may be to those whom it would interest to hear how, and in what manner of speech, a productive artist once busied himself with problems generally left to the professional critic (309). "Opera and Drama," which goes into almost

SUMMARY. 401

the finest detail, must have had more interest for me than it can for others; a private meditation, with a polemical tinge. A brief outline of it :—Mistake of those who deemed the Dramatic ideal, if not reached, yet well prepared-for in actual Opera; Gluckists and Piccinists, Voltaire, Lessing, Goethe and Schiller; Goethe's trivial opera-texts. Opera's constitutional defect could shew itself to neither the musician *per se* nor the literary poet; truly great poets, with unfavourable exceptions, have never written for Opera, whilst the musician was engaged purely in maturing his specific musical forms. The ideal poetic stuff; I believed I found it in Mythos, the purely-human, freed from conventions (312). The Form for this 'stuff' only our modern music could furnish. Since Renaissance two arts, Music and Painting, have gained a development quite unknown to former ages; Harmony and Polyphony the invention of latter centuries. With the Greeks Music was always the attendant of Dance; thence she and Poetry gained their laws of Rhythm; the earliest Christians took over this melody, but left out its rhythm as ungodly. But the Christian spirit next invented Harmony, the changes of the four-part chord at once supplied an expressional motive akin to that lost when Rhythm was dropped; then the subordinate voices took independent action—Counterpoint. With the relapse into Paganism the worldly longing re-appeared, and Melody recovered in Italy its rhythm, but knew not how to take advantage of Christian music's own invention; a periodic structure quite childish in its threadbare narrowness (315). German masters also went back to rhythmic melody, still surviving in people's dance-tunes, but combined it with harmony and polyphony—e.g. Bach's motett. Through formation of string-quartet polyphony extended to orchestra, emancipating it from its subordinate position, still occupied in Italian Opera; dance-form extended in Fugue, then several dance-melodies combined; birth of Symphony. Haydn broadened it and gave expression to its linking passages; Mozart imparted the full euphony of Italian Song; Beethoven deepened it, forming a landmark in history of Art itself (317). This Symphony a revelation from another world; Logic ousted by Feeling. Metaphysical necessity for discovery of this new language in *our* times, as word-speech had become a mere convention; Feeling, downtrod by Civilisation, seeks itself a new outlet; uncommon spread of Music's popularity and interest in its deeper-meaning products. Poetry now has only two ways open: either to become Philosophy, or to blend with Music in the Drama; the poem to penetrate the musical tissue's finest fibres, and spoken *thought* to dissolve into *feeling*; answering the fateful question "Why?" (320).

Abnormal state when I wrote my theoretic essays, for I was struggling to abstractly express what had become clear enough to me in my artistic intuition and production; impatience in style, trying to give in each sentence the *whole* subject of my thought. From this brain-cramp I returned to my artistic work, as though recovering from a serious illness, wrote and partly composed the *Ring*. A change now came over my relations to publicity: my operas were spreading and becoming popular; character of their performances; the pessimist's advantage and thanks. Critics had not been able to alienate the public, and individuals experienced a total change of taste; this confirmed me in my views of Music's all-enabling efficacy (324). Share taken by spirit of Music in the conception of my opera-poems; these poems will shew you

SUMMARY.

the line of my artistic evolution; even my boldest theories were thrust upon me through my carrying in my head the plan for the *Ring*—in *Tristan* also I had clean forgotten my so-called "system," while going beyond it; the artist's sense of wellbeing when inhesitantly producing. *Rienzi*, a work full of youthful fire, written under dazzling influence of Grand Opera (327). This five-act opera followed by one originally meant for *one* act, *Flying Dutchman*; in its poem I already felt differently; once for all I forsook History for Legend. Advantages of Legend: its purely-human content, facilitating the poet's answer to the "Why?" and doing away with a mass of outer detail and explanation. Only gradually did I grow conscious of, and profit by this advantage; the increasing volumen of each poem shews this, as I brought out more and more the inner springs of action, till *Tristan* is nothing but inner motives and soul-events—no longer a trace of word-repetition—the melody's *structure* is here foreordered by the *poet*. Even the poem's workmanship has probably gained thereby; but how about the musical form, the melody? (331).

Shrill cry of dillettanti for "melody!"—they take their idea of Melody from works in which long stretches of scarcely musical noise, for conversation's sake, parcel off the separate melodies, i.e. Italian Opera. But Music's only form is melody, so we have less a question of melody before us, than of its first restricted dance-form. Now this earliest rudiment of melodic form is the basis also of the Symphony, but developed at last by Beethoven through division, re-combination etc., to one sole continuous melody (335). This Symphonic procedure applied to his Mass—text-words of the Church being almost purely symbols—but never yet to Opera; the traditional forms prevented it, but there must remain open the possibility of finding in the poem itself a counterpart to this Symphonic form. That counterpart supplied by orchestra giving voice to inner motives of dramatic action: as Dance-tune is to the Symphony, so is Dance itself to the Dramatic Action. The poet gains his freedom while meeting the musician half-way; the poet's greatness mostly to be measured by what he leaves unsaid, the musician's *endless melody* speaking out this thing unspeakable; the orchestra will thus replace Greek Chorus, and the chorus be banished save as an *active* personage in the plot (338). The forest and its voices; a silence growing more and more eloquent; what folly to try and trap one of the sweet woodbirds and train it to sing in a cage! (340). Long step from *Tannhäuser* to *Tristan*; should *Tann.* gain favour with Paris public it will largely be due to its visible connection with works of predecessors, especially Weber.

What I have proposed above had manifestly lain at heart of all our great masters—Gluck and his followers; even in works of frivolous composers [Meyerbeer etc.] I have met effects unattainable in the merely spoken play; but 'numbers' reckoned for lowest art-taste stand side by side with these gems of art; stereotyped *cadenza*, footlights and signal for applause. Through no continuous style being adopted, Un-nature could sally forth more brazenly than ever (342). Concessions made by even Weber—"rights of the Gallery." I believe you won't find these concessions in *Tannhäuser*, the whole musical adornment being meant merely to display the dramatic *action*; in this you may find its real distinction from works of my forerunners, and not in a "music of the future" (345).

SUMMARY. 403

TANNHÄUSER IN PARIS.

Projects for *Tristan* at Carlsruhe in 1859; amnesty impossible then; removal to Paris in autumn, for sake of hearing good orchestra etc. at last; Carlsruhe plan falls through. Idea of *Tristan* at Théâtre des Italiens, inviting German Directors to a model-performance; the three Paris concerts were to prepare the public, but they proved the plan's impossibility (350). Princess Metternich and the Emperor; order for *Tannhäuser* at Grand Opéra a complete surprise. Difficulties about a ballet in act ii for the late diners; plan for new Venusberg scene; carte blanche for engagements and mise en scène; Niemann, Morelli and young talents; Vauthrot and his pains with pianoforte rehearsals; taken with a new liking for this early work, I carefully revised the score (353). Gradual disheartenment; reporters prophesy failure to Niemann; spiritless orchestral conducting; offer to withdraw score (354). Performance and false accounts; magnanimity of Paris public proper. First night: clique of reviewers, cues and roars of laughter, especially in third act, which promised so well; uproar, but opposition beaten down at end by public—in reality a victory for the work (356). Second night: Jockey Club and dog-calls for the ballet-less opera. Second offer to withdraw the work, but management persisted, and refused to announce third night as "final." Jockey Club's alarm at stratagem of Sunday performance; scenes of second night renewed, indignation of public; only social standing of Messieurs Disturbers-of-peace saved them from rough handling (358). Definite withdrawal prompted by artistic considerations—the house was sold-out for several nights in advance; circular protest signed by musicians, authors etc.; Empress's offer to intervene. Let the inadequacies of this production lie buried beneath the dust of its three nights' war! Project for a new theatre in Paris, to realise my reforms (360).

THE VIENNA OPERA-HOUSE.

Distastefulness of writing to papers, instead of to official authorities, about things which every scribbler thinks he knows much better; but only way of reaching the few who care for Art. The reporter the only present censor of the Theatre's taste. Why not attach genuine experts to boards of control? Difference between duties of subventioned and non-subventioned theatres; former should be conducted on definite principles, and none better than Joseph II.'s dictum: "*It should contribute to ennobling the nation's taste and manners*" (365). Present state of Vienna Opera-house: viewed from without —a medley of styles, blunders in inscenation, singers forcing themselves out of the frame, etc.; from within—overwork where we expected to find mere laziness, the best of musicians, the bandsmen, thrown away on musically-emptiest operas, prima-donna-tyranny and no *esprit de corps* (368). Troubles of directorate, money fines, and singers bound to tasks for which they are unfit. Fault lies in *giving representations day by day*; these should be reduced by about a half. Théâtre Français and Burgtheater may well play daily, as (1) there are more good plays than good operas; (2) relays of actors available for different classes of play; (3) plays can be largely studied at home, thus fewer stage-rehearsals needed. These conditions reversed in

404 SUMMARY.

Opera, and dearth of Comedy-operas (370). Exegesis of Kaiser Joseph's dictum: Art cannot operate directly on public Morals, but only through raising quality of taste by *good performances*; the Public knows nothing of Poetry or Music, but simply of the Theatric Representation, and Music cannot work purely *as such* in Opera where the Dramatic Action stays unclear; style=a complete harmony of musical with dramatic tendence. Owing to great expenditure of time required for preparing good performances, their number should be reduced, and even of these a part should fall to Ballet. But mere edicts will never create good taste and feeling; measures for appeal to conscientiousness, for spurring emulation (372). German theatres and their Kapellmeisters—people who haven't the remotest idea of music's application to the stage, as shewn by their own operas. Arrangements at Paris Opéra: a *chef du chant, chef d'orchestre* and *régisseur*, in constant touch with one another; method of rehearsals. The correctness of Parisian representations the result of a *judiciously devised co-operation of judiciously divided functions* (375). Method of German rehearsals by "unser genialer" so-and-so; blunders in tempo and Kapellmeister's surprise at seeing the stage on evening of performance. One might well adopt the Paris constitution: Vocal-director, Orchestral-director, Stage-director; and a Director-in-chief, chosen from past working-directors, to carefully watch and follow the performances, keeping them to the required standard (377). Financial aspect of reducing number of performances: no loss need arise, with the new, much larger auditorium and a single, instead of double company; if it should, *time* for preparation is just the thing whereon to spend subventions, not on costly mountings and singers. Social aspect: outcry of pleasure-seekers; let them maintain an Italian Opera at their own expense, with *Italians*—beauty of Italian voice and language; even in Paris Italian Opera is unsubventioned, but the speculation always succeeds. Grant an independent theatre for this purpose, and seasons of lighter French Opera; perhaps a fraction of the subvention might go to form a pledge of good work and correctness of taste here (381). The *Ballet d'action* should be retained, as its performances are quite a model to the Opera, for sureness, precision and spirit; advantage here of one-man management; this graceful dissipation for those in the humour (383).

The above reforms are practical, no overthrow, and their execution well might lead to high results in *creative* art; but present management—save when sheer luck has favoured, as at time of Eckert—affords no encouragement such as in Paris; an earnest creative artist, were he to arrive, would meet the cold shoulder at present Vienna Opera-house. Rule of Director 'Quandary'; French visitors' surprise at finding in the home of German music, of Gluck, Mozart and Beethoven, the cast-off trash of vulgarest Parisian taste. Shame felt by the true artistic members of Vienna Opera, bandsmen and conductors. Better take away the subsidy, and leave Vienna to its own devices; has it not produced Raymund's magic-dramas and Strauss's waltzes? Things not to be made light of; Stephen's-tower and boulevard-pillars. Appeal to the reader's honour (386).

INDEX

As in the previous volumes of this series, I have adopted the following plan of numeration for the references in this Index, viz. :—the figures denoting tens and hundreds are not repeated for one and the same *subdivision*, save where the numbers run into a fresh line of type; thus 7, 14, 17, 21, 27-35, 37, 101, 107, 117, 119, would appear as 7, 14, 7, 21, 7-35, 7, 101, 7, 17, 9. Where the reference is merely to notes &c. of my own, it is placed within brackets.—
W. A. E.

A.

Abnormal state, see Mental.
Above and Below, 91.
Absolute Music, 95, 247 ; Musician, 14, 6, 375.
Absolute-musical, 183, 331, 44. See also Purely-musical.
Absolution, 201.
Abstract and Concrete, 1, 80, 2, 270, 279, 95, 310, 2, 25, 6.
Abstract Reason, 312, 8.
Abstractions, 18, 113, 243, 302, 19.
Absurd, the. See Ridiculous.
Abusive, 102. See Calumnies.
Academies, Singing, 141, 281, 373.
Accent, Melodic, 314 ; Theatric, 136, 173, 211, 374; of Voice, 178, 81. See Rhythm.
Accidental, the, 64, 92, 249, 302.
Accommodation, an endless, 199.
Accompanying voices, the, in Counterpoint, 314, 6, 7.
Acting, its importance for Singers, 46, 7, 173, 9, 92, 3, 202-3, 12, 97, 305, 66.
Action, athirst for, 181 ; Dramatic, see D.
Actors, 198, 201, 59. See Performers, Singers &c.
Actress and Iambics, 66.
Actress and her lover, 27.
Actuality, 100 ; and Thought, 10, 1, 15, 8. See Reality.
Adagio-ensemble and Stretto, 180.
Admiration, Craving for, 40, 202, 367.
Admiration for great Masters, 311. See M., Reverence, &c.

Admonition, a Mother's, 226.
Advertisement, love of, 287.
Æschylus, 289, 307.
Æsthetes and æsthetics, 22, 65, 113, 308 ; Musical, 105, 13-4, 7, 22, 239, 48.
Affected *v.* popular, 159.
After-speak &c., 85, 9, 95.
Agamemnon, in *Iphigenia*, 162.
Agitation, inner, 92, 215.
Agnes von Hohenstaufen, 139, 40.
Agreeableness, an art of sheer, 116, 122, cf. 334.
Ahasuerus, redemption of, 100.
Aim, Artistic, 16, 45, 125, 60, 73, 4, 176, 80, 95, 7, 248, 89, 97, 8, 339, 344. See Poetic, Tendence.
Aim, a definite, 21.
Akin, 49, 148, 52.
Alexandrines, the, 68-9.
Allegro and Andante, 157-8, 60.
Allegro and Moderato, 149.
Allgemeine Zeitung, 264, 5.
(Alliance Israélite Universelle, vi).
Alps, the, 151, 266.
"Amateur," W. an, 161, 2.
Amateurs, 291 ; acting, 54.
Ambition, 240, 87 ; a worthy, 372, 374, 6.
Amphitheatric auditorium, 274, 6.
Amusement, shallow, 35, 6, 94, 277, 306, 32, 79.
Analogy in Myths, 268.
Anarchy in art, 300, 1.
Angel, 201, 11, 6, 32 ; a fallen, 211.
Animation on stage, 177, 82.
Anonymity, see Pseudonym.
Anschauung, 79, 238, 48, 50, 2, 78, 302, 21, 38.

405

INDEX.

Antigone, Mendelssohn's, 141.
Antique, the, 302, 3, 13, 4; Frenchified, 137.
Antique arrangement of stage, 141.
Antiquity, relics of, 263.
Apathy, 28, 88, 92. See Indiff.
Apparatus, Mechanical, 10; Operatic, 368; Scenic, 37. See Mise en scène &c.
Appeal, a Motive of, 162.
Applause, 40, 105, 37-8, 80, 202, 350, 355, 6, 7, 66; Signal for, 342.
Aptitudes, natural and artistic, 46, 48, 53, 4, 275, 9, 81, 375.
Appreciation, 120; quick, 355, 7.
Architect, the, 19, 67; no Jewish, 86; for Wagner's theatre, 274.
Aria, 297, 338, 41-2; at least one, etc., 332, 3; Duets etc., 328.
Aristocracy of France, 357, 8, 84.
Aristocrat in disguise, an, 66.
Armistice, though no full peace, 163.
Armoury, laid up in the, 243.
Arouse and satisfy, 179.
Arrogance, 223, 7.
ART, 163, 381; Living, 11, 63, 73, 172; Modern, 64, 82, 313; Native, 49-50, 260, 301; Public, 48, 72, 126, 275, 89, 97, 386. See Friends.
Art, a new atmosphere of, 260.
Art and art-varieties, 8, 14, 9, 22, 87, 88, 95, 8, 289-90, 307-8.
Art as a Livelihood, 36.
Art and Life, 9, 52, 63, 4, 71, 89-91, 99, 246-7, 9, 89, 301, 7, 20, 65.
Art and Morals, 371.
Art and the Public, 36, 41, 52, 289. See Theatre.
Art-bazaar, an, 32.
Art-creation, 15, 48. See Artist.
Art-enabling import, a life of, 90.
Art-fiend, 82.
Art-forms, 243, 8, 302, 17, 34; a Childish, 315, 33. See Ideal.
Art-history, 32, 101, 6, 21, 7, 50, 306, 13, 7.
Art-impressions, 278. See Infl. and Impr.
Art-industry, 367. See Ind.
Art-music, 91.
Art-philosopher, 291.
Art-taste, 79, 81, 108, 9, 282, 370, 372; the lowest, 324, 42. See T.
Art-trade, the, 8, 13, 108.
Art-understanding, or -intelligence, 9, 10, 6, 22, 62, 126, 58, 61, 5, 86, 365.
Art-unions, 8, 15, 7.

Art-work, the enacted, 9, 19, 45, 9, 63, 269, 89, 95, 305, 24, 40; Greek, 307-8.
Art-work of the Future, the, 63, 4, 71, 3, 271, 90, 303, 8.
Art-world and the artist, 205.
Artificial art, 98.
Artillery of debate, heavy, 102.
Artist, Creative, 89, 91, 152, 238, 242, 53, 96, 321, 7, 85, cf. Productivity; Vocal, 205, see Performer &c.
Artist and artist, 291; and Critic, 62, 73, 172, 242, 91, 309, 43, 63; and Man, 204.
Artistic consideration, a weighty, 359.
Artistic faculty running dry, 64, 98.
Artistic quality of an aim, 45.
(Aryan, Wagner an, ix).
Assimilation of races, 121.
Associations, 118, 281. See Unions.
At one, 71.
Athenian youth, bringing-up of, 68.
Athéniennes, Spontini's, 139.
Athens, 306, 7. See Greek.
Athletic competitions, 52.
Atonement, 200, 31.
Attention, continuous, 31, 189, 244, 275, 339, 55, 9, cf. 92, 332, 67.
Attraction and repulsion by opera, alternate, 301, 4, 5, 22, 41.
Attractive hubbub, an, 334.
AUBER, 327.
Audience, number of, 42, 378. See Public.
Auerbach, Berthold, 120.
Augmentation and diminution, rhythmic, 190, 317.
Augsburg bellelettrists, 264.
Austria and its Government, 383.
Authority, Respect for, 158, 61, 5.
Autobiography, 127, 269, 304.
Autograph-hunting, 8.
Awaitings, dramatic, 162, 79, 277, 307, 36, 40, 3.
Awe, sense of, 181, 232, 303.

B.

Bacchantes, 230.
BACH, J. SEB., 94, 116, 300; compared with Mozart and Beethoven, 95; Motett, 149, 316.
Back-door for pedants, a, 161.
Ballad, a popular, 329.

INDEX. 407

Ballet, 324, 37, 51-2, 70, 2; and its Entreteneurs, 352-3, 7; at Paris, 36; at Vienna, 382-3.
Ballet-dancer, 68, 297.
Ballet-master, 194, 369, 83.
Banal, 31, 334, 44; Chord, 342.
Banck, C. (Dresden critic), 159.
Bandsmen, 259, 366, 7, 85. See Orchestra.
Bankruptcy at theatres, 25, 7.
Banner, my, 260.
Banquets, 278. See Table-music.
Bar, strict value of, 175, 210.
Bars, four to a tune, 316.
Barred out from Press, 108.
Barriers and boundaries of the arts, 95, 290, 308, 12, 36, 7.
Basses (double) in *Dutchman*, 314.
Basso buffo, Fischer as, 152.
Bassoons in *Tann.* overt., 188.
Bathos, 88.
Bâton and Spontini, 129-30, 4.
Bavarian Government, W. denounced to, 115, (256).
(Bayreuth idea, the, 256).
Beat, musical, 175, 373.
Beautiful, the, and Schiller, 113.
Beauty, Musical, 105, 59, 342; of Passion, 47, 305; Sense of, 147; of Tone, 134, 87, 317, 79.
(Becker, vii).
BEETHOVEN, 95, 9, 104, 14, 303, 5, 385; the daring, 247; the later, 116; and Mendelssohn, 105; post-Beethovenian, 112, 8.
BEETHOVEN'S *Fidelio*, 300.
Missa Solemnis, 335.
Overtures, 244; *Coriolanus*, 225-8; *Leonora*, 245, 300.
Sonatas, 240.
Symphonies, 155, 300, 17-8, 9, 334-6; Heroic, 221-4; Ninth, 114, 49.
Beggar and alms, 40.
Beholdings, 45, 238, 78; the Artist's, 68, 338; Feelings and, 68, 9, 86, 89; Poetico-musical, 248, 50.
Being-no-more, 230.
Belief in oneself, 143.
Belief in one's part, 204.
Belief through Love, 152.
Belisario, a march from, 193.
Belittling, 192, 311. See Depreciate.
Bellini, 126; *Romeo*, 305.
Berlin, (6), 32, 97; *Lohengrin* at, 270; and Spontini, 127, 31, 5, 8, 139, 40, 1, 3, 59, 304; Theatre, 111, 209, 61, 72, 370.

BERLIOZ, 286-91; *Romeo*, 249-50; at Spontini's deathbed, 142.
Bible-student, a famous, 114.
Birchrod and dustbroom, 66.
Birchpfeiffer, Frau Charlotte, 33, 4.
Bird, the wood-, 340.
Bischoff, Prof., 103, 66, 288, 91.
Bizarre, 248.
Blabber, an intolerably jumbled, 85.
Blond musicians, 101, 13.
Blood of generations, 82.
Blurring, 117, 280, 371.
Boards of Control, 41-2, 363, 4, 5; of Education, 44, 52, 3. See Directors, Theatre.
Bodily motion and Music, 247.
Body, Animal, 95; Culture of, 52, 68.
(Böhme, vii).
Bologna, *Lohengrin* at, 270.
Book-trade, the, 8, 13, 101.
Book-writing, 2, 22.
Boredom, 36, 96, 7, 306.
Börne (writer), 100.
Botschafter, Wiener, (362), 363.
Bourgeoisely devout, 203.
Bourse, the, 109.
Brain-cramp, 321.
Brain-fag, 277, 8.
"*Braut*" and Spontini, 132.
Bread-givers, Art's, 8,
Breadth and Broadening, 316, 7, 29, 335, 41.
Breathing-pauses, 175, 88.
Brendel, Franz (vii-ix, 60, 6), 101-2.
Bricabrac, mannered, 82.
Brilliance and display, 29, 36, 49, 191, 273, 305, 27, 8.
(Brockhaus, F.A., 6).
Brünnhilde and Siegfried, 268-9.
(Bruyck, C. von, 161).
Budget, a Prince's, 281-2, 386.
Bugbears, 158.
Bühnenfestspiel, 1, 257, 8, 79, 80, 1, 282.
Bunglers, 104, 246, 8.
Bureaucratic priggishness, 379.
Burgher Artists, 56; Society, 42, 3, 51, 2, 4, 96, cf. 226.
Business worries, 277, 306, 69, 77.
By-play, 173, 92, 4, 366. See Gesture.
Byzantinism, musical, 67.

C.

Cabinet-minister and *Tann.*, French, 352, 7, 9.

408　INDEX.

Cackle and chatter, 67, 109, 14, 290, 343, 55, 64.
Cadenza, 217, 342.
Calchas in *Iphigenia*, 157.
Calls for the author, 138, 80.
Calm, 93, 224. See Repose.
Calumnies, 104, 6, 7, 65, 355.
Candid avowal, 64, 121.
Cantilena, a lugubrious, 135.
Canto fermo, 314, 6.
Canvas bare of contents, a, 337; a great historical, 225.
Caprice, 35, 42; a musical, 171, 93, 344.
Care (*Sorge*), 150, 1, 277.
Carelessness after first few nights, 184.
Caricature, 33, 5, 91, 246, 8; a human, 143, 259.
Carlsruhe for *Tristan*, 349-50.
Carte blanche at Paris, 352, 3.
Cast-off operatic trash, 385, cf. 49.
Cataclysm, an imagined, 259, 60.
Catchwords, 107, 13, 288, 90, 309, 355.
Categories, accustomed, 265, 6, 369.
Causa finalis and efficiens, 119.
Causality, laws of, 318, 20.
Cause, The, 101.
Caution-money, theatr., 25, 6.
Celebrities, acquaintance with, 50.
Centralisation of Art, 48, 299.
Centre of world, inmost, 330.
Chamber-music, 350.
Champfleury, 267, (286).
Chance, 27, 114, 55, 384, 5.
Change, constant, 27, 92, 299.
Changefulness, musical, 162, 3, 245, 249, 317, 8.
Chaos, shouldered back to, 273.
Characteristique, 96, 126, 79, 276, 81, 305, 30.
Charm, musical, 164, 317, 86.
Chastening sorrow, 223.
Chastisement, 103, 253; disdained, 115, 65.
Chef du Chant, and d'Orchestre, 353, 354, 73-4.
Chief-Moments, 194; -Motives, 249, 334.
Childhood, Wagner's, 303.
Childish Art-form, 315, 33; Pretext, 356.
Childlike Glee, 129, 42; Pleas, 226.
Chimeras, 258, 61, 71, 380.
Choice, the artist's, 296, 328.
Choir-master, 149, 52, 72, cf. Vocal-cond.

Chorales, 314.
Chord, the, 314.
Chorus: Greek, and Modern, 338; Operatic, 36, movements of, 193, 375-6; -Singing, 149.
Christian, a, 104; Baptism, 87; Nations, 313; Spirit, 314. See Civilis.
Christians: bamboozled, 114; early, 314.
Christian - German: Fame, 113; Rulers, 81.
Church, the: Fall of, 315; and the Jews, 109; Reform of, 120.
Church-music, 298, 314-6; Litany, 335.
Circles, wider, 21, 56, 103, 48, 261, 274.
Circular appeal for theatre, 54-5, 281. Cf. 359, 60.
Citizen and civic, see Burgher.
City's din, the, 339.
Civilisation: Christian, 84; Conventional, 56, 319; and the Jews, 66, 78, 100.
Clairvoyance, 329.
Claptrap, 40. See Applause.
Claque, the, 342.
Clarinet in *Tann.*-overt., 189.
Classical, quite, 240, cf. 246.
Classics, study of the, 303.
Clatter, muisical, 92. Cf. Noise.
Clergy, the lower, 120.
Climax, dramatic, 177, 86.
Clique, a, 355-6, 7, 9.
Clouds: Castles in, 289; Conjured from, 258; Fighting the, 81.
'Coach' for singers, 375.
Co-creative artists, 175, 92.
Coercion, 244, 71, 97, 302, 11.
Coldness, Spohr's, 147. See Indiff.
Collectedness (*Sammlung*), 277, 339, 356, 9.
Colossus crashes down, 228.
Colour, legendary, 329; musical, 94, 317; turned to Action, 330.
Combinations, dramatico - musical, 305.
Comedian-dom, 72, 152, 259.
Comedy-operas, 47, 370.
Comic, The, 217.
Comings and goings, stage, 173, 93, 375.
Commercial world, a, 260. See Ind.
Common: good, a, 61; a need in, 42, 3; working in, 308, 80, 4.
Common-places, æsthetic, 105.
Common-sense, 258, 364, 84.

Community, the, 84, 8, 231.
Complacency, contemptuous, 100.
Complex: Institution, 384; Scene, 178, 94, 276; Works and undertakings, 115, 247, 51, 334, 70, 2.
Composer and the Singer, 174-5, 297-8. See Musician.
Composition at any price, 98.
Composure to be ruffled, 202.
Compromise, 160-1; with existing Theatre, 258; with Ital. Op., 379-81.
Comrades, artistic, 71, 3, 148, 50, 1, 164, 205, 71.
Concealment, 106, 21; of Opera's evil, 311, 37; of Origin, 104; of Technical means, 276.
Concentration, a period of, 116, 8; of forces, 275.
Conception: Musical, 251, 66, 327; Poetic, 264, 9, 87, 305, 12, 25; and Rendering, executive, 132, 3, 159, 60, 70, 5, 83, 202, 70, 6, 366, 374, 5.
Concepts, mental, 318, 9. See Abstract.
Concerts, 9, 14, 5, 55, 72, 119, 64, 165, 350, 79; -performances of dramatic music, 156, 7, 63, of Beethoven, 240.
Concessions, 176, 258, 343, 4.
Conditions antecedent, 306. See Life.
Conductor, 112, 30, 4, 58, 60, 1, 4, 171, 88, 354, 73-6, 85; and singer, 175, 81, 373, 6. See Kapellmeister.
Confidence, 330, 44, 5; empty, 114.
Conflict, the artist's, 296, 303. See Tragic.
Connexion, or inner coherence, of phenomena, 268, 318, 29.
Connoisseurs, 9, 86, 186, 239, 308, 39.
Conscience of Judaism &c., 100.
Conscientiousness, 160, 372, 7.
Conservatism, 57, 64, 161, 259; Old-, 109.
Construction, musical, 315; Rules of, 247. See Form.
Consumptive art, 49, 126, 265.
Contemplation, Poetic, 89, 204. See Behold.
Contempt, 100, 226, 62, 89.
Content, æsthetic, 382; an entire, 269; a foreign, 32; a nugatory, 95; poetic, 162-3, 221; purely-human, 328. See Emotional, Form.
Contradiction: in Jewish nature, 93; in Opera, 311; and Spontini, 138.

Contrast, musical, 160, 2, 245; dramatic, 198.
Contributions, 8, 55, 281.
Contrition, see Penitence, Remorse.
Contumely, ten years', 290, 324.
Convenient penance, 200.
Conventions, 312, 8, 9; Dramatic, 298; Operatic, 171, 3, 7, 341, 76.
Conversation, audience's, 31, 332, 4.
Conversion, a sudden, 104, 6.
Convictions, 102, 92, 238.
Convincing, 290, 318, 20, 1, 38.
Coolness of mind, 321.
Co-operation of managing artists, 170-172, 373, 5, 7.
Copying-out old music, 151-2.
Cords, ropes and laths, 276.
Correctness of Performance, 112, 58, 164, 71, 80, 209, 51, 72, 3, 5, 9, 99, 324, 66, 72, 4, 82; of Taste, 381.
Cortez, Spontini's, 127, 31, 9, 40, 304.
Costume, Stage-, 36, 52, 202.
Counterpoint, 314, 6, 7; Exercises in, 304, 27.
Courage, 16, 8, 78, 178, 223, 81, 343, 58.
Court-Theatres, 27, 30, 111, 2, 363-386.
Cowardice, 72, 229.
Creative faculty, 18, 49, 50, 86, 93, 126, 241, see Artist; Singer, 175.
Creditor of Kings, 81.
Creed, Hear my, 246.
Crescendo and decr., 164, 88.
Crisis in my life, 288, 97.
Criticism, 45, 68, 79, 160, 1, 290; Modern, 62, 263, 4; Paradise of, 65; Revolutionary, 64, 73.
Critics, 160, 1, 251; Wagner-, 2, 62, 66, 109, 159, 65-6, 254, 67, 71, 83, 295, 309, 23-4, cf. Æsthetes.
Cross themselves and flee, 229.
Crucifixion, The, 114, 232; picture of, 83.
Crumbs from Paris, 49.
Cry to poets etc., 51, 70.
Culture, (viii), 48, 78, 85, 7, 8, 260, 306; -needing, 43-4; Downfall of, 121; Period in, 95, 8, 9, 106, 16-117, 9, 312, 7; Public, 44, 51-3, 382.
Cultured men, 63, 8, 265, 308, 77; musically, 367, 84.
Curiosity, 25, 7, 39, 125, 263, 95; if only out of, 279.
Curse resting on: the Jew, 100; Tenors, 202; Vanderdecken, 100, 228.

410   INDEX.

Cut off from music, 155, 266-7.
Cuts, 38, 135, 76-85, 92, 273.

D.

Daily performances, 274, 6, 369, 78, 379.
Damned, torments of the, 229, 31, 367
Dance, 225, 44, 7, 313, 4; in the Venusberg, 194, 230, 352.
Dance-form, 244-8, 316, 33, 7, idealised, 334, 6; -tune, 313, 5, 6, 35, 6.
Dancing to a Beeth. Sym., 336.
Dandies and Theatre, 119, 352.
(Dannreuther, E., v).
DANTE, 116, 367.
(David, vii).
Davison, Bogumil, (actor), 83.
Davison, J. W., 109-10.
Day, glare of operatic, 267.
Dead, when a master is, 243; when I am, 259, 82.
Death, 125, 42, 7, 8, 51, 2, 303; inner, 99.
Death, Athirst for, 228; Elisabeth's, 183, 6, 201; Love-, 268; -Warrant, his own, 227.
Decency: Artistic, 276; of Argument, 102, 8, 13.
Deed, 18, 48, 57, 117, 223; an unfree, 268; "In the beginning was the," 278, 82.
Defamation, 103. See Calumnies.
Defiance, 200, 1, 22, 6.
Definition and distinctness, 88, 9, 224, 246, 51, 90, 303, 38, 41, 83. See Feeling.
Demagogic Jew, a, 83.
Democrats, the, 66.
Demon of denial, 100.
Demoralisation, 37, 258, 366.
Dependence of the Jews, 120.
Depreciate, I don't, 244, 333, 41.
Depreciatory tone, 77, 105-6, 14-5.
Deriding the artist, 385.
Description, mere, 211, 320.
Desire, 232. See Yearning.
Despair, 18, 181, 201, 10, 1, 6, 74, 282, 306.
Despléchin, 356.
Destiny (*Schicksal*), 78, 150. See Fate.
Destroyer, the, 222, 3, 5-7.
Details: Attention to, 191, 4, 8, 257, 259, 79; -Work, 309, 28, 30, 1, 9.
Determinant (*bestimmend*), 158, 62, 179.

(*Deutsche Allgem. Zeitung*, 348, 54).
Deutsche Museum, 7.
(*Deutsche Rundschau*, 104).
Development, 44, 5, 245-6, 317, 32. See Evolution, Musical working-out.
Devil's scandal, a, 36.
Devotion (*Andacht*), 278, 339.
Devrient, Eduard, 132, 5, 365.
Dialectics, 104, 5, 13, 7, 248.
Die cast on the world, 205.
Difficulty in W.'s works, 198, 270.
Dilemma, a, 265, 88.
Dilettanti, 155, 332.
Dining too late for first act, 352, 7.
Dinner at Frau Devrient's, 138-41.
Diplomacy, 128, 41.
Directors (theatr.), 3, 25, 72, 191, 259, 79, 363, 8, 9, 79, 85; -in-Chief, 377; French, 351, 2, 7, 8, 373-4; Inviting the, 279, 350; Musical, 170, 1, 4, 6, 87, 98. See Conductor.
Discretion, 200. See Prudence.
Discussion, artistic, 71, 3, 101, 3, 6, 108, 13, 6, 9, 263, 4, 325.
Disgust at Opera, 257, 303, 4, 6, cf. Attraction &c.
Disheartenment, 268, 341, 54, 66, 380, 6.
Dishonesty of critics, 62, 106.
Disillusionment, 277. See Undec.
Dissipation and distraction, 12, 31, 36, 125, 277, 8, 82, 306; a graceful, 383.
Disturbers-of-the-peace, 358, 9.
Disturbing, 244, 320, 38, 51, 66.
Diversity of tongues, 302, 19.
Dodgery of managers, 111.
Dog-whistles, 357.
Dogma, a musical, 113.
Doing and Suffering, 223, 47.
Donizetti, 126.
Dorn, H., 261, (? 267).
Double Companies, 46, 378.
Doubled Prices, 137.
DRAMA, 19, 41, 163, 262, 82, 9, 320 :—
Complete, or perfect, 307.
French, 29, 298.
Genuine, or acted, 11, 7, 8, 51. See Artwork.
German, 32-3. See Poetry.
Higher class, 34, 5.
Ideal, 310. See I.
Inner kernel of, 35, 6.
Literary, 11, 263-4.
Modern, 53.

INDEX. 411

DRAMA—*continued*—
Musical, 35, 47, 193, 305, 38, see Music.
Opera's make-believe of, 31, 5, 6, 37, 289, 97, 309.
Spoken, 369, 72. See Play.
DRAMATIC:—
Action, 34, 249, 79, 320, 9, 31, 7, 372, 4; before all else, 344; compared with Dance, 336; and Greek Chorus, 338.
Aim, 36, 8. See Poetic.
Artwork, the, 96, 309, see A.
Bent, 52, 303.
Catastrophe, 178, 86, 330.
Characters, 34.
Coherence, 171, 9, 85.
Composition, German, 373.
Declamation, 47, 174, 299, 374.
Development, 162, 344.
Music, 300; puissance of, 304, 41.
Portrayal, 11, see P., Repres. &c.
Representation, 30, 4, 371, 3, 5, 383, see R., Perf.
Singer, 201, 375, see S., Perf.
Situations, 38, 173, 7, 9-81, 6, 90, 192, 8, 214, 374; thrilling, 97; treated finely by composers, 341-342.
Stuff, 32-3, see S.
Drapings, concealed by, 37, 260, 71.
Drastic, 131, 5, 257.
Dreamlike state, a, 329.
Dreamy nature, a, 216, 303.
Dregs, stately sober, 37.
Dresden, (ix), 61, 127-51, 5, 60, 303; Chorus, 131, 5, 49; Orchestra, 159, 164, 367; Theatre, 112, 27, 34, 56, 159, 76, *et seq.*, 322, 7.
Drum, big, and Spontini, 139.
Drum-solo in *Holländer*, 213, 4, 5.
Dubious, 103, 15, 277, 95, 7, 323, 71, 375, 86.
Dumb Scores, 267. See Music, lit.
Dumb-show, Elisabeth's, 185.
Duping, 97, 100, 253.
DÜRER, ALBERT, 14.
Duty and Morals, 69. See M.

E.

Ear: entrancing the, 35; leaving it indifferent, 333.
Ear and Eye, 68, 226, 32, 79, 305, 39.
Earnestness, 101, 2, 10, 22, 7, 270, 303, 71; in Art, 140, 7, 51, 2, 258, 275, 80, 300, 60, 3, 4, 82, 4, 5.

Eckert, Karl, (Vienna, 279), 384.
Ecstasy, 320; frenzied, 178, 230; holy, 231, 3; and horror, 222.
Eddas, the, 262, 3.
Educated, the, 44; half-, 291. See Culture.
Education, 52, 4, 6, 158, 65, 319; Greek, 68; Wagner's, 303. See Board, Theatre.
Effect: Dramatic, 177, 82, 6, 7, 94, 196, 204, 304; Musical, 341; Stage-, 83, 135, 6, 7, 263.
Egoism, 70, 85. See Self.
Eidgenössische Zeitung, 142.
Elect, the, 232, 48.
Elisabeth, see Tannhäuser.
Emancipation of, and from, the Jews, 80, 1, 2, 121.
Emotional: Catastrophes, 97; Content, 225, 49; Expression, 86, 183-184. See Expr., Feeling.
Emperor: of Austria, 378; Brazil, 269; the French, 350, 2, and Empress, 357, 9.
Emphasis, false, 343.
Emulation, 327, 72.
Encouragement of the artist, 16, 40, 50, 148, 279, 323, 4, 7, 45, 50.
End, the, 212, 28.
End-rhyme, 312.
Enemies, my, 78, 106, 7, 11, 21, 60, 356.
Energetic action, leading into, 114.
Energy, 132, 5, 59, 81, 2, 90, 203, 211, 2, 22, 371; and Initiative, 364.
England, 77; public, 110. See London.
Enjoyment, artistic, 10, 45, 50, 4, 73, 185, 221, 5, 379.
Enlightened times, our, 102.
Ennobling, 83, 246, 81, 304; artistic creation, 382, 3; taste and manners, 365, 70-1.
Ennui, 36, 96, 7, 184, 306.
"Enough! I have it all," 251.
Enriching power of Love, 253.
Ensemble, 135, 367-9, 84; -pieces, 180; -singing, 380.
Entertainment, 36, 40, 2, 379; an allowable, 282. See Amuse., Dissip.
Enthusiasm, 104, 26, 31, 7, 303.
Entire man, the, 224.
Entr'actes (Festival), 278.
Envy, 98, 102, 7.
Erard's sister (Md. Spontini), 138.
Error of Opera, the, 333.

Esprit de corps, 368, 85-6.
(Esser, H., Viennese cond., 279).
Essentials, overlooking, 291, cf. 160.
Eunuchs, 68.
Euphony of Ital. singing, 317, 79.
Evangel of the Stage, 41.
Everlasting laws, 302.
Evolution: Artistic, 81, 90, 3, 9—
  Wagner's, 304, 26, 7, 9; Free,
  120; of German art, 301; Histri-
  onic art, 46, 53, 298; Human, 78,
  121, 296; Individual, 241, 52, 96;
  Moral, 318; National, 84, 8; of
  Painting, 313; Solitary phase of,
  158; of the World, 296. See Music,
  Opera, Speech.
Exacting, too, 205. See Exorbitant.
Exaltation, 216, 23, 4.
Example, 50, 147, 279, 380. See
  Model.
Exceptional: and excellent, 306, 22,
  341; means, 45, 187, 91, cf. 150,
  273.
Executioner's axe, the, 137.
Exile, 150, 1, 69, 205, 67, 349.
Existing, The, 16, 8, 44, 5, 7, 57,
  258, 9, 81.
"Exorbitant demands," 173, 272,
  385.
Expectancy, 162. See Awaitings.
Experience, 17, 48, 53, 71, 204, 363,
  377; New, 27, 158, 200, 60, 80,
  322, 4, 44, 52; Personal, 62, 184,
  186, 257, 9, 81, 8, 328, 65, 80.
Experts, theatric, 360, 3, 4, 77, 8.
Explanations in Drama, 329, 30.
Exploitation, 27, 364, 8.
Exposure, open, 122.
EXPRESSION (*Ausdruck*), 238 :—
  and Aim, 35, 6, 89.
  Clearness, or definiteness of, 96,
    248, 90, 308, 38, 9. See D.
  Dramatic, 47, 312.
  Executive, 159, 71, 3, 82, 204, 10-
    217, 356. See Phrasing.
  a Heated, 85.
  Individual, 94. See I.
  Means of, 19, 29, 34, 7, 44, 5, 7,
    92, 270; choice of, 296; complex,
    251. See Musical.
Externals, mere, 33, 5. See Inner.
Exuberance of spirits, 177, 223.
Eye, see Ear.

F.

Factory-like excess of labour, 367.

Faith in Art, 57, 147.
Fallacy of the Theatre, 17.
False notions and judgment, 52, 7,
  202, 21, 309, 20, 5, 6, 55, 71, 3.
Falsetto in the *Holländer*, 217.
Falsifications, 102. See Calumnies.
Fame, 50, 97, 102, 13, 48, 52, 311;
  imperishable, 282.
Familiar Circle, a, 86, 138, 48, 240;
  Sensations, 198.
Fancy-picture, 57, 83, 94, 6, 183, 296.
Fantastic, 96, 248, 308, 80.
Fashionable scoffs, 118, cf. 106.
Fastidious, 131.
Fate, 255, 87, 328. See Destiny.
Fatherland, 226, 7, 70. See Native.
Faust: and the Evangelist, 278;
  Gounod's, 273.
Favourable demonstrations, 103, 49,
  264, 355, 6, 7.
Favourites, stage, 33, 9, 192, 353, 4,
  367.
Feather-brained rejoinders, 384, 6.
FEELING :—
  Addressing the, 51, 73, 222, 320.
  Bewildering the, 62, 166, 343, 71.
  Breath of, 90.
  Definite impression on, 158, 62, 78,
    179, 251, 312, 8, 24, 33, 8, 71.
  Expresssion of, artistic, 68, 86;
    natural, 65, 86, 175, 83-4.
  and Faculty, 222.
  Fellow, 17, 162, 92, 200, 4, 27, 9,
    290, 386.
  Fill of, 198, 221, 2.
  Healthy, 94, 160.
  Instinctive, 80, 3, 199.
  Language of, 302, 18-9.
  Man of, 223.
  Purely-human, 86, 221-6, 312, 9,
    324, 43.
  Stimulus of, a, 35, 320.
  Unbiased, 63, 343.
  Understanding by, 16, 45, 62, 318.
  Wholeness of, 198, 201.
Feeling Discourse, 174; Singers, 317.
Feelingless, 99; loungers, 184.
Feelings held in check, 158.
(*Feen, Die*, 304).
Fellow-knowers, 57, 192.
Fellow-suffering, 179, 367, 86.
Fellowship, artistic, 16, 51, 4, 368.
Festival-performances, 52, 307; An-
  nual, etc., 20, 280, 1, 2; Musical,
  20, 119, (220), 251, 75; Wagner-,
  275, 7-9.
Fétis, 166, 254.
Few, the cherished, 148, 205, 363.

INDEX. 413

Fidelio and Frau Devrient, 137.
Finales, &c., 180, 328.
Fine-feeling, 204, 41, 53.
Finery and voice, 202.
Fire : of Life, 199, 230; Mental, 7, 117; of Performance, 136, 89, 215; Youthful, 327. See Warmth.
Fire and flame in Israel, 114.
First nights, 184-5, 355.
Fischer, W., 130, 1, 47-52.
Five years without composing, 266, 330.
Fixity of form etc., 90.
Flourish, a decorative, 159.
Flower and sucker, 334.
Fluency of study, 276.
Flutists and lyre-players, 69.
FLYING DUTCHMAN :—
the Ballad, 216.
Berlin production, 209.
Composition, 326, 31.
Daland, 212-4, 7.
Eric, 216-7.
Omissions, allowable, 217.
One act, first meant for, 328.
Overture, 228-9.
Poem, 326, 8, 30, 1.
Senta, 214-6.
Ships, sea and steersman, 209.
Title-rôle, 209-16, 28.
Folk, the, 65, 80, 260; and Art, 89; Culture of, 18, 53, 307, 8; Poem of, 312; Spirit of, 89, 90.
Folk-: Dance, 91, 313, 5, 36; Life, scenes from, 52, 120; Play, 53; Refrain, 329; Song, 91.
Foot feeling for ground, 336.
Footlights, the, 342.
Force, 221-7; fill of, 300.
Foreign element, a, 99, 121, 270, 1.
Foreign products, 12, (24), 30, 2, 5, 44, 9, 51, 97, 298-9, 301, 79, 85, 386.
Foreign tongue, a, 84. See German.
Forerunners, 340-1, 3.
Foreshadowing the melody, 331.
Forest, 223; its melody, 339-40.
Form, 242-50, 300-2, 16, 28, 40, 3; and Content, 32, 90, 312, 7, 25, 44, 383; Modern, 271; Poetic, 312, 328, 9, 36. See Art-form, Ideal, Musical.
Formalism, 94-5, 239.
Formlessness, 247, 51.
Forte and fortissimo, 188-90.
Fount of Art, 90, 1, 385.
(Fouqué's *Held des Norden*, 261).
Four-bar melody, 316.

Frame, the artistic, 298; out of the, 33, 366, 7.
France and Wagner's works, 77, 112, 287, 91. See Paris.
Frankfort, *Lohengrin* at, 272-3.
Franz, Robert, 103.
Freedom : in Acting, 175, 7; of Action, 78, 120, 271; Development, 300, 2, 32; Folk, 80; Musical, 244, 318, 27, 32; Poetic, 337.
Freigedank, K., (viii, ix, 76), 102. See Pseudonym.
Freischütz and Spontini, 140.
French : Academy, 140; Art, 271, 302; Character, 271, 98, 358; Composers, 140, 385; Designs for *Tann.*, 196, 356; Friends, 267, 271, 344, 55, 8, 60; Musicians, 373; Singers, 353; Wagner speaking, 128, 41-2. See Opera, Paris.
French and Italians *v.* Germans, 14, 281, 97, 379, 85; treatment of native composers, 115.
Frenzied riot, 194, 230.
Friedrich, playwright, 33; (probably a printer's error, of old date, for the Christian name of the playwright F. Kaiser, as Hermann Friedrich was a novelist, and did not write his one play until 1862).
Friendly circle, Liszt in a, 240.
Friends of Art, 54-5, 74, 104, 260, 275, 9, 81, 360, 3-5; of Ital. Op., 380.
Friends, Wagner's, (x), 77, 8, 106, 8, 120, 1, 46, 55, 205, 57-8, 60, 7, 271, 4, 323, 44, 50, 63; Former, 104, 7, (110), 118, 267, 87, 8, 90.
Friends and foes, judgment of, 237.
Friendship, 148, 50. See Comrades.
(Fritzsch, E. W., pub., 256).
Frivolous, 36, 77, 125, 90, 289, 306, 341, 63, 84.
Fröbel, Julius, 115.
Frontiers of Music, 95. See Barriers.
Fugue, 304, 17, 27.
Full houses, 138, 358-9.
Funambulists, 68.
Funeral march, *Eroica*, 222.
Furtherance of Art, 9, 15, 6, 8, 20, 50, 379.
Fuss, a painful, 98, 102-3, 6.
Future, 57; Life of, 73. See Art work.

G.

G sharp or A, taking, 202.
Gaiety, buoyant, 223.

Gallantry, too much, 243.
Gallery, Rights of the, 343.
Gallimathias, a musical, 324.
Gaps in music, 334.
Gauze veilings, 195, 6, 7, 209.
Gems of art, 342.
Genius, Creative, 16, 239, 41, 385; decay of the nation's, 17.
Genius, Managing, rarity of, 375.
Geniuses of the past, 17, 51, 82, 4, 88, 9, 94-5, 106, 9-10, 6, 47, 61, 165, 244, 8, 308, 41, 3.
Genre, Opera as an art-, 34, 6, 125, 126, 69, 92, 277, 98, 300, 1, 3, 5, 309-10, 27, 71, 2, 80, 2.
Gentleness, 96, 131, 264, 6.
(Gerber, E., 261).
German: Art, re-birth of, 116, 260, 271; Art-taste, 108, 14, see A.; Character, 117, 258, 70, 80-1; Choirs, 14, 135, 366; Composers, 373, travelling to Italy, 299, 300; Culture, (viii), 116, 9; Disadvantages, artistic, 301-2; Embassies, 350; Empire, 260; Gruffness, 131; Heads, 113; Language, 287, 99; Poetry, 280, see P.; Princes, 281, 299; Public, 265, 75, 324, see P.; Singers, 275, 9, 366, 8, and Italian music, 276, 379-81, for Paris, 270, 350, 3; Spirit, (viii), 12, 9, 49, 117, 8, 260, 81, 2, 383. See Music, Opera, Orchestra.
Germany, a German in, 115, 271-2, 349, 50, 2, 3.
Gesture, 182, 92, 210-6, 26.
Ghost, grim impression of a, 216.
Gipsies roving, 260.
Given time, place &c., 45, 64, 275.
Gladiators and wild beasts; 308.
Gladness, 223, 9, 31, 3.
(Glasenapp, C. F., vii).
Glitter, 36, 191. See Brilliance.
GLUCK, 163, 341; Operas, 156, 9, 300; Successors, 125, 39, 341; and Vienna, 385. See *Iphigenia*.
Gluckists and Piccinists, 309.
Go-betweens, critical, 67, 290.
Goblin laughter, 128.
God: Hymn of, 231; Nature and Love, 231; Service of, 90, 7, 314; Will of, 72.
God all to himself, a, 82, 4.
God Himself must bless him, 201.
Gods, Rites of heathen, 314.
GOETHE, 11-4, 7, 8, 20, 99, 301; in Jewish jargon, 92; his opera-texts, 310, 1.

(Goethe-Museum, 6).
Goethe-Stiftung, 7-21, (60).
Going-under, 100, 212, 29.
Good will, appeal to, 170, 205.
(GÖTTERDÄMMERUNG, DIE, 262, 326).
Gounod, 273.
Government institutes, 118.
Grace, maidenly, 162, 99, 226; musical, 386.
Grail, The holy, 231-3.
Grand Duke of Baden, 349.
Grand Opera, see O., Paris.
Gratitude, 152, 75, 203, 5, 37, 323, 345.
Greek: Art, 302, downfall of, 307; Music, 68, 313; Rhythm, 314; Statue, 95; Tragedy, 289, 307, 338.
Grenzboten, (x), 66, 263.
Grey in the heavens, 155, 66.
Grief, 181, 200, 21, 2, 3, 4, 7.
(Grimm's law, 268).
Groupings, stage, 193, 4.
Guarantees, 359, 72, 7.
Gueux of the Netherlands, 107.
Guitar, a huge, 338.
Gymnastics, 52, 68, 71.

H.

Habit, 39, 57, 134, 59-61, 73, 202, 213, 51, 74, 9, 333.
Hagen and vengeful Grimmhilde, 262.
Halévy, 327, 74.
Half-closes, Mozart's garrulous, 334.
Hamburg theatre, 32; and *Tann.*, 273.
Handicraft, artistic, 52.
Hanslick, Dr E., (2), 104, 13, (248).
Happiest time in my life, 61.
Happiness ne'er dreamt before, 233.
Happy beings, supremely, 158, 65.
Happy songs of crew, 229.
Harmony, 313-5; Christian, 314, 6; Embodied, 315, 38; and Melody, 314-5, 37, 40; Progressions, rare, 252, 337.
"Harshness" &c., musical, 252.
Hatred, 78, 80, 2, 201, 26, 7, 31.
(Hauptmann, vii).
HAYDN, 105, 317, 34.
Hazard, 28. See Chance, Luck.
Hearing: good works, 155, 221, 5, 350; with new senses, 278, 339; things which don't exist, 291.
Heart, 35, 62, 85, 92, 117, 51, 2, 99,

INDEX. 415

200, 1, 23, 4, 6, 7, 9, 30, 1, 2, 63, 329; an Affair of, 344; Elsa's, 330; a Full, 237; and Head, 57, 120, 248; Rigor of, 216; Tones from, 94, 181.
Heart-searching music, 94, 223, 314.
Heartless, 87, 201.
Heat of expression, 85, 321.
Heaven's height, from, 232, 3.
Hebbel, F., 115, (262).
"Hebraic art-taste," (ix), 79.
Hebrew language, the, 84.
(Heckel, Emil, 256).
Hegel's dialectics, 104, 13.
Heightening the situation, 182. See Climax.
(Heine, Ferdinand, 146).
Heine, Heinrich, 99-100.
Hero, the, 221; dramatic, 83; pianoforte, 240.
Heroes of art, 94, 5, 165. See Geniuses.
Higher efforts, 63, 4, 125, 275, 306, 339, 69, 81, 3, 5.
Hiller, Ferd., 103, (161), 288.
"Hilt," Liszt's, 243, 50.
Historic: Dramatist &c., 225, 328, 330; Period, a, 95; Scenes, 52.
Historico-conventional, 328.
Hindrances, see Obstacles.
(Hinze, Bruno, pub., 60).
Hitzschold, Town-councillor, 155.
Hofburgtheater, Vienna, 369.
Home, near approach of, 229.
Honest artists, 99, 289; critics, 101, 113, 290.
Honour, sense of, 32, 93, 8, 258, 385-6.
Hope, 121, 82, 211, 3, 28, 60, 71, 279, 322, 45, 54, 9, 83; I no longer, 78, 282.
Horns, the, 223.
Horror and the Absurd, 91, cf. 222.
Horseback, Prima donna on, 262.
Hostile, 77, 84, 103, 47. See Calumnies &c.
How and What, 17, 39, 85, 8, 90, 5, 173, 251, 2, 371.
(Hueffer, Dr, v).
Hugo, Victor, 34.
Hum it he cannot, 340.
Human being, the true, 65, 216, 22; search for, 63. See Purely-human.
Human race, organising the, 307.
Humanising of Art, 52, 6.
Humanists, 82, 386.
Humanity, pure, 224: wide, 95.
"Hundred thousand Thalers," 33.

Hurried study, 38, 276, 366.
Husk without a kernel, 36.
Hybrid genre, a, 32. See Dubious.
Hypocrisy, 100, 26; humble, 225, cf. 385.

I.

Iambics written in prose, 66.
Idea: Artistic, 126, 260, 90; General, 80; Musical, 244, 5, 8, 9; and Representment, 51.
Ideal, the, 137, 271, 301, 3, 5-6, 8, 313, 22, 41.
Ideal Form, 249-50, 301-2, 38.
Ideal Reality, 249, 307.
Idealist v. Realist, 15.
Idiomatic, 84.
Idiosyncrasies, native &c., 9, 30, 1, 45, 9, 50, 78, 83, 252. See Indiv.
Ignominious modesty, 385.
Ignoramuses, happy, 158.
Ignored, 121, 267.
Illusion, 121, 268; artistic, 156, 276-7.
Imagination, 163, 231. See Phant.
Imitations, 12, 32, 44, 9, 240, 99.
Impartiality, 237, 73.
Impatience, passionate, 321.
Imperative conditions, 112, 73.
Imperfect things, 29. See Correctness.
Impossible, the, 44, 56, 96, 121, 239, 270, 90, 5, 349.
Impresarios, 25-8, 380.
Impressions: clear and unclear, 29, 162, 3, 5-6, 79, 83, 6, 239, 76, 9, 324, 60; disquieting, 186, 202; emotional, 198, 222; first, 174, 84, 185, 303, 27; new, 251-2, 79; overpowering, 198-9, 272, 339; personal, 143, 56, 250, 2, 303-5, 327; warm, 323.
Impressions from Life on Art, 91, 204, 46.
Impulse-to-impart, 63, 345.
Incitation, affording an, 50, 4, 163.
Incomprehensible, the, 126, 329, 341.
Independence, Music's, 246; of separate voices, 314, 6.
Indifference, 27, 8, 39, 40, 1, 85, 8, 92, 3, 100, 56, 8, 84, 299, 315, 55.
Indiscretion, 109, 264.
Individuality, a strong, 222, 4; artistic, 9, 16, 49, 51, 94, 6; essence of, 250, 2, 96.

INDEX.

Industrial, 12, 8, 52, 4, 6, 67, 70, 364, 78.
Ineptitude, present musical, 98.
Inertia, 93, 108, 17.
Inexpressive, 92, 4, 341.
Influences from without, 274, 322, 4. See Exper., Impress.
Ingratitude and intolerance, 323.
Inner Man, 68, 9, 318; Movement, 43, 271.
Inner and Outer, 35, 9, 329-31.
Innig (Inward), 49, 304, 6, 14, 43.
"Innovations," my, 344.
Insinuations, 108.
Instinct, 213; artist's, 40, 241, 96, 324; physical, 204; woman's, 241.
Instinctive, The, 91, 226.
Institutes, art, 15, 50, 118, 9, 280, 281, 2, 9, 97, 8, 306, 66, 81; ecclesiastic, 373.
Instrumental Music, 170, 316-7; limits of, 163, 245-8; mixed, 335; *versus* Dramatic, 300, easier of performance, 251, 87. See Orchestra.
Intellect, World of, 104, 5.
Intelligence a rare thing, 365.
Intelligibility, artistic, 13, 7, 30, 8, 44, 5, 90, 1, 169, 78, 83, 203, 21, 238, 45, 7, 8, 9, 51, 78, 87, 9, 90, 302, 7, 8, 12, 9, 29, 37, 71.
Intendants, theat., 259, 72. See Directors.
Interest, active artistic, 26, 7, 8, 31, 34, 5, 6, 9, 40, 126, 73, 8, 9, 80, 2, 204, 14, 22, 306, 19, 20, 9, 32, 8, 350, 66, 71.
Interests, mutual, 90.
Intonation, purity of, 374.
Intrigue in Drama, 330.
Introduction (musical) to drama, 157, 163, 231, 2, 44, 5.
Intuition, artist's, 296, 321 See Instinct.
Intuitive apperception, 343.
Inventiveness, musical, 242, 4; poetic, 310-2, 31.
Invisible orchestra, 274, 6-7.
Invitation to Brazil, 269; to give works in Paris, 345, 51.
Iphigenia in Aulis overture, 155-65, 245; Mozart's close, 156, 61; New close, (154), 155, 6, 61, 3-4; Paris ed., 157, 9; Themes in, 157, 62.
Iphigenia in Tauris, 156, 8.
Israel, tents of, 114. See Jews.
Italian Audience, 31, 332.
Italian Church-music, 298, 314.
Italian Composers at German Courts, 299.

Italian Language, 299, 380; Singers and vocalisation, 116, 269-70, 97, 317, 79-80. See Opera, Theatres.
Italian Singing-teacher, an, 369.

J.

Jehovah, 84; -rites, 90.
Jerusalemitic realm, a, 80.
Jessonda, Spohr's, 147.
Jesting, 110, 34, 42, 243.
Jesuits, the, 80.
Jew-anecdotes, 120.
JEWS, The, 66, 77-122, 40 :—
 Baptism of, 87, 101.
 Bondage, internal, 120.
 Civic rights, 80, 1.
 Cultured, 87, 8, 9, 91, 3.
 National dislike, (ix), 79, 80, 2, 90, 3, 8.
 Peculiarities, 80, 3, 5, 6, 7, 9.
 and Plastic art, 83, 6.
 as Poets, 88, 99.
 (Polish, viii, ix).
 and Press, 108-12, 5, 8.
 and Schumann, 117-8.
 Social standing, 88, 9.
 and Speech, 84, 6.
 and Stage, 83.
 Tactics, 102, 9, 18, 21.
 Tragic history, 81, 7.
 Victory, 119. See Music.
Joachim, (vii), 107.
Jockey Club, Paris, 353, 7-8.
Jodel etc., 91.
Jordan, Wilhelm, 262.
Joseph II. of Austria, 365, 70, 2, 7, 381, 4.
(*Journal des Débats*, 286, 8).
Journalism, 1-2, 264-5, 363-4; Æsthetic, 63, 5, see Æ.; Musical, 61, 3, 5, 6, 7, 9, 70, 3, 103, 5, 10, 156. See Press.
Joy and Sorrow, 200, 1, 31, 3.
Joy-in-life, 199, 200.
Jubilee-overture-writers, 163.
Judaism the mightiest organisation of our times, 118. See Jews.
Judæophobia, a medieval, 102.
Judicious constitution, 375, 84.
Jugglery, tone, 70, 184.
Justice, 80, 355, 8, 80; Eternal, 211.

K.

Kaiser, F., playwright, 33.
Kaleidoscope, a musical, 94.

INDEX.   417

KANT, 113.
Kapellmeister, 187, 267, (304), 369, 373, 5, 6; Wagner as, 61, 127, 304, 22, 67. See Cond.
Kapellmeister-operas, 267, 373.
Kettledrum in *Holländer*, 211.
Key, 162.
Keyhole of a garret, 109.
Kind deed, the first, 148.
Kindle, Art's function to, 163.
King of Denmark, 142; the Jews, 80; Prussia, 139, 40; Saxony, 134. See Ludwig.
(Klengel, vii).
Knowledge, true, 71, 80, 2, 172; new, 116, 240.
Kölnische Zeitung, 103.
(Krüger, Dr, viii).

L.

Laisser-aller, 258, 366.
Land of the living, no longer in, 267.
(Lang, J., vi).
Language, see Speech.
Laughter, 67, 128, 223, 8, 67, 9, 70, 355, 6.
Law, artistic, 302, 10, 3, 8, 20.
Laziness, 99; and Leisure, 367.
Legacies of matchless masters, 116, cf. 317.
Legend in Drama, 328-30, 44.
Leipzig, 101, 10; (Brühl, ix); Conservatoire, (vii), 101, 2; Theatre, 152,*Lohengrin* at, 270; University, 101.
Length, tedious, 180, 3, 7, 278.
LESSING, 308, 10.
Leverage, we lacked the, 119, 385, cf. 343.
Liberals, the, 80, 1, 108.
Librettists, see Textbook &c.
Lies, 99, 100, 201.
Life: of Everyday, 217, 49, 51, 330; Freshness of, 177, 96, 223, 66; Instinctive, 89, 204; a New, 182, 199; Outlived, 228; Real, imitating, 193. See Art.
Life and Death, 331; struggle for, 199.
Life-: conditions, 247, 70; fill, 90; force, 227; glad, 200, 23; need, 99; pang, 224; view, 204.
Lifeless tools, 296, cf. 11.
Lifelike renderings, 221.
Lightning-flash, 137, 82, 99, 229, 304, 376.

Like-minded, 74. See Sharers.
Likeness, a deceptive, 89.
LISZT, 7, 106-8, 254, 61 :—
Agitation against, 107.
compared with Berlioz, 250.
Faust and *Dante*, 248.
Most musical musician, 246, 53.
Orchestral compositions, 107, 8, 237-54; distinctness, 251; form, 242-3; surprise the critics, 239, 241, 52.
Orpheus and *Prometheus*, 247.
Playing Beethoven, 240.
Prose-writings, 239.
Pupils, 251.
What I owe to, 237, 53.
(*Liszt-Wagner Corresp.*, ix, 6, 24).
LITERARY WORKS, WAGNER'S, 56, 61, 9, 73, 103, 55, 253, 309, 323; style of, 321. See also Theoretic :—
Art and Revolution, 63, 307.
Art-work of the Future, (ix), 63, 103, 288, 309.
Communication to my Friends, (62), 257.
Epilogue, 1.
German Art and Politics, 111.
Judaism in Music, (vi-x,) 2, 101, 6, 108, 12, 9.
(*On Musical Criticism*, 7).
Opera and Drama, (vi, x), 22, 66, 71, (224), 257, 309, 11-3, 20.
Performing of Tannhäuser, 3, 168.
Remarks on Flying Dutchman, 3.
Literary historian, a, 263.
Literary hodmen, 299.
Literary rubbish, 66, 265.
Literati, 71, 283; and Opera, 309.
Literature : *versus* Art, 8, 65, 302, 8; German, 301; -Poets, 8, 262. See Poetry.
Literature "in general," 66; fungoid growth of, 72.
Lithographs, cheap, 8, 13.
Little, never a, 198.
Lively and quiet movements, 245.
Local allusions, 32, 3; conditions, 44, 45, 51, 4, 274, 5; patrotism, 101, 10.
Lodestar, 229.
Logic, 4, 318, 9, 35.
LOHENGRIN, 232; Composition, 326; Poem, 330; Prelude, 231; Unheard by me, 267, 87, 322.
Lohengrin - performances : Bologna, Leipzig and Berlin, 270; Frankfort, 272-3; Vienna, 272, 9; Weimar, 103.

INDEX.

London : article on *Judaism* from, (viii) ; Papers, 109-10 ; Theatres, 276, 380 ; Wagner in, 109, 287.
Loneliness, or Isolation, 70, 4, 87, 88, 100, 26, 66, 216, 29, 76, 308, 334, 9.
Longing : Artistic, 50, 63, 96, 278, 308, 19, 45 ; and Fulfilment, 199 ; and Living, 222 ; for Love, 213, 229, 31, 2.
Looking back, no, 100, cf. 199.
Lottery, an art-, 9, 15, 21.
Lovable, 148, 223.
Love, 41, 70, 80, 150, 2, 99-201, 4, 215, 21, 4, 31-3, 53 ; hallowed, 231 ; imperishable, 232 ; unblest, 230.
Love for an Artist, 50, 253.
Love as keystone of Society, 115, 231.
Love triumphant, Song of, 230.
Love-pangs of Tr. and Is., 268-9.
Lovelessness, 90.
Lucerne, 122, (256).
Luck, sheer, 26, 7, 43, 384.
"Lucky find," a, 261.
Ludwig II. of Bavaria, (xii, 115, 256, cf. 282).
Lust und Leid, 222.
Lüttichau, von, 128.
Luxury, arts of, 36, 87, 8, 9.
Lyric, literary and musical, 49.
Lyric moments, 174, 316 ; stage, 297, 385, see Opera ; tournament, 330.

M.

Machinations, secret, 103, 6, 9, 16.
Mad, (vii), 65, 258, 88, 327.
Magic of art, 242 ; banned from, 330.
Magic Dramas, Raymund's, 386.
Make-believe, 100, vid. sub. Drama.
Makeshifts, 378, 85.
Man : Godhood of, 224 ; Shores of, 228 ; the Whole, 221, 4. See Human, Inner.
Man-of-feeling, 223.
Manhood, redemption into, 100.
Manly and Womanly, 224, 5, 6, 41.
Mannerism, sickly, 112.
Manners, good, 32, 318, 65, 71.
March, the, 193, 244, 5, 7.
Marche des Pèlerins, 250.
Market, no, 13, 283.
Marvellous, The, 344.
Masses, the sheeplike, 290.
Masters, great, 116, 311, 4, 5, 7, 41-342, 67 ; almost unknown, 151-2. See Geniuses.
Material, living *v.* raw, 10-4, 296, cf. 160.
Maturing, 43, 50, 5, 98, 241, 98, 311, 326, 34, 71.
Maxims, 61, 237, 319, 24, 65.
Meadows, through the, 223.
Means and end, 15, 30, 3, 4, 9, 41, 3, 44, 5, 97, 203, 73, 96, 9, 341, 66, 369, 71, 83, 6.
Means, material or financial, 55, 118, 258, 74, 81, 352, 70 ; of Discipline, 368.
Mechanical movements of band, 276.
Medley of diverse styles, 25, 39, 92, 299, 366, 71, 9, 84.
Mediocrities, 46 ; world of, 237.
Meditation, abstract, 307, 9, 21. See Abs.
Medusa's head, 106, 7.
MÉHUL'S *Joseph*, 304.
(*Meister, The*, xi, 30).
MEISTERSINGER, DIE, (vi, xi), 111, 112, (256).
Melancholy, softest, 223. Cf. 96.
Melismi of the Synagogue, 91.
Melodic genius, inexhaustible, 332.
Melodic phrases heard before, 333.
"Melodies," forever, 324, 32, 3, 40.
MELODY, 333 :—
Abolition of, alleged, 104, 6, 324.
as Amusement, 332.
Christian, 315.
Dance-, 316-7. See D.
Endless, 335-40.
Evolution of, 314-6, 35, 7.
Expansion of, 344, 5, 40.
Greek, 313-4.
Harmonic and Rhythmic motives of expression, 314-7, 35, 7, 42.
Instrumental, 317.
Operatic, 331, 7, 40 ; structure of Italian, 315, 6, 7, 33, 4.
Symphonic, 335, 7-40.
in *Tristan*, structure, 331.
and Un-melody, 332, 4.
and Word-verse, 313, 5, 31, 53.
Memory, 127, 38, 79.
Memories : grievous, 367 ; pleasant, 271 ; sorrowful, 222, 3, 4.
MENDELSSOHN, (vi), 93-6, 8, 101, (104), 105, 10, 41.
Mental pictures (*Vorstellungen*), 247.
Mental state, 267, 71, 97, 303, 5 ; abnormal, 295, 320-1. See Moods.
Menuetto, 244, 5, 336.
Mercantile, 70, see Industrial.

INDEX. 419

Mercy, 227.
Merry ending, a, 136, 7.
Metaphor, 336, 9.
Metaphysical necessity, 318.
Metronome, 190. See Tempo.
Metropolis of Jewish music, 102.
Metternich, Princess, 351.
MEYERBEER, (vi, ix, x), 96-9, (104), 125-6, 42, 3, 203, 327, 41, 2.
MICHAEL ANGELO, 116.
Middle Ages, the, 82, 102.
Military bands, 191.
Minority, rule of, 359.
Minutiæ, 143, 98. See Details.
Miracle, 187, 232; if need be, 133.
Mirror, a faithful, 45, 91, 260.
Mise-en-scène, 29, 30, 6, 191, 209, 276, 305, 52, 6, 66, 70, 8. See Scenic, Stage, Tannhäuser.
Mistrust, 205, 52, 3.
Misunderstood, (viii), 74, 180, 6, 93, 205, 88, 90, 1, 309, 22, 5; Beethoven, 241.
Model, 94, 161, 245, 99, 300, 43; Performances, 118, 275, 80, 99, 350.
Modern Art, 64, 82, 313.
Modulation, 317, 35, 7, 42.
'Moment,' 9, 43, 52, 88, 186, 247, 9.
Money, 10; as bond twixt man and man, 88, 368-9.
Money lost, or squandered, at theatres, 26, 7, 30, 46, 55, 258, 368, 78, 86.
Money-making, 52, 306, 64; -princes, 8, 81, 2, 7.
Monkey and man, 303.
Monstrous undertaking, my, 257, 260, 1.
Monumental singleness, 9.
Moods, Dramatic, 177, 83, 245; Personal, 61, 205, 57, 95, 328, 44.
Moods and interests, 32, 5, 42, 9, 279, 383.
Moral evolution, 318; world, 201.
Morals, public, 41, 3, 69. 365, 71.
Morality, artistic, 282. See Demor.
Morbidness, 216.
Morelli (barytone), 353, 6.
Morose and peevish, 117.
(Moscheles, vii).
Moscow, Wagner in, 110.
Mother, wife and child, 225, 6.
Motivation, 183, 92, 8,
Motives: Inner, 330-1, 8; Dramatic, 162; Musical, 160, 2, 3, 80, 1, 9, 249, 317, 35—of *Ring*, 266; Poetic, 246, 7, 9, 312; Scenic, 249; Soul-, 329, 30, 6.

Mountain air, 266.
MOZART, 95, 104, 5, 47, 56, 61, 300, 385; symphonies, 317, 34.
Muchanoff, Mdme., 77.
Muckers, the, 115.
Munich (3), 115, (256).
MUSIC, 246, 7, 333:—
 Absolute, 69, 88, 9, 95.
 Capability of, 248, 9, 320, 4.
 Christian, 298, 314-6.
 Degraded, 246, 8.
 and Drama, 201, 82, 98, 372, 3, 6. See Poetry.
 Easiest art to learn, 88.
 in Education, 319. Cf. 68.
 as Expression, 319, see Musical.
 French, modern, 385, see Opera.
 "of the Future," 103, 4, 6, 288, 290, 1, 309, 24, 44.
 German, 106, 16, 280, 300, 5, 15, 367; downfall of, 98, 119, 90, 385; compared with Italian, 317.
 Grammar of, 290.
 Greek, 313; word for, 68-71.
 Idealising effect of, 137, 316, 20, 9, 341.
 Italian, downfall, 298, 314.
 Jewish, 85-99, 102, 5, 14.
 Latent, 247.
 Literary, 8, 9, 10, 4, 49, 50, 382.
 versus Logic, 319-20.
 is Melody, 333.
 Modern, 66, 9, 93, 105, 291, 308; evolution of, 61, 9, 116-7, 300, 313, 9.
 Naïve and popular, 91, 2, 386.
 Passion for, W.'s, 303.
 Popularity of late, 319.
 the Redeeming art, 246.
 Sounding, 66, 8.
 versus Speech, 238, 319-20.
 Spirit of, 325.
 Standing of, 116.
 Universal tongue, 94, 226, 302.
 Weighty office of, 122, 324.
 Writers about, 66, 114, 239. See Journ.
Music-: Director, 304, see D.; Goods, 67; Jewdom, 104, 12, 8, 119; Making, 70, 89, 98, 240, 386; Man, 95; Piece, 300; Thrummers, 67, 72.
MUSICAL:—
 Adornment, 183, 312, 44.
 Boxes, 67.
 Dramaturgy, 259.
 Expression, 35, 88, 90, 4, 173, 5,

MUSICAL—*continued*—
202, 25, 44, 5, 8, 314, 6, 7, 8, 320, 37, 41; bounds of, 336.
Faculty, 49, 94; my "poverty" of, 264, cf. 324; specific, 93, 8.
Forms, 140, 71, 242, 6-7, 8, 311; operatic, 328, 9, 31-2, 6, 7, 40, 341, 3; scaffolding of, 310-1. See Symphonic.
Jesters, 264, 90, 364.
Thread, losing the, 249.
Working-out, 162, 224, 66, 317, 327, 31, 5.
"Musically-Beautiful, The," 104-5, 113.
Musically-emptiest operas, 367, 85.
Musician: Educated, 315, 33, 84; Executant, 259, 373; Solid, 98, 270; Specific, 93, 8, 373, 4; Unconsecrated, 246, 8. See Absolute, Poet, Professl.
MUSICO-DRAMATIC WORKS, Wagner's, 73, 103, 15, 52, 291, 304, 326; Earlier, 170, 322, 3, 7, contrasted with later, 329, 31; Later, 111-2, 55, 267; Popularity and spread of, 104, 5, 11, 2, 51, 69, 264, 83, 322-4, 7, 50, 4, 8; Supervision, personal, 112, 69-70, 98, 205, 72, 323, 49-50, 2, 4, 9; no blind affection for, 185, 352; so as to hear my own, 270, 88, 326; not witnessed for many years, 266, 287, 322, 49.
Musico-theatric art, 278.
Mystery of Individuality, 250.
Mystic orchestra, 278.
Mythos, 262, 8, 9, 312. See Legend.

N.

Nägeli, H. G., 52.
Naïvety, 91, 216, 44, 51, 90, 333, 9, 343.
Nakedness of Opera &c., 337.
Nameless, 199, 312.
Naples Opera-house, 29.
Narrowness of art-forms, 315, 33, 7, 341; of nationality, 302, 80.
National: Customs, 302, 15; Form, 271, 80, 1, 99, 301; Spirit, 282; Stuff, 262.
Native: City, 110, 225, 6; Land, 112, 5, 51; Products and talents, 49-50, 6. See Idiosyn.
Naturalism, 52, 193, 209. See Mirror.
Naturally-gifted musicians, 93, 253.

Nature, 93, 198, 216, 23, 31, 96; a Freak of, 83; -Motives, 266; My own true, 322.
Necessity, 73, 91, 306, 18; Artistic, 15, 64, 9, 81, 8, 95; Dramatic, 329; Inner, 119, 64, 98, 9, 296.
Need, 48, 99, 326, 36; and Satisfaction, 28, 42, 3, 9, 50, 231, 319.
Needs, Life's vulgar, 39, 238.
Nervelessness: of Art, 114; of newer Poets, 18.
Nesselrode, Countess, 77.
Nestroy (comedian), 115.
Neue Zeitschr. f. Musik, (vii-ix, 6, 7, 60, 2, 6, 76), 79, (80 *et seq.*), 101, 117, 9, (146, 54, 68, 220, 9, 31, 6, 286, 7, 91, 348, 54).
New Actors and Singers, 258.
New-Birth of Art, 63, 116, 313.
New Lights, 268, 78, 90, 5.
New and Old, 51, 94, 147, 52, 288.
New Paths, or departures, 9, 16-7, 8, 73, 108, 40, 52, 8, 69, 221, 41, 3, 246, 8, 52, 65, 301, 17, 35.
New, Saying something, 79, 288.
Newspapers, see Journalism, Press.
NIBELUNGEN, RING DES (vi, xi), 257-83 :—
  Conception of, 1, 73, 257, 9, 321, 326.
  as Literary product, 260, 3, 5, 73, 83.
  Musical composition, 155, 266, 82, 322, 6.
  as Opera!, 265, 6.
  Plan for production, 258, 60, 1, 4, 265, 73-8, 322; effect on audience, 279; repetitions, and at other theatres, 280.
  Poem, private publication, 260, 1, 274; full (xi), 263, 73, 4, 82.
  and Press, 120-1, 264-5.
  Provisional theatre, 274, 7; its guests, 277, and signal, 278.
  Rival poets etc., 261-4.
Nibelungen, Die, Dorn's, 261.
  ,,   ,,   , Hebbel's, 262.
  ,,   ,,   , Jordan's, 262.
Nibelungen-epics, 262.
Nibelungen-myth, 262; a supplementary Act (*Tristan*), 269.
Niemann, Albert, 353, 4, 6.
Night, 229, at dead of, 230, 59.
Nimbus, a larger, 105.
Noble, 18, 21, 34, 41, 2, 52, 69, 90, 93, 5, 121, 7, 47, 93, 213, 23, 53, 304, 7, 41, 2, 85.
Noise, non-musical, 277; nothing-saying, 31, 333, 4.

INDEX. 421

Nook, a quiet, 274, 349.
Norma, March from, 193.
Norräna, names from, 263.
Norway, 216.
Notables, world of, 36, 380.
Notes, getting by heart, 173, 375.
Nôtre Dame, Hugo's, 34.
Novelty-hunting, 25, 32, 9, 299.
Now thus, now otherwise, 88.
Nuances, 165, 209, 318, 37, 66, 74.
(Nuitter, Charles, 294).
Nurmahal, Alcidor &c., Spontini's, 139.

O.

Object, the, 92, 252 ; and subjective feeling of it, 318.
Objective view, 204, 52, 96, 302.
Oboe-players, the two, 130, 4.
Obstacles and hindrances, 16-7, 62, 63, 114, 5, 20, 70, 269, 300.
Obscurantism of Press, 266, 355.
Obscure young artist, 50, 148.
Ocean of harmonic waves, 316, cf. 337.
Offenbach, 108, 14, 272, 385.
Offence, an old, 253.
"Old-Frankish gear," 263.
Olympia, Spontini's, 127, 39-41.
Omen, an, 135.
Once, but not again, 295.
One-man management, 375, 83.
Onesidedness, 51, 156, 380.
Open air, entr'actes in, 278.
Open mind, 147, 52.
Open secret, 109, 244.
OPERA, 179, 282, 7, 98, 305 :—
 Aim of, 35, 7, 8. See Drama.
 Downfall of, 143, 73.
 Dramatising the, 125, 6, 310.
 Earnest, or serious, 157, 279.
 Evolution of, 125.
 French, 298, 9, 379 ; light, 381 ; modern, 385 ; *opera seria*, 136, 157.
 Genre, see G.
 German, 140, 267, 75, 99, 303, 4, 373.
 Good, dearth of, 48, 369-70, 9.
 "Grand," 34-7, 327, 8, 70, 9.
 Great poets and, 310-1.
 Italian, 31, 140, 71, 276, 97-8, 304, 16, 32, 4, 8, 79-81, old, 309 ; introduced into Germany, 298-9.
 Legendary v. Historic, 328.

OPERA—*continued*—
 Modern, 303, 22, 40.
 Previous attempts to elevate, 309-311, 41, 3.
 and Public, 343-4. See Theatre.
 Rise of, 297-8, 300, 14, 71.
 "Romantic," 140.
 Spontinian Heroic, 327. See S.
Opera-cantata, 125.
Opera-composer, posing as, 327.
"Opera-composer as poet!" 262, 4.
Opera-house, 257, 65, 81, 9, 97, 300, 21, 6, 63, 72, 9, 82. See Theatre.
Opera-performances, Ordinary, 173, 191, 3, 278, 82, 304, 6, 23, 54.
Opera-poems, my, 295, 322, 5-31.
Opera-singers, 31, 6, 173, 83, 259, 287, 342 ; pure and simple, 170, 181, 92, 202. See S.
Opera-worries, 142, 79, 84, 267.
Opposites, 162, 80, 99, 225, 45.
Opposition, an organised, 114, 55, 251, 95, 355-6. See Machinations.
Optimist, 116 ; and pessimist, 323.
Oratoria, 94, 300.
ORCHESTRA :—
 as mere Accompaniment, 316, 38, 373.
 Balance of, 134, cf. 277.
 Choral effect, 188.
 French, 36, 134, 90, 350, 4.
 German, 14, 134, 90, 251, 9, 367. See Dresden.
 as Greek Chorus, 338-9.
 Invisible, 274, 6-7.
 Language of, 317.
 Number etc. of, 128, 89-91.
 Playing fairly together, 376.
 Polyphonised, 316.
 Seating of, 130, 4-5.
 and Singer, 175, 81, 366.
 and Stage, 171, 92, 4, 5, 209, 12, 374, 6.
Orchestration, 133, 9.
Orders, Spontini's, 138, 42.
Orestes in a tail-coat, 156.
Organic work, an, 177, 85.
Organism, inner, 92, 173 ; a living, 99 ; v. Mechanism, 11, 37.
Organs, living artistic, 18, 169, 270, 275, 96, 350.
Origin stamped on every form, 334.
Originality, 14, 20, (24), 30, 1, 2, 3, 35, 44, 8, 51, 241, 80, 1, 333, 86.
Original-performances, grand, 280.
Orpheus, Liszt's, 247.
Otiose pastime, an, 308.

422 INDEX.

Outcries, 246, 332.
Outlandish, the, 85, 92, 263.
Outlaw, 178, 82, 201, 27.
Ovations, 273.
Over-acting, 136-7.
Overfill, driven to vent its, 222. Cf. 198, 300.
Overstrain, mental, 266, 77, 8.
Overture, the, 157, 62, 3, 243-6; origin in dance, 244, 6.
Overwork at theatres, 39, 150, 367, 376.

P.

Paganism, relapse into, 314-5.
Painstaking, 43, 257, 353, 80.
Painters, Jewish, 86.
Painting, modern, 313; and Poetry etc., 8, 10-4, 6, 9, 67, 303, 8.
PALESTRINA, 116, 298.
Pantomime (Dumb-show), 185, 226; and choreographic art, 194, 351. See Gesture.
Paper artworks, 8, 10, 2, 7. See Print.
Paradoxical, seemingly, 313.
Paris: and modern music, 49, 97, 385; Opéra, 29, 30, 6, 7, 271, 98, 305, 27, 51-9, 70, 3-4, 6, 80, 4; Press, 109, 355; Project for new theatre, 360; Public, 307, 25, 40, 344, 5, 50, 5, 6, 8; and Spontini, 128, 33, 4, 42.
Paris, Wagner in, 146, 8, 304, 27, 344, 5; reasons for going, 270, 349; Wagner-concerts, 270, (286), 350.
Parisians v. Berliners, 32.
Parrots, 89.
Particles of Art, lifeless, 19.
Party-feeling, 237.
Passion, 47, 79, 85-6, 92-3, 160, 81, 182, 210, 2, 3, 5, 6, 22, 30, 336; in *Ring*, 266.
Passiveness, 117. See Inertia.
Past and Present, 51; Future, 199.
Pathos, 270, 99.
Patience, 237, 82.
Patrons, 114-5, 258, 67, 350, 9.
Peace, 163, 227, 8; Disturbers, 358, 359.
Peaceably disposed, 155.
Peasant's hats &c., 263.
Pedantry, 22, 94, 173; crude, 52.
Peerage, a, 142.
Penance, a time of, 330.

Penitence, 181, 98.
Pensioning-off (band), 135.
Perception, instantaneous, 186, 343, 355.
Perceptive faculty, 91, 239, 319, 39.
Performable at once, 268, 70, 326.
Performance, a live, 9, 257, 305, 71; the moment of, 169, 252, 304, 76; spirit of, 323, 54. See Correctness, Stage.
Performances: Good and bad, 26, 127, 149-50, 221, 5, 58, 79, 306, 16, 22-323, 49, 52, 4, 5, 9, 71, 2, 5, 382, 3, 5; Number of, 55, 275, 280, 369-70, 2, 7, 9; Preparation of, 43, 55, 130, 1, 5, 49, 72-5, 272, 366, 9, 72, 4, 6. See Daily.
Performer, the, 20, 6, 33-5, 45, 6, 51, 172, 92, 204, 9, 79, 98, 305, 56, 7, 359; demoralised, 37-8, 40, 258, 366; groups of, 46, 370; higher standing, 53-4, 72, 259; maintenance, 55. See Singer.
Perils of the deep, 228.
Periodic structure, Ital., 315, 6, 40.
Periwig, Bach's, 95.
Persecution, (vii), 103, 7, 10, 21, 47.
Personal: Animosity, 2, 102, 6, 288; Considerations, 2, 85, 110, 5, 47.
Personality, the, 41, 96. See Indiv.
Personnel (Stage), 25-7, 40, 6-7, 51, 54, 272, 5, 368, 9; size of, 46, 55, 56, 370, 8. See Perf.
Pessimist and Optimist, 323.
Pettiness, 147.
Pewter tokens, 32.
Phantasy, 35, 89, 94, 6, 232.
Phenomenal world, 318, 20, 9, 31. (Philology, 268).
Philosopher: Art-, 291; and Language, 238; Music, 114.
Philosophy, 68, 105, 13, 319.
Phrase, structure of verbal, 85.
Phrasing: Orchestral, 159-60, 4-5, 87-188, 366; Vocal, 174, 204, 12, 366.
Physical show, 11, 6, 8. See Portrayal.
Physiognomic exterior, 41, 83, 6.
Physiology, 89, 121.
Pianoforte, 173, 240-1, 373. See Rehearsals.
Picked troop, a, 270, 6, 350.
Pictures of human life, 221, 5, 49-50, 312, 20.
Pietists, 80.
Pilgrims and pardon, 200.
Piquant, modern-, 97.

INDEX. 423

Pity, 210; a motive of, 162.
(Plaidy, vii).
Plans, 20. See *Nibel.*, Reform.
Plastic: Art, 7-19, 67, 83, 6, 289; Expression, 303, 35; Shape, 96, 117, 224, 66; Subject, 225.
Plates and dishes, a prince's, 334.
Platoon-fire of the Press, 109.
Play and Opera, 34-5, 46, 7, 173, 92, 201, 71, 341, 69-70, 2; difference in public judgment of, 34, 311, 43.
Play-wrights, 18, 33, 262.
Player-caste, 51-2, 4, 259.
Playing at composing, 240, cf. 373.
Pleasing every one at once, 21.
Plot, the, 173, 298, 329, 30, 6; a foolish, 343. See Dramatic.
POET, the, 8, 10, 1, 7, 89, 204, 312, 320, 9:—
  and the Composer, or musician, 9, 15, 9, 70-2, 173, 225, 48-50, 62, 310-1, 20, 31, 7-8.
  Dramatic, 296. See Drama.
  Great, and Opera, 311-2.
  Greatness in what he leaves unsaid, 338.
  Historical, 328, 30.
  Literary, 262, 4, 310. Vid. inf.
  foreordaining the Melody, 331.
  -Performer, 307.
  as Prophet, 88.
  and the Publisher, 264.
  as Servant, 310.
  and the Thinker, 88.
Poetic, 312; Aim, 162, 73; and its Realisement, 11, 2, 3, 6, 9, 35, 45, 61, 126, 62, 9, 80, 3, 6, 98, 203, 296, 371, 85.
Poetic Diction, 312; gentry of, 264.
Poetic element of Modern Life, 100.
POETRY:—
  Art of, 8, 69.
  Future of, 319.
  German, 280; decay of, 17-9.
  become a Lie, 99.
  Literary, 8, 10, 2, 3, 7, 8, 49, 50, 66, 9, 70, 116, 283, 382. Vid. sup.
  and Music, 68, 9, 289, 97, 301, 8-310, 2, 9, 20, 4, 31. Vid. sup.
Poets, two brand-new every year, 264, 5.
Polemics, 155, 309.
Police, the, 27, 42, 364; "in general," 66; Russian, 65, 6.
Political: Canvas, a, 225; and social Life, 63; Newspapers, 105, 8, 9, 364.

Politician, the, 68, 226.
Politics, 79, 80, 109; High, 117.
Polyphony, 151, 313, 5, 6.
Pontifex, Spontini's, 133.
Pope and Spontini, the, 142.
Portioning etc. melodic themes, 335.
Portrayal, physical, 10, 4, 45, 337; art of, 11, 47, 71, 203, 98, 305, 82. See Repres.
Possibilities, Artistic, 44, 5, 51, 6, 269, 304, 5, 8, 12-3, 22, 3, 40, 52-353, 63, 72.
Poverty, German musician's, 118.
Power, a motive of, 162. See Force.
Powerlessness, 96, 283, 352.
Practical, 44, 6, 148, 50, 257, 9, 67, 276, 81, 304, 22, 63, 77, 83.
Practice, Stage-, 55, 279. See Training.
(Praeger, Ferd., 110, —? viii).
Prayer, 228; Elisabeth's, see *Tann.*
Precision, 131, 5, 6, 371, 82.
Predestined bride, 268.
Prejudice, 246, 95, 355.
Present, the, 51, 6, 64, 126, 309; Artist of, 63, 73.
Press, the, (x), 77, 103, 4, 6, 8-10, 112, 5, 8, 21, 261, (286); and Public, 265, 355; Writing to, 108, 363.
(*Presse Théatrale*, 286).
Presumptuous, more than, 262.
Pride, 133.
Priests and populace, 133, 307.
Prima Donna, 31, 261, 7, 97; tyranny, 175, 368, 73.
Prince, the dreamt of, (xii), 281-2.
Princes, 8, 299.
Printer's ink, 12, 72, 282.
Private meditations, 309.
Prizes for Art, 15, (20, 262), 280. Cf. 52.
Problems, artistic, 152, 250, 78, 89, 297, 301, 9-10, 36, 72.
Processions in costume, 52; Stage, 131, 2, 87, 93.
Procurable, the, 45, 273.
Productivity, artistic, 48-9, 91, 4, 147, 66, 241, 57, 66, 96, 321, 2, 326, 82, 5.
Professional: Critic, 94, 309; Musician, 156, 60, 2; Poet, 264 Theorist, 290, 321.
Profit, reckonings of, 85, 90, 6, 217, 231, 368.
Programme, explanatory, 220-33, 48, cf. 239, 337; -Music, 246, 9-50, cf. 163.
Progress, Men of, 108.

Promise of atonement, 182, 228.
Pronunciation, Niemann's French, 353 ; Semitic, 85. See Accent.
Propaganda, a curious, 106.
Property, 231.
Prophet, 88, 105.
Prosody, faults of, 299.
Protest, re *Tann.*, 359.
Pseudonym, (ix), 102-3, 21, 254.
Pseudo-original, 33.
Provincial towns, 30, 3, 274.
Prudence, 103, 9, 200, 26, 37, 53, 67, 343.
Psalm-singing, 104.
PUBLIC, the, 10, 110, 251, 60, 4, 272, 5, 83 :—
  Brisk, 138, 386.
  its Contempt for theatric art, 35, 36, 9, 40, 258. See Interest, Theatre.
  and Critics, 323-4, 33, 43.
  Dresden, 137, 49.
  Familiar, a, 49, 240.
  Greek, 289, 307.
  Italian *v.* German, 31, 270, 332.
  Judgment of, 40, 57, 105, 371. See Taste.
  of Large city, 274, 5, 7, 89, 379, 381, 2.
  Local, 33, 5, 44, 51, 275.
  Modern, 62.
  Opera-, 96, 126, 277, 343, 51, 9.
  and Philosopher, 291.
  Reading, 3-4, 239, 82, 363, 83, 6.
  Travelled, 28-9.
  Unbiased, 186, 343, 58.
Public : Life, 43, 52, 289, 307, 9 ; Spirit and Weal, 41-4, 53.
Publicity, 42, 322 ; Spirit of, 265.
Publisher, 264 ; my, 112.
Puffs, newspaper, 265.
Pure of heart, 232, 3, 343.
Purely-Human, 62, 84, 5, 95, 6, 148, 225, 63, 90, 328-9 ; form, 271, 301-2. See Feeling.
Purely-Musical, 163-4, 71, 4, 83, 270, 318, 376.
Purism, musical, 163, 4.
Purity of Art, 147, 342, 79.
(Puschmann, Dr, vii).

Q.

Quandary as Director, 385.
Quartet, hearing a good, 350.
Quavers and semiq., 157, 9.
Question, the, 320. See Why.
Quiet movement after lively, 245.

R.

Rare, the, 306. See Exceptional.
Raupach (dramatist), 261.
Rawness, 81, 134, 366.
Raymund's magic-dramas, 386.
Read, *not*, 3, 21, 205, 90.
Ready-made : Culture, (viii), 87-8 ; Forms, 299, 301.
Real thing, without saying a, 89.
Realisement, 10, 1, 4, 44, 72, 353. See Poetic Aim.
Realist and Idealist, 15, 20, 249.
Reality, 18, 301 : Horrible, 137 ; Ideal, 231, 2, 307 ; Material, 81. See Actuality.
Reason (*Vernunft*), 318. See V.
Rebel, 227.
Receptivity, 290. See Percep.
Recitation, mere, 201. Cf. 173, 341.
Recitative, 210, 6, 324 ; Italian, 174, 341 ; Melodic and *secco*, 342 ; for Orchestra, 183.
Recollection, endless, 223.
Reconciliation, 150, 99, 227.
Recovery from illness, 322.
Recreation, 151, 5, 277.
Redemption : of Artist, 72, cf. 246 ; Cry for, 181, 229 ; by Love, 201, 213, 6, 28, 9 ; through Self-annulment, 100 ; Won, 231.
Reflection, 91, 296, 7, 319, 21, 3, 4, 327, 38, 41.
Reflective Criticism, 290, 343.
Reform : not Overthrow, 383, 4 ; Spirit of, 91 ; Theatric, 306, 60, 3, 382, 3, 6. See T.
Refreshed and responsive, 278.
Regeneration, 100.
Regiments, well-drilled, 193, 258.
Regisseur (Stage-manager), 170, 92-195, 375, 7 ; and Conductor, 171-172, 91, 4, 209, 374, 6.
Rehearsals, 38, 47, 130, 2, 50, 275 ; Orchestral, 174, 5, 354, 67, 74, 6 ; with Pianoforte, 132, 353, 4, 74, 375 ; Reading, 172-4, 92 ; Stage and Dress, 173, 4, 82, 4, 272, 356, 370, 4, 5 ; Vocal, 172, 370, 4.
Reissiger, G., 156.
Relations (social &c.), 32, 41, 264, 8, 306, 12 ; political, 225 ; of a whole world, 269.
Religion, 79, 115 ; and Art, 307 ; Christian, 80.
Religious rites, 307, 14. See God.
Remnant, 260. See Few.

INDEX.

Remorse, 182, 201, 27.
Renaissance, The, 8, 301, 13.
Repertoire, 34, 47, 55, 267, 74, 6, 299, 321, 70, 9.
Repetition in Overture, 245. See Word.
Reporters, theat., 264, 354-6, 63-4.
Repose, 93, 213, 4; terrible, 210.
Reprehensible cravings, a few, 203.
Re-present, bent to, 296.
Representment (*Darstellung*), 11, 8, 30, 4, 7, 48, 51, 61, 72, 169, 258, 305, 20, 71, 3, 4, 81. See Portrayal.
Reproduction and production, 30, 2, 150, 240-1, 302.
Research, literary, 262, 8.
Resignation, 12, 93, 6, 114, 322.
Respect, 41, 105, 26.
Responsibility, artistic, 373, 4, 86.
Restoration, 64, 91.
Retirement, complete, 103, 26, 303, 352.
Revelation from another world, a, 318. Cf. 137.
Reverence, 126, 7, 43, 7, 8, 289, 306.
Revival of neglected operas, 279.
Revolution, 307; German, 289; in the Singer, 202.
Revolutionary Criticism, 64.
Reward, 9, 10, 3, 6, 40.
Rhapsodist, a wandering, 262.
RHEINGOLD, DAS, 155, (256), 266, (339); Scenery, 276.
Rhetorical phrases, 299.
Rhyme and rhythm, 312.
Rhythm, 313-4; of Folksong, 91; Marking the, 135, 74, 88. See Melody.
Rhythmic pauses, 335.
Rich, the, 36, 87, 90, 217, 380.
Rich man, some, 258, 81.
Riddle of Being, the, 259.
Ridiculous, the, 85, 6, 91, 3, 8, 110, 143, 59, 288, 90, 9, 311, 8, 66.
RIENZI, 327-8; Dresden production, 148-9; Spontini on, 133, 9.
(Rietz, vii).
(Riga, 304).
"Right," 69.
Rio de Janeiro, 269.
Ritornello, 212, 6, 342.
(Ritters, the, 220, 36).
River, Orchestral, 337. See Stream.
Robert the Devil, 38, 203.
Roeckel, August, 141, 2.
Rolling gait of seamen, 210.

Roman world, the, 82, 308.
Romanic nations, 301-2.
Rome, 142, 82, 7, 201; "or I," 227.
Rose, the tainted, 115.
ROSSINI, 125-6, 43, 288, 303, 23.
Rothschild, 80, 1.
Rounding off its nature, 222, 4, 9.
Routine, 46, 9, 51, 63, 99, 173, 276, 279, 378, 85; Un-thinkers by, 69.
(Rubinstein, Joseph, x).
Rulers of the Opéra, 257.
Rules, 247, 50, 98, 318, 26, 77.
Runs and a forced last note, 342. Cf. 202.
Russian police, 65; soldiers, 258.

S.

Sacred flame, the, 147.
Sadness, 213, 7; manly, 222, 4; and Sweetness, 222.
Sagas, see Legend, Myth.
S. Gall, people of, 251.
S. Petersburg, 110.
Salaries, Singers', 25, 7, 39, 46, 150, 202, 352, 3, 68.
Sale of a daughter, 217.
Sammlung, 356. See Collectedness.
Satisfactory ending, 163, 87.
Saturated with feeling, 198, 200, 22.
SAVIOUR, the, 231; garments, 114.
Sax, Fräulein, 356.
Scandal, a public, 27, 98, 102.
Scenas by great masters, 342.
Scène aux champs, 250.
Scene-painter and Machinist, 172, 87, 195-7, 209, 76.
Scenic or emotional incidents, 171, 92; Show, 282, 320, 37.
Scherzo, 244, 336.
SCHILLER, 17, 83, 99, 113, 301, 10.
Schmidt, Jul., 263. See *Grenzboten*.
Schnorr, Ludwig, 3.
Schöll (writer), 7.
Schröder-Devrient, Frau, 127, 8, 30, 132, 6, 8, 41, 2, 76, 7, 86, 305.
SCHUMANN, 105, 17-8, (161).
Score-reading, 344, 73, 4, 6. See Silent.
Scores for theatres, 151. See *Tann.*
Scorn, 201, 10, 26-7.
Scribbling about Art, 61, 7, 290, 363.
Scruples and head-shakings, 148-9, 152, 242, 52, 327.
Sculptor, The, 8, 10-3, 9, 67; no Jewish, 86.

Sea of Music, 337, cf. 316.
Sea-folk, 210, 7, 29; spoils of, 228.
Secret, the, 250-2, 302, 30, 7, 8.
Secreting it, 261.
Secularising Music, 315.
Seer, the, 248. Cf. 88.
Seizable, swiftly, 225, 51, 329, 33, 7.
Selbstverständlich, 114.
Self, sense of, 222, 6.
Self- : Annulling, 100, 200, 27, 33 ; Consciousness, 143; Deception, 62, 81, 97, 100, 85, 359; Offering or sacrifice, 178, 83, 99, 200, 4, 227, 9, 68; Reliance, (24), 106, 17, 237, 81, 304, 27 ; Seeking, 40, 137, 201, 367, 8 ; Surrender, 232.
Semblance *v.* inner wish, 360.
Semitic talk, 85.
Semper, G., 141, (274).
Sense-and-sound-confounding, 91.
Senses, the: Appeal to, 35-7, 9, 66, 72 ; Daring of, 230; Displaying to, 169, 86, 320 ; Solace of, 231.
Sensuality in Art, 72, cf. 324.
Sensuous, 317 ; absolutely, 36, 125.
Sentimental, 112, 7, 216.
Sentinels of classic music, 240, 6.
Separate-art, 22, 69, 70, 88, 9, 290, 308.
Severance, 46, 84, 307 ; and re-union, 100, 281, 335.
Shadow-forms, fantastic, 96.
SHAKESPEARE, 83; and Berlioz, 249-50.
Shamed musicians, 165, 386.
Shape, Individual, 312. See Form.
Shaping, artistic, 18, 96, 224, 96, 338 ; -force, 91, 223 ; -impulse, 11, 117.
Sharers in ideas, 57, 238, 321.
Sharp-cut, 96, 138, 83, 298, 329.
Ship, the Dutchman's, 209, 28.
Shock, 246, 58 ; a sudden, 251, 79.
Shop-signs and gravestones, 13.
Shrewdness, Meyerbeer's, 203.
Sick list, the, 150.
Sickliness, 112, 385 ; as mystery, 117.
Side-thrusts in the dark, 263.
SIEGFRIED, (73), 243, 66, 8, 76, (326).
(*Siegfried's Tod*, 262, 326).
Sigh of yearning to become a Man, 72, cf. 100.
Signal for fest. perf., 278.
Significance (in artworks &c.), 48, 116, 221, 37, 41, 65, 81, 91, 300, 302, 5, 34, 45, 75.

Silence, 103, 14, 43, 9, 59, 214, 38, 239, 40, 50-1 ; a sounding, 337-9.
Silencing 'the question,' 320, 9.
Silent scores, 267, cf. 344.
Simplicity, 45, 183-4, 224, 73, 330, 6.
Simrock, Carl, 263.
Singer and Hearer, 277.
Singers : Eminent and expensive, 26, 36, 132, 79, 368, 73, 8-9 ; First-rate, 269, 74, 305, 6, 50, 67, 84 ; Freedom for, 175. See Opera, Trained, Young.
Singing-Academies, 141, 373, 9 ; Unions, 52.
Single acts from operas, 37.
Singlemindedness, 201.
Singspiel, 299.
Sips of Art, 97.
Siren-call, 230 ; Rossini's, 323.
Sitte, 69, 199, 365, 71.
Sixteen bars, the first, 251.
Sketch *v.* Working-out, 185.
Slanderer and slandered, 115. See Calumnies.
Sleep-walker, 267.
Sluggishness, 93. See *Trägheit*.
Smaller towns, 33, 274, 99, 349.
Smile, a roguish, 258.
Snuffle, a buzzing, 85.
Sobered down, 252. Cf. 37.
Social problem, 10, 307.
Socialists and Art, 289.
Society, 80, 115 : Civic, 51, 2, 4, 7, 102 ; Foundations of, 90, 307 ; High, 36, 379, 84 ; Modern, 78, 87, 9, 99, 100, 11, 259.
Softness, 96, 222, 4.
Soldiers, German and Russian, 258.
Solecisms, revolting, 175, 342.
"Solid," 98, 112.
Song, 86 : Italian, 317, 79 ; Jewish, 86, 7 ; Natural gift, 46. See Singers, Voice.
Song the earliest language, 318.
SOPHOCLES, 307.
Soul and Senses, 231.
Soul-events, 330, 1.
Souls, to heal their own, 200, 1.
Sounding-board, acoustic, 277.
Spain, Art in, 301.
Spanish grandee, 129.
Speaking for sp.'s sake, 88-9, 92.
Speaking tone, the, 47 ; in Opera, 137.
Specific mus. talent, 93, 8, 311, 73.
"Spectacles," conductor's, 134.
Speculation, theoretic, 295, 322 ; on the Public, 27, 40, 9, 344, 64, 80, 6.

INDEX.   427

Speech, 237-8, 312; Diversity of European, 302; Emotional, 85-6, 312, 9; Evolution of, 84, 318-9; Jewish, 84-6; Ringing, 68, 9.
Speech-making at banquets, 278.
Spell of magic, 230, 2, 305, 12, 30.
Sphinx, the, 95.
Spirit of a thing, the, 160.
Spirit is the life, the, 99.
Spirited dramatic compositions, 171; performance, 382.
Spiritless perf., 323, 54, 9, 66.
SPOHR, LUDWIG, 147, 52.
SPONTINI, 125-43, 59, 304, 27:— Aims, 125-6, 32; Death, 125, 7, 142; Demands, 128, 31-2, 5; and German tongue, 130; Majesty, 128, 9, 33, 8, 40; Opinions, 126, 140, 3; Short sight, 131, 4; Sundays at Berlin, 138; Value, 125, 127, 43; on W.'s career, 138-9, 42.
Spring, 274; morning, 196; of '57, 266.
Stabat mater, Palestrina's, 298.
Stability in ruins, 93, 302, 15.
Stabreim, 263.
Stage-: Business, 193, 374; Conversation, 193; Directions in Scores, 172, 92, 4, 209, cf. 375; Feast, 278; Lighting, 195-7, 209; Music, 191. See Effect, Theatre.
Stahr, Adolf, 103.
Stars, Night's multitude, 339.
'Stars,' 25, 31, 354, 66, 8, 79.
State, the, 56, 118; Antique, Art, and downfall, 307; "ruled from an opera-house," 115.
Statue, Greek, 95.
Statutes and edicts, 372. See Rules.
Staying-power, (x), 181, 2.
Stephen's tower and boulevards, 386.
Stereotype, 171, 84, 93, 342, 53.
Stimmung, 177, 83, 209, 12, 78, 339, 356, 9.
Stimulating contact, a, 270, 305, 36, 349, 50.
Storm, 147, 209, 17, 28, 30.
Stormy: and sombre, 216; *v.* Sturdy, 150.
Strauss, David, 114.
Strauss, Johann, waltzes, 386.
Stream of Music, 305, 35, 7, 8, 9.
Strength and delicacy, 224.
Stridings to and fro, 210.
String-quartett, the, 316; and Wind, 134, 89, 90, 214.
Strong and the Weak, 199.
Stubbornness, 85, 226.

Study, 152; personal, 262, 8, 303; Singers' course of, 173, 92, 8, 202, 270, 5-6, 374, 6.
Stuff (poetic), 32-3, 225, 57, 61, 2, 4, 269, 328, 9; ideal, 312.
"Stupid stuff," my, 268, 88, cf. 263.
Style, 46, 275, 98, 341, 3, 53, 69, 72, 381, 2; a truly German, 118, 280, 282; modern Operatic, 171, 275, 299, 342, 66.
Subject, musical, 248-51.
Subjective mood, a, 295.
Sublime, 137, 225, 7, 9, 31, 2, 98.
Subventions, theatr., 282, 364-5, 78-381, 6.
Success, 9, 25, 65, 151, 239, 91, 355, 375; true artistic, 56, 7, 149, 59, 177, 85, 97, 202, 3, 10, 2, 58, 70, 4, 275, 356, 9.
Successes, 83, 97, 8, 104-6, 11, 9, 26, 180, 203, 39, 322-3, 7, 40, 58.
Succumb, we will not, 223.
Süddeutsche Presse, 115.
Suffering and sorrow, 100, 200, 11, 222, 3, 7, 9; Fellow-, 367, 86.
Suggestiveness, musical, 342.
Summer evening, 278, 339-40.
Summer season, 55, 275, 7.
Sun, the ascending, 231.
Sunday performances, 138, 358.
Supers, stage-, 150, 77, 93.
Superficial, 39, 40, 9, 92, 160, 262, 277; Analogy, 203.
Superfluous, 172, 338, 68.
Superintendent, offspring of Christian, 104.
Superlative, using the, 202.
Superstition, 133, 43.
Suppose a genuine artist came among you, 385.
Suprasensual, the 231.
Sureness, 57, 185, 246, 50, 318, 27, 382.
Surrounding, the, 31, 178, 80, 1, 2, 200, 330, 67.
Survival (? of the fittest), 199.
Suspended sixths, 139, 40.
Switzerland, German, 50.
Swords without blades, 242.
Symbols, 231.
Sympathy, 80, 6, 7, 8, 96, 143, 8, 9, 224; Artistic, 178, 90, 204, 329, 59.
Symphony, the, 317; and Opera, 170, 303, 34.
Symphonic Form, 225, 44, 8, 300, 334-7.
"Symphonic Poem," 243, 8, 9.
Synagogue music, 90-1, 7.

INDEX.

Syntax, verbal, 318.
Systems, 113, 326-7.

T.

Table-music, 278, 332, 4.
Tableaux vivants, 52.
Tail-coat and ball-dress, 156.
Tailors, hair-dressers &c., 259.
Talent, composer's lack of, 333. See Aptitude, Unknown, Young.
'Talent,' the, 30, 3, 56, 354.
Talk at all hazards, 89, 92; small, 332, 3; and Song, 86.
TANNHÄUSER:—
 Act iii, 356.
 Applications for, 169, 70, 351.
 Axis of, 179-81.
 Ballet in act ii, 351-2.
 Composition, 326, 40, 4.
 Contrasted with other operas, 173, 191, 3, 340, 3, 4, 59.
 Cuts (Dresden) in, 176-85 : Song to Venus, 176-7, Close of act i, 177-8, 94, Prelude to act ii, 178, Adagio in act ii, (x), 178-81, 2, Close of act ii, 181-2, Prelude to act iii, 183, Elisabeth's Prayer, 183-5, 201, 356, Closing Chorus ("Heil!"), 187.
 Elisabeth, 178, 80-3, 99, 200, 1, 4.
 Entry of Guests, 193.
 Even-star, 356.
 Favourite passages, 357, 9.
 Heinrich der Schreiber, 187.
 New liking for, 353.
 Overture, 188, 229.
 Paris booking, 359.
 Performances: Dresden, vid. sup. Cuts; Hamburg, 273; Paris Opéra, 271, 95, 325, 40, 4, 349-60.
 Pilgrimage, recital, 179, 81, 356.
 Pilgrims' entries etc., 194, 356.
 Plot, 330, 44.
 Protest, Parisian, 359.
 Recitative in, 174-5.
 Revision : of act iii, Prelude, 183, Close, 185-7 ; Parisian, 351-2, 353.
 "to Rome," 182, 200-1.
 Scenery etc., 186-7, 93-7, 356.
 Singers' Tourney, 187, 93, 6, 200, 204.
 Tempi, 188-90.
 Title-rôle, 178-82, 98-203, 30, 351, 353, 4, 6.

TANNHÄUSER—*continued*—
 Translation, French verse-, (294), 325, 44, 53.
 Tristan, compared with, 340.
 Venus, 176, 86, 98, 9, 200, 4, 30.
 Venusberg scenes : first, 194, 5, 230, 351-2, 3 ; second, 196-7.
 Walther, (x), 187.
 Wartburg valley, 195-7, 231.
 Wolfram, 180, 204.
 Younger Pilgrims, 182, 7, 94.
Taste : French, 271 ; Individual, 42, 277, 9, 324, 77, 83 ; Public, 9, 25, 87, 125, 6, 323, 64, 5, 71, 81, 382 ; Ruin and confusion of, 41, 62, 95, 6, 279, 343, 70, 1, 82.
Teacher, Wagner's, 304, 27.
Tears, 200, 1 ; of Love, 222.
Technique, 49, 183, 296, 312, 20, 74, 377, 83.
Tempo, 149, 56-60, 4, 5, 71, 5, 88-90, 192, 5, 215, 6, 374, 6.
Tendence : Artistic, 9, 111, 26, 271, 289, 96, 306, 8, 12, 20, 1, 3, 4, 5, 327, 8, 31, 6, 9, 45, 51, 78, 84-5 ; Culture-, 121, 383 ; Heroic, 222 ; Operatic, 125, 40, 3, 289, 98, 321, 324, 51, 72, 84.
Tendentiose acting, 83.
Tenor, Costumed, 202, 67 ; Rôles, 31, 202, 3.
Terms and epithets, mus., 239.
Testament, New and Old, 110.
Tetralogy, 322.
Textbook, 172, 263, 311, 28, 44, 375.
"Text-concoctions," my, 264, 83.
Text-words, 299, 335, 53. See W.
THEATRE, the, 25-57, 296, 363-86.
 Abuse of artistic forces, 258, 367, 386.
 Business aspect, 25, 7, 55, 191, 281-2, 306, 51, 8, 64, 8, 70, 7, 378, 80, 4.
 Classes of, special, 30, cf. 380.
 Constitution for, 365, 72-6, 84.
 and Creative artist, 9-21, 385 ; as example for, 50, 298.
 Debarment from, W.'s, 267, 353.
 as Educational institute, 41, 4, 53, 371, 82.
 Faulty management etc., 17, 43, 72, 170-1, 92, 258, 9, 364, 6-70, 373, 5-6, 82, 3.
 Fines, 368-9.
 proper Functions of, 365, 71, 2, 81.
 -Goers, 46, 55, 274, 7, 81, 99, 364, 366, 78. See Public.

INDEX. 429

THEATRE—*continued*—
Good work, 28, 363, 4, 9, 84. See Perf.
Lease, 25, 7.
Little, 29, 32, 3, 304, 51.
Managing-committee, 44, 53-5.
Model, 298, 9.
Modern, 22, 306, 82; downfall of, 111, 258, 384.
Officers, relation of, 373, 7.
Official authorities, 363, 4, 9, 86. See Boards, Directors.
Original, 20, 4, 9, 45-8, 51, 281.
Paid entrance, 28, 36, 9, 137, 324.
Parsimony, 191, cf. 351.
Permissive, 25, 282, 381.
and Press, 111, 5, 364.
Projects for new, 360. See *Nibel.*
Provisional, 274, 7.
and Public, 26-31, 4, 5, 8, 9-45, 9, 54, 6, 125, 83, 204, 74, 7, 80, 9, 299, 306, 8, 32, 43-4, 58-9, 67, 8, 371, 81, 4. See Interest, and P.
Social standing and dignity, 54, 259, 306, 9, 78, 9, 84.
and State, 56, 115.
Subscribers, 55, 352, 8.
Subventioned and un-, see S.
effect on Young, 53, 152, 303.
Théâtre de l'Ambigu comique, 34.
,, Français, 298, 369.
,, des Italiens, 350, 80.
,, Lyrique, 351.
Theatres, German, (x), 3, 11, 22, 30, 31, 72, 111, 68, 9, 90, 257, 8, 72, 274, 5, 6, 9, 322, 73, 5-6; an end to, 259; of first rank, 280, 366, 8, 369, 85; friendly, 3, 350; attempting tasks beyond their strength, 34, 37, 9. See Court.
Theatres, Italian, 29, 31, 51, 332; London, 276, 380; Parisian, 30, 51, 276, 369; Suburban, 30, 380.
Themes as thoughts, 156, 64.
Theoretic writings, W.'s, 1-4, 73-4, 7, 104, 7, 11, 3, 6, 55, 291, 5, 303, 322; Origin of, 62, 326; Repugnance against reading, 295, 321, 5, 340, 5.
Theory, 290, 5, 321, 3, 5, 7.
Thinker and Poet, 88.
Thinking Artists, 126; Men, 41, 2, 57, 369, 86.
Thorwaldsen, 14.
"Thou," the brotherly, 150.
Thought: and Feeling, 319, 20; the Poet's, 10, 3, 7, 8; Reasoning, 318, 9.

Thraldom of Jews, internal, 82, 120.
Threadbare form, 315, 7.
Throat-dexterity, 299.
Thrust, instinctive artistic, 71.
Tichatschek, 132, 5, 49, 76, 9, 81.
Time: and true Being, 259; Expenditure of, 10, 372, 8, 85; and Place, 31, 275; and Space, 297.
Time-length of tone-piece, 317.
Time-motive, the, 268.
Times, The, 109.
Tinsel pomp, 191.
Titan and the gods, a, 222.
Titles of music-pieces, 221, 43.
Tolerable and Good, 150, 323, 68.
Tone, Art of, 47, 68, 9; Hall-marked, 161.
Tone-: Artist, 70, 1; Figures, 159, 178, 210, 4, 317; Jugglery, 70; Pictures, 96, 221, 3, 5, 6, 32; Piece, 226, dramatic, 339; Poem, 221, 8; Poet, 222, 3, 5, 32; Speech and word-, 224; Works, 242, 4, 247, 8.
"Too much seriousness" &c., 278.
Tortures, 200, 321, 67.
Trade, by, see Professional.
Traditional, 157, 93, 244, 5, 62, 87, 329, 36.
Tragedy, W.'s first, 303. See Greek.
Trägheit, 93, 117.
Tragi-comedy, 98.
Tragic Conflict, 93, 162, 200, 22, 7; Trait, 96.
Training one's faculties, 152.
Training, Conductors', 373, 5; Singers', 46-7, 56, 183, 202, 75, 299, 300, 66, 7, 80; in one specific rôle, 270, 5, 6, 9, 353, 74.
Transfiguration through Music, 246.
Transfigured sound, 277.
Transition, Advance by, 46.
Transitional and linking passages, 162, 4, 315, 7, 34, 41, 2.
Translated operas, 38, 47, 276, 99, 379.
Translation of W.'s dramas, 287, 95, 322; literal, 326; verse, 325, 44.
Transport, 200; cries of, 223, 30.
Treason, political, 225.
Tribschen near Lucerne, 122, (256).
TRISTAN UND ISOLDE, (vi, xi), 120, 268-70, (294), 326-7, 30-1; for Carlsruhe, 349-50, Ital. singers, 269, 70, Paris, 350, Vienna, (xi), 272, (362) cf. 385; compared with *Tannhäuser,* 340.

430 INDEX.

Triviality, 88, 93, 7, 105, 58, 89, 310, 1.
Trombones, 133, 88, 90.
Troth, eternal, 216.
Troubler of musical religion, 165.
Troyens, les, Berlioz', 291.
Trumpets (in *Dutchman*), 210.
Trust him !, 253.
Truth, 330 ; eternal, 302 ; telling the, 237, 360 ; a Woman's, 213, 6.
Tuba, bass, in *Rienzi*, 133.
Tuileries, advocacy at, 350.
Turgid blurring of surface, 117.
Turning back, no, 199, cf. 100.
Twilight darkness, 82.

U.

(Uhl, Friedrich, 362).
(Uhlig, Theod., ix, 7, 73, 220 ; *Letters to*, 24, 43, 66, 89, 146, 68, 220).
Ultramontanes, the, 109.
Unconscious and Conscious, 28, 43, 63, 71, 80, 8, 91, 238, 41, 68-9, 296, 7, 308, 21, 9, 67.
Unconstraint in acting, 177, 93, 204.
Undeceived, 50, 107, 221, 8, 77, 354, 9.
Underlay for melody, an, 331.
Understanding (*Verstand*), 62, 226.
Understanding (*Verständniss*) of drama : by the audience, 203, 12, 278, 307, 44, 71 ; by the performers, 38, 173, 280, 353. See Intelligibility.
Undertakings, my, 114-5, 257, 67, 71, 345, 50, 2.
Undeveloped faculties, 52, 169, 278 ; forms, 302, 34.
Union and disunion, 8, 46, 281.
Union of German Musicians, 118.
Unions, Musical, 118, 373. See Art-, Wagner.
Unisono, an adamantine, 159, 60.
Unit, the, 73, 4, 84.
Unitarian whole, a, 280, 307.
Universal music, a course of, 270.
Unknown talent, 50.
Unmanly, 202, 3.
Unmated being, an, 229.
Un-Nature, 33, 92, 342.
Unpractical, unsingable &c., 267.
Unproductiveness, 48, 70, 93, 106, 114, 302, 85.
Unrest, a prickling, 93, 118.
Unruliness, youthful, 222, 3.

Unspeakable, the, 238, 42, 50-1, 338.
Un-thinkers by routine, 69.
Unwonted, 169, 73, 91, 203, 5, 39, 241, 52, 79, 359.
Uplifting (*Erhebung*), 238, 52, 304.
Upper-court-poetess, an, 33.
Useless officials, crowd of, 379.
Usury, 87.
Utopian, 383.
Utterance, or manifestment, 68, 9, 84, 92, 198, 204, 46, 301.

V.

Vagueness, 95. See Definition.
Vanity, 26, 161, 202, 88 ; wounded, 85, 98, 375.
Vapid and invertebrate, 202-3.
Variation-form, 245.
Variations of one theme, 4, 126, 222, 224, 68, 97, 315.
Vaudevilles, French, 30.
Vauthrot, 353.
Vengeance, 178, 82, 225-7.
(Venice, 236).
Venture, lust of, 228, 30.
Venus : in *Vestale*, 136 ; in *Tann.*, see T. ; Knight of, 178, 99, 200, 30.
Venusberg, redeemed, 231. See *Tann.*
Vernunft, 62, 70, 318.
Verse and Music, 247 ; Rhythm of, 312, 3. See Melody.
Versifiers, 100.
Vestal virgins, 132, 6, 47.
Vestale, Spontini's, 127 *et seq.*
Victory : of Jews, 119 ; Spiritual, 216, 229 ; of *Tann.*, 355, 6.
Vienna, 105, 283, 379, 86 : and Ital. Op., 380 ; *Lohengrin* at, 272, 9 ; New work for, 272 ; Opera-house (xi), 32, 111, 272, 9, 363-86 ; Public, 379-81, 5, 6 ; Worthies, 385, 6.
Viennese jurist, a, 104.
View, power of, 92 ; -point, 61, 251-3, 321, 70, 9. See Beholding.
Villot, Fr., 293, (294).
Violas, 191, 210 ; "is't Death in ?", 135.
Violins, the, 178, 88, 9, 210, 2.
Violin-virtuoso, a great, 107.
Virtuosity, 29, 36, 107, 239-40, 97, 9, 315, 67, 8, 80.
Vischer, Prof., 113.
Visiting-card in a keyhole, 109.
Visits in the boxes, 31, 332.

INDEX. 431

Vocal Art, 184, 204; Conductor, 149, 374-6; Forces, 52, 187; Practice, 47, 173, 270, 6, 353, 74, 80; Trickery, 184, 202.
Vocalism, Italian, 116, 269, 380.
Voice: an endurable, 368; strain of, in acting, 47. See Training.
Voice, Human, the noblest organ, 317.
Voices waking in the wood, 339.
Void and null, 30, 69, 95, 105, 161; a, 180, 229.
VOLTAIRE'S saying, 310, 1.
Volumen of the poems, 329, 30.
Voluptuous, 126, 230, 324, 51.
Vorstellung, 247.
Voyage, a raving, 228.
Vulgar interests and needs, 238, 306, 368; music, 385.
Vulgarity of expression, 108.

W.

WAGNER, "enough of the name for the present," 272.
Wagner, Johanna, 136, 84.
(Wagner, Uncle Adolph, 54).
(Wagner-Verein, 256, cf. 281).
Waking eye, the, 329.
WALKÜRE, DIE, (155, 256), 266.
Want (*Noth*), 9, 39, 48, 72, 100, 49, 163, 76, 269, 97, 330.
Wanton whir, a, 230.
Warmth, artistic, 177, 202, 23, 78, 323; of heart, 355; mingled with bitterness, 353. See Fire.
Wartburg, Singers' Hall, (20), 196.
Washiness, 95, 112.
Weaker natures, 199, 343.
Weaknesses in great works, 245, 311, 352.
Weil and woe, 222, 4, 9.
Wealth and penury, mus., 333.
Weariness, utter, 210, 3, 28, 78, 367.
Weather, 27, 155, 66.
WEBER, 340; death, 303; and wife, 343; *Freischütz*, (30), 140.
(Weber, J. J., publisher, 76, 294).
Wedding of Poetry and Music, 69.
Weimar, 21, (24), 107, 261; *Lohengrin*, 103; *Tannhäuser*, 177.
"Well-meaning," 203.
Well-printed poets, 263.
Well-to-do, the, 87.
(Wenzel, vii).
"What is German?", 270.
"Whence?", 330.

Whim and Whimsical, 88, 95, 155.
Whirlpool, 228, 335.
Whole, a, 19, 38, 170, 91, 271, 80, 282, 321, 59, 68.
Whole and half, 156, 98.
Whole human being, 95, 223, 4.
"Why?", 320, 9, 30, 6, 7.
Wild Hunt, the, 230.
Will: Artistic, 63, 7, 114, 25, 6; Force of, 16, 21, 44, 52, 6, 7, 64, 71, 3; Free, 72; Poet's, 331.
Will and Can, 71, 97, 253.
Will of God and Directors, 72.
Will-less, 158.
Winds and storms of life, 147.
Winter Season, 25, 55; of '53, 266.
Wire-pullers, 109.
Wish and fulfilment, between, 328.
Witchery, 186, 95, 230.
Withdraw my work, 173, 7, 354, 7, 8.
Within and without, 242, 52, 366-7.
Without: no tonic from, 266; an offer from, 269. See World.
(Wittgenstein, Princess M., 236).
Woman, 226-7; and the Critics, 66.
Woman's: Intuition, 241; Look, 229; Offering, 215, 29; Prayer, 201, 226-8; Sensibility, 184, 204.
Womanly, the Purely, 224.
Wonder-seeing, 230.
Wonder-working, 96, 232, 8, cf. 242.
Wont, Use and, 199, 244, 51.
Woodlands, the, 223.
Wood-warblers trapped etc., 340.
Wooing of lovers in dance, 336.
Word and Deed, 278, 82.
Word: Sense of, 38, 85, 312, 8; Toneless, 282.
Words copied into orch. parts, 175.
Words and music, 246, 99, 353; easily heard, 277. See Melody.
Words and syllables, 160.
Word-repetitions, 329, 31, 5.
Word-roots and modern speech, 318, 319.
Work, Wagner's, 151, (168), 257, 66, 282, 321, 7.
Workaday cares, 277.
WORLD:—
  Best-regulated, 273.
  Beyond, 151, 2, 318.
  Centre of, 330.
  for common good of the, 116.
  Displayed in the Artist, 296; by Logic, 319.
  -Fame, 50.
  -Metropolis, 36.
  Outer, 238, 9, 42, 52, 331.

WORLD—*continued*—
Reconciliation with, 199.
whole Relations of a, 266.
This, 199, 200, 1, 31, 43, 7.
Two at once, 137.
-Upheaval, 212.
Wrecker of a, 222.
Worldly and ungodly, 314, 5.
Worm of ruth, the, 226.
Worm-befretted carcase, 99.
Worn out at last, W., 282.
Worship and annihilation, 233.
Wotan, 276.
Wrath, embodied, 201, 11, 26-7, 9; or Laughter, 67.
Written communications, 170, 363.
Wrong-doing from ignorance, 217.
(Wurzburg, 304).

Y.

Yearning and Burning, 194, 230; Over-earthly, 232; for Rest, 213, 228; for Sorrow, 200. See Longing.
Young talents, 46, 279, 353, 4.
Youth: and Age, 42, 52, 151; Impressions on, 53, 158; Unresting, 222. See Education.

Z.

Zeal, 133, 49, 74.
Zukunftsmusik, 103, 7, 293. See M.
Zurich, 24-57, 74, 103, 13, 42, 66; Government, 41; Musical Society, 155, 61, 4; Public, 26, 7, 33.
Zusammenhang, 268, 318, 329.

www.ingramcontent.com/pod-product-compliance
Lightning Source LLC
Chambersburg PA
CBHW021912180426
43198CB00034B/135